King's Vibrato

DUKE UNIVERSITY PRESS
Durham and London   2022

King's Vibrato

Modernism, Blackness, and the Sonic Life of Martin Luther King Jr.

Maurice O. Wallace

© 2022 DUKE UNIVERSITY PRESS
All rights reserved
Project editor: Lisa Lawley
Designed by A. Mattson Gallagher
Typeset in Portrait Text, Canela Text, and Optima
by Westchester Publishing Services

Library of Congress Cataloging-in-Publication Data
Names: Wallace, Maurice O. (Maurice Orlando), [date] author. Title: King's vibrato : modernism, blackness, and the sonic life of Martin Luther King Jr. / Maurice O. Wallace.
Description: Durham : Duke University Press, 2022. | Includes bibliographicalreferencesandindex.
Identifiers: LCCN 2021044935 (print) | LCCN 2021044936 (ebook) ISBN 9781478015741 (hardcover) | ISBN 9781478018407 (paperback) ISBN 9781478022992 (ebook)
Subjects: LCSH: King, Martin Luther, Jr., 1929-1968. | King, Martin Luther, Jr., 1929-1968—Oratory. | African American preaching—United States—History—20th century. | Sermons, American—African American authors. | Voice—Social aspects. | Elocution—Social aspects. | Vibrato—Social aspects. | BISAC: SOCIAL SCIENCE / Ethnic Studies / American / African American & Black Studies | RELIGION / Christian Ministry / Preaching
Classification: LCC E185.97.K5 W355 2022 (print) | LCC E185.97.K5 (ebook) | DDC 323.092—dc23/eng/20211230
LC recordavailableathttps:/ /lccn.loc.gov/2021044935
LC ebookrec ordavailableathttps:/ /lccn.loc.gov/2021044936

Cover art: *Martin Luther King Jr., Brown Chapel A.M.E. Church, Selma, Alabama, March 3, 1965.* Photograph by Dan Budnik.
© 2022 The Estate of Daniel Budnik, All Rights Reserved.

Duke University Press gratefully acknowledges the Rutgers University Research Council, which provided funds toward the publication of this book.

In memory of my mother,
Tommie Catherine Wallace,
who would have been excited past words

And for my father,
Ronald Van Buren Wallace,
my pillar

CONTENTS

Acknowledgments ix

Introduction 1

I. Architectures of the Incantatory

1. Dying Words 21
The Aural Afterlife of Martin Luther King Jr.

2. Swinging the God Box 43
Modernism, Organology, and the
Ebenezer Sound

3. The Cantor King 71
Reform Preaching, Cantorial Style, and
Acoustic Memory in Chicago's Black Belt

II. Nettie's Nocturne

4. King's Gospel Modernism 97
The Politics of Lament, the Politics of Loss

5. Four Women 138
Alberta, Coretta, Mahalia, Aretha

III. Technologies of Freedom

6. King's Vibrato 185
Visual Oratory and the "Sound of
the Photograph"

7. Dream Variations 229
"I Have a Dream" and the Sonic Politics
of Race and Place

Epilogue. "It's *Moanin'* Time" 273
Black Grief and the End of Words

Notes 281 Bibliography 325 Index 343

ACKNOWLEDGMENTS

I wish this book had been finished years ago. I know now, however, that *that* book would have been very different from the present one. *That* book I might have wrestled into being with the critical tools of literature, cultural studies, religious studies, and gender critique. This one, however, would not be forced by any means; I had to tarry for it, wait for its coming in the fullness of these shocking times. Perhaps I am a slow study; I admit that possibility. But slow study or no, I doubt I could have written this book before the Black Lives Matter movement or the Black Studies debates or, indeed, before my time in the Christian pulpit came to its current close in 2017. I needed critical distance from the last of these, the pulpit, and to experience the felt urgency of Black Lives Matter and Black Studies to realize the subtleties of argument I hope are plain and not hidden to scholarly readers in particular. Moreover, my mother's passing in 2017 opened me up to thinking deeply about black mother-loss in this book, and I owe to her memory, which still brings heartache, gratitude for the guidance her spirit gave me along the way. That I endured her loss was a miracle all its own. Only lasting through the darkest, most despairing days of the COVID-19 pandemic to finish *King's Vibrato* came remotely close to vying with that wonder of wonders. My mother's hand is throughout this book, then. What's more, from a deep-seated place of grace invisible in me, she urged it done.

Many others, too, tarried patiently with me for the delayed coming and completion of *King's Vibrato*. No one, though, has been more patiently present with me than my wife, Pamela Sutton-Wallace. I can't imagine the mediocrity that might have been produced if she hadn't believed that my thoughts had merit. She, too, is my pillar. I hope my strengths buoy her as hers do mine. My daughters, Sage Alexandra and Amaya Olivia, were both entering college at the time *King's Vibrato* was finally taking shape. As members of Generation Z, they were mostly amused by my thought-trances and old-man fixations on all things "Dr. King." Pam, on the other hand, would not allow me to only write and theorize black sociality. She encouraged my work *and* my presence in the world.

If my family was even more patient than my friends who have also looked forward to this book with me, this is not to discount my friends' support. Since the inception of this project, I have enjoyed invaluable encouragement from a small informal council of professional friends, field and institutional leaders at a half-dozen major campuses whose generosity with research leads, urgent reading recommendations, critical improvement to underdeveloped ideas of mine, and collective wisdom about the peculiar exigencies of black work-life balance rescued this book when it threatened to sink under the weight of fatigue brought on by overcommitment or the social climate nationally. I owe Cynthia Young, P. Gabrielle Foreman, Jacqueline Goldsby, Anthony Foy, Psyche Williams-Forson, Andreá Williams, and Daina Ramey Berry profound thanks for their direct and indirect advice on the direction and arguments of this book, and for helping me always to stay on task. I was also inspired in this work by my brotherly connections to Michael A. Walrond Jr. and Scott H. Adams, both brilliant churchmen. In the context of *King's Vibrato* and beyond it, Michael and Scott have been my most reliable interlocutors. Though their work in black religious practice and its futures is not often reflected in print, both are scholars in their own right and my engagements with them are reflected in many of the most ambitious ideas of this book. Also, without always knowing it, Johari Jabir and Ed Pavlic have pushed me to ever higher levels of excellence in black sonic and musical reflection. Their understanding of the musicking of black thought and worldly reimaginings is deep. I hope I've captured some of the depth of their insights here. Perhaps only my onetime colleague at Duke, Fred Moten, has had as significant an influence as Johari and Ed have on my thinking about the depths of blackness obtaining to Martin Luther King Jr.'s sound and oratory. Fred's influence is conspicuous in these pages. I am appreciative of his early encouragement to stay with this project. Also, Richard Lischer at Duke Divinity School could not have been a warmer interlocutor as I undertook my first efforts to outline a theory of the affective power of Martin Luther King Jr.'s preaching and speech-making. I hope *King's Vibrato* flatters him and his essential scholarship on King, the preacher and orator.

At Duke I have others to thank, no less important to the finish of this book. But for the incomparable Karla FC Holloway, of course, there'd be no book or academic me to speak of. My most faithful mentor and supporter, Karla has been an advisor, dean, advocate, counselor, best teacher, interlocutor, and, with Russell Holloway, trusted friend. My debts to Karla are infinite. She, too, pushed me to finish this book and be heard. Mark Anthony Neal, Tom Ferraro, Priscilla Wald, Wahneema Lubiano, Robin Weigman, Charlie Piot, Kerry Haynie, Richard Powell, Len Tennenhouse, Luke Powery, Ashon Crawley, Allison Curseen, Pete Moore, Jonathon Howard, and Chris Ramos also lent me early and diverse audience for this work when it was still unformed. At the University of Virginia, a new set of colleagues aided my thinking about King. The collegiality of Steve Arata, Marlon Ross, Lisa Woolfork, Anna Brickhouse, Sylvia Chong, Mrinalini Chakrovorty, Njelle Hamilton, Jennifer Greeson, Chris Krentz, Carmen Lamas, Andrew Stauffer, Charles Marsh, Claudrena Harold, Jennifer Geddes, Charles Mathewes, Matt Hedstrom, Martien Halvorson-Taylor, Nichole Flores, Larycia Hawkins, Grace Hale, Sandya Shukla, Andrew Kahrl, Talitha LeFlouria, Kwame Otu, Sabrina Pendergrass, Lisa Shutt, Ann Rotiche, Bonnie Gordon, John Mason, Deborah McDowell, Francesca Fioroni, Bill Wylie, Lawrie Belfour, James Hunter, Garnette Cadogan, and Tony Lin was deeply valued. I want to extend special thanks to Caroline Rody, Asher Biemann, and the members of the faculty of the Jewish Studies Program at UVA for the kindness of giving me an audience for, and a set of important criticisms concerning, this book's third chapter, "The Cantor King: Reform Preaching, Cantorial Style, and Acoustic Memory in Chicago's Black Belt." A Sesquicentennial Sabbatical Fellowship at UVA afforded me valuable writing time in the fall of 2017.

My present appointment at Rutgers University afforded me exactly the close community of Black Studies thinkers I needed to polish this work. The ground for this sort of synergy across periods and fields was cleared early at Rutgers by one of the most generous figures in the entire professoriate: the late (and irreplaceable) Cheryl A. Wall. I was fortunate to come on board at Rutgers just before the last year of Cheryl's service to Rutgers English began. The Board of Governors Zora Neale Hurston Professor of English at Rutgers, Cheryl was a widely admired colleague and expert in African American literature, American literature, and feminist criticism; she spent nearly fifty years at Rutgers and helped transform the institution. Today, the State University of New Jersey is led by an African American president, Jonathan Holloway, whose appointment, I do not doubt, owes something to the decades of quiet institution-building Cheryl helped see to before her abrupt passing in 2020. Cheryl read many of the pages of this book in draft form. In them, she encountered my debt to her writing on the gendered construction of genealogical lines in African American literary and cultural history and black women's critical and creative renegotiation of the idea of lineage in *Worrying the Line: Black Women Writers, Lineage, and Literary Tradition* (2005). I won't soon forget her seeming assent to this effort of mine to have us all hear Martin Luther King Jr. again with new ears. Nor her humility or her gentle prodding to get this book done.

Though Cheryl's loss has been deeply felt, I am grateful to belong to a genuine community of others who continue her work. The deeply cooperative and yet still critical conversations about black life and literature I enjoy with Carter Mathes, Erica Edwards, Doug Jones, Evie Shockley, Abena Busia, Ryan Kernan, Imani Owens, Bode Ibironke, Stéphane Robelin, and Mukti Mangharam have been gratifying past words. In whatever ways this book may succeed at the level of thought, it is owing, in no small part, to the deep dedication and intelligence of these colleagues' adjacent ideas about blackness and gender and sound, and the further influence of their published works on thinking about King. Also, the support of Rebecca Walkowitz and Michelle Stephens (especially, but not exclusively, in their roles as departmental and university leaders), Meredith McGill, Brad Evans, Jeff Lawrence, Dana Luciano, David Kurnick, Colin Jager, and, at nearby New Brunswick Theological Seminary, Nathan Jérémie-Brink has contributed significantly to an environment perfectly congenial to this work. At Rutgers I have also drawn inspiration from the examples of Deborah White, Brittney Cooper, Nicole Fleetwood, Nelson Maldonado-Torres, and Donna Murch.

Today, it is impossible for me to conceive I could ever have succeeded in getting these pages in print-ready condition without the editorial support of Sara Appel. Sara entered into dense thickets of prose where I had nearly lost myself and helped me recover my vision and my voice, all the while affirming my determination to give my mind breathing space on the page. This, of course, is no easy tension to hold in balance. Wherever I may succeed, it is to Sara's credit; where I do not, she bears no accountability. Her struggle to keep my excitable mind on track was mighty. I owe debts, as well, to more than a couple of research assistants. Dionte Harris, Landon Wilkins, Heidi Siegrest, Bria Page, and Angel Dye were all tremendous in their talents and commitment to this work. All were indispensable to bringing this book into being.

Anyone who has had the privilege of working with Ken Wissoker at Duke University Press knows how generous and committed Ken is. I've known Ken from way back, as the expression goes, and he is the same engaged editor today leading the press as he was so many years ago when he gambled on *Constructing the Black Masculine: Identity and Ideality in African American Men's Literature and Culture, 1775-1995*. Given the remarkable output of Duke University Press in African American literature, black cultural theory, cultural studies, and critical theory since then, I am flattered by Ken's early and continuous investment in the realization of *King's Vibrato* among so many other fine works in the Duke catalogue. These few lines don't come close to conveying my appreciation to Ken and, of late, Ryan Kendall for their labor on my book's behalf.

Here, too, it seems appropriate to express thanks for the ongoing support of three friends whose interest in this project kept it going when the writing or inspiration lulled. Cathy Davidson, Shawn Michelle Smith, and Robert Patterson have, each in their own way, moved this book along. Similarly, I would be unprofessional not to acknowledge the services of the staffs at the Stuart A. Rose Manuscript, Archives, and Rare Book Library at Emory University, Vivian G. Harsh Research Collection at the Chicago Public Library, and the National Park Service National Register of Historical Places. Chapter 5 of *King's Vibrato*, "Four Women: Alberta, Coretta, Mahalia, Aretha," would have been diminished by half without the attention it pays to Dameun Strange and Venessa Fuentes's "Mother King." I am grateful to them both for permission to quote from their unpublished libretto.

A few of the ideas developed in this book have had polite audiences at the University of Georgia, the University of Virginia, the annual meeting of the Canadian Anthropology Society, and the Harriet Tubman Institute at York University (Toronto). Profound thanks to those from each of these institutions who invited me to lecture on their campuses or participate in their conferences. Finally, a part of chapter 4, "King's Gospel Modernism," was previously published in the journal *Religions* 10, no. 4 (April 23, 2019): 285 under the title "'Precious Lord': Black Mother-Loss and the Roots of Modern Gospel." The special issue, "Between Self and Spirit: Mapping the Geographies of Black Women's Spirituality," was edited by Carol Henderson. I thank the Multidisciplinary Digital Publishing Institute (MDPI) for permission to reproduce those pages here.

And before those demonstrations and underneath the melee and after the bleeding and the lockups and the singing and the prayers, there was this magical calm voice leading us, unarmed, in the violence of White America. And that voice was not the voice of God. But did it not seem to be the very voice of righteousness? That voice was not the voice of God. But does it not, even now, amazingly penetrate/reverberate/illuminate: a sound, a summoning, somehow divine? That was the voice of a Black man who had himself been clubbed and stabbed and shot at and jailed and spat upon, and who, repeatedly and repeatedly and repeatedly, dared the utmost power of racist violence to silence him.

June Jordan, "The Mountain and the Man Who Was Not a God" (1992)

Introduction

The vibrato is present in all King's preaching.
Richard Lischer, *The Preacher King* (1995)

The prehistory of this book is both academic and autobiographical.

King's Vibrato: Modernism, Blackness, and the Sonic Life of Martin Luther King Jr. had its first tentative articulations in a talk at the Dartmouth College Black Theatricality conference a decade ago. Then, as now, I wanted to understand the sonic power of preaching in the life and career of Martin Luther King Jr. I proposed a reading of what has regularly passed as transcendent preaching but which I eventually came to consider a function of the acoustic calculus of voice, architecture, organology, and audience. Together, the acoustical considerations of modern ecclesial architecture in the United States, the pipe organ as a statement-object of cultural and theological cultivation (even and especially among middle-class African American congregations in the first half of the twentieth century), and that experience of black audition Hortense Spillers describes as "a special relationship of *attentiveness* to the literal Word that liberates" established the conditions for the natural vibrato in King's voice to "speak" to and for black audiences in tones well past words.[1] As a figure for the sound of black cultural memory and its modern reflections, I argued at the Black Theatricality Conference, King's vocal vibrato opened up his unique voice to new possibilities in hauntological theory like that posited by Jacques Derrida in *Specters of Marx: The State of the Debt, the Work of Mourning, and the New International* (1994) and, later, Avery F. Gordon in *Ghostly Matters: Haunting and the Sociological Imagination* (2008). In the final analysis, I concluded, greater sonic sensitivities to King's career invite glimpses of the new world possibilities King not only saw (*I looked over and I s-e-e-e-e-n the Promised Land*) but heard like a slow-gathering storm. In the sound of his voice was the sound of a people's racial hope and resistance.

Later I was to learn that my sense of the significance of King's iconic timbre had been shared by others long before it came to me, even if it had not been one of the prevailing currents in the abundant scholarship on King's life and career. Not long after King was assassinated in 1968, in fact, the surviving leadership of the Southern Christian Leadership Conference (SCLC) proposed "An Audio History of Martin Luther King, Jr." The national civil rights organization that King cofounded with Ralph Abernathy, Joseph Lowery, Fred Shuttlesworth, Bayard Rustin, and Ella Baker had already conceived and mounted a weekly thirty-minute radio program, *Martin Luther King Speaks*, airing speeches and sermons by King to over ninety broadcast stations across the country with an audience totaling five million people nationwide. Although the broadcast format for *Martin Luther King Speaks* grew over time to include a variety of voices—Abernathy, Andrew Young, and other SCLC staff members were frequent on-air guests—clips of King speaking opened and closed every broadcast. Committed to "the collection, preservation, organization and dissemination of the auditory record of Martin Luther King, Jr.—in action,"[2] the audio history SCLC leadership aimed to tell from these clips would not just archive the public life of *Martin Luther King Speaks* for posterity; it would essay a more expansive record of King's own public life and work than written testimony alone allowed.

The brainchild of William S. Stein, the producer of *Martin Luther King Speaks* and director of SCLC Radio, the idea for the audio archive followed from Stein's belief that "at this juncture in history . . . the printed word neither inscribes a total scope of narrative events nor provides perspective for an overview of such events."[3] The new technology of the twentieth century, he proffered, "with its concomitant emphasis on audio-visual forms of communication,"[4] was especially pressing to the project of modern historiography he proposed to engage in the preservation and expanded narrative effort. To Stein, the audio archiving of King's sermons and speeches was particularly urgent because the pace of King's activity as a Baptist preacher and public orator left him little time to keep a diary, maintain a travelogue, or compose his memoirs—those traditional genres in which the development of a moving figure's thoughts are usually to be found. So far as Stein was concerned, King's recorded speeches thus constituted "the definitive documentation of this man and his ideas."[5] To be clear, this was no mere cataloging of speeches "A Proposal for an Audio History of Martin Luther King, Jr." suggested, however. Rather, the SCLC avowed that "Dr. King's words—*the sounds themselves*—have a special importance in this transitional and critical period in our history. We are in a remarkably favorable position to retain these words and thereby to *retain the sound of the man*. The nation does not have the voice of Washington or of Lincoln, and our knowledge and understanding of the impact of these men would have been immeasurably expanded if such audio history were available. An audio history of Dr. Martin Luther King will clearly become more and more important as time passes."[6]

"Dr. King's words" projected an essential aurality onto the civil rights struggle, the SCLC maintained. To their imagining, he who called himself, famously, a "drum-major for justice" didn't only establish the beat of black political and economic activism nationwide; in a very literal sense he set its tone, too—lent it a sound. Unlike Washington or Lincoln, the SCLC theorized, "much of Dr. King's public impact was *because* of the particular 'sound' of his words."[7] "An Audio History of Martin Luther King, Jr." aimed to track that sound.

For all of the visionary effort that went into its planning, the Martin Luther King Jr. audio archive never materialized. *King's Vibrato* is my attempt to pick up on the scent (mixing metaphors) of the "particular 'sound' of [King's] words" Stein and others discerned as a triply historical, acoustical, and racial phenomenon. I depart from those countless volumes of study about King's career intent upon deriving a coherent ideology or social philosophy from King's sermons and speeches. Instead, I propose to demonstrate how King's words sounded with vagaries of an imminent irruption poised to break in sonically on the racial order, one aimed at a disordering of the expressive terms of engagement under the Western logocentric regime. Like King's SCLC contemporaries, I have heard these vagaries in King's voice for as long as I have known of a "Dr. King." Until I undertook the research and deep thought I committed to for the sake of this book, however, I did not know a great deal about what they meant.

Just as a five- or six-year-old today comes to know, unconsciously, the lyrics and rhythms that issue from a parent's regular playlist without having actively listened at all, I came to recognize, very early in my life, King's deep, measured, Southern tones as commonplace features of my youth's soundscape. Before I came to a conscious awareness of the performative peculiarities of King's oratory, that is, his voice was already living with me.

Its "undulating tones," "lyrical, idiosyncratic diction," improvisatory enjambments, and "the towering majesty of his concluding words," to repeat Eric Sundquist,[8] all inhabited our house, and thus my life, from bare-butt infancy to adolescence. As a matter of fact, it would not be too romantic to say that in routinely filling the house I was formed in with its incantatory sound, King's oratory came to dwell in *me* just as fully. Over extended periods of my boyhood, my father—a small-town activist and deputy organizer in Havre de Grace, Maryland—set playing most weekend mornings *The 1963 Great March on Washington DC, August 28, 1963*, a vinyl 33 recording he spun on a turntable inside the console stereo we knew as the living-room hi-fi. From its built-in speakers, A. Philip Randolph's theatrical introduction of "the moral leader of our nation" (the expressiveness of which my father especially loved) and King's radiant "I Have a Dream" oration were trumpeted into my sleep. To my father, a former Air Force police officer, King's leonine eloquence was the perfect Saturday reveille.

My parents met and married in the Air Force as enlisted personnel in 1965. Upon being honorably discharged some months after they married, Ronald and Tommie Wallace made their home in Maryland only fifteen minutes from my father's hometown. Swan Meadows was a public housing complex just south of Havre de Grace in Aberdeen and bordering Aberdeen Proving Ground (APG), a US Army installation. Although the barracks-styled duplexes populating Swan Meadows must have felt familiar to my ex-military parents, Swan Meadows was not formally a part of APG but a federal housing development constructed during World War II to house civilian construction workers tasked with APG's wartime expansion. In 1966, Ronald and Tommie rented the unit at 70 Liberty Street, where thunderclaps of large munitions testing from the proving ground were every day's weather. It wasn't until decades later that I considered those daily explosions, so routine as to be banal, as an especially deleterious form of sonic pollution, the environmental impact of which was to be unfairly and disproportionately borne by the overwhelmingly black, low-income community where my family lived opposite the base. I imagine, though, that my mother had considered them threatening from the start.

Eight hundred miles away from Aberdeen, in segregated Birmingham, Alabama, sounds more ominous than ordnance exploding just a few thousand feet away had beset the black residents only a few years earlier. Between 1949 and 1965, black Birmingham saw so many homes bombed at the hands of hate-filled segregationists that the city where my mother lived with her own mother, stepfather, and eight siblings gained the ill-famed nickname

"Bombingham." She had been away from her home city just five years when she settled with my father in Aberdeen to start our family. The sounds of the munitions blasting close behind our little house must have unnerved her for a time; or, they didn't and she accepted them as part of the natural soundscape of black life in America.

Sometime later, with my sister and me added, our family reached the low rungs of the middle class and moved out of our Swan Meadows duplex into a split-level single-family home a couple miles away. There, on Walker Street, Saturday mornings resounded with the incanted preaching of he whom Daddy loved to hear introduced as "Dr. Martin Luther King, *J-R!*," the voice that connected me, by way of a public housing unit on the edge of a military weapons testing installation and my mother's girlhood in Bombingham, not only to the sound effects of America's long history of racial terror but to the black insurgent countersounds of hope-in-resistance as well. As a boy, I was not yet awake to the intimacy between this history, this hope, and me. Today, though, as an academic, an erstwhile preacher/pastor, and something of a contemplative, my sense of black cultural hearing—what I will call later *black audition*—is acute and well developed. *King's Vibrato* is a demonstration of this avowal.

Expressed less personally, *King's Vibrato* argues that however systematic or intimate our scholarly knowledge may be of the rhetorical style and strategies obtaining to Martin Luther King Jr.'s celebrated speeches and sermons, neither the structural grammars of King's orations nor their "strategies of style," to quote Richard Lischer,[9] disclose as much as they might about the effectual *sound* of those orations. For the sound of King's voice—the "grain" of it, I propose—is, if not also *something else*, then clearly *something more* than so much admiring description. Very little about his "mesmerizing style," "undulating tones," "lyrical . . . diction," or the "towering majesty of his . . . words" as descriptives deepens our understanding of the aural charms of King's voice. Roland Barthes's "grain of the voice," however, affords one of several generative tropes this book applies in approaching the exorbitant condition in King's speech.

To summarize, "the grain of the voice" refers to "that very precise space (genre) of *the encounter between a language and a voice*" in Barthes's theory of voice.[10] It is "the body in the voice as it sings" or performs.[11] "Listen to a Russian bass," he invites the doubtful, "something is there, manifest and stubborn . . . beyond (or before) the meaning of the words, their form . . . and even the style of execution: something which is directly the cantor's body, brought to your ears in one and the same movement from deep down in the cavities, the muscles, the membranes, the cartilages.... Above all, this voice bears along *directly* the symbolic, over the intelligible, the expressive.... The 'grain' is that: the materiality of the body speaking its mother tongue."[12] Similarly, the grain of King's voice, that something else that was there "beyond (or before) the meaning of the words," is dimly discernible in that soaring vibrato-speak whose pathos and authority are so gripping to King's listeners. Embodied as much in him as the singing voice is embodied in the singer, King's vibrato—the play of overtone and resonance, lament and ecstasy—is the approach of one to a black metavoice of accumulated black injury, rage, creative suffering, and *jouissance*, the sound of which the adjectival obsession with his speech-making seems often enough to foreclose.

Although this complex of insurgent black sounds—the sounds of injury, rage, suffering, and jubilee routinely repressed in black oratorical representation—is indeed the main object of my inquiry in *King's Vibrato*, I cannot avoid the epistemic and methodological implications that follow from the sensorially restorative ambitions of this study. King, therefore, is not so much a *biographical* figure in this work as *a figure for the aural exorbitance of black cultural history itself* and for the insufficiency of the normative grammars and protocols of historical practice to thoroughly apprehend the black witness to history in sound. Moreover, as the embodiment of the sound of modern black thought and protest in the South, King's preaching and speech-making as platform performances of black speech and audition challenge the hegemony of dominant historical methods, those carrying the day though hard of hearing. Jacques Attali posited that hegemony as an exceptionally long and epistemically visual one. "For twenty-five centuries," he wrote, "Western knowledge has tried to look upon the world. It has failed to understand that the world is not for the beholding. It is for hearing. It is not legible, but audible ... Nothing essential happens in the absence of noise."[13] Against our enduring Enlightenment predispositions, then—against the habits of those who conceive of history visually in discrete sequential frames, I mean—it is crucial we acknowledge that the past, per Attali, is also intensely acoustic. The audio record of King's public career (such as it is) powerfully discloses this.

Following Attali, I insist that history generally, and black cultural history in particular, is—or ought to have presently attained to—a considerably noisier recording of events than is conventionally rendered in scholarly discourse. Fortunately some historians, as Mark Smith attests, have started "listening to the past with an intensity, frequency, keenness, and acuity unprecedented in scope and magnitude."¹⁴ According to Smith, "this intensification holds out the prospect of helping to redirect . . . the visually oriented discipline of history."¹⁵ Smith's own edited volume *Hearing History: A Reader* is a valuable intervention toward that reorientation. In it, Shane White and Graham White's "Listening to Southern Slavery" is a compelling example of the sort of challenge posed by (black) sound to traditional historical foci. "Listening to Southern Slavery" hints at, and is a part of, a shadow archive of black sonological and acoustical thought largely submerged beneath and between the lines of the history of modern aural experience. This imagined shadow archive of historical and critical attention to black musical and extramusical soundways includes representative musings by W. E. B. Du Bois, Zora Neale Hurston, Ralph Ellison, Amiri Baraka (LeRoi Jones), even Frantz Fanon.¹⁶ Not a few later thinkers, hewing closely to the formulations of these forerunners, have followed a more formal academic path toward black sound study. If Du Bois, Hurston, Ellison, Baraka, and Fanon are ancestral to the present formation of black aural history and the theoretical interventions of black sound studies, then scholars as various as Houston Baker, Paul Gilroy, Fred Moten, Alexander Weheliye, Emily Lordi, Ashon Crawley, Shana Redmond, Nina Sun Eidsheim, Kara Keeling, Josh Kun, and Carter Mathes are the present future of that ancestral call to acoustic cultural memory. As a work devoted to exploring the modern acoustemologies of black speech, song, and spatiality informing the peculiar vocalic acts and aesthetics of Martin Luther King Jr. himself, *King's Vibrato* is an experiment in the tradition of the present future.

While the past fifty years of scholarly reflection on King's life as a modern civil rights leader and icon have never *not* made a point of noting his oratorical style, I examine the deep sonic properties inhering to King's unique preaching and speech-making powers. Rather than viewing these properties as the innate inheritance of a familial legacy of black preachers dating back to the Civil War, however, I consider them as absorbative instincts developed within the totality of sounds and silences animating black lifeworlds across modern time and space including King's own curated voice, other ensemblic voices, the environmental sounds of black peril and progress, architectural acoustics, new sound technologies, and the general tenor—or keynotes—of his day. While I dedicate further space to each of these features of the black civil rights soundscape in the section that follows, this last reference to the general tenor of the times and the historicist approach to King's speech-making power that the keynote trope helps to crystallize merits a more immediate commentary.

To sound historian R. Murray Schafer, "keynote sounds" convey "the anchor or fundamental tone" of a soundscape. Analogizing their significance to the "ground," which visual phenomenologists say "give[s] the figure its outline and mass," Schafer conceptualizes keynote sounds uniquely in spatial terms. Setting-specific, they are largely the emanations of "geography."[17] Yet the titular "world" in Schafer's *The Soundscape: Our Sonic Environment and the Tuning of the World* is more than the geographical sum of the earth's environments; it signifies temporality, too—the time of the earth's becoming. The "tuning of the world," therefore, is also necessarily the tuning, or intonation, of time's/the times' keynote sounds, the ubiquitous surround (i.e., the "ground") by which one differentiates and comes to know past, present, and future worlds aurally. Not only the world environment, then, but the very history of the world and its constitutive lifeworlds is sonic to those with ears to hear. History's acoustic condition is not a property of the audible objects of its deliberation projected onto the nonobject of the past's pastness, but the ontological reality of history as the memory of time gone by. In other words, to argue for history's sound (by means of which I approach the sound of blackness in the modern era in this book) is to maintain belief in a sonic materiality immanent to history *as such*. It is to hold truck with the mystic conception of "the angel of history" Walter Benjamin advanced as at once an onlooker and *ear*witness to the past of history's concern formally, which Benjamin portrayed as a long-drawn-out cataclysm "which keeps piling up wreckage upon wreckage and hurls it in front of [said angel's] feet."[18] The thunder of this crashing wreckage is the keynote sound of history experienced from above. From below, the sound is elegiac, funereal, dark, and tremulous.

Out of this mournful surround that is the sonic ground of black aural history in the West comes the figure of the particular sound (we shall call it), asserting itself over and against the sonic surround. Like that which Schafer calls, in a word, a "signal" sound, the particular sound of blackness evolves, bends, and modulates its tenor over time, as historical listening practices, black phenomenologies of audition, and new technologies for the black "tuning of the world" adjust to the imperatives of the political or cultural economy of race in their moment.[19] Just as "sound signals may often be organized into quite elaborate codes permitting messages of considerable complexity to be transmitted to those who can interpret them," so with the particular sounds of blackness covered in this book—namely, the vocal vibrato, the shout, vocal growls, and laughter, among them.[20] The title, *King's Vibrato*, refers to one such particularity of the complex encryption of black signs and signals into the twentieth-century racial soundscape. While I foreground the vibrato sound in King's preaching and speech-making, specifically, I am clear that King's vibrato did not develop out of a vacuum, but out of a promiscuous interplay of figure and ground—out of the ensemble of signals that reflect black speech and audition in the foreground as they materialize from the background sound, or ground, of modernity itself in its constitutive violence against black people.

Still, the near-universal recognizability of King's dark-toned and measured voice, arguably first among black public voices in modern memory, is sui generis. Perhaps no national voice is more readily identifiable by Americans of any generation. Well beyond the intimate familiarity many Americans have with King's most remembered idioms—"I have a dream," "I may not get there with you," and "Tell 'em I was a drum-major for justice," to cite only three of many more of these known set phrases—who can dispute that this far-reaching knowledge of King's voice has a great deal more to do with the singular grain, cadence, and tone of it than with its discursive pronouncements? To lionize King's *oratory*, then, with its too-narrow and specific concern for argumentative proofs and rhetorical formulas, above the supralingualism of his *preaching*, by contrast, is to risk the protraction of a habituated deafness to the material sound of blackness enlivening King's speeches to propheticism. With a similar worry in mind, Richard Lischer hoped *The Preacher King: Martin Luther King Jr. and the Word That Moved America* would go a considerable ways to "restore its hero's voice" from formalistic domestication by classical homiletics and rhetoric.[21] In *The Preacher King*, Lischer set out, "to the extent it is possible for a book to make a sound,"[22] to re-sound the particular voice of the preacher King. *King's Vibrato* follows a similar inclination—to give spoken soul its voice back.

In the spring of 1968, a young black writer, new on the scene, sketched out in broad irreligious terms a portrait of what he referred to as "spoken soul" in *Esquire* magazine. His article "The Language of Soul" defined spoken soul as the "incorrect . . . language" of black American speaking subjects over against the linguistic and grammatical correctness of speech ascribed to white Americans. Claude Brown was still a neophyte at the time compared to more visible black prose writers like Baraka, James Baldwin, Julius Lester, Maya Angelou, and Alex Haley, but his debut work, a gritty 1965 autobiography titled *Manchild in the Promised Land*, made for an auspicious start to a professional writing career. Pointedly, Brown's "The Language of

Soul" explained what the freshman writer took the task of black writing to be and mean. It took on the blackness of modern black literature by way of a meditation on the politics of sound black speech acts coolly, if subversively, voice.

Tucked discreetly behind *Esquire*'s April feature on Muhammad Ali, Brown's piece cast spoken soul as "more of a sound than a language."[23] Published just days after King's assassination, as it would happen, "The Language of Soul" posited that spoken soul "generally possesses a lyrical quality which is frequently incompatible with any music other than that ceaseless and relentlessly driving rhythm that flows from poignantly spent lives. . . . To the soulless ear the vast majority of these sounds are dismissed as incorrect usage of the English language and, not infrequently, as speech impediments. To those so blessed as to have had bestowed on them at birth the lifetime gift of soul, these are the most communicative and meaningful sounds to ever fall upon human ears."[24] Coming so close to King's death, Brown's *Esquire* article seemed a fitting nod to the lyrical expressiveness of King's own "poignantly spent" nights and days. Even as Brown's article tended to identify spoken soul with the hardscrabble soundscape of the industrial urban North, the linguistic sounds of blackness that "The Language of Soul" posited were not wholly separate from the South. Growing up on the segregated east side of downtown Atlanta, King was far from a small-town country boy. Not unlike Beale Street in Memphis, the Auburn Avenue neighborhood that formed his youth and young adulthood was in fact a social laboratory of black middle-class achievement and aspiration. Decidedly urban in its commercial and cultural life, "Sweet Auburn," though still yet a Southern community in sensibility, projected enough cool black urbanity and industrial hum to have imparted a discrete soulfulness into King's speech and manner worthy of Brown's reflections. By virtue of space, place, time, and tribe, a broad form of spoken soul, I mean to say, was part of the preacher King's heritage as well, heredity meekly giving way to the aural force of history and culture on his most public speech habits.

In this connection, King's sermonic voice boasts a musical quality in *The Preacher King*. "It is a beautiful voice," Lischer enthuses, "with a breathtaking range." Lischer's wonder at King's genius goes on: "Within a few minutes his voices moves from husky reflection to the peaks of ecstasy. . . . Like a good singer, he will open his mouth wide to hit the notes but will not reach or strain. His voice never breaks."[25] Lischer focuses not on the preaching lessons King received from instructors at Crozer Theological Seminary and Boston University—lessons heavily slanted toward matters of form—but on "tonality, timbre, [and] rhythm," all issuing from "a second, nondiscursive, track on which the [black] sermon proceeds."[26] Keenly attuned to what he calls the black sermon's "sound track," Lischer's approach to King is as much an acoustemological one as it is a study of rhetorical strategy. His concerns for pitch, blue notes, cadence, and glissando, for instance, tend to ally King more closely to a vernacular preaching tradition than many scholars, playing to respectability politics, have allowed. In its designs to not only parse and catalogue the rhetorical and affective distinctives of King's preaching, but represent them on the page in a phonological script—*to sound them out*, in print[27]—*The Preacher King*, thirty years on, remains perhaps the most estimable work on King's oratory.

Enduring as Lischer's study is, however, and despite his best effort to lay down the "nondiscursive track" of sacred black sound typographically, reproducing King's preaching voice on the page also proves its own impossibility in *The Preacher King*. "The written word cannot adequately convey the pathos of King's voice."[28] This scarcely comes as any surprise—for Lischer, it is a kind of self-own—since a certain disability constrains words, Fred Moten reminds us, "by their implicit reduction to the meanings they carry—meanings inadequate to or detached from the objects or states of affairs they would envelop."[29] Too, "an absence of inflection; a loss of mobility, slippage, bend; a missing accent or affect; the impossibility of a slur or crack and the *excess*—rather than loss—of the meaning they imply" all undermine any attempt to either describe or transcribe King's preaching verbally.[30] And yet despite this disability, Moten considers words' impossible representation of nondiscursive communication enabling insofar as it necessarily calls up that which has been occluded by the very adjustments to normative spelling or pronunciation intended as a remedy or, at the least, a work-around for words' impairments.

Nothing about the irony of "the enabling disability" of words to portray pathos, say, or indignation appears lost on Lischer as *The Preacher King* betrays *exactly* that which it is helpless to faithfully represent in its pages: namely, the vibrato which "is present in all King's preaching."[31] Though occluded from his sermons' manuscripts and transcriptions, the vibrato sound in King's preaching haunts every graphic mark quieting or silencing—or attempting in vain to reproduce—what is clearly heard "in all King's preaching." In a word, King's vibrato essays to name "the *excess*" Moten describes shorn of the presumptuousness of words alone to convey meaning in King's musical speech-making. Not unlike the incessant hum or hiss of currents running all but noiselessly to and from an electric receiver, say, not wired to code,

King's vibrato, diffused into the aural atmosphere, goes on against the quiet which pretends to have overcome it. The sound of King's vibrato is thus unrepresentable and irrepressible all at once. It bears a spectral aspect. Try as the critic might, none can amply re-sound, nor, on the other hand, utterly repress, the luminous resonance of the vibrato-effect in King's public speech and preaching. *King's Vibrato* theorizes why.

By way of the power of metonymy, I give a name to the full range of aural occlusions written words, especially, may strain to ventriloquize but cannot entirely exclude from hearing in any case. I take the vibrato in its fullest signification to be a figure for what I call *diacritical noise*, those an-archic[32] flights or inflections of speech away from the systematized pronunciations of printed words—those tones or tenses of utterance, one might also say, that the diacritical marks attending to written representation aim to approach, laboring in that effort because they are simultaneously antecedent to writing and outside the logic of pronunciation and the proper. Diacritical noise is resistive sound, profligate, against the law. It is sound refusing the control of words' graphic and phonic coercions, sound figured as external to representation in otherwise-than-sonic modes of signification.

To put this another way, I mean to subsume under the sign *vibrato* a symbolic range of nondiscursive sound effects arising from the notional and expressive energy of black hope and insurgency condensed in, and reflected by, King's spoken soul. Within this range of noise, from eloquent roar to indistinct inflection, lie the diffusive sounds of blackness one hears in the gospel intensities of Ray Charles, for instance, or James Brown's mighty scream. One hears them, too, in Mahalia Jackson's melisma, and, more subtly, in the whistling sibilance beneath W. E. B. Du Bois's late-career speech.[33] These effects, stemming neither from "incorrect usage of the English language" nor "speech impediments,"[34] as Brown stresses in "The Language of Soul," color the soundscape blue. Unlike black slang, which is to be understood in its adaptive function to the extant rules of conventional English, as Brown argues, the vocal intensities belonging to the vibrato-as-metonym are opposed to such adaptations. In relation to the rules slang adjusts to, these effects are resistant, irregulative.

In this way, King's vibrato is a natural trope for the insurgent operations of black sounds. No simple adornment or overwrought force of sermonic expression, his vibrato is the aural index of an irrepressible counterwitness of fugitive sounds the preacher-orator has harnessed to black liberatory ends. But what Lischer calls King's "natural vibrato" isn't natural in the way one might expect if by that descriptor one means having developed out of a hereditary endowment or biologic accident of ability. King's vibrato is naturally only insofar as it is born of the everyday complex of sounds and feelings that make up the common history of black life in twentieth-century America. It is the reflexive sound of blackness no one who fears black freedom in modern contexts wants to have to hear. It is the storm warning of the counterthreat of black modernism stirring. Unfortunately, however—and lessening our sense of its material force on historical experience—notice of its exorbitance has mostly gone lacking.

Until Baker's *Modernism and the Harlem Renaissance* in 1987, that is, scant attention was paid to the influence of black expressive culture on modernism and still less to the *"modern Afro-American sound"* as a consideration in modernist thought.[35] In fact, as Douglass Kahn has written, though "read and looked at in detail," modernism has been "rarely heard" at all.[36] *Modernism and the Harlem Renaissance*, though, took up precisely sound—even more precisely, "the meaning of speaking (or *sounding*) 'modern'"—in interrogating modernism's specifically black expressivities.[37] Baker's appeal to African American poetics, and to black "speaking manuals" and "singing books" like Booker T. Washington's *Up from Slavery* and Du Bois's *The Souls of Black Folk* as prefigurings of the sounding of black literary modernism, very plainly inferred its critique of the visual prejudice easily obtaining to US and European modernism even if it did not assert the tone-deafness of traditional modernist history and criticism outright. Vital as Baker is to approaching here what I have referred to as *the particular sound of blackness* for which King is a key figure, Kahn's *Noise, Water, Meat: A History of Sound in the Arts* reckons explicitly with the unhearing history and criticism of (white) artistic modernism in its generality. For the sake of the general, I want to turn again to Kahn so that I may say somewhat more about the broad historical and cultural conditions within which *King's Vibrato* posits black modernism temporally.

While modernism's audible past would seem to have escaped others, not so Kahn. Astutely, he notes that "the early days [of artistic modernism] were concurrent with the advent of the phonograph,"[38] for instance, and the coincidence is far from insignificant. For the phonograph produced more than new sounds mediated by its machinic preservation and reproduction designs; it also engendered, as Kahn writes, "a new status for hearing."[39] Phonography, that is, ushered in "a new day in aurality" in America.[40] Midwife to the new era, phonography was an active agent in modernism's proud arrival. Because it did more than produce new sounds and new ideas about sound, but "produced audibility," Kahn explains, phonography "heard past physiological constraints to the imaginary realms of conceptual sounds, ancient and future sounds, voices of inner speech and the dead, subatomic vibrations, and so on."⁴¹ Phonography, therefore, helped effect a stirring of the imagination of what the modern was, or might become, in historical time. Imbricated with science, technology, war, and imperialism, cultural modernism called up more sounds and placed greater emphasis than ever on listening. One could say, in fact, that for all the *new* attention (since Kahn significantly) to the constellation of soundings recently narrated into Anglo-American and British modernism (e.g., mechanical engines, early automobiles, radio, the gramophone, typewriters, dialect speech), it was the metaphysics of *audition* that most forcefully intervened on thought and time to modernize the world. Perhaps, as Julian Murphet, Helen Groth, and Penelope Hone have together suggested, Edvard Munch's 1893 painting *The Scream* does indeed index well the scale and impact of the aural revolution.⁴² The desperation of the figure of Man in Munch's painting to close his ears to the rumble of new earsplitting auralities is not only a defense against more sounds that it cannot sanely bear but also a panic triggered by the prospect of a more crushing sensorial regime than one dares imagine, which more sounds now threaten to install.

Somewhat against this picture of white American and European modernism that Virginia Woolf famously proposed as having arrived around December 1910, a peculiarly black modernism was unfolding in tensive contradistinction. To the extent it seems appropriate to locate its appearance in time, no more precise hypothesis than Baker's has been offered for historical consideration. On September 18, 1895, in an oration by Booker T. Washington at the Cotton States and International Exposition in Atlanta, Baker proposes, black modernism spoke its first tentative words behind the disarming sound of a few well-staged minstrel inflections. But if Washington's oratory and its strategic manipulation of "Afro-American *sounds*" set black modernism to a slow blaze, then I believe it was King's oratory, a half-century on, that set it roaring. Whereas Washington's speech-making may have heralded a New Negro movement, in other words, it was King who bore it in haunted tones from 1957 to 1968, the clear and woeful end of a *longue durée* of black modernist optimism and racial opinion.

This study, which focuses little on the historicity of concrete events associated with King's life and work or on King's social thought systematically, labors instead to theorize the historical force of King's voice at the level of sound. Moreover, it aims to contextualize that force within the cultural field, to attend to the wider range of sonic material in the black cultural milieus of the urban church, the public auditorium, and the civil rights protest march as an intrinsic part of this theoretical exercise. In general terms, *King's Vibrato* doubles as a cultural history and critical theory of black modernist soundscapes, North and South, that helped produce the vocal timbre and time signature of the figure whom Lischer crowned "the preacher King." These soundscapes include the acoustic energy and imprints of black women's musicianship, urban "renewal" and industrialization, embodied black listening, and other vital soundmarks. This book is as much about those influences as it is about King imagined as a singular figure of black modernist speechcraft. My Martin Luther King Jr., I mean to suggest by this, contains multitudes.

King's Vibrato is organized in three parts. Part I, "Architectures of the Incantatory," explores the acoustical architectures of those African American churches in Atlanta and Chicago where history records King having held forth with especial eloquence. Specifically, chapter 1, "Dying Words: The Aural Afterlife of Martin Luther King Jr.," considers King's voice as a sound object for "acousmatic" or reduced listening. It posits King's April 9, 1968, funeral (and Coretta King's insistence on her late husband's own recorded voice in place of a eulogy) as an unparalleled occasion for the study of black voice *in itself*, the sign and signifier of a black radical critique of the modern order of things.

Chapter 2, "Swinging the God Box: Modernism, Organology, and the Ebenezer Sound," is concerned with how the history of Protestant church architecture helped to give rise to the sound of what Lischer has called "the Ebenezer gospel," that soundscape which is perhaps most directly responsible for the texture and tenor of King's preaching and speech-making voice. Chapter 2 devotes considerable space to the evolutionary history of Protestant church architecture in the United States with the particular acoustic design of Atlanta's Ebenezer Baptist Church in mind. It also gives important attention to the history of the modern pipe organ. Behind and beneath the modern black preaching voice, from the 1920s to the 1960s, the vibratory and aspirational sounds of the pipe organ were essential instrumentation for the sacred soundscapes of black modernity. Ralph Ellison, whom Alexander Weheliye has called "one of the foremost intellectual architects of Afro-modernity," is the key theorist in this chapter.[43] His unfinished second novel, *Three Days before the Shooting...*, I show, illuminates the cultural power of the pipe organ as "God box" in the material culture of black modernism.

Chapter 3, "The Cantor King: Reform Preaching, Cantorial Style, and Acoustic Memory in Chicago's Black Belt," contemplates King in cross-cultural context. On August 27, 1967, at Mt. Pisgah Missionary Baptist Church in Chicago, King preached a sermon titled "Why Jesus Called a Man a Fool" based on a Lukan parable. Considered one of King's great sermons, it was successful partly because of the acoustical design and sonic memory of the former Jewish synagogue where the preaching event took place. Chapter 3 traces the early history of Mt. Pisgah to two prominent Jewish Chicagoans—an architect, Alfred S. Alschuler (1876–1940), and a radical Reform rabbi, Emil Gustav Hirsch (1851–1923). The space designed by Alschuler to maximize the dynamic preaching of Hirsch at then–Sinai Congregation was acoustically suited to King's own "reform" preaching decades later.

Part II, "Nettie's Nocturne," comprises two chapters, "King's Gospel Modernism" (chapter 4) and "Four Women: Alberta, Coretta, Mahalia, Aretha" (chapter 5). Chapter 4 locates in the gospel blues of gospel-music pioneer Thomas Dorsey a productive tension between the imagined primacy of voice in black expression and the print imperatives of cultural moderns. This tension, I argue, is reconciled in Dorsey's early gospel compositions as a voice-and-vellum miscegenaeity exemplified by King's 1963 book of sermons *Strength to Love* and his repertory preaching of those sermons for the five more years of his life and career to come. King's stylized, resistive preaching in those years was in sync with the modern gospel sound popularized by Dorsey and overtaking the religious landscape of black Chicago. King's 1966 reprise of "A Knock at Midnight" at Ebenezer Baptist Church in Chicago, three years after its appearance in *Strength to Love*, powerfully demonstrates this aesthetic harmony. Chapter 4 ends with a consideration of the politics of loss reflected in and by Dorsey's most famous composition, "Take My Hand, Precious Lord," a dark hymn inspired by the death of his wife, Nettie, and their firstborn son, Thomas Jr., in childbirth. The history (past and present) of black maternal and infant mortality is, I argue, at the social and sonic foundations of the history of modern gospel.

Chapter 5 is a black feminist critique of the modern gospel sound and its influence upon King's resonant sound. I explore the radical meaningfulness of King's mother, Alberta Williams King, in her role as the main organist and musical director at Ebenezer (and where, seated at the organ, she was fatally shot during a Sunday service in 1974). I not only mean to underscore here how profoundly formative the organ's vocalizations were on the tone and texture of King's preaching and oratory, but I posit a black feminist genealogy of influence for King's oratorical talent, one that sets aside King's much-vaunted descent from a long line of African American male preachers for another that shows King in sonic relation to Alberta King, Coretta

King, Mahalia Jackson, and Aretha Franklin. I appeal to black feminist theorists Hortense Spillers and Alexis Gumbs and to contemporary feminist musicologist Susan McClary in this chapter, to show King's debt to black feminist sound and performance.

Like part II of *King's Vibrato*, part III, "Technologies of Freedom," is constituted of two chapters. In chapter 6, "King's Vibrato: Visual Oratory and 'the Sound of the Photograph,'" I bring together Slavoj Žižek, Fred Moten, and Shawn Michelle Smith to explore a brief history of visual culture associated with King's speech-making and the repressed sounds of terror and triumph that photographs of King holding forth bear for those with ears to hear. A new reading of "I've Been to the Mountaintop," one that extrapolates from the collision of visuality and aurality obtaining in the sermon's close, is at the heart of this chapter. It is about the deadly perils of black speech-making as a spectacle event, and the fugitive threat of black vocality to visual (i.e., "photographic") thought. In chapter 6, as well, a black performativity of gesture stands in for the liberative impulse of black subjects to escape their framing under the modern colonial capture of pictures and politics.

Chapter 7, "Dream Variations: 'I Have a Dream' and the Sonic Politics of Race and Place," considers the evolution of two deliveries of "I Have a Dream"—in Detroit in June 1963 and, famously, in Washington, DC, in August 1963—against the memory of an earlier one in Rocky Mount, North Carolina, in November 1962, with a view toward contrasting the acoustical conditions of each. Variations in sound amplification, microphonic technology, and even the built and natural environments in Detroit and Washington (the street versus the reflecting pool) lent themselves to quite different deliveries, and therefore auditions, of the same speech, differences having more to do with available technologies than with essentialist ideas about black speech and improvisation.

Combined, it is hoped that these chapters, with an epilogue-meditation on black grief in the aftermath of George Floyd's death spectacle in May 2020, open up to keener hearing the sounds of blackness in their historical time and aid us the more in hearing history in black for a change.

I

Architectures of the Incantatory

1

Dying Words
The Aural Afterlife of Martin Luther King Jr.

There is . . . a mode of production of the phantom, itself a phantomatic mode of production.
Jacques Derrida, *Specters of Marx* (1994)

Power can be invisible, it can be fantastic, it can be dull and routine. It can be obvious, it can reach you by the baton of the police, it can speak the language of your thoughts and desires. It . . . can exhilarate like liberation, it can travel through time and it can drown you in the present. . . . It causes dreams to live and dreams to die.
Avery Gordon, *Ghostly Matters* (1997)

Disappearance is not absence.
Fred Moten, *Black and Blur* (2017)

The morning of April 9, 1968, was wet and muggy in downtown Atlanta. Already, by 10:30 a.m., a humidity nearing oppressiveness had set in. Steamy as it was for the long parade of mourners crowded outside of Ebenezer Baptist Church, inside the sanctuary felt almost airless. One thousand or more, brows beaded with Georgia sweat, packed Ebenezer's pews. The church's seating capacity was only 750. For the "lucky" thousand—family members, intimate associates, celebrity supporters, and political dignitaries—the start of the memorial service for the late Martin Luther King Jr., solemn and overcrowded, was its own relief.[1] First, a prayer prayed for comfort and for a redoubled commitment to nonviolence. Then, solemn readings from the Old and New Testaments. A brief panegyric of the decedent. And six classic hymns threading the speaking elements together. King's closest friend and lieutenant leader, Reverend Ralph Abernathy, steered the memorial program, taking occasional liberties of eulogy and admonition in the transitions.

Although simple in outline, King's memorial service, the first of four discrete funeral events to take place over a full day's obsequies, was not without weight or emotional expense. For starters, it was an exceptionally slow-moving service, its sixty minutes feeling interminably protracted as each somber hymn or solo, and Abernathy's ponderous speech, obeyed a lugubrious meter. Neither speech nor song moved according to any "natural" pace of its own so much as both seemed led—which is to say, taken over—by the drawn-out elephantine tones of Ebenezer's Hillgreen-Lane pipe organ playing loudly over top of the choir and only more subtly under the speech of nonsinging program participants. Too, the press of so many packed into the pews, and the sticky humidity that beset Ebenezer, made for uncomfortable sitting and a rather restrained grief. Inside and outside the church, mourners were alternately inspired and staid. Their mood was stately and, for the most part, composed. With scores of journalists and several television cameras to record everything, King's funeral was a national and international news event airing live to more than 120 million people throughout the United States and making headlines throughout the world.[2] As a global image event, much was at stake for the first funeral of an African American to air on network television.

Still, the morning memorial, solemn and scrupulously delineated, was not self-contained. Missing from the morning obsequies was a proper eulogy, for which the short "TRIBUTE" by Dr. L. Harold DeWolf, King's dissertation supervisor at Boston University and a mentor, was no realistic substitute. For all the care taken by Coretta King to script a worthy, if not beatifying, memorial liturgy, the omission of any eulogistic reference from the printed order of service must have seemed peculiar to some. No doubt it made the service feel, in a word, unanchored to those expecting a full-out funeral drama, not the prelude to one. Perhaps Abernathy felt this way. With the glare of the world upon the service, Abernathy's responsibility for the fluid conduct of last rites could only have weighed heavily upon him as the memorial's appointed officiant. Pointing to just this sort of angst, King's trusted aide-de-camp, it seems, could not resist interposing his own eulogistic remarks into the prescribed order of speech and song where none was planned or called for. Perhaps it was just some *feeling*, an irrepressible instinct, or some acute sense he had of the incommensurability of the morning rites at Ebenezer to the scale of King's monumental importance that inspired him to try, on his own, to counterbalance the felt lack of a properly homiletic remembrance. Only Abernathy missed the printed cue that might have, had he noted it, prompted him to recognize the homiletic intent behind Coretta King's phonographic designs for the morning's last rites. Archival transcripts and video footage of the service that day suggest Abernathy may not have altogether apprehended what Coretta King and her sister-in-law, Christina King Farris, envisioned by their reference as organizers of the Ebenezer obsequies to "Sermon Excerpts" in the printed program that was to guide Abernathy's officiating.

"Sermon Excerpts" appears on the official memorial program as one of the last acts in the service's liturgy. Only a choral rendering of "Balm in Gilead" remained between it and the King family's recessional from the Ebenezer sanctuary to the street outside, where a walking procession to the Morehouse College campus was to begin behind a mule-drawn wagon carrying King's casket. As if Abernathy took "Sermon Excerpts" to refer to an officiant's responsibility, he took the liberty of going off script to proclaim Martin Luther King Jr. his "dearest friend and closest associate"—perhaps to authorize himself for the task, immediate and organizational, he then and there assumed to himself—before narrating a scene from recent days illustrating their unique amity and proceeding without pause to read extracts from two of King's classic messages, "The Death of Evil upon the Seashore" and "A Tough Mind and a Tender Heart." Abernathy read King aloud for fully ten minutes. When he was finished, he closed the book from which he'd read King's words (very probably *Strength to Love*, King's 1963 collection of sermons) and commenced to bring the service to its end with "that favorite spiritual of Martin's" and general instructions for the congregation eager for the fresher air outdoors.[3]

> Whenever we would gather at the close of mass meetings and wonderful experiences fighting for justice and equality for all men, Martin always wanted to get the staff in the mood for singing. We would seek to sing our troubles away and bring joy into our hearts. We bring this service to a close now by ending with one of his favorites. And then we will take his body from this sanctuary to the mule-train which is waiting in front of the church. And the thousands of impatient people who say that Martin

belonged to them. And as I take the body to that train I am going to ask that Reverend English will remain and keep the congregation seated until we have cleared the way out in front of the church. May we sing that favorite spiritual of Martin's now.[4]

If Abernathy misconstrued "Sermon Excerpts" as the occasion to curate, in *his* voice, a public audition of some of King's best preaching, presuming to establish himself as King's heir by such sermonic sampling,[5] then Andrew Young quickly disabused him of that arrogation. Young, another King intimate and SCLC adjutant, on hearing Abernathy directing the service's close ("We bring this service to a close now by ending with one of [Martin's] favorites"), broke protocol and approached the podium with a discreet message whispered in Abernathy's ear. His gaffe quietly corrected, Abernathy returned to the lectern to announce a change in course. "Mrs. King," he spoke, not too sheepishly, "has requested that we have the tape of his last sermon played to us now."[6]

In his 1989 autobiography *And the Walls Came Tumbling Down*, Abernathy made no mention of his apparent misunderstanding of what the funeral program was calling for by "Sermon Excerpts." He recalled only that "they played a tape recording of Martin's instructions concerning his own funeral."[7] In reality, the scene was far more gripping than this. "A moment of silence, then a few crackles of static and King's unmistakable voice echoed through the church."[8] In "rich tones," Rebecca Burns offers in *Burial for a King: Martin Luther King Jr.'s Funeral and the Week That Transformed Atlanta and Rocked the Nation*, King delivered "his own eulogy" to an audience all but overwhelmed by the paradoxically near and distant sound of King's resonant voice issuing as from the tomb. Young was visibly shaken by it. Reverend E. H. Dorsey, who served neighboring Tabernacle Baptist Church, struggled to keep his priestly composure while more than a few choir members, visible in the choir stand behind him, pressed limp handkerchiefs to their faces for long stretches of the recording's play to cover their grief. King's four children, seated alongside their mother before the casket, appeared poignantly nonplussed. Shouting *and* sentimental, King's leonine delivery shattered the placid solemnity of the assembly's mourning with a rumbling ghostliness, "as though something," James Baldwin later mused, "perhaps the heavens, perhaps the earth, might crack."[9] Abernathy's attempt to fill the imagined void of a sermonic performance fit to the occasion was perfunctory and uninspiring in comparison.

Ghostly Materialities: Voice and Funereal Sound

Stirring as the experience was for many, King's funeral event was far from the first time sound recording was exploited to self-eulogizing ends. In his book *The Audible Past: Cultural Origins of Sound Reproduction*, historian Jonathan Sterne claims "there are many cases reported in the early phonograph industry press" of clergymen who have, with the aid of phonography, preached, like King, their own funeral sermons.[10] As early as 1892, a Reverend Thomas Allen Horne of Larchmont, New York, recorded a full funeral ceremony "complete with hymns and sermon," while a Reverend Henry C. Slade of Rideout, Kentucky, drew residents of neighboring towns to his funeral in Rideout "to hear the 'wonder' of the minister's final sermon."[11] It was the late nineteenth-century advent of the cylinder phonograph that enabled Horne's and Slade's postmortem sermonizing three-quarters of a century before King's own funeral oration played to hundreds over Ebenezer's public address system. If calling the "tape recording of Martin's instructions concerning his own funeral" *funereal phonography* (after Sterne) seems an anachronism, this does not preclude the tape on which King's February 4, 1968, preaching of "The Drum Major Instinct" was stored from being figured, like the tinfoil strips Sterne documents mediating early phonographic recording and transmission, "a resonant tomb" in any case.[12]

As Sterne explains in *The Audible Past*, phonographic technology before the twentieth century succeeded by abstracting the human voice from the human body and "preserv[ing] it indefinitely on record." Nothing underlined this power of phonography to preserve and archive human sound so forcefully as its ability to play back into the present a person's voice long after their death. "Is this [not] the ultimate and shocking power of sound reproduction," Sterne asks, "that it finally set the voice free from the living and self-aware body (if only for a few moments)?" Death, he explains, "appears as the philosophical limit case for sound reproduction, and sound recording becomes a philosophical index for sound reproduction in general."[13] To the extent that the audiotape of King's funeral preaching, like its phonographic antecedents by Horne and Slade, resists the certainty of death for the corpse it manages to ventriloquize, it approaches what Sterne outlines as a "canning" function, the determined mechanistic preservation of that which commended King universally—his luminous voice—by new technological means.

According to Sterne, "the practical and imagined possibilities of recording's permanence existed as part of a longer history and larger culture of preservation."[14] Specifically, Sterne traces the evolution of modern canning practices to nineteenth-century preoccupations with preservation including, especially, the preservation of food from spoilage and the dead from decomposition. Although the cultural and practical imperatives of canning foodstuffs and embalming expired bodies were in the main wartime interests, by the time the phonograph was invented a decade after the Civil War, both practices, canning and embalming, were regular rituals of American cultural life. It is no surprise then that the phonograph itself came to be as fulfilling a similarly preservationist end. Famously, John Philip Sousa referred to phonographic music (as distinct from the live performance of it) as "canned music" in this regard. No doubt he would have considered Horne's and Slade's posthumous preaching canned performances as well. But who could fitly call King's funeral oration "canned" seventy-five years later? Unlike its two nineteenth-century antecedents, King's "last act"—his first-person accounting of his own death to come, even as he orchestrates "the mood and response of the survivors" in his hearing—seems appreciably less concerned for embalming King's voice than for realizing its *un*canning—which is to say, its flight from the terminal silence of the grave to a material afterlife beyond it.[15]

To put this still another way, if King's assassin, James Earl Ray, was after some perverse poetic justice when he felled King with a bullet to the jaw that shattered King's lower face as if to silence him twice over, then Coretta King's insistence on the priority of King's still-living voice preaching in the place set to solemnize his irrevocable loss was not only a subversion of the fact of her husband's death but a dramatic vindication of his silent repose on the handsome bier at the foot of the pulpit. Ray had indeed killed King's body, but the miracle of magnetic tape did not let King's voice die within him. Coretta King, it seems, had abetted its escape from interment in and with the host body. Heard well outside Ebenezer in the bright air overhead, King's uncanned preaching rendered the finality of the civil rights leader's Memphis murder strangely uncertain. The magnetaphonic playback of "The Drum Major Instinct" could only have left those on whose ears his sermon extracts fell most sensitively spooked, as though it were a visitation.

Alternately transfixed and forlorn, a host of bereaved friends and allies, variously unnerved by the spectral voice, occupied the sanctuary: black sportsmen Wilt Chamberlain, Jim Brown, and Floyd Patterson; presidential candidate Richard Nixon; New York Governor Nelson Rockefeller; Jackie, Robert, and Ted Kennedy; Supreme Court Justice Thurgood Marshall; Vice President Hubert Humphrey; UN Under-Secretary General Ralph Bunche; and, by one reporter's count, "more than twenty ambassadors" representing

"Britain, Nicaragua, Morocco, Norway, Jamaica, Guyana, Liberia, the Netherlands, Chad and New Zealand."[16] Entertainers as admired as Harry Belafonte, Diana Ross and the Supremes, Sammy Davis Jr., Bill Cosby, and Aretha Franklin brought ever wider attention to the funeral event. Forced to linger outside by the full house of mourners within were black power apostles Stokely Carmichael (later Kwame Ture) and Ron Karenga, outraged that they'd been denied entrance into the sanctuary: "But," they protested, "you're seating white dignitaries!" Though the two would eventually get inside (probably only standing), rapping again and again on one of the exterior church doors until an usher on the opposite side relented to their determination, still, inside and out, the crowds scarcely resembled the Ebenezer faithful at all. Few of the people who heard King preach on Sundays, in fact, found seating among the celebrity class crowded into their Auburn Avenue church.[17] It hardly mattered, though. The funereal sound King brought to "The Drum Major Instinct" live was surely as haunting then as its premonitory speech seemed to others on tape.

Two months before his early April obsequies, King had delivered "The Drum Major Instinct" from the very platform before which his remains lay. Borrowing nearly whole-cloth from a 1952 sermon preached by the Florida Methodist Rev. J. Wallace Hamilton, King recast Hamilton's "Drum Major Instincts" in the light of an unfolding nuclear age.[18] Where Hamilton had decried the continuing world peril of global fascism, King condemned the US–Soviet arms race as a symptom of a "suicidal thrust we see in the world today." His energy intensifying, King leaned in: The problem of man's "drum major instinct," he pronounced, "goes into the struggle between nations."

> And I would submit to you this morning that what is wrong in the world today is that the nations of the world are engaged in a bitter, colossal contest for supremacy. And if something doesn't happen to stop this trend, I'm sorely afraid that we won't be here to talk about Jesus Christ and about God and about brotherhood too many more years. (*Yeah*) If somebody doesn't bring an end to this suicidal thrust that we see in the world today, none of us are going to be around, because somebody's going to make the mistake through our senseless blunderings of dropping a nuclear bomb somewhere. And then another one is going to drop. And don't let anybody fool you, this can happen within a matter of seconds. (*Amen*) They have twenty-megaton bombs in Russia right now that can destroy a city as big as New York in three seconds, with everybody wiped away, and every building. And we can do the same thing to Russia and China.

But this is why we are drifting. And we are drifting there because nations are caught up with the drum major instinct. "I must be first." "I must be supreme." "Our nation must rule the world." (*Preach it*) And I am sad to say that the nation in which we live is the supreme culprit. And I'm going to continue to say it to America, because I love this country too much to see the drift that it has taken. . . .

But God has a way of even putting nations in their place. (*Amen*)[19]

Though the greater part of "The Drum Major Instinct" evinced as reliable an evangelical strain as any in southern black sermon, the preacher King's excursus-transfiguration within the sermonic performance from Sunday preacher to prophetic crier, from a brooding moralistic displeasure in the ego-driven ticks of black moderns and their "quest for attention and recognition and importance"[20] to an impassioned desk-pounding against warmongering between nations, is not a move or modulation in real time from parochial moral concerns to global theopolitics. Rather, "the Ebenezer gospel," Lischer argues in *The Preacher King: Martin Luther King, Jr. and the Word That Moved America*, was parochial and global all at once. A capacious "interpretation of God's will for Ebenezer and the world,"[21] King's ecclesiology in "The Drum Major Instinct," like Ebenezer itself, was influenced by progressive black clergy, professors, and labor activists from Benjamin Mays and Howard Thurman to Mary Gurley and Bayard Rustin, whose common view of the social and material conditions of modern black life and labor in the Cold War period was expansive.[22] Tyranny at home in the United States was not disconnected from that abroad in Africa and Asia.

If the arc of the Ebenezer gospel in "The Drum Major Instinct" begins with the individual's affection for Jesus and approaches its mathematical limit as it follows King's "quest for justice, yearning for redemption, insistence on nonviolence, embrace of suffering, prophetic rage, and all else that emerged from his Sundays in Atlanta," then that theological vision Sarah Azaransky calls "religious black internationalism" sets at its other, forward-looking, end.[23] For all the generativeness we may today recognize and commend in the Ebenezer gospel for its coextensively broad and particular theopolitics, in the ears of the Ebenezer faithful, "the sermon was thoughtful but strange."[24] A discourse on death from such a young man—King was only thirty-nine—made for the most improbable climax to a message warning its listeners of the threat of premature ends ("If somebody doesn't bring an end to this suicidal thrust . . . none of us are going to be around"). How much stranger it must have been for those who had come to know King's voice intimately to hear the recent sermon preached again, postmortem, one can only guess. Cued exactly to the sermon's self-eulogizing coda, the April audience listened despondently as the ghostly King, dead in fact but living on in voice, mused over his death and the sermon he hoped would flatter it if he lived and labored well.

> Every now and then I guess we all think realistically (*Yes, sir*) about that day when we will be victimized with what is life's final common denominator—that something that we call death. We all think about it. And every now and then I think about my own death and I think about my own funeral. And I don't think of it in a morbid sense. And every now and then I ask myself, "What is it that I would want said?" And I leave the word to you this morning.
>
> If any of you are around when I have to meet my day, I don't want a long funeral. And if you get somebody to deliver the eulogy, tell them not to talk too long. (*Yes*) And every now and then I wonder what I want them to say. Tell them not to mention that I have a Nobel Peace Prize—that isn't important. Tell them not to mention that I have three or four hundred other awards—that's not important. Tell them not to mention where I went to school. (*Yes*)
>
> I'd like somebody to mention that day that Martin Luther King, Jr., tried to give his life serving others. (*Yes*)
>
> I'd like for somebody to say that day that Martin Luther King, Jr., tried to love somebody.
>
> I want you to say that day that I tried to be right on the war question. (*Amen*)
>
> I want you to be able to say that day that I did try to feed the hungry. (*Yes*)
>
> And I want you to be able to say that day that I did try in my life to clothe those who were naked. (*Yes*)
>
> I want you to say on that day that I did try in my life to visit those who were in prison. (*Lord*)
>
> I want you to say that I tried to love and serve humanity. (*Yes*)
>
> Yes, if you want to say that I was a drum major, say that I was a drum major for justice. (*Amen*) Say that I was a drum major for peace. (*Yes*) I was a drum major for righteousness. And all of the other shallow things will not matter. (*Yes*) I won't have any money to leave behind. I won't have the fine and luxurious things of life to leave behind. But I just want to leave a committed life behind. (*Amen*) And that's all I want to say.
>
> If I can help somebody as I pass along,
> If I can cheer somebody with a word or song,

> If I can show somebody he's traveling wrong,
> Then my living will not be in vain.
> If I can do my duty as a Christian ought,
> If I can bring salvation to a world once wrought,
> If I can spread the message as the master taught,
> Then my living will not be in vain.[25]

Even on tape, King's preaching was passionate and felt; his temperament, earnest. By turns composed and thunderous, he quickly found his rhythm. "I'd like somebody to mention that day," he offered, then roared, "that Martin Luther King, Jr., tried to give his life serving others."[26] Seated near Coretta King before the bier, King's younger brother, A. D. King, came suddenly undone, so much alive with force and familiarity was the sound of that voice.[27] Perhaps it was a sudden awareness of the new meaning obtaining to the phrase "to give his life" that bore hardest on him and others who struggled to stay composed. It is one thing to dedicate one's best energies to a chosen course or cause—to give all one's heart to a thing. But to lay down one's life—to give one's life for a thing by dying for it—that is something else altogether. Whatever the provocation, a phrasal sensitivity or the shock of his name uttered vigorously in his own voice, no accounting of either its source or power in that surprising magnetaphonic moment of public speech is credible that does not include deep thought about its impact on the very youngest of King's mourners that day, five-year-old Bernice King, and her unforgettable reaction to the disembodied sound of her father's postmortem preaching.

Perhaps too little thought or serious attention has been given to "the shock of . . . death or, more truthfully, the shock of death as a reality" in black children's lives.[28] Too few of us have contemplated the depth of consequentiality that the mournful condition of black life Claudia Rankine recorded in *Citizen* imposes on black boys and girls as targets, losses, and survivors in the war on black political yearning and democratic freedom. Still, a handful have bucked this trend. Literary and cultural critic Karla Holloway was early to do so for the contemporary period. "Despite our best efforts in the 1960s," she wrote in 1995, reflecting on the Atlanta child murders of 1979 to 1981, "despite our attentiveness to the legislative inequity and social imbalance, despite our newly integrated classrooms and all our affirmative action, we were not safe. And especially, our children were not safe."[29] Poignantly, Holloway rued "the threat against [the Atlanta] children's lives came not only from a murderer who marked his victims by their color, but from the color which marked the children as vulnerable."³⁰ A little more than a decade before the twenty-four child and six adult murders terrorized black Atlanta and black people across the country, King's four children sat at arm's length from their murdered father's casket, taking in the lesson all of Atlanta's black children would come to confront as a community of potential murder victims themselves: namely, that "being black was a necessary danger in the United States."³¹ So there they were, blankly silent at their mother's side, like the "bewildered and frightened and very small" innocents who sat with Baldwin, afraid at their father's funeral in Harlem. Small as the King children looked to be, uncomprehending alongside their suddenly widowed mother, an aspect of their grief was "very gallant," as it is generally with "children at such moments," according to Baldwin. "It has something to do with their silence and gravity and with the fact that one cannot help them" as they puzzle over death and the impenetrable shock it is to youth.³²

Likely no black child in public memory has ever shown how "bewildered and frightened and very small" the murderous threat against black life can leave a black child feeling as vividly as Bernice King restless on her mother's lap when "The Drum Major Instinct" played in high fidelity overhead. The voice she recognized immediately, but locating it was a mystery much too cryptic for a five-year-old. Hearing her father preaching, Bernice King looked "startled." "She jerked her head around, expecting to see him. She stared at the casket intently."³³ Bemused by the disorienting strangeness of experiencing her father's voice outside of his body, which she knew very clearly to be immured in the floriated box before her, Bernice leaned in on her mother's lap, now looking into Coretta's face and silently searching for answers. In time, words would come to Bernice. Many years later, the memory of that experience returned to her. Not surprisingly, she recalled it as a "traumatic" event:

> To prepare me for seeing my dad in another form, my mother had told me that he wouldn't be able to talk to me or hear me. That's hard for a child of four, five, or six to understand. I was on my mother's lap, more faced toward her, resting on her lap, tired and frankly, cranky; it was boring for a little kid. So I now hear my father's voice. I was jerking my head around, looking at the casket like he was going to come out. . . . I was looking around—where is he?—of course, he was dead. I remember that specifically. It was traumatic.³⁴

Perhaps predictably, given the traumatic force of the paternal soundings of his version of funereal phonography on Bernice, memory of her father's Ebenezer undying discloses a vague Freudian dynamic enlivening it. Inasmuch as the father in Bernice King's narration could only be heard by her, not seen, while a brooding mother, *saying nothing*, turns her studied gaze away from the solicitous look of the child and toward the vacant thought-space in front of her, a primal scene of sound and subjectivity obtained as the child, her senses shocked nearly to horror, comes to an unwelcome awareness of the essential alienation of voice from the body. That human speech (or "the sonorous substance," by which I mean, after Derrida, "the voice phenomenologically taken"[35]) should be separable from the fleshly materiality of its source-body (in its "opaqueness," in its condition as "*Leib*"[36]) is a shock, in other words, equal to the Oedipal surprise.

The scene of the child's recognition in Bernice King's flashback to her father's postmortem powers of speech and sound thus argues for a subjectivity apart, I contend, a mode of time and being at once deep within and far beyond the strictures and structures of being and knowing exercising power within the visual regimes governing modernity. None has pointed to this radical otherness, this manifestly *sonic* subjectivity apart, more vividly than the five-year-old little girl to whom it revealed itself obliquely at King's funeral. In video and photographic memory, the picture of her gesturing as she innocently searches the sanctuary for a live speaker evokes the phenomenological voice of "my dad," as she said, "in another form."

By the otherness of King's "phenomenological voice," I mean to call up Derrida's notion of speech that is before or above or after the body, a vocalism which dwells "in the breath" separate from the physicality of verbalization. The "phenomenological voice" is disembodied, "continu[ing] to speak and be present to itself—*to hear itself*—in the absence of the world" it would otherwise expect to be addressing.[37] Bernice King may have been the only one to properly look for the phenomenological voice ("I was looking around—where is he?—of course, he was dead"), but the one thousand others who didn't look wondered at it all the same. The tape of King's last sermon mystified many by its impression of unmediated (black) aliveness. "There was his voice echoing through the church. It was amazing—where was this coming from?"[38] a great many wanted to know. Why did the sound of King's voice seem so palpably ghostly? Nearly a century after the introduction of funereal phonography, the surprise King's voice elicited was hardly in its technological novelty. To what extent, then, was the *vox dei* effect, which so clearly disquieted King's children and overwhelmed his brother and closest friends, produced out of an *architectural* complicity—the high roof lines, for instance, or the reflective properties of wood and plaster—lending to the tape's broadcast an exceptional acoustic intensity? Might not the redbrick building on Auburn Avenue have offered up its physical design and materials as a built-in acoustic supplement to the tape- and public-address technologies responsible for the first soundings of King's acousmatic afterlife that day? I aver that wholly separate from the unique blues-grain of King's voice and the prevailing technofashion of magnetic tape recording, the acoustic architecture of Ebenezer was no small variable in exciting both "amazing" and "traumatic" listening responses.

I will explore this matter more and in greater detail later, but let it be said presently that whatever the depth or dynamic of sound King's postmortem preaching had on Bernice King and other mourners that haunted melancholic morning in 1968, Coretta King setting right Abernathy's misunderstanding of what "Sermon Excerpts" was to signify emphasizes another key aspect of the black modernist soundscape within which I am situating King's career as a black preacher and orator. Specifically, at the scene of death's formal acknowledgment, King's funeral, a surprising *dis*articulation of death happens as an upheaval or ghostly irruption upon that which might be aptly called the *death sentences* spoken over King's remains in DeWolf's tribute and Abernathy's misguided sermonizing. The strong, stentorian rumblings of King's recorded voice "anarranges every line"[39] of ceremonial speech and text delivered by one or the other as his own exorbitant tone of voice militates against death's claim on him. Against the grave as against the church walls, a sonic materiality "vibrates against its frame like a resonator, and troubled air gets out," takes to the air.[40] Overhead, King's "stolen life," by ghostly means his again, re-sounds.[41]

Well past such para-ontological provocations about King I have already considered, the echoing playback of "The Drum Major Instinct" inside Ebenezer set in motion another crisis altogether, one obtaining between two discrete modes of listening: direct listening and acousmatic (or "reduced") listening. In his pioneering 1996 work *Traité des Objets Musicaux*, the late French music theorist, Pierre Schaeffer, famously distinguished *acoustical* from *acousmatic* sound. Shaeffer's student, Michel Chion, explained Schaeffer's thought concisely: "Acousmatic listening is the opposite of direct listening, which is the 'natural' situation where sound sources are present and visible."[42] Whereas the acoustical field is constituted by a physics of sonic waves, vibrations, frequencies, and durational time within empirically defined spatiotemporal frames, acousmatic listening, or "the acousmatic experience of sound," on the other hand, disavows the "visible, tactile, and physically quantifiable" imperatives valorized in acoustical science; rather, the acousmatic "reduces sounds to the field of pure listening."[43] More simply put, we refer to the acousmatic as that sound the source of which is unseen to the listener, invisible as the great and powerful pretender ruling Oz. Issuing from an indeterminate source, acousmatic sound is the distillation of the acoustical event reduced to the nakedness of the "sound object" itself or "the autonomous sonic effect" in the world.[44] For Schaeffer, as Brian Kane explains, "the acousmatic experience of sound"—which Kane, echoing Chion, has called "the acousmatic situation"—"opens up the possibility of identifying modes of listening more *essential* than those that depend primarily on context" or source-specific narratives.[45]

Since acoustical sound, by contrast, "is always in danger of being apprehended as something other than itself," acousmatic listening, Kane continues, "only truly emerges when a sound no longer functions *for another* as a medium, but rather is perceived *as such*."[46] In this way it "grant[s] auditory access to transcendental spheres, different in kind from the purely sonic effect—a way of listening to essence, truth, profundity, ineffability, or interiority" even if we must admit that "we cannot specify precisely the kind of transcendence heard in the sound."[47] As much a cultural practice as a specialized technique or technology of musical or pedagogical audition,[48] acousmatic listening, encouraging if not simultaneously encouraged by a *cultural* form of what in brain science is an expression of cross-modal neuroplasticity, posits "a shared, intersubjective practice of attending to musical and nonmusical sounds, a way of listening to the soundscape that is cultivated when the source of sounds is beyond the horizon of visibility, uncertain, underdetermined, bracketed, or willfully and imaginatively suspended. The term 'acousmatic listening' should be understood as a rubric intended to capture a set of historically situated strategies and techniques for listening to sounds unseen."[49] With just this sort of listening in mind, I intend to explore the acousmatic disturbance at King's funeral further. In the section that follows, I propose that King's audio inbreaking upon the final rites of his own funeral event realized nothing other than (as Moten would surely have said it) a visitation, the revenant King as phenomenological or acousmatic voice which, giving the impression of coming out of nowhere, calls notice to several surprising effects of physical space on sound and audition even as it raises the unexpected metaphysical question derived from the acousmatic situation: *Where was this coming from?*

Disarticulating Death

Just as the acousmatic experience of (King's) sound is resistant to scientism and other positivist forms of knowing, there are sounds in and touching the earth that are, conversely, inapprehensible to properly aesthetic judgment, instinct, or impression. Those sounds, such as the sound of the Ebenezer congregation affirming King's live preaching with their answering murmuration and intermittent outbursts, or that of the asphalt shuffle of an estimated 100,000 mourners moving en masse through downtown Atlanta three miles to Morehouse College for the public memorial, or the whistle of an infrequent breeze lightly gusting through a barely raised window, or indeed the dramatic tone and timbre of King's own amplified voice, at times too awful for words, constitute the greater part of the soundscape of King's burial. Against this backdrop of preaching and procession, and the affective framework of mourning and memorialization inflected by, and giving rise to, the expansive repertoire of fugitive sounds in all their ensemblic expressivity, I want to interrogate that which can only be called the *sonic ecology of black emancipatory hope and political resistance*. Within this historical economy of sound's black political effects, King's vibrato-spectrality alternately comes and goes, enters and exits, departs and returns, as the twentieth century's lead voice-in-relation.[50]

But for the serendipity of the automortographic conclusion to "The Drum Major Instinct," King's enduring sermon of last wishes might not have been of great historical importance, in the final analysis. To be frank, not a great deal of its text (heavily cribbed) recommends it alongside "I Have a Dream," "A Knock at Midnight," "Remaining Awake through a Revolution," or "I've Been to the Mountaintop." And yet there is an acoulogical property in the voicing of "The Drum Major Instinct" that commends it all the same, a materiality of affect and (dis)articulation exceeding mere lexical intelligibility and straining after that which *comes after* words, which is to say both that which remains in the wake of words (ἐπί, *epi* + λόγος, *logos*) and that which in thought is in pursuit of them (πρό, *pro* + λόγος, *logos*). Insofar as this second-level signification coming after words inheres in "The Drum Major Instinct," listening closely to King's preaching on tape, one hears not what passes as exceptional wordsmithing so much as the very passing of words, their own dying, that is, to normative verbal units and grammars. Inasmuch as "The Drum Major Instinct" is remembered by King's "dying words," I mean to say, its distinction as a black cultural sound object also lay in King's feeling for "dying words" as a black speech act. Even as he speaks of death,

King's voice, by turns rolling and rumbling, denies death the presumption of its power to impose arbitrary ends—denies death, I mean, the privilege of *sentencing* black life as an exercise of sovereign (necro)power in language.

Despite its debt to J. Wallace Hamilton's "Drum Major Instincts," as a sound object King's "The Drum Major Instinct" peroration, reproduced above, not only departs from Hamilton's text as an extempore coda to it; unlike Hamilton's, tonally King's sermon *rages*.[51] In earnest the prophetic voice comes on, full-throated, not only to assail the nations for the "bitter, colossal contest for supremacy" they've entered but to declare an impassioned defense for his life and work ("I want you to be able to say *that day* that *I did try-y-y* to feed the hungry!"). It was hardly the subdued expression of traditional funeral oratory he communicated. Instead, King finished his preaching shouting, his voice thunderous over the quiet bereaved. Words became glass bursting in a back draft of rapture and righteous indignation. As Lischer writes,

> What God expects of the prophet is not flowery ritual but a kind of divine madness that shatters the complacency of religious people. The origins of prophecy are in ecstasy. The root meaning of *to prophesy* may be "to slaver," "to foam at the mouth," hence the utterances of one whose sensibilities the spirit has completely alienated from civilized life and discourse. Hebrew scholars contend that prophets are "maladjusted" figures whose "pathological" visions are given utterance in tones "one octave too high for our ears."[52]

While the argumentative and affective value of the store of rhetorical devices Lischer traces in King's preaching is beyond question,[53] not even those considered sonic (e.g., alliteration, assonance, onomatopoeia) yield utterances sufficiently indeterminate (insofar as they remain, after all, identifiable as "devices") to produce "tones . . . 'too high for our ears.'" By the time King delivered "The Drum Major Instinct" at Ebenezer in February, he was altogether given over to, which is to say he was resignedly receptive toward, the transportive power of the prophetic utterance to overwhelm words with an-archic sounds.

The dramatic moment "The Drum Major Instinct" reached its climactic peroration, departing radically from the temporal pretensions of the sentence as the finished work of words, King dealt his death a double undoing. For brooding over "that something that we call death" and the hoped-for praise of those left behind "allows the dead," in Derridean thought, "a sort of *survivance*, a kind of living on" in the face of (if not the very jaws of) that death which all death-bound subjects know is surely to come "not only after their death [sic] . . . but even before." It is as though the ones contemplating their death beforehand and what is to be conveyed after it "were already living on posthumously before their death, as if they had found a way, not simply to utter some prophetic intimation of their own death," as Pascale-Anne Brault and Michael Naas have written on the work of mourning, "but to enact the impossible speech act . . . : 'I am dead.'"[54] In the same way, King's "prophetic intimation" of the death that was to befall him before most of the audience hearing "Sermon Excerpts" knew of its original auguring afforded his death a narrative tense otherwise than the perfectly past, which physical death pretends to accomplish at the end of one's biological life. Rather, "a kind of living on" approached by way of a ghostly remainder in and after death—not the occurrence of death itself but "something *in* what occurs [as death], something to come that conforms to what occurs"—urged the assumptive pastness of King's life rather toward a resolutely anterior futurity instead.[55] In "The Drum Major Instinct," as King directs his obsequies to come, he imagines that his life shall have expired already as he thinks on—indeed, *feels*—the fatedness of an ever approaching dying. In "The Drum Major Instinct," that is, death is not an *event* set apart from the materiality of living by a biological limit so much as an enduring *eventuality*, an indefinite tense "out of joint," as Derrida says, with what is and was and will have come to pass. In its ontotheological half-life, extended by the ghostly aliveness of "Sermon Excerpts," King's death "de-synchronizes, [and] recalls us to anachrony," that is.[56] It is "a ghost waiting" ahead of time at the end of words.[57]

Notwithstanding Burns's reading of King's funeral as "a deliberately staged 'image event,'"[58] the haunting of the mourning space inside and outside by the ghostly sonority of the dead man disappearing words into plainchant, vibrato-speak, lyrical flights and organ tones was, by any standard, epiphenomenal. Everywhere King's voice filled hollow space. Everywhere "this non-object, this non-present present, this being-there of [the] absent . . . departed one" sounded a disarticulating power.[59] His effect was felt directly as that of someone else, some other quantity, strange, perhaps transfigured in death, the disorientation to be expected. The work of mourning a specter is disquieting to the extent that "one does not know if it is living or if it is dead. Here is—or rather there is, over there, an unnameable or almost unnameable thing: something, between something and someone, anyone or anything, some thing, 'this thing,' but this thing and not any other, this thing that looks at us, that concerns us [*qui nous regard*], comes to defy semantics and much as ontology."[60] Here the politics or "work" of mourning Derrida theorizes, to which I shall turn more fully below, has its most reliable witness not in the widow staring at the casket as the recorded sermon plays but the little girl "resting in her lap," jerking her head and "looking around—where is he?" Here, we sit with her, recognizing "something, between something and someone," between something strange and someone frighteningly familiar but mystified as to the source of it since we are blind to see "'this thing'" which has already presciently seen us. Audibly addressed ("If any of you are around when I have to meet my day . . ."), we feel ourselves seen sitting silently by, but seeing no body address us, "we must fall back on its voice" disembodied.[61] "This thing and not any other, this thing that looks at us," as Derrida helps us understand, "comes to defy semantics," comes not only to be "almost unnameable" except by its thingly properties; it comes to defy the denotative drive in speech and communication as well, so much so that even what "comes to defy semantics" is not irreducible.

Bernice King's visible bewilderment at her father's voice sounding, bodiless, "over there," which is to say somewhere separate from his body which she had already seen *up there*, expressionless, is an important heuristic for all. Her child-wise acceptance of the acousmatic situation, the little girl having regained the stillness of a big girl soon enough, calls us to a similar attitude of reduced listening, one more abstractly called for by the theory-wise wonderings of Fred Moten. In Moten, we have a scholarly model of reduced listening for the page as *he* listens with sensitive, adept, and generatively *over*hearing ears to poet and free jazz genius Cecil Taylor. Taylor's *Chinampus*, a performative assemblage of poetic and percussive experimentation, opens up the free jazz enthusiast to "frequencies outside and beneath the range of reading,"[62] frequencies of black language and sociality that "defy semantics" and supplant words. Admittedly, "The Drum Major Instinct" is scarcely in the vein of Taylor's avant-gardism, but who can deny the vague an-archic closeness between them as King's voice grew increasingly and palpably prophetic from 1965 to his assassination and, thus, inclined him to similarly an-archic ends of expression? Pointing up the unfathomed "depths of his militancy" largely overlooked by liberal historiography, Lischer writes, "In his latter years [King] accused America of genocide and compared its conduct of war to Nazis'. He warned an audience in Montgomery that any country that had treated its natives as America had would not blink at putting blacks in concentration camps. He warned of long hot summers in the ghettos and began calling for radically new ways of distributing wealth. His final rhetorical strategy was the abandonment of strategy and his own surrender to prophetic rage."[63] Like Taylor's search for a poeticism expressive of certain elemental principles of music that are *prior* to their organization into musical structure, the prophetic names a kind of devolutionary drive, an "abandonment of strategy" *as* strategy for de-forming the (death) sentence that words commend to homiletics as a science of proper preaching. Thus, between the late King and the late Cecil Taylor an an-archic kinship obtains, one set free from the laws of sentence, syntax, and signification to *sound out* (from the outside of the visibly textual) a black aesthetic radicality for revolutionary and would-be revolutionary times.

Specters of King

"Vigilance, therefore: the cadaver is perhaps not ... dead," warns *Specters of Marx: The State of the Debt, the Work of Mourning and the New International*. Under this 1994 title, a late-career Derrida, turning to the political and cultural work of mourning in late capitalism, means "to speak first of all about Marx. About Marx himself. About his testament or his inheritance. And about a specter, the shadow of Marx, the *revenant*."[64] Grounded in a close reading of *Hamlet*, specifically the scene of visitation by the (voice of the) late king on Prince Hamlet grieving his father's murder and the abrupt loss of the throne to Claudius, *Specters of Marx* reflects on the work of mourning as "attempting to ontologize remains, to make them present" before everyone in order to certify—"to know," absolutely—that the decedent is securely in his place.[65] And yet what of remains which, like King Hamlet, refuse their proper place among the dead-and-forever-buried? The ghostly effect of King's dying words in "The Drum Major Instinct," heard out of time and place ("There was his voice ... —where was this coming from?"), suggests that perhaps *King's* legacy, no less than Marx's, has also been inhabited by a haunting spirit, one set on a disruption of the left-behind order of things, as terrible in its consequentiality as what was portended by the villainy of Claudius. Even at his funeral, King is no more dead than he who "usurp'st" the night in "that fair and warlike form / In which the Majesty of buried Denmark / Did sometimes march."[66] *Hauntology* is the term Derrida conceives for this persistent beingness of the (un)dead in the temporal present, a phenomenality exemplified by the fantastic power of King's spectral voice. In appealing to *Specters of Marx*, I am positing an analogous hauntology to Marx's, one that sheds light on the peculiar ontology of King's voice and vibrato as they refuse his death and threaten a return while the national mourning, abstracted and ritualized into a holiday, keeps the disruptive spirit of the drum major for justice sentimentally at bay.

As Derrida explains, contrary to capitalism's repeated pronouncements of communism's permanent defeat at the collapse of the former Soviet Union, a Marxian return from the dead is an acute worry of the West. The threat the United States and Europe claimed was overcome around 1989 is feared to be undead. Thus, the move "to adjust all of politics to the frightening hypothesis of a visitation" by the spirit of communism reveals that very spirit as the source of angst modern liberal politics produces with every radical critique of capitalism.[67]

> There is today in the world a *dominant* discourse, or rather one that is on the way to becoming dominant, on the subject of Marx's work and thought, on the subject of Marxism (which is perhaps not the same thing), on the subject of the socialist International and the universal revolution, on the subject of a more or less slow destruction of the revolutionary model in its Marxist inspiration, on the subject of the rapid, precipitous, recent collapse of societies that attempted to put in into effect at least in what we will call for the moment, citing once again the Manifesto, "Old Europe," and so forth.[68]

Sensing the world-dominant discourse aurally as it is canted "to the rhythm of a cadenced march," Derrida lays bare the capitalist colonial fantasy: "Marx is dead, communism is dead, very dead, and along with it its hopes, its discourse, its theories, and its practices. It says: long live capitalism, long live the market, here's to the survival of economic and political liberalism!"[69] Derrida's theorizing, or what we might try to imagine him enacting as a political dialectics of the legacy of Marx, explodes this fantasy of a teleological, triumphalist politics according to which liberal capitalism comes to prevail as though by providential will.

An analogous fantasy not yet deconstructed persists in American life until this very day. It is born not of the fear of a resuscitated communism so much as of an alarm triggered by portents of black protest and white racial comeuppance threatening to hobble the racial scaffolding supporting expansionist liberal-market dreams. This, the dominant neoliberal discourse feigns obliviousness to, while it disappears the specter of black rebellion into public statuaries, memorial gardens, inner-city odonyms, and a day off—all in King's name. However, unlike the hauntology of Marx, which has as its totem Marx and Friedrich Engels's *The Communist Manifesto*, the specter of King in those postintegrationist formulations against poverty, racism, and militarism that neoliberal actors so cheerily co-opt in their facile domestication of ideas like "civil disobedience," "nonviolent resistance," and "political noncooperation" has no philosophical tract or treatise to immortalize him in print. No Bible, no compendium or codex—no *corpus*, I mean—only the cadaver of him who, though dead, orates a conjuring of the revolutionary spirit in print's place.[70]

King's spectral presence at the Ebenezer service solemnizing his death, then—his being-there estranged from his own corpse—was as much a hailing of the revolutionary spirit of the times as a startling return to public voice, though dead. Ebenezer's complex acoustic, instrumental, and audio technologies aided the hailing effect. But whereas the specter of Marx "announces and calls for a presence *to come*," a *future* "manifestation of the manifest" resistance already clearly coming, to quote Derrida again,[71] King's hailing is a calling-up that is rather like a dialing-into on a frequency immanent and audible in the present. In his acousmatic delivery of what Abernathy called "his last sermon," King blurred benediction with invocation in much the same way Langston Hughes described the blended operation of death in his poem "Drum."

> Bear in mind
> That death is a drum
> Beating forever
> . . . .
> Death is a drum,
> A signal drum,
> Calling life
> To come!
> Come!
> Come![72]

With a similar bidding, the spectral King—he who was thought to have been silenced for good and yet speaks—sounded life(-like) from (the beyond of) Atlanta. His voice a trumpet of conscience, he hailed his listeners into the new Black International of emancipatory thought, action, and feeling from Aimé Césaire, Léon-Gontran Damas, and Léopold Sédar Senghor to Kwame Nkrumah and Malcolm X. Quite apart from *what* he said, though, it was *how* King said what he wished to be said about him upon his death— rumbling, thundering, *shouting* it—that rattled the listening to consciousness. King's "dying words," both in the sense of a self-referential valediction and the practice of straining against words' limits in the performative mode (as rumbling, thundering, *shouting*, etc.), seemed intent on getting a hauntological hearing: "I *triiiied* to be right on the war question. . . . I *did* try to feed the hungry. . . . I *did* try in my life to clothe those who were naked. . . . I *did* try in my life to visit those who were in prison. . . . I *triiiied* to love and serve humanity." Italics hardly express the volume, pitch, or fever of King's preaching voice. However impoverished their struggle to reproduce King's sounds and cadence, though, as aural indices of articulatory stress (rather than a typographic spotlighting of some utterance's most consequential terms), they gesture nonetheless to a dis-articulating of regulative pacing and pronunciation. By just such means the revolutionary spirit is welcomed to "Come!"

Thus did King, by a force stronger than death, portend (something like) resurrection even as he was being funeralized. Implicitly, his spectral voice troubled the planned close of the funeral liturgy as it sounded its own hauntological undying. The printed order of service complete, King's remains were carried out of the church and hoisted onto a wagon pulled by two mules. Behind them, a procession numbering more than fifty thousand trailed the casket ceremonially to Morehouse. Passing the Georgia State Capitol building, the Democratic governor, Lester Maddox, scrambled to barricade himself inside for fear of the procession.[73] Armed troops, authorized to kill, guarded the Capitol's perimeter, vividly testifying to a much wider worry of the state that King's death might inspire a black revolutionary spirit it could not quell. For Maddox, particularly, the mules pulling King's funeral wagon might just as well have been stallions and the parade of mourners a black army advancing on Atlanta. Who knows but that he had previously heard King's vibrato voice himself—heard King's exorbitant tones, his vocal inflections and verbal breaks, the tremulant terribleness (un)hidden in his speech—and sensed its latent world-shaking power? If so, he would not have been alone among Georgia's segregationists or the state's oligarchs in his dread of the imagined drumbeats of a coming racial and economic justice foreboded in King's voice. For this same terribleness which provokes the segregationists' dread stirs the disinherited to strength with a promise, hauntologically conveyed, that the last shall be first and a new kingdom was surely coming.

2

Swinging the God Box

Modernism, Organology, and the Ebenezer Sound

If preserving the memory of her late husband's stirring voice was Coretta King's principal objective in re-sounding his dying (of) words in "The Drum Major Instinct" at the end of the funeral liturgy memorializing his martyred life, Atlanta's Ebenezer Baptist Church could not have been more fitted to her intention. Beyond the obvious consolation Ebenezer offered as the center of spiritual life and leadership for three generations of the Williams/King family, Ebenezer lent arresting realism to the audio playback of King's preaching, an acoustic fidelity owed to more than the mimetic power of magnetic tape technology. Those intimate enough with the Kings to have seating inside Ebenezer when "The Drum Major Instinct" played overhead heard King at his own funeral, as those who had been present two months earlier had heard it live from the very pulpit it seemed it might possibly be issuing from again, transcendently. For the late preacher's mourners heard not only his hauntological voice preaching but theirs as well—the antiphonal voices of the sermon's listening community, that is—and the greater soundscape shaping its hearing in black ears.

In this chapter, I want to argue for a black sacred soundscape and audition of miscegenated middle- and lowbrow exigencies informing the (theo)social and aesthetic sensibilities animating what I call "the Ebenezer sound." What's more, I shall show how this matrix of mixed musical, oratorical, and modern environmental sonorities shaped, even as it would also come to be shaped by, King's preaching practice at Ebenezer and similar settings. Specifically, to understand the etiology of the Ebenezer sound, I look to a history of modern (black) building design—here, Ebenezer, but I have in mind other modern (black) architectures, too, which I shall consider in more than one of the chapters to come—and to the related matter of organology as a concern for modern church architecture and its acoustic interests. Architecture and instrumentation, then, are key to the mood and meaning of black religious modernism as it prevailed in the embodied and disembodied sounds of blackness at Ebenezer between 1922 and 1974. I take Ebenezer in these years as a cultural index of the social and material aspirations of a black ascendant class, Northern and Southern, to racial modernity. Like the composition of Ebenezer itself, I have this caste in mind as overlaying but not precisely reproducing the traditional black middle class. These desiring moderns are recognizable not by the formulaic determinants of social science but according to a sounded sociality Houston Baker once called "cultural performance," which refers to a "distinctively Afro-American sounding of events" achieved, in no small measure, by the "blending ... of class and mass."[1] In a way, this investment in "cultural performance" was built into Ebenezer's walls.

Divine Designs: Ecclesial Architecture and the Ensoniment of America

Ebenezer Baptist Church has sat on the southeast corner of Auburn Avenue and Jackson Street since 1914.[2] Organized in 1886 by John A. Parker, who was almost certainly born enslaved in Georgia in 1844, the church first occupied a small "box-like building" on Airline Street in the city's fourth ward before moving into a larger structure on McGruder Street in 1895. The move to McGruder Street was deftly shepherded by Adam Daniel Williams, King's maternal grandfather and Ebenezer's second pastor. Under Williams's leadership, Ebenezer flourished. By 1901 its membership had outgrown its McGruder Street structure, forcing Williams to relocate the church again, this time into "'a beautiful, spacious structure, 40 × 80,' at 176 Gilmer Street," formerly (white) Fifth Baptist Church.[3] For a sum of $2,500, the wood-framed building was purchased "together with ... all furniture in said church except organs, pulpit set, communion set and desk."[4] Ten years on, Ebenezer had become one of Atlanta's most significant black churches, with a membership well above four hundred. To reflect its impressive growth—Ebenezer was scarcely a dozen congregants when Williams took over—Williams was soon laying out plans for an imposing *new* construction. In 1913, on behalf of the Ebenezer congregation, Williams "received bond for title to a lot at the southeast corner of Auburn Avenue and Jackson Street."[5] The edifice that was to be built there would take forty thousand dollars and nine more years of effort to complete. Finished in 1922, the new building in southeast Atlanta was to be Ebenezer's home for seventy-seven years.

Although church and city records show clearly A. D. Williams's leadership in all the legal and financial transactions related to Ebenezer's Auburn Avenue construction, just whose design plan was realized by Ebenezer's completion is unknown. In its Late Gothic Revival style, Ebenezer's architecture, like the architecture of so many other early twentieth-century Baptist, Methodist, Congregationalist, and Presbyterian houses of worship, reflected significant cultural changes and theological shifts in American evangelical identity and practice—namely, the democratization of ecclesial polity in US Christianity and the aural emphases in the new Protestant theology of the Word saw material expression in the new ecclesial architecture of the fin de siècle and the decades immediately following.[6] Specific as these two vital shifts were to the late nineteenth and early twentieth centuries, however, the Late Gothic Revivalism in the United States endured many decades more as a preferred style in mainline church architecture. Thus, it was not separate from the acoustical resonance of King's mid-century witness as it was preached within Ebenezer's lofty walls.

As significant an architectural movement as it was in Europe, Gothic Revivalism was slow in coming to America. It was three centuries after it flourished in England, France, and Germany before a late stage of Gothic Revivalism finally dominated nineteenth-century public architecture in America. Part of a renaissance movement, the turn to Gothic Revivalism in American public architecture was not by chance or, looking back, surprising. Its aesthetics, after all, were well suited to America's "ensoniment," that stage of American scientific and cultural history when—and this largely on the strength of phonography's nineteenth-century invention—"sound itself became an object and a domain of thought and practice."[7] According to architectural historian Jeanne Halgren Kilde, "the sixteenth-century Christian reform movement that quickly escalated into the Protestant Reformation minimized the essentially visual nature of centuries of Christian worship, which had been dominated by the celebration of the Eucharist, and emphasized a new linguistic, particularly aural, experience."[8] In challenging the visual ritualism of the Roman Catholic Mass, in other words,

Martin Luther and other Reformed theologians also led early Protestantism to a new aurality of faithful listening and devout hearing engendered by the sacralization of the proclaimed Word of God in Protestant thought and liturgy.

As the expository sermon replaced Mass as the liturgical center of worship in Protestant practice, closer cognitive attention to the sermonic presentation was demanded. The design of church buildings where the new liturgies were enacted thus evolved to reflect new theological imperatives. Writes Kilde,

> Not surprisingly, this shift in focus of Christian worship brought radical changes to the spatial arrangements of churches. Protestant services . . . required the fixed attention and participation of audiences. Listening became a primary worship practice, and in a remarkable shift in Christian design priorities, facilitating listening emerged as an important principle in Protestant worship space. The existing Christian (i.e., Roman Catholic) churches of the Reformation period, however, had not been designed to facilitate listening. . . . Protestant reformers immediately recognized the need to modify traditional worship space to aid worshippers' reception of the sermon.[9]

Protestant architecture lowered the pulpit, for example, to stage height from its former placement on an interior wall high overhead. Centuries on, the nineteenth-century search for "new measures" to radically increase and accommodate the number of converts in Christian churches during the Second Great Awakening inspired another Protestant design convention, one that formalized the greater role music would come to play in Protestant worship settings. The "neomedieval auditorium church" in the United States borrowed from the public theater and opera house not only their front-center performance focus but the majestic ornamentality of gleaming organ pipes prominent above the stage-level lectern.[10]

In her book *When Church Became Theatre: The Transformation of Evangelical Architecture and Worship in Nineteenth-Century America*, Kilde draws attention to an 1886 layout of Minneapolis's First Baptist Church as an early model of this auditorium ecclesiality in America. She notes how "the lavishly articulated stage" inside First Baptist "functioned as the focal point of the room." More notable, however, was the arrangement of liturgical space and furniture emphasizing the new acoustical imperative: "A portable lectern, which served a pulpit, claimed the center but was dwarfed by the features located behind and above it—the baptistery and choir, partially obscured by a short curtain, the grand organ console, and the stenciled organ pipes that soared to the ceiling."[11] Taken singly, these perspectival details, against the still broader backdrop Kilde paints of a balcony above the main floor and a proscenium arch backgrounding the pulpit, suggest a theatrical opulence meant to inspire the devout visually. Taken together, however, organ pipes and pulpit, choir and console, so far from only signposting First Baptist's wealth or churchly formalism, disclose in their spatial contiguity the aural priorities of Gothic and Late Gothic Revival styles. In this respect (among others), First Baptist Church was, according to Kilde, "highly representative" of its era.[12]

Following in the same architectural vocabulary as First Baptist, Atlanta's Ebenezer Baptist Church fashioned a similar aural ecology of worship and ritual practice. More to the point, the neomedieval structure on Auburn Avenue and Jackson Street established the brick-and-mortar conditions for the peculiarly Protestant ensemble of sounds reflected in and as the synchronicity of sermon, song, and sacred instrumentation in modern liturgical thought and activity. Ironically, the same design also afforded Ebenezer the possibility of a counteracoustics that the high-church ritualism of First Baptist almost surely suppressed as irreverent. The din of black audition—of verbal and extraverbal antiphon, congregational musicking, and the audibility of ecstatic experience, for example—at times answered the principal sounds of authoritative speech and choral song in Ebenezer's worship with interpellations of unratified black noise. It was within this acoustic environment where sermon, song, and fugitive sound were keyed to an emergent black religious modernism that Martin Luther King Jr.'s rare voice and rhythm took shape and tone. If the Late Gothic architecture of Ebenezer helped to realize the spatial conditions in which a modern black Protestant soundscape might powerfully influence King's *hearing* the sacred sounds of blackness, then it was the church's commitment to the sonic affordances of pipe organs over many years that lent King tonal intelligence. Blurring respectability and resistance for the better part of the church's one-hundred-year Auburn Avenue history, Ebenezer, like countless other black religious moderns, privileged the sound and stateliness of the pipe organ early in its liturgical life. A significant element in the evolution of what I call "the Ebenezer sound," the pipe organ was one of the church's earliest investments and a signal feature of the church's interior design as early as 1922. Vital though they were to the sacred soundscape within which King developed as a preacher and orator, Ebenezer's earliest organs did not create the Ebenezer sound in and of themselves. Rather the Ebenezer sound

2.1 Ebenezer Baptist Church, Atlanta, GA. Interior showing pipes of the Wurlitzer pipe organ. Courtesy of Ebenezer Baptist Church of Atlanta.

was realized in ensemblic relation to the voices, technology, and acoustical architecture they variously melded with as equal palimpsests, I shall argue, of black modernist angst and assertion, a tension King would inherit and grapple with in pulpits and on speaking stages his whole career.

Organology and the Ebenezer Sound

In *The Soundscape of Modernity: Architectural Acoustics and the Culture of Listening in America, 1900–1933*, historian Emily Thompson derides as, "well, shortsighted" those "scholars who assume that consideration of the visual and the textual is sufficient for understanding modernity."[13] With reparative aims in mind, Thompson sets her study to the task of "restoring the aural dimension of modernity." Specifically, *The Soundscape of Modernity* maps "a history of aural culture in early twentieth-century America. It charts dramatic transformations in what people heard, and it explores equally significant changes in the ways that people listened to those sounds." Crucially, Thompson argues that "a new kind of sound" came into being, "the product of modern technology."[14] Not only does Thompson's claim forcefully intervene upon the visual prejudices of modern historiography, however; it also posits a philosophy or phenomenology of history radically different from what scholars seeking to understand modernity characteristically "assume." The implication here is that history in itself, so far from presenting as mute experience, inheres in a complex materiality of sound as much as it does in the facticity of historical objects and events visually remembered. Sound, then, may disorient normative historical temporalities. *Early-, late-, pre-, post-, middle-* and *modern* may be differentiated by a more deliberate *listening* to historical records as new organizing logics reframe, or explode, their former presumptions under a scopic regime. More concretely than the radical epistemic inferences it makes, however, Thompson's argument lends itself to understanding how the modern technological evolution of the pipe organ and its appropriation by black religious modernism gave rise to the elegiac allusiveness of the Ebenezer sound in its brooding, atonal, and *black* feeling. For, in the main, it was the sound of the electric pipe organ (in historicosonic contradistinction to the cast bronze bells of nineteenth-century ecclesial culture[15]) that struck the keynote of black modernist hope loudest at Ebenezer, its undulant echo resonant in King's preaching voice.

Importantly, between 1922 and 1974, pipe organs occupied a central place at Ebenezer. The earliest, an "old John Brown pump organ,"[16] believed to have been brought to Auburn Avenue from the church's Gilmer and Bell Streets location, operated on a mechanical system. Requiring a human hand to supply it air with bellows, the John Brown organ relied upon a tracker action to produce sound—that is, to produce its sound "the organist opens up the wind channel by direct mechanical action: each key is directly connected via strips of wood called trackers and a mechanism called a roller board to the palettes that cover the openings to the pipes. The result is a very direct connection between the organist and the sound the instrument makes."[17] Somewhat later, with Ebenezer's membership and reputation still emergent under Williams's successor, Martin Luther King Sr., and with its musical life flourishing under Alberta Williams King, wife and mother of the elder and younger King, respectively, Ebenezer replaced the old mechanical tracker organ with a "crack new" Wurlitzer, said to be "the most modern type available."[18] Manufactured by the Wurlitzer Company of North Tonawanda, New York, the new organ, with its two thousand electrically operated pipes, eliminated the need for a manual supply of air. Dedicated

November 1, 1940, the organ sat dramatically at the front of the church, its gilded pipes raised ceiling-high. For black Atlantans it was a marvel to behold. Floor to gallery, locals packed the dedication event to see and experience it firsthand.

That Ebenezer's new organ should attract so many to its dedication probably came as no surprise. The "Mighty Wurlitzer" was, after all, a theater organ—"the 'Rolls Royce' of the theatre organ world."[19] Originally built to replace early-century silent film orchestras, the Wurlitzer represented "a whole new medium of musical accompaniment—the introduction of the pipe organ into film theatres."[20] While the organ made possible a more intimate correspondence between the cinematic vision and its musical accompaniment, as the organist "could play music from memory, making smooth transitions from one piece to another" and improvise to extend or shorten accompaniment as needed, "the organ [also] helped create a certain atmosphere of luxury and culture"—a mood, that is, as suitable to the aspirational architecture of a neomedieval auditorium church like Ebenezer as it was to Radio City Music Hall (which, since 1932, has kept the largest Wurlitzer organ ever built).[21] Against the opinion of sacred music purists who disavowed the Wurlitzer's capacity for light and nimble sounds (perfect for theater and fairground settings but not churches, they complained), the music leaders at Ebenezer embraced the Wurlitzer's greater flexibilities: its wider range of tones, its whispering *pianissimo possibile*, its thundering *fortissimo*, and, most crucially for this study, its marked tremulant functionality.[22]

But it was hardly the organ's theatrical possibilities alone that fit it to Ebenezer's aural environment. As modernist architectural tastes brought the pipe organ console out from hiding behind concealing walls and partitions designed to obscure its mechanics and render the source of its sound celestial, the Wurlitzer asserted a new kind of subjecthood in American social and religious life. Although architectural historians who have closely studied Ebenezer's structure surmised that the Wurlitzer console was "so large and heavy that it [simply] could not be placed in the choir loft but had to be placed on the floor near the east end of the stage,"[23] it should not be overlooked that the Wurlitzer's electropneumatic action made possible the separation and movement of the console from other parts of the instrument earlier organs did not allow. The compelling logic of size and weight notwithstanding, I mean to suggest Ebenezer's placement of the Wurlitzer console at stage level was also in keeping with the cultural and design logic of the Late Gothic Revival period in the United States. Though not exactly center stage, the console's prominent and front-facing placement "near the east end of the stage" brought the technical and human operations behind the organ sound into plain view. Together with the low-droning neon sign radiating "Ebenezer Baptist Church" over the building's main entrance,[24] the "Mighty Wurlitzer" made Ebenezer's communicants (black) moderns by default. Thus, the pipe organ became, in a phrase borrowed from the title of Jeremy Begbie and Steven Guthrie's 2011 book, a "resonant witness" to, and the unlikely instrument of, a distinctively black religious modernism King would come to sound movingly before black and white publics the same.

From a purely organological vantage point (not to be confused with, or reduced to, scholarly concern with organs or organ-playing specifically), it was the organ, then, rather than the piano, the other most commonplace musical instrument in the modern history of Protestant worship before 1960, that established the tonal foundations of the Ebenezer sound that, in turn, produced King. The elevation of the Wurlitzer, in particular, to sonic and visual prominence in public theaters and houses of worship was not unimportant to this influence but, safe to say, the Wurlitzer was not the last of Ebenezer's pipe organs helping to form its unique sound. In 1956, a Hillgreen-Lane organ replaced the Wurlitzer, and by 1974 an electric Baldwin organ had supplanted the Hillgreen-Lane organ as Ebenezer's primary liturgical instrument until 1999. If Ebenezer's now century-long engagement with the pipe organ seems anomalous in the black church tradition, it is only because so little attention has been paid to the pipe organ in black sacred settings. Still, the keenest observers of black religious life in the twentieth century did not fail to mark the broad appeal of what some styled "the God box" to African American religious moderns.

In 1903, for example, W. E. B. Du Bois depicted "a small organ and stained-glass windows" in his delineation of "a typical [Negro] church in a small Virginia town" in *The Souls of Black Folk*.[25] A few years on, in 1916, he called more specific attention to the efforts of First Baptist Church of Roanoke, Virginia, to purchase "a $2,300 pipe organ." So close to the church's last campaign to finance a $3,300 parsonage, a $750 terrace wall around the church property, and the installation of new gallery pews to the tune of $800,[26] the organ's cost was significant—significant enough that, separate from its leaders' appeal for donations from the readers of *The Crisis* magazine, which Du Bois oversaw, philanthropist Andrew Carnegie was prevailed upon for support. *The Crisis* announced that Carnegie "has subscribed half the fund" for the pipe organ purchase, while the congregation managed to collect $900 on its own.[27] It seems Du Bois's mention of the campaign helped First Baptist raise the needed balance externally. When the new organ was installed sometime later, First

Baptist (today, First Baptist Church–Gainsboro) exulted in its elevating vision and sound. After 1916, one church historian wrote, "many generations sat in awe and admiration of the tall stately pipes set in majestic columns atop the pulpit area and the glorious tones emitting from the great organ."[28]

Despite the dearth of more significant attention to the pipe organ as image and instrument of black cultural modernity, however, there are, in any case, myriad other instances like First Baptist of an implied acoustical modernism in tune with the times of black social critique and ambition. In other words, neither Roanoke's First Baptist nor Atlanta's Ebenezer further south was an exception to the strong desire for a new sacred sound of New Negro piety. Rather, they were the unheeded rule—"typical," to repeat Du Bois's term. Pipe organs of various sizes and sounds were not unusual in modern or aspirational black churches before the 1970s. They could be found among Baptist, African Methodist Episcopal (AME), African Methodist Episcopal Zion, Episcopal, and, if less often, Pentecostal churches.[29] If a complete history of the pipe organ in black ecclesial contexts is still unwritten, though, this is not to say that the pipe organ's importance to the sacred soundscapes of black modernism has gone entirely missing in print. Given the depth of black music's influence on (the sounds of) African American literary practice historically (effecting, over time, a "musical-literary reciprocity," as Emily Lordi argues[30]), we might have expected that an African American novelist would be first to interrogate the pneumatic power of the pipe organ to sound out black religious thought and feeling in the modernist period. Ralph Ellison—novelist, essayist, music critic, instrumentalist—was not an unlikely theorist of the pipe organ's black life. Against those who held the "mistaken notion . . . that classical music had nothing to do with the rhythms, relaxed or hectic, of daily [black] living," Ellison mused over the pipe organ (which Mozart had called "the king of instruments") both in fiction and nonfiction, as personal memories of Oklahoma City's Avery Chapel AME Church and Ira Aldridge Theater, as well as those of Tuskegee Institute Chapel in Tuskegee, Alabama, helped him explore the religiosonic sensibilities of black moderns when he was perhaps least trusted by many as a purveyor of the critical mood of modern black life.[31]

Swinging the God Box

To be sure, Ellison is a contested figure in black cultural politics, although it is not often one says so aloud. The author of what is widely agreed to be among the finest American novels of the twentieth century, *Invisible Man*,

2.2   Interior of First Baptist Church–Gainsboro, Roanoke, VA. Courtesy of the Virginia Room, Roanoke Public Libraries.

and some of the most discerning essays in modern black literary and performance history (e.g., "Harlem Is Nowhere," "Living with Music," "The Little Man at Chehaw Station"), Ellison famously set himself at a distinct remove from the public struggle for racial justice and its vanguard of artists, intellectuals, and activists. Though rarely publicized in deference to the unarguable achievement that was *Invisible Man*, Ellison's elitist reputation has troubled many black critics. Houston Baker's criticisms of Ellison in *Critical Memory: Public Spheres, African American Writing, and Black Fathers and Sons in America*, for example, were cutting, to say the least. For all Ellison's celebrity as one of the most significant black writers of the twentieth century, Baker charged that Ellison was painfully out of touch with the material black world of civil rights thought and activity.

> Ralph Waldo Ellison—the valedictorian of African American letters—reads the black public sphere as a white-instigated and controlled battle royal. His reading misses, of course, all the nascent energy of Civil Rights and Black Power. And when Civil Rights and Black Power became American— indeed global—realities, Ellison reclined in butter-soft seats at exclusive Manhattan clubs, explaining to whites why he could *not* take any active

part in the liberation politics of black Americans. . . ."Alas, Poor Ralph!" He completely missed the *real* modernity of America.³²

Severe as Baker sounds, his appraisal of Ellison's "asymptotic" relationship to "that great curve of *actual* black life" is not unsupported.³³ In "miss[ing] so completely the black spirit of his times," Baker concluded, Ellison demonstrated a failure of black critical memory for the sake of individual gain.³⁴ As much as black liberation politics may have sought his sympathy when his voice was most absent from its concerns, the black civil rights movement did not so much miss Ellison, Baker maintains, as Ellison "missed the *real* modernity."

And yet, to be fair to both critic and author, within *Invisible Man* and, later, *Three Days before the Shooting* . . . , another class of memory—Ellison's black cultural memory, let us call it—far from missing modernity entirely, recalls that essential instrument of modern African American religious thought and feeling, the organ, in his fiction. Whatever else may be true about Ellison's absent identification with the black "spirit of his times," his memory of the material sound and significance of the pipe organ in black cultural contexts suffered little to no lapse at all. That such a detail, prominent in chapter 5 of *Invisible Man*, goes so easily overlooked in Ellison criticism is ironic since *Invisible Man* portrays the organ as "looming" imposingly above the dais in the college chapel and "stretching to the ceiling."³⁵ Although evidently dwarfed by the black metal monstrosity that is the nearby power plant, the organ nevertheless dominates the chapel environment with a rhythm and sound all its own. I look to both novels (at some length) to explore Ellison's clear comprehension of the material investment and sonic depths of experience in the pipe organ as a figure, in black musical performance and sound, of what I will establish as our miscegenated modernity.

First, *Invisible Man*. Early in chapter 5, Ellison's protagonist and scores more, all students, descend onto the walkway leading to the campus chapel. It is the college's Founder's Day and a ceremony in the founder's honor is set to soon begin. The students' measured, winding procession into the chapel is part funeral procession, part zombie apocalypse, the chapel a sepulcher "with its sweeping eaves, long and low as though risen bloody from the earth like the rising moon; vine-covered and earth-colored as though more earth-sprung than man-sprung" (*IM*, 110). Unhurried automatons all, they heed the "doomlike bells" (*IM*, 110). The Invisible Man gets on more mechanically than any:

> Into the doors and into the soft lights I go, silently, past the rows of puritanical benches straight and torturous, finding that to which I am assigned

and bending my body to its agony. There at the head of the platform with its pulpit and rail of polished brass are the banked and pyramided heads of the student choir, faces composed and stolid above the uniforms of black and white; and above them, stretching to the ceiling, the organ pipes looming, a gothic hierarchy of dull gilded gold. (*IM*, 110–11)

Curious as Ellison's mechanical obsessions are ("Modern man, for Ellison, is man attuned to the rhythms of the machine, to the currents and undercurrents of a raceless industrial capitalism," Baker insists[36]), it is not the mechanical interpolation in itself amplifying the significance of the organ in *Invisible Man*, but rather that precise tension which is at root a miscegenation obtaining between biological and mechanical modes of sound and sociality. Here, that is, biology and mechanics meld into a gothic behemoth as the "banked and pyramided heads of the student choir" repeat the visual pattern of the organ's pipes ranked overhead. Similarly, the students' "black and white" uniforms blur that "vague and shifting line" between the biological and technological Mark Seltzer has theorized in *Bodies and Machines*, as the choral chiaroscuro transfigures the singing bodies behind the pulpit into so many keys on the organ keyboard and reverses the original teleology of the organ sound toward a *vox humana* with prospects for a voicing every bit as mechanical as "natural."[37] What Seltzer highlighted as "the problem of the body" in the new machine culture of American modernity is even more starkly illustrated in *Invisible Man*.

The Founder's Day event opens with a voluntary. "Instead of the bells" (*IM*, 110) that dominated the auditory landscape of public summons in nineteenth-century civic and ecclesial cultures, the organ plays "carols to the distances" (*IM*, 110). Soon, though, the prelude comes to its end as the anthropomorphized "organ voices" (*IM*, 116) give way to an a cappella strain rising from a "thin brown girl in white choir robe standing high against the organ pipes, herself become before our eyes a pipe of contained, controlled and sublimated anguish" (*IM*, 117). Separate from the ensemble of other human voices who will shortly join hers, the thin brown-skinned soloist, amalgamated into the organ's architecture, sings, Ellison writes, as if "a disembodied force . . . sought to enter her, to violate her, shaking her, rocking her rhythmically" (*IM*, 116). The girl's stiff body stands caught between several discursive straits: technology and biology, discipline and frisson, generativity and profligacy, respectability and fugitivity, modernity and primitivism, body and flesh. Little surprise, then, that the novel's hero "could not understand the words, but only the mood, sorrowful, vague and ethereal, of the singing" (*IM*, 117) as the singer stands trapped, moreover, between the structure of "A Mighty Fortress Is Our God," on the one hand, and sounds "sorrowful, vague and ethereal," wholly unstructured, on the other. At pains to balance music and mood, rhetorical mastery and the idea-emotion of song, the singer's labor to reconcile these unreconciled strivings recapitulates a vital tension in Ellison's own coming-to-musical-consciousness as a young trumpeter and jazz enthusiast in the 1930s.

In "Living with Music," a narrative essay which, as Ellison biographer Arnold Rampersad averred, "charmingly captures [Ellison's] love of music from his early days in Oklahoma City . . . to his life in contemporary New York,"[38] Ellison recalled being "caught mid-range between my two traditions [i.e., black jazz and European classical], where one often clashed with the other, and one technique of playing was by the other opposed." Resolving to lean into that tension rather than dissolve it, "whole blocks of [neighborhood] people" were made to suffer the blaring din of Ellison's adolescent playing.[39] But whereas the suffering created by the conflict in Ellison's playing is borne by others, it is the black girl artist herself who is made to suffer the conflict's irresolution *in her own body*. "Throbb[ing] with nostalgia, regret, and repentance" (*IM*, 117), her performance is—in a word—tortured. A violence has come against the black girl artist, a theft namely, "a *willful* and violent (and unimaginable from this distance) severing of [a] captive body from its motive will, its active desire," as Hortense Spillers writes.[40] She is a figure for the modern misnaming of black womanly power and racial resilience to which the pipe organ, appropriated to patriarchal ends, is made an accessory.

In "Mama's Baby, Papa's Maybe: An American Grammar Book," Spillers deeply probes the "mythical prepossession" attending to the sign "black woman" under the particular hegemony of "the sociopolitical order of the New World."[41] The overdetermined figuration of that historical subject variously interpellated as "Peaches," "Brown Sugar," "Sapphire"—more recently, "Bitch"—survives, Spillers makes clear, through a metonymic fantasy whereby "the rule of dominance" preserves difference, in all its historical fortunes and losses, for now and forever.[42] The sociopolitical order of modernity has been prepossessed by the signifying excess of "the black woman" since slavery ("signifying property *plus*" under that regime[43]) which made her captive body "a defenseless target for rape and veneration, and . . . in its material and abstract phase, a resource for metaphor."[44] In Ellison's black girl artist, Spillers's outline of the complex of discursive effects named "theft" is symbolically evident. Even in *Invisible Man*, the social grammar governing the sublimits of black women's identity and experience as constituting "a particular figuration" of historically American "investments and privations" imputes, in Spillers's words, "meanings and uses" of her flesh far removed from the prerogatives of self-possession. In other words, with respect to black women's standing in bondage and nominal freedom, we see

> (1) the captive body as the source of an irresistible, destructive sensuality; (2) at the same time—in stunning contradiction—it is reduced to a thing, to *being* for the captor; (3) in this distance *from* a subject position, the captured sexualities provide a physical and biological expression of "otherness"; (4) as a category of "otherness," the captive body translates into a potential for pornotroping and embodies sheer physical powerlessness that slides into a more general "powerlessness," resonating through various centers of human and social meaning.[45]

In Ellison, Spillers is economically corroborated: The white-robed body of the black girl singer, pressed against the "dull" metal of the organ pipes reaching carcerally high to the chapel ceiling, appears all but "contained, controlled" in the chancel space, a snared bird singing a sad, "sublimated anguish" for all to hear. More imprisoning still is the common gaze of the platform guests, white captains of industry and liberal benevolence, "turn[ing] to look behind them, to see the thin brown girl in white choir robe" (*IM*, 116–17), her captive body effectively powerless to escape the "potential for pornotroping" toward which prurience white men in the novel have been previously shown to be inclined—including especially Mr. Norton, at once fixated and scandalized by Trueblood's incest story, and the tuxedoed "big shots" (*IM*, 17) howling their hedonism at the battle royal event one chapter earlier.

Concerning Mr. Norton, specifically, Spillers discerns a desublimating effect on the college trustee by Trueblood's storytelling. Trueblood's tale, she shows us, manages to educe a repressed miscegenation desire Norton himself can scarcely confront. As Spillers argues in "'The Permanent Obliquity of an In(pha)llibly Straight': In the Time of the Daughters and the Fathers," "Trueblood tells his story because he cannot help himself, and he has no idea why white men, in their exhibitionist urge, need to pay him (somebody-anybody) to hear what they would love to perform."[46] But if Trueblood is authentically oblivious to "why white men . . . need to pay him . . . to hear what they would love to perform," I argue that Bledsoe, the college president directing every detail of the organ-accented chapel event, has studied white men closely enough to know. Whereas Trueblood's story succeeds only in effecting in Norton a guilt-tripping incest-arousal imagined via a black-girl proxy, Matty Lou—Norton's is a repressed desire barely concealed in the memory of his own daughter as "more beautiful, purer, more perfect and more delicate than the wildest dream of a poet" (*IM*, 42)—Bledsoe wears a darker mask.

More beguiling than Trueblood, Bledsoe aims to fulfill that which can only be thought of, against the chapel backdrop of a dozen well-heeled dignitaries looking lecherously on the brown girl strenuously singing, as the philanthropists' money shot. Their concupiscence, which Bledsoe exploits to the college's material advantage and to his own ego-gain, is depicted in the tumescing and detumescing phallicism suggested in the sounds and exercise of the singer's performance. Notably, her song begins "softly" (*IM*, 116). As its volume "gradually . . . increased" and the music approaches "shaking . . . [and] rocking," the text hints at a lewd phallic readiness shared, it would seem, by the barons holding her captive under their common gaze. Although it is her voice that is portrayed as "throbb[ing] with nostalgia, regret and repentance," and her very own body slackening "as she sank slowly down" (*IM*, 117), the genital subtext is clear: When the singing ends, she executes "not a sitting but a controlled collapsing, as though she were balancing, sustaining the simmering bubble of her final tone by some delicate rhythm of her heart's blood" (*IM*, 117). More than a masturbatory projection of a miscegenation fantasy enjoyed by white men of power and means, however, the scene betrays a greater violence, as if she had been sexually taken by those looking, or by an incubus that possessed her as "a disembodied force that sought to enter her, to violate her, shaking her" (*IM*, 116). As if, so "violated," she were felled by a burden—a "theft," to recall Spillers—impossible to bear. Thus, as the singer attains to a phonemic sounding of the experience of pornotropic exposure ("I could not understand the words, but only the mood, sorrowful, vague and ethereal, of singing"), the "more general 'powerlessness'" of black womanhood in American social life (which, to be clear, Spillers does not mean to deny the particular power of black women to nobly suffer struggle) is represented literally "resonating" (after Spillers) above the chancel in the chapel where, in that compressed quarters blurring holding pen and performance platform, the captive body of the girl—now a caged bird—sings "not a carol of joy or glee," to evoke the poet Paul Laurence Dunbar, "but a prayer . . . a plea."[47]

This sad picture of a lonesome black girl, naked-seeming against the ranks of organ pipes high overhead with the lascivious eyes of a dozen trustees leering at her, is made sadder still—and, thus, more maddening—by Bledsoe's misogynistic orchestration of the entirety of the exploitive affair. As he starts the chapel service with a nod, "it was as though [Bledsoe] had given a downbeat with an invisible baton" (*IM*, 115). From the beginning, the fix was in. Bledsoe had not merely seen to the specific moment of his guests' indulgence in the "thin, brown" singer's libidinal availability but had devised, it seems, a full-on burlesque, start to finish, for their pleasure and the college's profit. On cue, "the organist turned and hunched his shoulders. A high cascade of sound bubbled from the organ, spreading thick and clinging, over the chapel, slowly surging. The organist twisted and turned on his bench, with his feet flying beneath him as though dancing to rhythms totally unrelated to the decorous thunder of his organ" (*IM*, 115). With a "high cascade of sound bubbl[ing] thick and clinging" to introduce his production, Bledsoe enlists the organ itself into the erotic economy of the scene as music spills from its phallic pipes and its organist "twist[s] and turn[s]" orgasmically in his place. The college chapel is hardly the place of inspiration its sounds pretend to; Founder's Day—to this point, at least—seems more a bawdy revue than a religious service.

Despite Bledsoe's disdain for black peasants like his coarser counterpart, Trueblood, he is not unlike Trueblood in their common consciousness of the serviceability of sexual excitements to extract money from white wealth. The shared metaphoricity of their names' hematic root betrays a closer consanguinity, in fact, than Bledsoe would allow. Both men, Bledsoe and Trueblood, traffic in the general powerlessness of black girls to the precise end that they may get a rise out of their benefactors and profit by it. But whereas Trueblood exacts a payment from Mr. Norton through narrational cunning, Bledsoe directs a pageant of black sexual signification toward white male concupiscence, relying strategically on the suggestive spectacle and moaning tonality of the pipe organ to help transform the chapel into a gentleman's club for those with cash to spend.

To recognize the pipe organ's part in establishing the exploitive undertones of Bledsoe's burlesque, let me be clear, is not to diminish its mechanical power to intone black modernist thought and feeling acoustically, Bledsoe's offenses notwithstanding. Nor is this black modernist acoustical emphasis, on the other hand, a pretext for looking past the troublesome legacy of misogyny and historical neglect that that power has been appropriated to underwrite. The full story of the pipe organ's hold on Ellison's imagination, in fact, is, like the double modernist/misogynist expression of the organ I am positing, a conflicted one, a good deal of it lying beyond *Invisible Man*. That other side of the modern life of the pipe organ, which the flying feet and dancing rhythms of Bledsoe's accompanist dimly hint at, is ultimately laid bare in Ellison's unfinished second novel, *Three Days before the Shooting*. . . .

In this thousand-page assemblage, a tome of dangling scenes, narrative sequences, and episodic improvisations often repeated and revised toward their eventual integration, what had been but the low sensuous groaning of black striving in *Invisible Man* is made to swing in *Three Days*, this new tonality emanating from the God box, which certain hep black cats of the time came to call the instrument that furnished both church and theater with the sounds and sights of material modernism.[48]

Broadly, the plot of *Three Days* is constituted in a rescue mission: Alonzo Hickman is a grizzled black jazzman-turned-Baptist-preacher who sets out from Georgia to his old home in Oklahoma, then to Washington, DC, in order to save the life of a racist US senator, Adam Sunraider. Sunraider, who grew up an orphaned child of indeterminate race, had been taken in and raised by Hickman until Sunraider was a teen. As an adult, Sunraider assumed a white identity, becoming, rather improbably, an unreformed racist congressman along the way. Hickman, on his way to thwart an assassination attempt on the senator and to solve the mystery of Sunraider's young-adult disappearance into obscurity before reemerging as a hate-filled politician, encounters a colorful array of secondary figures who, one after the other, serve the ends of his journey to save Sunraider (again). Critic Adam Bradley maintains "Ellison intended each of these characters and their corresponding episodes, though at a seeming remove from the novel's central action, to build on the 'basic themes' embodied in the novel's core narrative."[49]

Notably, to return to the organological emphasis in this chapter, in one sequence, "Hickman in Washington,"[50] Hickman lingers briefly over a memory of lazily killing time in an empty music theater once, early "for an orchestral rehearsal" he was to join (*TDS*, 593). Waiting, he "heard the sonorities of Bach's 'Sheep May Safely Graze' pouring from the theater's pipe organs." Seated on the organ bench, he observed "the usually irreverent, derby-hatted Fats Waller fingering the keyboard while swaying in time with the music" (*TDS*, 593). Considered alone, Ellison's proposal to place Waller, a marginal figure in the novel, at the organ console in his thoughts only hints at the organ's black cultural second life as it is illumined in *Three Days*. But taken as one figure in a large cast of characters, each "build[ing] on the 'basic themes'" of the novel, as Bradley proposes, Waller helps *Three Days* realize a more critical functionality for the pipe organ, one that allows to it a radical openness to tones obeying none of the conventional rules or rhythms of piety that the pipe organ's liturgical life in Europe and the United States had sought to sacralize. In the later "Hickman in Georgia and Oklahoma" sequence (a variant of which, titled "A Song of Innocence," Ellison published in 1970, an excerpt from his novel in progress[51]), Ellison illustrates the pipe organ's radical new possibilities for sounding black(ness) comedically.

Not much is known about the novel's Cliofus, another ostensibly minor character, except that he is a young jazz performer at the Cave of Winds nightclub, where his flair for improvisation, instrumental and rhetorical, is showcased live. In one amusing "lie" in particular (i.e., in one improvisational tale) he cannot resist telling, Cliofus, who is widely known for "saying filthy toasts" and "telling ... *stories!*" on stage (*TDS*, 853; emphasis Ellison's), does Ellison's strategic bidding. Playing philosopher and funnyman at the same time ("He'll tell you stories, he'll give you toasts as juicy as our good beef roasts. He'll give you speeches, poems, and orations—" [*TDS*, 864]), Cliofus likens the waywardness of words from intention—that impulse "forc[ing] you to say" not what "you think you're saying," but "what comes out"—to the fugitive fingers of a piano player he'd heard of

> "who claims that when he's in his liquor he doesn't worry about how his music sounds because he leaves it up to his educated fingers, and that when his fingers take off he just sits back and goes along to wherever they take him.
>
> "Which I believe, because once upon a time after he staggered into the biggest white folks' church in town they took off and got him thrown in jail for knocking out the Jelly Roll Blues on the God-box!"
>
> "Hey, Cliofus," a man shouted through the roar of laughter, "I remember that! You're talking about old Derby Brown, the piano player—but what's a *God-box?*"
>
> "A God-box? Why, that's the great Fats Waller's name for a *pipe* organ."
>
> (*TDS*, 866)

Not too surprisingly, the inebriate's "educated fingers" are connected to a covertly sexual criminality against the formal strictures of white hymnody and organ play. Jail seems a logical consequence for one whose playing just "take[s] off," especially since it is the disciplining imposition of *bars* white musical and juridical traditions alike rely on for the regulating of black insurgency. Unfettered from the affectations of correct or even legible playing, Derby Brown's wayward hands mirror those of the church organist observed by yet another secondary character, Love New, when he visited with some of the "State Negroes" in their church. "Even the organist sitting with his back to the pews is feeling [something], because once or twice he loses control of his fingers and something which ain't exactly church music reels from the organ" (*TDS*, 785). In both scenes, the nightclub and the church, it is the pipe organ's potential for speaking in tones "which ain't exactly church music" and in tongues which aren't exactly words I want to highlight. Try as they might, "even the words on a church organ's stops—such as *Vox Excelsis* or *Vox Angelica*," Cliofus explains playfully, "can get you into trouble. Especially if your fingers start messing around like Derby's did" (TDS, 866). Following Cliofus, what I mean to say here is that when the "educated fingers" and "dancing feet" of black soundmakers are applied, even the pipe organ *swings* and plots against the rule(s) and regulative logic of its own organological kingship. With irregular rhythms, strident overtones, and quiet undertones, the swinging of the organ undermines everything. This is why Fats Waller's name for it, the God box, is finally so ironic. Who can keep God in a box? How long before God breaks God-self out, violently? And yet to imagine the pipe organ as possessing as radical an ontology as this is to risk misapprehending its *being-for-others* and the racial politics of space and sound its history in sacred settings, especially, reflects. In other words despite its pretense to sacrality, and thus to solemn practices of faith and tradition, the pipe organ's thunderous power all but precludes the possibility of outright withdrawal from the carnal materiality of the flesh. Classical codes of religious conduct notwithstanding, no organ's sound-offering is ever wholly or precisely what it is permitted to pretend since that "which *ain't* exactly church music" (my emphasis) is already always prior to—in fact, constitutively internal to the emergence of—that which *is* church music.

I have devoted extensive space to *Invisible Man* and *Three Days before the Shooting* . . . here not with ambitious literary intentions but in the interest of the most descriptive portrait possible of the organ's specifically black expressions of cultural modernity. Routinely passed over as standard furniture (if of an imposing, sound-making kind), the pipe organ in black sacred and secular settings is far more than the requisite appointment it may seem for sounding religious and theatrical space. In other functional terms, it could be said that it also keeps time. It is self-historicizing, I mean, insofar as it is, in both religious and irreligious settings, a temporal materialization of modern black middle-class aspiration as well as a figure for a historical sound of blackness that might best be styled *mixed*, caught as it is between high and low drives. Verging on a theory of black organology in America, I point out this greater work of the pipe organ to keep time, after a fashion, as it is appropriated into, and comes to reflect, the soundscape of twentieth-century black performance and cultural politics. To be sure, this approach to a theory of black instrumental performance, however, is not without an extraliterary history also informing it.

At Ebenezer in Atlanta, the Wurlitzer and Hillgreen-Lane pipe organs struck the keynote chords of black religious modernism between 1940 and 1975 by way of the "educated fingers" of both resident and guest players. Their tremulant soft-chording and finger-furious disidentifications with the instrument's imperialist unconscious sounded out the "vibratory frequency of black thought," broodingly, at mid-century.[52] When the Ebenezer congregation dedicated its two-manual Wurlitzer in honor of A. D. Williams, for instance, with "music lovers throughout the city jamm[ing] the church to hear the thrilling program," as *Atlanta Daily World* reported, it was to hear the renowned African American organist, Graham Washington Jackson, perform.[53] A close friend to President Franklin Roosevelt and a regular White House performer, Jackson had trained formally only briefly. A young virtuoso from Portsmouth, Virginia, Jackson was largely self-taught, accompanying silent movies at age seven and mastering several other instruments before adulthood. In 1926, at the age of twenty-three, Jackson found his way to Atlanta, where his desire for a college education led him somewhat belatedly, and only temporarily, to Morehouse. Soon enough, he would forgo books for a baton as orchestra leader at Bailey's 81 Theater and give up being a student to head the music department at Booker T. Washington High, where young Martin Luther King Jr. was shortly to enroll. Playing many times at Bailey's 81 himself, Count Basie remembered how Jackson "owned that town when it came to playing some organ."[54] In fact, he was even bigger than that. His close friendship with the Roosevelts brought him ever wider (and whiter) audiences, including a record-setting twenty-four command performances at FDR's "Little White House" outside Atlanta in Warm Springs, Georgia.[55]

At the Ebenezer dedication, Jackson's virtuosity did not go unappreciated. The *Atlanta Daily World* noted Jackson's November 1 performance early the next day: "Of widespread interest were two numbers done by the nationally prominent musician, Graham Jackson, on the new organ. Applause after applause was tendered the famous musician who took the audience by surprise when he rendered a number depicting bombs falling in Europe, breaking it off with a piece in which one could still hear the praise of God."[56] Departing from his usual repertory of religious, popular, and patriotic songs, Jackson seems to have approached playing the new pipe organ with uncharacteristic freedom as he improvised "something which ain't exactly church music," to recall the fictional organist heard by Love New in *Three Days*. Jackson's earsplitting simulation of "bombs falling in

Europe" may have entertained the Ebenezer audience with the Wurlitzer's surprising range of sound effects, but coming just one year after the Nazi army invaded Poland to provoke the second world war in half a century, the blasts heard from Jackson's *diapason magna* sounded the sound of a titanic rupture of the structuring structures of race, nation, and global power in the West. Not just the bombs Jackson mimicked but the abstract pieties of sacred sound as apolitical bromides were exploded that night by the Crusades-sound of the break Jackson played and the exulting hymn which followed.[57]

Ebenezer Modernism

If Jackson set the tone and tempo for the pipe organ's an-archic potentialities that evening, his lead was followed closely by the Ebenezer choir, accompanied by Alberta King at the console this time. Together, choir and accompanist "scored with two request numbers: 'Rough and Rocky Road' and 'You Have Got to Cry Sometime before You Get to Heaven.'"[58] On the heels of "several enjoyable selections" prepared for the dedication, the choir's readiness to render the unrehearsed selections extemporaneously demanded an equal readiness by King's musician-mother, and an intrinsic, anoriginal intractability within the physical mechanics of the organ itself. Like Ellison's fictional organists, Count Basie, and Jackson, Alberta King was apt to "swing it out," even against the fundaments of classical hymnody she had rehearsed assiduously to showcase the church's aspirational aesthetics in sound, architecture, and organology. So reflexively attuned to, if not always already seeking after, the break, the breakdown, the cut, and the decomposition of that which they strained to present practiced and composed were Mother King and the Ebenezer choir that the "two request numbers" noted by the *Atlanta Daily World* were not, it turns out, two distinct numbers at all but a single song that must have *seemed* like two to the paper's reporter. A young black preacher himself, Taschereau Arnold was writing from within the circle but, like the young Frederick Douglass, misapprehended the radical materiality of the break(-down of the proper) in black sacred singing.[59]

To put this misunderstanding of the Ebenezer performance another way, Arnold's reporting of the dedication event missed the improvisatory (il)logic of the choir's performance, being unaware that "You Have Got to Cry Sometime Before You Get to Heaven" was not itself a proper song title, but the refrain of a song titled "Rough and Rocky Road."[60] Recorded circa 1948–1949 by the Stars of Harmony gospel quartet, and again in 1956 by a little-known doo-wop group, the Mello-Tones, it seems likely that "Rough and Rocky Road" was already popular in many black churches when Alberta King pushed the new Wurlitzer to keep pace with the up-tempo request. Its definite bounce notwithstanding, "Rough and Rocky Road" surely fingered the jagged grain of blacks' blues-life in the city:

> There's a rough and rocky road
> Before you get to heaven
> There's a rough and rocky road
> Before you get to heaven
> There's a rough and rocky road
> Before you get to heaven
> And I feel like shouting all the time, all the time.
>
> You have to cry sometime
> Before you get to heaven
> You have to cry sometime
> Before you get to heaven
> You have to cry sometime
> Before you get to heaven
> And I feel like crying all the time, all the time
>
> You have to moan sometime
> Before you get to heaven
> You have to moan sometime
> Before you get to heaven
> You have to moan sometime
> Before you get to heaven
> And I feel like moaning all the time, all the time
>
> It's a rough and rocky road
> Before you get to heaven
> It's a rough and rocky road
> Before you get to heaven
> It's a rough and rocky road
> Before you get to heaven
> And I feel like shouting all the time, all the time
>
> You have to bow so low
> Before you get to heaven
> You have to bow so low
> Before you get to heaven

> You have to bow so low
> Before you get to heaven
> And I feel like bowing all the time, all the time
>
> You have to stop your wicked ways
> Before you get to heaven
> You have to stop your wicked ways
> Before you get to heaven
> You have to stop your wicked ways
> Before you get to heaven
> And I feel like shouting all the time, all the time.

Despite few recordings of it, "Rough and Rocky Road" was not short-lived in the history of modern gospel. In 1961 ethnomusicologist Alan Lomax recorded Bessie Jones, a lead member of the Georgia Sea Island Singers, buzzing "It's a rough and rocky road before you get to heaven . . . *Ohhh*, I feel like praying all the time."[61] Though exchanging "rocky" for "rugged," and "shouting" for "praying" somewhat deepened the sense of the singer's Christian sufferings ("rugged" surely resonating with the preferred image of the cross in black popular hymnody), Jones reprised the recorded performances faithfully for Lomax. Like the Stars of Harmony and Mello-Tones recordings, the brisk beat of Jones's a cappella belied the deep blues sensibility beneath it. There is little doubt the version raised by the Ebenezer choir was similarly buoyant as the pipe organ was made to swing and the singers set free to follow their song leader wherever her improvisations might lead. This "intrinsic duality" of opposing mood and meter in gospel song that Michael W. Harris traced in his book, *The Rise of Gospel Blues: The Music of Thomas Andrew Dorsey in the Urban Church*, meant that however much Ebenezer aspired to high musical modernism by their repertory of George Frideric Handel, Giaochino Rossini, William MacFarlane, and concertized sorrow songs, the cultural force of a "trained choir" (as the *Atlanta Daily World* thought it important to point out about the Ebenezer singers[62]) did as little in Atlanta to "dissuade the longing for traditional songs" as it did in Dorsey's Chicago. Like the choirs at Chicago's Metropolitan Community Church, Bethel AME, and Quinn Chapel AME, that is, the Ebenezer choir "showed irrefutably that the practice of the old religion—southern and truly black—could be curtailed but not denied."[63]

Even so, the insurgent, improvisatory conditions of the "truly black" instincts of African American religious song remained moored to high modern opinion in black aspirational musical practice. That is to say, whether or not the Ebenezer organ played in the break created by and for the off-script interpolation of "Rough and Rocky Road," the organ's object power, if not its irreducibly mechanical limitations, almost certainly kept the fervor inspired by "Rough and Rocky Road" from spilling too far outside the understood bounds of American modernist legibility—for the evening ended not with the sort of "improvisatory exteriority" that "can occasion something very much like sadness and something very much like devilish enjoyment," dually, but with L. B. Byron, Ebenezer's second chair organist, "pleas[ing] with two selections as he gracefully presided at the console."[64] After the clapping countertones of "Rough and Rocky Road," Byron's distinctly graceful manner was scarcely more than a proxy enactment of communal re-composure as sober-minded black moderns, an organological sounding forth (if not exactly a putting on) of new *airs*.

By new *airs* I do not mean to refer primarily to such pretensions or affectations as those aimed at dissembling class-inflected social anxieties behind overwrought performances of bourgeois identification, although this idea is certainly a secondary or tertiary signification in the phrase's designedly ironic cast. Primarily, I mean for *airs* to be understood as an entanglement within, rather than a spectacle display of, a complex of felt social *lack*. Airs comprise a constellation of relative wins and losses, often unspoken but always betrayed in performativity, formed within that briar patch of tensions and contradictions obtaining to what Baker styled "mulatto modernism." "What I call 'mulatto modernism,'" he explains, "defines a gospel and dynamic of uplift. For me," he continues, "'mulatto modernism' is race- and class-inflected along a distinctive axis of representation. Bourgeois, middle-class individualism, vestimentary and hygienic impeccability, oratorical and double-conscious 'race pride,' and proto-nationalism are defining characteristics of 'mulatto modernism.'" Importantly, Baker describes this strain of black modernist struggle (to which he has also attached "a decent job at a decent rate of pay" and the vote as its concrete ends) as "a project in ambivalence,"[65] which I take to underline the double bind of uplift as an aspirational mission. However noble it pretends to be, the mission of racial uplift cannot escape the "ironic absurdity"of its reliance upon an abiding belief in the essential brokenness of black vernacular life.[66] This racial disability, this *lack*, may well be helped, the logic goes, but it is as necessary as it is aversive. It is uplift's prior and ongoing condition of possibility apart from which black cultural elites cannot know themselves as (also) moderns of the West.

Even as an entanglement, though—that is, as a "project of ambivalence" within black modernism's "mulatto" condition—*the new airs*, I want to be clear, obtain inextricable from the sounds by which they lend said ambivalence "voice." Black modernism's new airs are not so much productive of a modern black sound, either active or ambient, as they anticipate said sound, in and as "aria." Literally "air" in Italian, *aria*, though usually denoting an operatic solo performance, is irreducible rather to breath, to the "plural movement and displacement of inhalation and exhalation to enunciate life" itself, as Crawley writes, "life that is exorbitant, capacious and, fundamentally, social."[67] Air, then, or "aria"—as in the wind or a whisper, a peal of thunder or a faintly heard outbreath—is before *airs*, is the very precondition, inherently aural, to *airs* as a performativity of mixed "broken" and bourgeois impulses. However important black musical expression is to the sound(s) of black modernism, the latter, I aver, is antecedent to the former. It is there, in the air, ahead of that out of which black musicality is drawn. Heard as "nothing" in that special sense Crawley has posited as the theomusical unconscious of Blackpentecostal organ play, it is "said to *be* nothing."[68] What is "said to *be* nothing" however, risks the unhearing of history—risks, that is, a historical tone-deafness to the sonic materiality of black nothingness, which is not "nothing" at all but is rather the "vibratory frequency of black thought" out of which what Schafer calls "keynote sounds" marking the times issue. Inside these black keynote sounds, specifically (*vibrato, melisma, overtone, undertone, extemporization, swing*, etc.), black values and a vision of black flourishing are so deeply embedded, these *airs* "do not have to be listened to consciously" as sound objects in themselves, even as they contain "the possibility of a deep and pervasive influence on ... behavior and moods" all the same.[69]

In black cultural contexts, *airs*, then, are keynotes of racial memory and dreamwork, black pride and injury, uplift and its color-struck absurdities. *Airs* bespeak not a way of *doing* so much as an insider's way of *hearing*; they bespeak an aural habitus of black rhythms and blues notes that risks being overlooked precisely as/because it is being over-heard as "nothing" to the uninitiated. As it is, at root, the freedom to *breathe* freely that even the putting on of *airs* has wanted so badly to achieve, the pipe organ's place at the center of this modern search after an aestheticization, high and low, of the sound of black breath and its strivings comes as no surprise. A natural source and symbol of the fraughtness of black *airs*, the twentieth-century pipe organ is as much a monument in sound as it is in structure to the lived, double-conscious tension between black aspiration historically and aspirational blackness in the age of modernism. Odd as it seems, then (since black religious history has tended not to linger much over its own discernibly bourgeois yearnings and exertions), the Ebenezer sound specifically and the modernist soundscape of Afro-Protestantism broadly owe themselves not insignificantly to the deeper, darker tones of pipe organ play and accompaniment within the acoustic architectures of twentieth-century Afro-ecclesiality.

Said another way, within the modernist soundscape of Afro-Protestantism, scholarly attention has been focused primarily on the ecstatic performativities of black religious identity, from ring shouts to praise breaks and the diverse panoply of vernacular acts and addresses in between. Very little ground, it seems, has been given to those largely imitative aspects of black ecclesiality "in which the tone is set [primarily] by people with middle-class aspirations,"[70] as pioneering black sociologists St. Clair Drake and Horace Cayton once lamented. Perhaps the seemingly bourgeois strains of black religious history—hierarchical ecclesiologies, neomedieval architectures, dispassionate preaching, and sheet music, to name a few—embarrass black religion's blackness, or diminish the force of its historical witness as a radical agent in the struggle for black freedom and human dignity. Whatever the case for their invisibility to critical reflection, the class-inflected pieties of Afro-Protestantism are never singularly, or reductively, conformist, in any case.[71] At Ebenezer and other "mixed-type" churches, "elements of storefront Pentecostalism *coexisted* with upper levels of black society,"[72] in other words. Highbrow and lowbrow held together. In aural terms, specifically, this meant, as Lischer observes, that the Ebenezer congregation not only "sang metered hymns with lugubrious dignity [read: highbrow] but saved their excitement [read: lowbrow] for the gospel songs and preaching"; despite many black elites in his congregation—a major newspaper editor, a bank president, and various other professionals—"Daddy King [MLK Sr.] saw to it that Ebenezer never lost its mass-identity as a talk-back, whooping, gospel-singing, workingman's church."[73] To be sure, Ebenezer combined low and high sensibilities. Nowhere was this miscegenation of past and future, mundane and modern, instincts—nowhere were the "warring ideals" (Du Bois) of black sociality and the overestimations of racial uplift, I mean—more clearly reflected than in the overlapping acoustic and organological drive to the otherwise world of life and breath in the Ebenezer sound.

Constituted by a gospel field of intermingled sounds and rhythms in the sanctuary, Ebenezer baptized King into a unique tuning of the Southern black world. Insofar as "King carried the sanctuary with him as a state of mind and soul," in Lischer's words, Ebenezer acculturated him into a keen apprehension (or knowingness) and command of the alternately competing and harmonious timbres and time signatures of black southern sacrality. The "reedy baritone" Lischer describes as King's preaching voice was born of exactly this intimate auralism.[74] If the elder King was what intimates of black preaching traditions call "a whooper," one who "in moments of high intensity gave certain words and phrases both a rhythmic and a musical value," then, by contrast, the younger King's preaching more nearly approached that of a "moaner," one whose rhythms of public speech tend to a "more sustained and predictable pattern of intonation,"[75] slow-going and stately, deforming right speech into black aria. Although the performative force of the former King's whooping to inspire the expressiveness of the latter King's near-moaning cannot be doubted,[76] tonally King Jr. drew more fully from the wider sonic environment at and around Ebenezer even as he lent his voice to its peculiar polyphony, reciprocally.

With gripping vocal power, vaguely Robesonian in its baritonic flights, King (*fils*) enlivened the very soundscape that formed his aural education. Make no mistake, he "fully inhabited this holy space of Ebenezer by internalizing its sense of order and its spiritual values" so deeply that Ebenezer's living architectures of sociality and sound inhabited King in return.[77] Their politics and sensibilities he effectively exteriorized through his vibrato speech. King's vocalization of the sense of Ebenezer's peculiar gospel and sound, "without intention or decision [but] by simply absorbing the universe in which he was enveloped," suggests an educative sociality, an ecology of influence, far different from those romances of rare genius and genetic endowment that commonly attend to King's biography.[78] For all his uncommon rhetorical talents and linguistic facility, King's virtuosity was not primarily oratorical but was, above all else, auricular. With the sensitivity of an orchestral conductor, a bandleader, or, more exactly, a jazz ensemblist, King *heard* more acutely than most, heard more intensely than the average person the "interacting sounds and rhythms" of Ebenezer, the aspirational black church in the South, and black religious modernism, more broadly. Like Baldwin farther north, his ear was to "the beat of the language of the people who had produced [him],"[79] the people who bequeathed him his remarkable gift of audition.

3

The Cantor King

Reform Preaching, Cantorial Style, and Acoustic Memory in Chicago's Black Belt

O that i may give air to my people.
Honorée Jeffers, "Selah" (2020)

Who is considered conversant with prayers . . . He who is skilled in chanting.
Ta'anit 16a, Babylonian Talmud

The degree to which Martin Luther King Jr.'s inspired vision of freedom and the sublime force of his speech developed out of the social, theological, and acoustic environment within and proximate to Ebenezer Baptist Church can scarcely be overstated. To be sure, Ebenezer's influence was far in excess of the eight short years that King served as the church's copastor between January 1960 and King's April 1968 assassination. But it was in those years, nevertheless, that he fashioned "an evolving, sometimes volatile, interpretation of God's will for Ebenezer and the world" that Richard Lischer has named "the Ebenezer gospel."[1] As he shared the church's leadership with his father, King "did not preach at Ebenezer every Sunday, but he spoke there enough to establish what Paul (and any preacher) would have called 'my gospel,'" in any case. "The Ebenezer gospel," writes Lischer, "is what the preacher King had to say to his people over the course of his one-hundred-month pastorate; it is his 'message.'"[2] If a distinct and coherent theological viewpoint, the Ebenezer gospel, seemed to Lischer to coalesce from King's preaching over the years he was his father's lieutenant, then it would seem as reasonable to posit "an Ebenezer sound" informing and sustaining it.

By "the Ebenezer *sound*," of course, I mean the acoustic ecology of black Protestant faith and ritual discussed in the previous chapter as obtaining from the long history of music, speech, technology, and architecture at Ebenezer from the installation of its first mechanical tracker organ in 1922 to King's self-memorializing funeral oration in 1968 and beyond. Distinctive as the Ebenezer sound surely was, however, it would be wrong to insist that the acoustic environment it distilled was altogether unique. Although the Ebenezer sound was almost certainly distinctive in Atlanta, discretely different from the city's half-dozen other mixed-type congregations that might have claimed characteristic sounds of their own (e.g., the Big Bethel sound, the Wheat Street sound),[3] Ebenezer was also significantly like them in its shared sense of the black world outside the church walls its interior sounds were pitched to succor, strengthen, sacralize, and save from Southern evils. Well past Atlanta, Ebenezer also shared a general tonal attitude with countless other churches, including churches "up South." A vague elegiac sensibility, equal parts lament, faith, and gladness, was common to many, preserved as it was in the sounds of black religious songs, sermonic performance, and sacramental acts that reinterpreted the Jesus story in light of black suffering and the Divine's sympathy. In this chapter, I show how the Ebenezer sound, specifically, and Afro-Protestant acoustemology, in general, played "up South" in and around the sacred architectures of black Chicago, where the sound of modern gospel expressed the spirit of black religious modernism for decades. King's preaching at Mt. Pisgah Missionary Baptist Church in Bronzeville in 1967 is a case study in just such a convergence of black cultural soundscapes—one North, one South, one spoken, the other musical—realized on a broad scale by the cultural and aesthetic tunings of black migration to the exigencies of the modern city.

On August 27, King preached a sermon at Mt. Pisgah titled "Why Jesus Called a Man a Fool" based on a Lukan parable. Venerated as one of his "great" sermons by Clayborne Carson and Peter Holloran in *A Knock at Midnight: Inspiration from the Great Sermons of Reverend Martin Luther King, Jr.*, "Why Jesus Called a Man a Fool" succeeded in large part owing to the facility with which King vocally navigated the acoustical space to its designed ends. Knowingly or unknowingly, King was clearly listening, in other words, as the room, designed by Alfred S. Alschuler in 1911 for Sinai Congregation, sounded sound on its terms. So hearing, King spoke into, not against, the acoustical design and sonic memory of the former synagogue, whose acoustic architecture seemed to fit the incantatory tonality of King's oratory. The neomedieval design also fit the tonal attitude of the ecclesial culture the black migrants to Chicago created and distilled in gospel blues. In very real terms, and continuous with acoustic and organological influences on the Ebenezer sound, Mt. Pisgah amplified the migrants' collective memory of "home" and sounded the sound of loss and the new urban precarity into which their freedom dreams fast dissolved. King's preaching resonated with the expressive sounds of their modern black thought and confessional instincts.

Approaching the Incantatory: Gospel Music, Black Toil, and King's Cantorial Sound

As a people's quest for the material safety and lived modernism of *new airs*, a new calculus of racial wins and losses, tensions and contradictions far away from the physical terrors and economic exploitations of the South, black migration to New York, Philadelphia, Washington, DC, St. Louis, and Chicago not only acted out large-scale African American discontent in the South but "to some extent," Michael W. Harris has argued, sounded "a search for cultural reorientation."[4] Harris's exceptional study *The Rise of Gospel Blues: The Music of Thomas Andrew Dorsey in the Urban Church* shows how the very sounds of the black South traveled north in the vernacular musicality of the secular blues-as-black-folk-art to influence and give birth to gospel blues as the music of black religious modernism in the North, nowhere more intensely than in 1930s Chicago. Gospel blues, however, quite apart from constituting an objective form or style of musical expression alone, Harris argues, "is *thought* [too] as opposed to mere music."[5] It is "the emergence of a concept" of lived experience brought north as "idea" rather than a cultural artifact transplanted into soundless fields of urban emptiness. For Harris's part, it is Georgia bluesman-turned-gospel preacher Thomas Dorsey who best represented the blues idea in migrant motion. Dorsey "personifies—almost uniquely so—the thought and social forces that forged the culture in which [gospel blues] was shaped."[6] Perhaps more important to my project, Dorsey's part in the introduction of blues thought to the assimilationist sounds of Afro-Protestantism in Chicago in the 1930s and 1940s began in the very city where the Ebenezer sound that formed King's preaching and oratory developed.

Dorsey was just ten years old in 1908 when his family relocated from rural Villa Rica, Georgia, to Atlanta with thousands of other peasant families who converged on the city from outlying country districts. Though his father, a graduate of Morehouse, had led a small congregation in Villa Rica years before and his mother had earned an estimable reputation as a well-regarded church organist there, in Atlanta the Dorseys' religious activities all but ceased. Young Dorsey was thus led away from churchly influence, gravitating instead to black Atlanta's downtown theater and entertainment district, where weary-blues pianists in theaters and brothels captured his youthful imagination. Soon Dorsey picked up playing. When, later, he sought formal training, "he realized that his improvisational playing style would have to yield to note reading."[7] Unwilling to make the adjustment, young Dorsey would ultimately give up taking formal lessons and return to selling popcorn at the Bailey's 81 Theater (through which legends like Count Basie and Graham Jackson also passed). In between shows, he squeezed in informal lessons from guest performers, persuading them to teach him the latest blues tunes and associated riffs. It was not long before Dorsey was accomplished in his own right, playing at various Atlanta clubs until 1916. That year, with local terrors peaking and far-off opportunity beckoning blacks north in record numbers, Dorsey made for Chicago—according to Harris, "clearly in an effort to find something new."[8] Joining throngs of others quitting the South, Dorsey's migration conveyed not the Ebenezer sound, of course, nor even a sound that could be said to issue from, or enliven, Atlanta's club and theater scene, but a sonancy of thought born from the blackness of rural Georgia and matured, *like* the Ebenezer sound, in the sensual cityscape of Atlanta. Eventually, after many years playing in the Chicago clubs and on the road as bandleader for blues queen Ma Rainey, Dorsey surrendered to the religious feeling of 1920s and 1930s Chicago and redirected his musical gifts toward the church, offering its mainline musicking an alternative blues-infused pitch, rhythm, and timbre.

As I shall pursue more intentionally in later chapters (4 and 5 notably), gospel blues, which would come to be irrevocably identified with Dorsey as its high priest and progenitor, had been a key element in the "cultural reorientation" of the black South in the North, and an irreducible property of the modern sound of Chicago for three decades when King ascended the pulpit at Mt. Pisgah. In time and tune with what we might call his mother-tongue, the sound-language learned at Ebenezer under the tremulant influence of the pipe organ, King adjusted easily to the key of black hope and toil in Chicago. Although the coloniality of Chicago's Black Belt—its slums and housing discrimination, above all—was a disturbing new reality to King's liberal middle-class sensibilities, the acoustic architecture and instrumental airs inside Mt. Pisgah were familiar.[9] There King stepped waist-deep into a Red Sea of racial and religious memory older than Mt. Pisgah itself. Echoes of a more ancient exodus than that realized by the dark itinerants facing him in the pews were all around, as much in the synagogal vestigiality of the church's physical plant as in the din of fugitive sounds accompanying his resonant discourse. Leaning into, rather than away from, the alchemy of racial identity, religious ritualism, and the soundmarks of ecclesial modernism, King held forth at Mt. Pisgah in an aptly incantatory mode of speech and with an irruptive phenomenological power, to boot.

To speak of an "incantatory" mode of black preacherly sound and sensibility is to call up an aesthetic tradition of black being-in-the-world that is constitutive of, but not reducible to, an eschatological performativity of black religious hope enacted in shouts, tongues, claps, and cries. Here, though, I mean to underline King's instinct for a radicality inhering in the tremulous *after* of thundered speech. I mean to call attention to the otherworldly witness of King's vibrato-speak, understood, in Fred Moten's words, "in and as irruptive and uncontainable, fugitive, phonic materiality on the plane of performance."[10] *Incantatory* reflects an especially material power within the acoustic architecturalism of Mt. Pisgah, whose very name suggests the liberationist prehistory informing the incantatory effect Moten locates in the philosophical disarticulations of black chant. In "Black Kant (Pronounced *Cant*)," his 2007 lecture at the Kelly Writers House in Philadelphia, Moten summoned the incantatory idea as he explained the unavoidable variability of his talk's title. "Black Kant (Pronounced *Cant*)," he offered, was sometimes "Black Kant (Pronounced *Chant*)."[11] "It just depends on kinda how I feel. But the resonance of both terms—and it's 'cant' without an apostrophe, although sometimes there's an apostrophe, too. [*Audience laughter*] So. It just depends on what's going on."[12]

Moten observed "the resonance of both terms," *cant* and *chant*, to his project, culling from the philosophical cant of Kant's *Critique of Judgment* an "irregulative opening of the regulative" as he emphasized the (en)chanted play of incantatory affects over the cant of the regulative principle in scientific and historical discourse.[13] He spoke pointedly of black poetry as "marking [and] . . . channeling a certain incantatory reach toward or projective structure for science and history" that "race, or the raced figure, particularly the figure of the black" in Kant concretized. "Race in Kant," he told his audience, "is incantatory gesture, the mark of an incapacity that drives philosophy, the black can't (with [an] apostrophe) of philosophy. Philosophy's indebtedness to the unmeaning jargon, and illegitimate rhetoric, of phonomaterial suasion it keeps trying to leave behind . . . [is to] the beautiful art of the unbeautiful."[14] Next, Moten interpellated poet Norman H. Pritchard into his lecture (by way of an audio recording) to exemplify the "incantatory gesture" of blackness traceable in Kant. He put forward Pritchard's "Gyre's Galax" as an "instance of black poetry, of black chant, of black-poetry-as-black-chant" enacting in its chanted materiality "a kind of transverse . . . performance of black Kant (pronounced *cant*), of blackness in Kant, insofar as it intones the foundational interplay of sense and nonsense at the racial crossroads where modern philosophy takes its own path."[15] According to Moten, blackness runs along an apposite trail at once ahead of and in the wake of modern philosophy. Thusly framed, "black is not just a color," Moten argued; it is a (counter)force of nature, an epiphenomenality. And, therefore, "also . . . [something like] a city, or more precisely, a field, a gathering of possibility . . . homelessly at home . . . Black, or the blackness of blacks, is a form, a garment, a continuing irruption against the very idea and/or representation of a deathly or death-driven nakedness marking the radical impossibility of social life."[16] I argue, following Moten, that this "underground city, this irreducible form" that is blackness in Kant dwells not only in the variegated performativity of Pritchard's unregulated incantations in "Gyre's Galax" ("Above beneath/abovebeneath/abovebenea/abobenea/abobenee . . .") but likewise inhabits the tonal space of play between moan, shout, flight, and fermata in King's cantorial preaching.[17] In "Why Jesus Called a Man a Fool," the incantatory worries preaching's exegetical drive as the hard edge of words softens into an acoustemological reduction interanimating the homiletical line with overtones and undertones of black speech, song, and modern prosody issuing from "abobenea" ("Above beneath"). Simplified, "Why Jesus Called a Man a Fool" put the incantatory otherwise of Pritchard's "abobenea" in resonant evidence. Although King had already preached early versions of "Why Jesus Called a Man a Fool" at Ebenezer and at Central Methodist Church in Detroit years earlier,[18] at Mt. Pisgah he set flowing new verbal intensities that he had not realized before.

As president of the Southern Christian Leadership Conference (SCLC) at the time of his August 1967 visit, King had gone to Chicago in support of the local branch there, presided over by Rev. Dr. Joseph Wells. It was Wells, the pastor of Mt. Pisgah, who had invited King to his pulpit. From the first, King struck a sober note. Weakening in "courage and vigor to carry on in the struggle for freedom and human dignity," King opened his sermon expressing gratitude to Wells and the unnamed but "charming" congregant at Mt. Pisgah tasked with his introduction for the "encouraging words" spoken about him.[19] His appreciation for such supporters, ready "to give you consolation in the darkest hours," eventually gave way, however, to a narration of the sort of trouble that was sapping his strength. Several minutes into "Why Jesus Called a Man a Fool," King told a personal anecdote to illustrate the "deep and patient faith" he was, in spite of himself, discovering through suffering.

> I never will forget one night very late. It was around midnight. And you can have some strange experiences at midnight. (*Yes, sir*) I had been out meeting with the steering committee all that night. And I came home, and my wife was in the bed and I immediately crawled into bed to get some rest to get up early the next morning to try to keep things going. And immediately the telephone started ringing and I picked it up. On the other end was an ugly voice. That voice said to me, in substance, "Nigger, we are tired of you and your mess now. And if you aren't out of this town in three days, we're going to blow your brains out and blow up your house." (*Lord Jesus*)

King recalled being "frustrated, bewildered." Vexed by a father's burden for his children and by a young husband's guilt over a life as public and dangerous as his, King recalled how he was close to coming apart: "I got to the point that I couldn't take it any longer; I was weak."

> Something said to me, you can't call on Daddy now, he's up in Atlanta a hundred and seventy-five miles away. (*Yes*) You can't even call on Mama now. (*My Lord*) You've got to call on that something in that person that your Daddy used to tell you about. (*Yes*) That power that can make a way out of no way. (*Yes*) And I discovered then that religion had to become real to me and I had to know God for myself. (*Yes, sir*) And I bowed down over that cup of coffee—I never will forget it. (*Yes, sir*) And oh yes, I prayed a prayer and I prayed out loud that night. (*Yes*) I said, "Lord, I'm down here trying to do what's right. (*Yes*) I think I'm right; I think the cause that we represent is right. (*Yes*) But Lord, I must confess that I'm weak now; I'm faltering; I'm losing my courage. (*Yes*) And I can't let the people see me like this because if they see me weak and losing my courage, they will begin to get weak." (*Yes*)

With this unhappy anecdote, King postscripted the two earlier iterations of "Why Jesus Called a Man a Fool," "The Man Who Was a Fool" in Detroit in 1961 and its essayistic revision (with the same title) in his first book, *Strength to Love*, in 1963. Considering the nature of its difference from these two early formulations of King's political theology, "Why Jesus Called a Man a Fool" may well be more helpfully styled a *super-scripting* of its pre-texts insofar as the preaching performance at Mt. Pisgah *exceeded* writing only and precisely by a radical departure from the manuscript performativity of those two prior trials. "Why Jesus Called a Man a Fool" succeeded not because it arrived at some exemplary condition *after* writing (i.e., a postscript) but because it passed *through* (perhaps also *over*) writing on to a noisy, diacritical beyond of printed and "correctly" pronounced words. This super-scripting of the sermon manuscript I cannot but see, and hope to show, as King approaching Pritchard's "abobenee"—his text-sound of the beyond *above, beneath,* and *through* words—in an acoustic, incantatory mode Mt. Pisgah was perfect for.

Off the Walls: Acoustic Architecture and Sacred Sounds

To be sure, King's preaching at Mt. Pisgah was re-sounding. It echoed in and from a place already ringing with the memory of insurgent sounds, sounds both modern in their blues-inflected gospel tones and, at one and the same time, distantly Judaic in acoustic memory. The former sound King engaged by way of what I referred to previously as the general tonal attitude of modern black ecclesiality and its drive to the incantatory; the latter sound-memory, as I turn now to show, was engendered, rather, by an accident of history and architecture that acoustically anticipated the politics of his preaching. More than the coincidence of the rise of gospel blues happening in Chicago alongside it, the prehistory of Mt. Pisgah as Chicago Sinai Congregation, Chicago's first Reform Jewish temple, also informed the "abobenee" acoustemology and meaning of "Why Jesus Called a Man a Fool," as the walls that reflected King's preaching voice in 1967 also spoke, as it were, in an antiphonal voice of its own as it harmonized Sinai's historical commitment to a reform politics of faith with King's black Protestant modernism.

My sense of Sinai's sonic memory as an element of the synagogue's intermural acoustics follows from the sound studies of the British poet, sound historian, and theorist Seán Street. In his 2015 book *The Memory of Sound: Preserving the Sonic Past*, Street claimed "walls have voices." In support of his proposition, he averred that

> great churches such as San Marco [in Venice] were designed not only with an intention to awe the senses visually, but also with the same care and attention to acoustic detail as an audio studio architect or the creator

of a modern concert hall would seek to build into a dedicated recording or performance space. Further, these spaces were invested with a unique *voice* distinct from other acoustic stages.... If we are able to remember the identity of a human voice, there is no reason why we cannot hold the memory of the voice of a building in our mind.[20]

If it is also true, as Street goes on to speculate, that "the attentive and sensitive ear, tuned to the various sound qualities of musical environments," which are Street's primary objects of study, "should be able to identify the location of a recording of a [musical] performance,"[21] this may indeed be owing to the recall of "our minds." But "the memory of the voice of a building" may just as easily belong to the building itself, I want to suggest. Walls that have voices, I mean, sound out not only the "echoes and ambiences ... of the stone that become part of the musical experience itself,"[22] but the memory of past musicking whose sound bears the same echoic and ambient trace. Thus are walls *envoiced* by their being aural palimpsests of the acoustic history of re-sounding architectures, recorders of the trace of interior sounds long since passed.

Crucially, voiced walls are not a generality in Street's reflections, but exist principally in "our great churches and temples."[23] Although none of the exemplary architectures discussed in the relevant parts of *The Memory of Sound* suggest that Street would have included the humbler neomedievalism of Ebenezer in the broad sharing of "*our* great churches and temples," Sinai's more significant proportions as well as the significant reputations of both its designer and influential rabbi, Emil Gustav Hirsch, suggest it as a more conceivable referent within Street's imagination of the "great" edifices of spatial and sonic synergy. I propose, then, to hold up Mt. Pisgah/Sinai as another "great" sacred architecture where cantorial memory and reform preaching have quietly re-sounded in the sanctuary, even as the Ebenezer sound, specifically, revealing echoes and ambiences of a greatness all its own, resonated, as we shall see, from the preaching platform.

Although the main stage of the structure that housed Sinai Congregation from 1912 to 1961 was designed "for the use of a single speaker, and the organ and choir were to be secondary," it was toward an ideality of "resonance," not speech per se, its architect drafted Sinai's design.[24] In a November 1909 letter to Alschuler from Wallace C. Sabine, a Harvard architect who was one of the turn of the century's most important acousticians,[25] Sabine underlined the resonant ideal Sinai's design was after. To a prior query from Alschuler about the advisability of constructing the stage floor of wood,

Sabine responded laconically: "Your choice of wood is good. Should you cover the platform with carpet, it should be thin; it will then serve to deaden footsteps without perceptibly diminishing resonance."[26] Wood paneling at the back of the platform, Sabine advised further, "should be thin and separated by an inch from the solid wall behind it in order to secure its best resonant effect."[27] Sabine was confident that a "resonant effect" would "on the whole . . . strengthen the sound" of the staged liturgies at the new Sinai and counteract "the possibility of echoes" predicted to otherwise muddle the acoustical conditions of the synagogue.[28] While Alschuler's objectives with regard to Sinai's sound (thus, his outreach to Sabine) were primarily aimed at showcasing the moving vocality of Rabbi Hirsch's increasingly celebrated speechcraft, Sabine's missives implied a keener awareness of the aural calculus complicating the architect's plans and the acoustical presumptions informing them. Which is to say, to whatever degree Alschuler set out to center what one observer called Hirsch's "perfect . . . form and diction,"[29] Sabine knew somewhat better than he that the walls of Sinai could speak just as eloquently.

Consistently, Sabine answered Alschuler's worries about the loss or "deadening" of sound within Sinai's built space with assurances that the solid surfaces covering the platform's lower face, above the platform, and surrounding the choir balcony would reliably "reflect the spoken voice,"[30] redirecting Hirsch's voice toward the audience in front of him. Looking at Alschuler's plans, what preoccupied Sabine was not the general direction accruing to the principal sounds defining the worship event as an expression of the meaning of Reform theology, but how effectively those sounds would be distributed, and thus heard, over the wide acoustical expanse of Sinai's yawning sanctuary ("the room is rather broad," Sabine offered in critique).[31] More than once, Sabine recommended the installation of "a somewhat broken surface" wherever possible for a more extravagant distribution of sound across the auditorium. "The shape indicated for the large cornice under the barrel vault is good, but irregularities are recommended on the surface, to make the reflection general rather than in a narrow direction. . . . [Additionally, a] somewhat broken surface at the back of the speaker is desirable and an architect is at liberty to use pilasters and other irregularities of that sort. The object is for the speaker's voice to be mirrored from several small surfaces rather than from one large surface."[32] Although the exchange between Alschuler and Sabine does not hint of a conflict between them—Sabine concludes by saying, "I have gone over your plans as a whole . . . I desire to express my general approval"[33]—nonetheless, a basic tension produced by the entanglements of the aural politics of "perfect ... form and diction," on the one hand, and those of resonant speech, on the other, is discernible in their correspondence. More particularly, it is the tension between the one's desire to enable the exercise of a verbal supremacy over the sonic environment through such "clean-cut polished sentences" and "right words" as Hirsch routinely delivered, and the other's concern to realize a more radically democratic aurality by way of "broken" planes of sound "very irregularly reflected" that their exchange discloses.[34] In a way, theirs was also the tension, recapitulated, inherent in most all of King's preaching: that obtaining between words and sound, scripted and super-scripting speech.

How much of Sabine's counsel Alschuler finally followed, or what portion of his acoustical philosophy Alschuler found agreement with, is difficult to say. Clearly, though, Alschuler's final design resolved the tension between the properly grammatical objectives of public speechcraft and the possibilities of synagogal preaching as excitable, resonant, "broken" speech. Certain mural enhancements recommended by Sabine ("the architect is at liberty to use pilasters and other irregularities of that sort"[35]) acted to scatter speech, diffuse it, and thus deform its dreamily impeccable projection. When King took to the preaching stage a half-century later, acoustically the old synagogue-become-Baptist-parish was already suited to—indeed, assuming Sabine's sway on its design, *built for*—the Protestant preacher's so-called natural vibrato. For whatever "echoes and ambiences" sounded the memory of Mt. Pisgah's Jewish past life, inevitably the irregular surround delineating the sacred world inside the main sanctuary conveyed waves of elegiac vibrato-speak over the entire vaulted expanse of the Mt. Pisgah nave, rendering King's preaching resonantly cantorial.

"Why Jesus Called a Man a Fool"

Not unexpectedly, given the miscegenated modernism of King's Ebenezer aesthetic and the re-sounding acoustemology of "great churches and temples" made great by the distinctive sonority of their built "voices," "Why Jesus Called a Man a Fool" just *worked* at Mt. Pisgah. Deftly, it harmonized precise speech and fugitive sound, oratory and "noise," rhetoric and resonance into a religious Afro-modernism figured in and by the ritual sound-play of black chant and/as the canted/cantillated Word.

> The great problem facing our nation today in the area of race is that it is the black man who to a large extent produced the wealth of this nation.

> (*All right*) And the nation doesn't have sense enough to share its wealth and its power with the very people who made it so. (*All right*) And I know what I'm talking about this morning. (*Yes, sir*) The black man made America wealthy. (*Yes, sir*)
>
> We've been here—that's why I tell you right now, I'm not going anywhere. . . . Before the Pilgrim fathers landed at Plymouth in 1620, we were here. (*Oh yeah*) Before Jefferson etched across the pages of history the majestic words of the Declaration of Independence, we were here. (*All right*) Before the beautiful words of the "Star Spangled Banner" were written, we were here. (*Yeah*) For more than two centuries, our forebears labored here without wages. They made cotton king. With their hands and with their backs and with their labor, they built the sturdy docks, the stout factories, the impressive mansions of the South. (*My Lord*)
>
> . . . And I feel that if something doesn't happen soon, and something massive, the same indictment will come to America—"Thou fool!"

Then, several minutes later and winding up, King recalled the slaves' legacy again:

> Centuries ago Jeremiah raised a question, "Is there no balm in Gilead? Is there no physician there?" He raised it because he saw the good people suffering so often and the evil people prospering. (*Yes, sir*) Centuries later our slave foreparents came along. (*Yes, sir*) And they too saw the injustices of life, and had nothing to look forward to morning after morning but the rawhide whip of the overseer, long rows of cotton in the sizzling heat. But they did an amazing thing. They looked back across the centuries and they took Jeremiah's question mark and straightened it into an exclamation point. And they could sing, "There is a balm in Gilead to make the wounded whole. (*Yes*) There is a balm in Gilead to heal the sin-sick soul." And there is another stanza that I like so well: "Sometimes (*Yeah*) I feel discouraged." (*Yes*)
>
> And I don't mind telling you this morning that sometimes I feel discouraged. (*All right*) I felt discouraged in Chicago. As I move through Mississippi and Georgia and Alabama, I feel discouraged. (*Yes, sir*) Living every day under the threat of death, I feel discouraged sometimes. Living every day under extensive criticisms, even from Negroes, I feel discouraged sometimes. [*Applause*] Yes, sometimes I feel discouraged and feel my work's in vain. But then the holy spirit (*Yes*) revives my soul again. "There is a balm in Gilead to make the wounded whole. There is a balm in Gilead to heal the sin-sick soul." God bless you. [*Applause*][56]

Here King closed his preaching, having brought the an-archic beyond of normative discourse to the edge of audibility by super-scripting words previously printed in *Strength to Love*. Against the midnight death threat he recalled to the congregation minutes earlier, King could be heard attaining to a tremulous countervocalism sounding through this sermon performance. Together, his "natural vibrato," heard in the variable long notes of such words as "here" and "history" and "heal" and "balm," as well as in the extemporal antiphony of the congregation vocalizing their own "different pitches, and *their* improvisational vocal 'riffs,'" to put it one way, called up the otherwise world where "that power that can make a way out of no way" is imagined to dwell.[37] Rising and falling, King's preaching and the people's improvisations rendered the priority of an unbounded "no way" indistinctly audible, admitting of an opening-up to hearing of an acoustically aided suprasonority, the effect of which could not but leave uncertain—or better, *ambiguous*—the point at which King's audience might have judged his sermon to be "winding up," as I've said. Or, equally ambiguous, just what that phrase might have finally meant, performatively speaking.

To put all of this more succinctly, "Why Jesus Called a Man a Fool" reflected that wavering between the high and heretical aspirations of black liberal hope, at one node, and, at the other, black radical resistance, which dualism, I submit, corresponds to the play of writing and voice composing the elemental miscegeneity of King's career. Like "A Knock at Midnight," also published in *Strength to Love* and preached memorably in Cincinnati in 1967, "Why Jesus Called a Man a Fool" was, as Moten would likely put it in that double-jointed syntax he favors, "not but nothing other than" a performative sight-reading of "The Man Who Was a Fool," the print representation of which served to materialize a form of what poet Ed Roberson calls "the calligraphy of black chant"[38] in its skeletal scoring of a cantorial—which is to say, loosely incantatory—ideal. In swells redolent of Jewish plainsong, King's audible vibrato added a cantorial intimation to the preaching act, sounding "that subtle undertone, / That note in music heard not with the ears" that James Weldon Johnson had versified decades earlier in the poem "O Black and Unknown Bards." King's preaching sonified "the elusive reed so seldom blown,/ Which stirs the soul" in ecstatic hope "or melts the heart to tears" that breaks under the weight of so awful a history.[39]

Not by accident did King's voice also reprise forty-two years of Jewish Reform preaching from the very same preaching stage that was Sinai's from 1912 to 1949. The resonant ideal in the Alschuler-Sabine building design made the very walls of the synagogue "resonant witness[es]" to the rhetorical powers of the congregation's most venerated rabbi—powers, his admirers boasted, that "scaled the heights of oratory" with "mellifluous tones" and "the cadences of the artist's speech."[40] Over and above their re-sounding of King's vibrato throughout its vast auditorium, Sinai's walls, I repeat, bore acoustic testimony to Hirsch's long career there as well. This they did by way of a palimpsestic aurality wherein the primary sound(s) of King's organ-voiced preaching also carried the trace memory of Hirsch's Reform sound in the latter's meticulously languaged articulation of the "great Messianic hope for . . . the kingdom of truth, justice and peace among all men."[41] In this way, Hirsch's Reform preaching, a mix of theological ethics, social activism, and classical oratorical technique, anticipated the social and ethical orientation of the exegesis informing "Why Jesus Called a Man a Fool." Together with what would come to be regarded as the most radical Reform theology in US Judaism, the memory of Hirsch's superior oratory—the trace of it, that is to say—had been preserved in the acoustic architecture of Mt. Pisgah well before King introduced his own Ebenezer sound into its twentieth-century aural history.

For more than four decades, Emil Hirsch served Sinai Congregation with great force of intellect and personality. Appointed in rabbinical literature and philosophy at the University of Chicago, Hirsch was, like King, no dry pedant. Not only "a brilliant intellectual" but a "charismatic speaker," Hirsh "regularly attracted up to two thousand Christians and unaffiliated Jews" to Sinai's services and, as Sinai's senior rabbi, built one of the largest Jewish congregations in the country.[42] Perhaps more notably, Hirsch's extraordinary aptitudes for intellectualism and public preaching placed him at the leading edge of the Reform movement in the United States. Departing deliberately from the mostly Orthodox rites of the two other existing synagogues in Chicago, KAM (Kehilath Anshe Ma'arav) Isaiah Israel and B'nai Shalom, Sinai "never belonged to (or regarded itself as part of) the Jewish mainstream," Tobias Brinkmann writes. "From its founding . . . the congregation provoked acerbic criticism for its radical reinterpretation and seeming disregard for Jewish tradition. Sinai was the first Jewish congregation in America to permanently adopt Sunday services in 1874."[43] More than a progressive congregation, however, as a "German" Jewish community, Sinai understood the historicity of its progressivism keenly. In his outstanding study *Sundays at Sinai: A Jewish Congregation in Chicago*, Brinkmann explains that although Chicago's Sinai sat within a large Jewish immigrant neighborhood at its start, "Sinai's founders understood [their] Germanness not in ethnic or national but primarily in spiritual and transnational terms and as a synonym for modernity." Even if the ground was then tilting toward the United States, Germany had long since been the center of Reform thought. Not satisfied merely to be regarded as moderns by others, Sinai "described *itself* as modern."[44]

Senior rabbi from 1880 to his death in 1923, Hirsch oversaw Sinai's golden years, leading with an uncommon rabbinical élan, revolutionary Reform convictions, and a radically ecumenical social vision.[45] Factors cohering to avow Sinai's modernism included Hirsch's high praise for Martin Luther as a model reformer as well as the congregation's modern scientific sympathies, the abolition of Saturday services, and an explicit rejection of circumcision rites; perhaps the most distinguishing element of Sinai's theological modernism, however, was "[its] strong emphasis on social action."[46] As the public face of the most radical Jewish congregation *"in the world,"* as the supercilious rabbi would boast in a tract for the 1893 World's Columbian Exposition, Hirsch "was very much in tune with the social gospel movement and was exchanging ideas with like-minded Protestants."[47] Hirsch's commitment to the social meaning of modern religion was so significant, in fact, that in 1912 he was called the "greatest living American Hebrew" by the *Chicago Defender,* Chicago's black daily, in recognition of his public demonstrations of solidarity with local black civil rights struggles.[48]

For about a decade, starting in 1912, Hirsch held forth weekly from the stage at Sinai that also launched the fourth NAACP convention in 1912, a generosity afforded the organization by Hirsch himself. Kicking off mere weeks after the new synagogue opened, the convention might have served Sinai's modernist preaching telos by baptizing the new preaching platform with several days' social action addresses, as if to stand with Hirsch's commitment to the theology and practice of Reform preaching—constructivist, ecumenistic, ethically concerned, socially conscious, and proclaiming "not rigid 'law,'" in the fundamentalist sense, "but progressive 'life.'"[49] Hirsch was clear that "the Jewish pulpit [should not] be silent on the injustices of earth, the maladjustment of society," but ought to bear "a vision of justice and freedom."[50] In a 1905 address to Sinai Congregation titled "The Concordance of Judaism and Americanism," Hirsch challenged the assembly:

> Remember great Rabbis exposed the iniquity of negro slavery from their pulpits. Remember that our greatest Reform preacher David Einhorn used

to say "no politics in religion but by all means religion in politics." Negro slavery has been wiped out, but alas! other and worse slavery still prevails in this world of ours. Shall they who hear the clanking of the chains forgo speaking though their old Jewish prayer-book praises God thrice daily for having led His people from bondage to slavery? . . . No, Judaism is for the world! Its genius of hopeful realism has syllabled the spiritual message which a people like that of the United States is in need of. Because its kingdom is not beyond the clouds but *a vision of justice and freedom* realized in the tents of men, Judaism strikes the note that sets vibrating the heart of America similarly attuned to energetic realism, similarly tender to the sufferer from injustice, similarly hopeful of the future dawn of universal peace and liberty.[51]

Holding to a liberative vision of American political and cultural life, Hirsch looked to "the genius of Judaism" to illumine and to "negro slavery" to give concrete tropic form to the oppressive conditions of social and spiritual captivity the best of Judaism had labored to overcome.

Hirsch may have overstated the political and moral force of American Judaism's activist tradition, however. His recall of "great Rabbis" who "exposed the iniquity of negro slavery" somewhat disagrees with Jewish preaching historian Robert V. Friedenberg, who has argued that only "on occasion" did early Jewish preachers in America "deal with social and political issues from the pulpit."[52] Slavery, particularly, "gave rise to relatively few Jewish sermons."[53] In Hirsch's time, Jewish sermons concerned with the memory of US slavery or its afterlife were "comparatively rare."[54] Hirsch's public refusal of precisely this strain of silence among Jewish preachers was surely the beginning of Hirsch's popularity with African Americans in Chicago. The high regard afforded him by African American religionists like the twelve hundred or more he addressed at Reverend Reverdy C. Ransom's Institutional Church on Chicago's South Side in November 1912 was almost certainly established on the strength of his will to identify straightforwardly (if sometimes condescendingly) with slavery's racial memory in his preaching. None of his rabbinic contemporaries preached the Reform message so baldly in racial-historical terms. Or so "loudly."

In "The Concordance of Judaism and Americanism," Hirsch set the noisy "clanking of the chains" of American slavery against the strongly "syllabled" sound of Reform preaching, "strik[ing] the note that sets vibrating" the hearts of hearers "attuned" to the hope of a perfected social order to come. With an aural instinct for comparative Jewish and African American racial histories, Hirsch posited a dialectical dissonance, it seems, between the amplified freedom-speak of Reform preaching he claimed as a heritage and black Americans' "clanging" captivity. In Hirsch's hands, "negro slavery" and Jewish abolitionism belong to modernity's enduringly audible past.

While formal rabbinical studies at Berlin and Leipzig quietly nursed Hirsch's historical knowledge of the Reform tradition's European antecedents, Hirsch's ear for history, which I have called his aural instinct, was almost certainly sharpened by, and likely sharpened, modern oratorical and acoustical considerations extending from the history of the US Reform movement itself. As a rabbinical student in Germany in the 1870s and as a young rabbi in the United States in the 1880s, Hirsch could not have avoided the influence of the pioneer Reformer Isaac Mayer Wise. Wise, an immigrant from Germany who was to serve as the founding president of Hebrew Union College (HUC), not only shepherded the Reform movement during its nineteenth-century infancy in the United States but, going "one step beyond virtually every other American Jewish preacher who had preceded him," promoted the assiduous study of classical rhetoric and homiletics.[55] Evidently, Wise impressed many with "a pleasing baritone voice," which he submitted to careful oratorical education.[56] Wise thus brought a discernible "rhythm and cadence" to the new measures that exemplified Reform preaching in the United States.[57] According to Friedenberg, Wise's tonal self-awareness and routine application of classical rhetorical techniques to preaching made clear that he was as concerned for "the way a speaker literally sounded" as he was for what a speaker said.[58] Wise's example almost certainly influenced Hirsch, who "as a speaker . . . could move audiences to tears."[59]

Hirsch's soul-stirring power of speech notwithstanding, no speech or sermon or public address by Hirsch or Wise or King sounded out of a temporal or spatial vacuum, as every address or oration "belongs to a vaster polyphony of perceptual and imaginative experience," as Don Ihde says.[60] Thus, it would be mistaken, and all too reductive, to locate the beginning of the history of Reform preaching in Chicago in Hirsch's talents alone. Rather, an ensemblic resonance, at once phenomenological and deeply historical, coheres in the sonic congress of (1) Hirsch's precise preaching, (2) Sinai's cantillating architecture, and (3) the vast scale of reflective tones generated by the towering electropneumatic Casavant Brothers pipe organ rising above the Sinai pulpit, not least of all.[61] This three-part harmony of oratory, architecture, and organology composes the tonal soundmark by which radical Reform, like the black civil rights movement to come, was to learn was the key of its own sonic ecology of hope and resistance and assured the Reform sound the force of survivance—Derrida's term for the living on of the departed—over vain ephemerality.

Inasmuch as "Why Jesus Called a Man a Fool" repeated Hirsh's modern Reform sensibilities, then, by way of a shared rhetorical commitment to liberal democratic values like "truth, justice and peace," King's preaching dimly echoed Hirsh's. Not so much Hirsh's tone or timbre, properly speaking, but "Why Jesus Called a Man a Fool" repeated the historical sound, which I have called *the general tonal attitude*, of the earlier sociality between liturgists (e.g., preachers, lectors, cantors, singers) and laypersons Hirsh set. Consonant with what Ihde has called the West's "religion of Word" and in particular "the ancient tradition of the synagogue in which the Word must be correctly *canted*,"[62] King, canting justice and freedom after and with Hirsch, sounded through and around the "somewhat broken surface[s]" Sabine commended to Alschuler, bending the shape of words past established pronunciation according to a pitch which "the congregation finds in tune with its [shared] expectations and needs," as the late Howard University theologian Evans Crawford put it.[63]

Even at its most autobiographical, "Why Jesus Called a Man a Fool" expressed doubly the lament and longings of black moderns in Chicago. When King thundered, for instance, "Martin Luther, *stand up* for righteousness, *stand up* for justice, *stand up* for truth," narrating the scene of divine deliverance many now recognize as his "kitchen table epiphany," he was reflecting the sound of *their* power over against *his* words; one hears the force of *their* insistent will-to-freedom in the rough grain of his voice formed around each "*stand up.*" King's pitch, in other words, was far from an arbitrary tuning or timbral affectation. At the level of sound, for one thing, it was "something else" to the sermon-text, "which something else," to invoke Roland Barthes, "is the particular language (and nowise the message)" that King came canting.[64] At another level, "Why Jesus Called a Man a Fool" was also "a witness to an ethical stance," as Crawford says, "an exercise of freedom in a way that was responsive to the rightful demands for justice and equality. The pitch of his preaching matched the pitch in the hearts of the people thereby giving them power to act for what was right and fair."[65] Thus, King's thunder hardly "called" at all in the conventional sense of a call-and-response. Rather, King's thunder, the emphatic and clapping rumble in his preaching's aural ascent to "something else," was the response to an always already calling sonority heard in the high-intensity, low-frequency surround of the sanctuary.[66]

3.1   Exterior of Mt. Pisgah Missionary Baptist Church, Chicago, IL (formerly Chicago Sinai Temple). Photo by Eric Allix Rogers.

3.2   Interior of Mt. Pisgah Missionary Baptist Church, Chicago, IL (formerly Chicago Sinai Temple). Photo by Erica Reggiero.

The mammoth two-thousand-seat neoclassical structure was always already hailing King, in other words, into its post-Reform future. At least since the second decade of the twentieth century, when Hirsch himself took up the marriage of Reform preaching to the defense of the rights of African Americans, the building's memory of the Sinai sound had been hailing King to its South Chicago afterlife, I suspect, ongoingly. The Baptists, then, did not *inherit* the property on Grand Avenue (now South King Drive) after Sinai Congregation vacated it in 1949; from a certain point of view, they fulfilled it.

Hearing Voices: Prayer as Aural Practice

However crucial to King's Mt. Pisgah preaching the (sonic) power of the people was, the significance of the sounds accruing to "Why Jesus Called a Man a Fool" lay only incompletely in his voice's resonance with their pitched protests and optimisms. Equally critical to the resonant effects of the preaching of "Why Jesus Called a Man a Fool," and, thus, to history's memory of King's Mt. Pisgah performance, was King's own fine-tuned audition of the beyond of religious experience which lent an apocalyptic property to the sermon's delivery. "A politics of hearing was always the paired complement to the politics of speaking in . . . churchly settings," Leigh Eric Schmidt tells us, and King's oratorical politics in no way breached this law.[67] In "Why Jesus Called a Man a Fool," buoying this claim, King represented himself as one given to what Schmidt calls "devout hearing," a sensitive "hearkening" and religious way of knowing "that emphasizes the aliveness of sounds, the power of scriptures to speak, the capacity of music to heal or to inspire ecstasy, the voices out there that become doubled voices within and the sympathetic vibrations that connect one body to another."[68] Schmidt's *Hearing Things: Religion, Illusion, and the American Enlightenment* chronicles the representation of audition as agency in early American religious experience.

To take one example from *Hearing Things*, Schmidt gives an account of Thomas Henry, who was born into slavery in St. Mary's County, Maryland, and was a convert to Methodism and who, in 1819, felt the call to preach. Like King, Henry got a midnight call. A demonic voice in the air mocks and scorns him: "You cannot be a preacher; you have not reached the requirements in education; the people will laugh at you." Disparaging as the antagonist is, Henry's torment proves generative in the end. He learns devout hearing:

> Then, one day, lying in the basement of a house, seeking shelter from a storm, Henry lapsed into "deep meditation" on what the Lord had in

mind for me: "There was a wonderful peal of thunder, and a great blaze of lightening ran around the room where I was lying. There was a short interval between the thunder and the lightening, and in this interval I heard a voice that was too distinct to be mistaken. I was perfectly awake; and the voice said this: 'I must work the work of Him that sent me, while it is called day.' I spring upon my feet and exclaimed: 'Yes, Lord! Yes!' I had no more doubt."[69]

Against the sneering voice of the devil, who had previously derided him, the clear voice of the Lord, "too distinct to be mistaken," calls Henry from the thunder. This same dialectic of terror and triumph is repeated in the concise chronicling of King's kitchen table epiphany in "Why Jesus Called a Man a Fool." The "ugly voice" gone its way, King was evidently moved to pray. Though prayer seems a human call in want of a telephonic reply, it is probably better put as "a closed-eye dialogue in which the devout [actively] *listened*."[70] Thus, it was not what King *prayed* that night that begs our attention (i.e., the litany of supplications reiterated in the preaching moment to recreate a scene of intimate dialogue for the benefit of those overhearing it); it is what he *heard* ahead of it all, the listening-to of praying, that set apart this preacherly performance.

> Something said to me, You can't call on Daddy now.... You can't even call on Mama now. (*My Lord!*) You've got to call on that something in that person that your daddy used to tell you about. (*Yes*) That power that can make a way out of no way. (*Yes*) And I discovered then that religion had to become real to me and I had to know God for myself. (*Yes sir*) And I bowed down over that cup of coffee—I never will forget it. (*Yes, sir*) And oh yes, I prayed a prayer and I prayed out loud that night. (*Yes*) I said, "Lord, I'm down here trying to do what's right. (*Yes*) I think I'm right; I think the cause that we represent is right. (*Yes*) But Lord, I must confess that I'm weak now; I'm faltering; I'm losing my courage. (*Yes*) And I can't let the people [supporting the boycott in Montgomery] see me like this because if they see me weak and losing my courage, they will begin to get weak." (Yes)
>
> And it seemed at that moment that I could hear an inner voice saying to me, (*Yes*) "Martin Luther, (*Yes*) stand up for righteousness, (*Yes*) stand up for justice, (*Yes*) stand up for truth. (*Yes*) And lo I will be with you, (*Yes*) even until the end of the world."
>
> And I'll tell you, I've seen the lightening flashing. I've heard the thunder roll. I felt sin's breakers dashing, trying to conquer my soul. But I heard the voice of Jesus saying still to fight on. He promised never to leave me, never

to leave me alone. No, never alone. No, never alone. He promised never to leave me, (*Never*) never to leave me alone."[71]

While this concise "oratory of prayer" might have easily merited printing in James Washington's 1994 volume *Conversations with God: Two Centuries of Prayers by African Americans*[72]—it is a small surprise Washington did not include it—the prayer succeeds not chiefly by its oratory but by the vindicatory power of its aural instincts as it repeated the aural intensities of religious experience emplotted within the early American spiritual narratives in Schmidt's study. "In a world of demonic menace and terrifying judgment," Schmidt shows, "the devout listened fearfully and yet also expectantly for the heavenly strains that signaled the final defeat of those terrors."[73] Though it is Henry's life and sufferings that lend Schmidt's argument authority, who can deny its further evidence in King's earnest example? The telephone standing in for modern religious hearing, King discerned "an ugly voice" on the other end which the congregation at Mt. Pisgah could only have recognized as a tonal description, a complex of timbre and overtone. It was the recognizable (and deadly) sound of the "ugly voice" of racist violence, over and above the foreboding content of the threat—for King "had heard these things before," he noted—that "for some reason . . . got to me."[74] It seems King's "devil" had reached him in a place deep within his aural imagination. Following Schmidt's typology, it shouldn't surprise us that "the final defeat" of the devil-caller would issue from this same deep place. Let us call it the place of prayer as an aural practice.

At the kitchen table, an "inner voice" answers King's sense of existential alienation ("You can't call on Daddy . . . You can't even call on Mama") with firm parental surrogacy: "Martin Luther, stand up for righteousness!" Hearing King hearing this holy consolation, we are led to see King's praying as revelatory of his preaching. Hearing King hearing, in other words, one cannot but see more clearly now than ever how, for all his formal preparation in the practice and theology of preaching at Crozer and Boston, the preacher King preached by ear so facilely, his published sermons and preaching manuscripts being but "calligraphies" of the oral mode, to recall Roberson.

Perhaps as much as any other detail that King's recapitulated prayer in Chicago offered up as key to the resonant sensitivities of his devout hearing, the sound of the thunderclap King evoked ("I've seen the lightening flashing. I've heard the thunder roll") brought an eschatological intensity to the scene of preaching. As Schmidt explains, in the eighteenth and nineteenth centuries "[t]hunder was a consummate sound of Judgment, and, like the trumpet blast, it made for an old refrain."⁷⁵ By 1967 it was even older, of course, and very familiar to modern black Protestant sensibilities. Ludie Pickett's 1897 composition "No, Never Alone" had long since been part of the canon of black hymnody when King appropriated its lyrics to evoke sounds that were too terrible to express in themselves: sounds of the approaching vindication of the weak by the Almighty. "I've seen the lightening flashing. I've heard the thunder roll," he intoned with a rumbling. Judging by their shouting approval, those who listened from all points in Mt. Pisgah's cavernous auditorium—those who would absorb the sound of the speaker's voice reflected off the walls in technical terms—heard "the thunder roll," too. Unscripted, King's preaching mimicked an abrupt inbreaking of the future upon the present past of segregationism. The present world, it seemed, had changed little from the one that Thomas Henry inhabited 150 years earlier. From a religious standpoint, at least, both Henry and King, past and present, gave testimony to "a world of demonic temptation and threatening judgment."⁷⁶ Like Henry's, King's "ears were well trained in fear and foreboding."⁷⁷ Still, as Schmidt points out in the Thomas Henry account and in the broader tradition of early American calling narratives, in life and plot structure "the devil never had the last word."⁷⁸

In the present past of 1967, then, not only did the sound of King's preaching prevail over the "ugly voice" of racial violence and intimidation, but the an-archic sounds of those exultant in their identification with it ultimately drowned out the devil and the last word with shouts of joy and wordless cries. A victory, it seems, was at once coming and already won.

II

Nettie's Nocturne

4

King's Gospel Modernism
The Politics of Lament, the Politics of Loss

By the time Martin Luther King Jr. visited Mt. Pisgah Missionary Baptist Church in 1967, the sound of blackness in Chicago had entered a new modernism all its own. Gospel music had revolutionized the black sacred sound in Chicago between 1931 and 1969, defining a radically new era of black sacred musical expression. Broad social and demographic changes in Chicago, especially the historic migration of thousands from the Deep South—Georgia, Alabama, Mississippi—to Chicago's South Side, brought insistent, irrepressible blues strains to antiseptic choruses of African-American Christian hymnody, distinguishing gospel's new sound and sensibility. I approached this people's history of twentieth-century gospel obliquely in chapter 2. But a bigger picture of the gospel aesthetic at mid-century calls, one that takes seriously modern gospel as a blues tradition and, thus, a parallel soundtrack to the history of black dispossession and material struggle that was the Great Migration north.

Although the blues undoubtedly had its genesis under slavery "when a man looked up in some anonymous field and shouted, 'Oh, Ahm tired a diss mess, / Oh, yes, Ahm so tired a diss mess,'" as Amiri Baraka (then LeRoi Jones) famously wrote,[1] modern gospel, first called gospel blues, did not come into being as a distinct genre until the twentieth century, though its roots too were surely bound up with those of the blues. Specifically, it was the religious feeling of black migrants in the Depression and New Deal eras, a feeling born of their wrestling between faith and despair in the new setting, that gave rise to gospel as "the most dominant form of African-American sacred music expression"[2] in the twentieth century. That the gospel sound should be inflected by social and material hopes and worries at its dawn shouldn't be surprising. Despite gospel's clear otherworldly orientation, it was at one and the same time "a vehicle of defiance and protest"[3] from the start. This is the argument of Robert Darden's 2016 *Nothing but Love in God's Water: Black Sacred Music from the Civil War to the Civil Rights Movement.* Some thirty-three years ahead of Darden, though, Anthony Heilbut had already made the claim Darden's two volumes of *Nothing but Love in God's Water* would confirm about the materialist history of modern black gospel. Heilbut's 1971 *The Gospel Sound: Good News and Bad Times* weighed how much gospel was composed of "coded political statements" in "barely disguised freedom song[s]." Not too rarely were these songs of imminence rather than transcendence, containing "coded references to social mobility and political empowerment," Heilbut noted.[4] Born of the mixed parentage of the blues and the new optimism of the New Deal, how could modern gospel be otherwise than a vital musical palimpsest of the political and material desires of black moderns cast in a sacred vocabulary?

Gospel blues, then, was not only inseparable from the cultural reorientation of the black South in the North, and an irreducible property of the modern sound of black Chicago from the New Deal to the Great Society (alongside blues, jazz, and, nascently, rhythm and blues). More than that, it could not avoid reflecting the political and materialist dream-keeping King was also keenly committed to. Even as the gospel sound grew clearer about its investments in the civil rights struggle (with the double-sided 45 bearing considerable weight in this evolution of gospel to intimated protest), by 1966, when the SCLC announced the Chicago Freedom Movement and King moved his family into a four-room flat on South Hamlin Avenue, King's stylized, resistive preaching was already very much in sync with gospel's improvisational priorities. King's sermon, "A Knock at Midnight," published in 1963 in *Strength to Love*, could hardly be said to have been familiar to King's followers when he resurrected it at the Blackstone Hotel in Chicago three years after publication. The relationship of the preacher King to the published sermon in *Strength to Love* was anything but faithfully recitational. King's improvisatory departures from the writtenness of "A Knock at Midnight" to its oration—what I have previously referred to as his *super-scripting* of the sermon-text, an overriding/overwriting of the paper imprint of words by their extraverbal envoicement—defamiliarized the published sermon by a certain "deformation of mastery," to call up Houston Baker on the strategies of black modernism,[5] as King afforded the Ebenezer (Chicago) congregation an interpretation of "A Knock at Midnight" that must have sounded like *something else* completely. King's translation of "A Knock at Midnight" from print to improvisatory proclamation was not a new dynamic but derived from the earlier attitude of gospel's insurgent sound toward its scored representation on musical manuscript paper. Long before King overcame the hegemony of vision underwriting print to recover "A Knock at Midnight" for sound, gospel had already settled the vexed relationship between inscription and envoicement. Thomas Dorsey provoked this very tension thirty-five years ahead of King, inaugurating a musical modernism in black sacred culture in 1931 at modern gospel's beginning.

Writing Sound: Thomas Dorsey

In 1931 three Chicago church musicians, Thomas A. Dorsey, Theodore R. Frye, and Roberta Martin, introduced a radically new musical aesthetic into African American religious experience. Against the prevailing tastes of black northerners for classical hymns and oratorios by Mendelssohn, Bach, Mozart, Rossini, and Handel—preferences indistinct from the musical repertories of white churches—they helped Chicago's black Protestants shift away from their high-church devotions toward more dynamic expressions of faith and God-consciousness such as those brought north by black southerners to the Baptist, Methodist, Episcopal, and Presbyterian establishment. The ecstatic displays and emotional freedoms that had been the exclusive purview of Holiness devotees and storefront Pentecostals were not long kept apart from the worship experiences of their mainline cousins, owing significantly to Dorsey, Frye, and Martin, and the revolution in black sacred sound they inspired. The new music was blues-based, heavily syncopated, and, above all, expressive.

It was early in 1931 that Alabama native Rev. Dr. James Howard Lorenzo Smith, senior minister at Ebenezer (Chicago), brought Frye and Dorsey, also southern migrants, to the historical church on Vincennes Avenue and 45th Street to revitalize the music department there. Like nearby Big Bethel AME, Ebenezer had been an "institutional" church of high local standing and a public voice dedicated as much to the social and formally political issues bearing on South Chicago as on spiritual matters. In 1935, for instance, Ebenezer's church board issued a formal declaration of support for Ethiopia

(Abyssinia) against Mussolini's fascist invasion halfway across the world. It even raised money for the defense of Ethiopia's independence. Important as the church's stalwart anti-fascism was, Smith yearned for a deeper spirituality at Ebenezer as well. He turned to Frye, an occasional singer at Ebenezer, for leadership. The new music director found his assistant in Dorsey, the erstwhile blues and jazz pianist. Soon Dorsey's original compositions and the hope-filled, sometimes even exuberant, performances of Dorsey's music that Frye oversaw at Ebenezer set gospel going and transformed the sacred soundscape of black Chicago. Called "Georgia Tom" when he was on the blues and jazz circuit, Dorsey was shortly to become the "Father of Gospel Music." Singing Dorsey's songs—"There'll Be Peace in the Valley," "If We Ever Needed the Lord Before," and "Take My Hand, Precious Lord," to name three Dorsey standards—Ebenezer's hundred-voice Senior Gospel Chorus made religious history in February 1932 as the first self-consciously modern gospel choir to be integrated into the principal liturgy of a mainline black church.

Short months later, Dorsey moved from assistant director of music at Ebenezer (Chicago) to director of the gospel chorus at the three-thousand-seat Pilgrim Baptist Church nearby, where the greater part of his musical legacy was created and preserved. Still, Ebenezer's standing as first among equals was firmly established. Under Frye, the new music's appeal grew rapidly and Ebenezer's roll swelled as a result. By King's visit for the seventh anniversary celebration of Smith's successor, Rev. Frank Kentworth Sims, gospel had all but displaced classical hymnody in Chicago's black churches and in black churches across the country. From 1931 to 1969, *pace* Boyer, gospel was golden. Perhaps no other word but "golden" fit gospel's dual popularity and mid-century commercial power so well.

While modern gospel drew the faithful to it on its own socioaesthetic terms, a keen entrepreneurialism underwritten by the print production associated with music publishing houses aided gospel's wide embrace by black church music leaders. "During the thirties," writes Heilbut, corroborating gospel's commercial circulation as a paper industry before it became widely phonographic, "the all-black National Baptist Convention sold its paperback collection of hymns, *Gospel Pearls*, by the tens of thousands. Taking a cue from the Convention's ministers of music, Dorsey began publishing his songs."[6] By 1942, Dorsey's music and that of others inspired by him were in such demand that gospel scores bankrolled "a good half-dozen" independent gospel publishing houses. "Where once every black Baptist home kept its copy of *Gospel Pearls* with the family Bible, Dorsey's sheet music took over, with Bible and *Pearls* both gathering dust."[7] Even more industriously, Dorsey set about personally training soloists and choruses in the new sound. With fellow pianist Roberta Martin and gospel ingénue Sallie Martin (no relation), Dorsey toured the country teaching gospel songs, vocal performance, and accompaniment style at black churches and auditoriums near and far. State to state, Dorsey, Martin, and Martin took to the road, blazing, as they say, a "gospel highway" out of the narrowest and most perilous thruways of Jim Crow travel. Their brave ambition paid off.

> By 1950, there were dozens of gospel hits heard everywhere in black neighborhoods, on street corners, through open windows, down alleys, in bars and restaurants. A whole generation grew up listening to the Trumpeteers' "Milky White Way," the Georgia Peach's "Shady Green Pastures," the Angelic Gospel Singers' "Touch Me Lord Jesus," Mahalia's "Move On Up a Little Higher," the Martin Singers' "Old Ship of Zion," the Pilgrim Travelers' "Mother Bowed," the Ward Singers' "Surely God is Able," the Five Blind Boys' "Our Father," and the Bells of Joy's "Let's Talk About Jesus." Not everyone remembered the singers' names, but . . . they all absorbed styles and standards of these early hits.[8]

Although Dorsey, R. Martin, and S. Martin would log countless miles on the road training black Baptist and Methodist choruses in the new style and instructing soloists "how to 'moan and roll,'"[9] it was their instinct to publish Dorsey's and R. Martin's piano-based compositions and to sell the scored music by mail order that fueled gospel's Trojan-horse insurgency against traditional pipe-organ propriety and the sounds of black religious respectability more broadly. Ironic as it sounds in light of gospel's essential commitment to improvisational vocal and instrumental play, the fast and steady growth of modern gospel in the 1930s and 1940s was owed to none more than those singers, directors, and pianists formally trained, many in colleges and conservatories, to read sheet music in the classical tradition. This was especially true of many old-line organizations like the National Baptist Convention which, though a voluntary association, helped establish the norms of black Baptist thought and liturgical life nationwide, having a powerful influence on its member churches in matters of theology, polity, liturgy, and, not least, hymnody. Although Dorsey's gospel music workshops and clinics for soloists and music directors were critical to broadening gospel's audience great distances away from Chicago, the gospel sound Dorsey is credited with having pioneered circulated primarily by means of its notational representation as sheet music for educated music readers. Ten cents per copy at the beginning, Dorsey's song sheets were only sketches of the gospel sound, however. More generic than mimetic, they stood rather as mnemonic guides for an essentially aural black choral pedagogy.

In other words, drawn upon to "move the music through a learning process (here only a link in a larger oral-transmission act)," as Horace Boyer explains, Dorsey's song sheets were *not* scores for imitative or tightly fixed forms of vocal intonation or instrumental play.[10] Consisting of "open rhythmic spaces for the obligatory improvisation that identified gospel,"[11] as Boyer's reflections on Dorsey go on to point out, Dorsey's song sheets, published and reproduced under his own Dorsey's House of Music imprint, observed the separateness of the gospel sound from its writtenness in musical notation precisely by the visual affordance of "open . . . spaces" and a corollary refusal of more and more paper against all hope of paper's sufficiency for gospel's recording. Kenneth Morris, another Chicago composer and Dorsey contemporary, elucidated gospel's minimalist composition strategies in a 1987 interview with Bernice Johnson Reagon:

> [In those days] I would have to write the music in easy keys, not too many florid passages. . . . A lot of runs, a lot of sixteenth notes and thirty-second notes; I had to cut them down. You have to change the time values and a lot of different chords. . . .
>
> If I wanted them [complex or dissonant chords] in there, naturally, when I played I could always add and interpolate. So the sheet music was a basic structure. The only thing limiting [the musician] was his ability.
>
> The majority of them [critics] said that it was not real music. It means that it ought to have been written up there what you are going to do. Whatever the composer intended for the person to do should be written on the paper.
>
> There was another way we were criticized. So many people would say, unless they could point out what note to use, they didn't know what not to use—and where is the tenor note? They saw three notes; which to use for the alto, and which to use for the tenor, and there is no bass? They wanted to teach four parts. . . .
>
> To write SATB [soprano-alto-tenor-bass] meant a different type of score. You had a clef for each part and you would have a piano score independently at the bottom. So all this meant space and paper. You were using up a whole lot of paper. From my angle, it wasn't necessary. . . . Most of our score was written for the pianist, incidentally. That was all that was necessary. We would try to incorporate as much of that into the piano score.[12]

Morris's memory of the material conditions of gospel songwriting in the 1930s and 1940s posits a very different relationship between gospel composition and musical notation on paper than that which is believed to obtain generally between classical composition and its inscriptive practice on musical manuscript paper. That is, while classical education in music has habituated readers of music to the song sheet, or score, as a meticulous notation of the composer's finished vision for the music's performance or audition ("Whatever the composer intended . . . should be written on the paper"), gospel scores called for another and special kind of musical literacy. Even on paper, modern gospel resisted a strict fidelity between what was "written up there" on manuscript paper and "what you are going to do" performatively. Its scoring was set to elemental notation, rather than simulacral symbolization. But Dorsey's song sheets no more disallowed "florid passages," "lot[s] of runs," "a lot of sixteenth . . . and thirty-second notes," and "complex and dissonant chords" than Morris did, even if their written music absented the more intricate grammar of gospel's deeper, soulful sonorities. Instead, they encouraged precisely what they omitted by preserving open space for music readers to "add and interpolate" freely.

Dorsey's notational writing was especially bidding to improvisationalists as the negative space created by his gospel notation tended to be, albeit accidentally, visually engaging as well. Writes Boyer,

> The tones employed in the melody of [Dorsey's] "Precious Lord" [for example] constitute its scale. Dorsey employed a scale, which in visual terms would look like a five- or six-year-old child with a tooth missing; there would be space to leap back and forth from. He liked scales that provided the same kind of space a Black speaking style conveys when African American people all of a sudden raise their voices in pitch and then return to a more comfortable pitch.[13]

In eschewing mimetic playing (or vocalism) and opening up scalar space for swing time ("space to leap back and forth from") directly on the page, Dorsey's songwriting reflected a doubly metrical and graphic materialization of what Moten describes as "the Afro-diasporic tradition's long, meditative, and practical concern with spacing, incommensurability, and rupture" on paper, though he refused "using up a whole lot of paper," as Morris put it, to achieve it.[14]

Although gapped scales set him apart and into the Afro-diasporic tradition, Dorsey also defied the orthodoxies of "real music" in other ways. As if the visual resemblance of the printed music to "a five- or six-year-old child with a tooth missing" was not hint enough of the general critique of gospel toward the material, even political, conceits of "real music" (like diatonic propriety, formalist harmonics, the extravagance of dedicated performance space, or, indeed, the cost of limitless paper), Dorsey's vague three-part notation (SAT), over against the written system's four-part convention (SATB), also opposed Western pretensions with an alternate logic inhering consistently, even constitutively, by the sense of "something missing," as Moten (I think) suggests[15]—which is to say (I think) by the sense of a *partial refusal* and, thus, a necessary improvisation (of unseen black notation) overwriting the (glaring whiteness of the) material space where paper wasn't necessary. Flouting publishing conventions (e.g., composing only three parts, writing in 4/4 but playing in 12/8), Dorsey and other gospel writers deformed the anthems, chorales, and arranged spirituals associated with the aspirational aesthetics of black religious modernism. Well before the New York School of notational expressionism (John Cage, Morten Feldman, Earle Brown) began experimenting with graph scores and other liberative organizations of musical notation in the 1950s,[16] in Chicago gospel song sheets were their own experimentalism, demanding to be read in the break in between the gospel sound and the gospel score where the Cartesian space-time otherwise insisted upon by the prescriptive formulism of prelined paper got de-formed. Thus, Dorsey pioneered not just a sound but a new musical literacy, one bearing analogously on the manuscript-as-preaching-screen. Perhaps it was just this duality—performance and notation, sound and score—that hooked King. In much the same way early gospel singers, choir teachers, and publishers learned to read gospel song sheets against the grain, King relied on preaching manuscripts in search of a sound for which print was mnemonically necessary but insufficient to mimetically reproduce the sound called for. "A Knock at Midnight" inhered in just this sort of elemental miscegeneity, reflecting the black modernist sensibilities of gospel's mixed musical and, in the breaks, political history.

Hearing "A Knock at Midnight"

When King approached the podium that had been set up in the events hall at the Blackstone Hotel in May 1966, one Ebenezer sound (Atlanta) met another (Chicago). Although the hotel was blocks away from the Chicago Ebenezer auditorium where gospel sounded its first insurgent notes, the acoustical otherness of the Michigan Avenue event space did not prevent the sonological invitation in the sermon's title from promoting the sermon's

4.1 Title page of Thomas A. Dorsey's "Take My Hand, Precious Lord." Courtesy Fisk University, John Hope and Aurelia E. Franklin Library, Special Collections Library, Thomas Dorsey Collection.

4.2 Sheet music for Thomas A. Dorsey's "Take My Hand, Precious Lord." Courtesy Fisk University, John Hope and Aurelia E. Franklin Library, Special Collections Library, Thomas Dorsey Collection.

aural objecthood. In marked contrast to its literariness in *Strength to Love*—it reads very close to an essay there—"A Knock at Midnight" resisted, but did not reject, its essayistic form. In May 1966, and again in June 1967, in Chicago and Cincinnati, respectively, King betrayed his desire to transfigure "A Knock at Midnight" into *something else*, to over-read the text of it so that it might *s(w)ing*, after the fashion of gospel blues. Emotive, full-throated, and pitched to black habits of hearing, King preached as one "not merely want[ing] to say, speak, or articulate the Word" but also intent upon "sound[ing] the Word."[17]

His determination to do so, though, was predicated upon the new reading practice Dorsey and others forged, one given much less to visual inquiry or sight-reading than to a keener listening for/in the breaks of homiletics' learned forms. A prior aurality, King's, occasioned before the general hearing of his sermon by the congregations in Chicago and Cincinnati, lifted "A Knock at Midnight" off the page, transfigured, to assert its difference from its own other life on paper by way of the play of speech and sound. Introducing "A Knock at Midnight" so languidly as to seem halting—"I come this morning, to try to preach"—the preacher King was not pretending false humility. In the pronounced caesura of the comma, and for several wordless seconds following the finished sentence, King was keenly listening while his audience listened to him listening, their ears keyed to the anticipated pitch of that moan of "trouble-glory" they knew was also theirs by proxy.[18] Before observing more closely King's reformulation of "A Knock at Midnight" as gospel preaching, however (adhering to no particular Christological claims in its aesthetic), I want to linger a while longer over the structuralist orthodoxies of homiletical composition and presentation that constituted the ground of King's gospel flights and refusals in "A Knock at Midnight" as he delivered it, postpublication, in 1966.

In print, "A Knock at Midnight" reflects King's early deference to the formal preaching education he gained years earlier as a seminarian at Crozer Theological Seminary. There, under the tutelage of Robert E. Keighton, King read closely Yale professor Halford Luccock's *In the Minister's Workshop* (1944). Luccock was a distinguished teacher of preaching who held strong convictions about the sermonic craft. In one illustrative chapter of *In the Minister's Workshop* titled "Structure and Outline," Luccock averred that "the power of a sermon lies in structure, not in its decoration. This is equally true of beauty, in spite of a common tendency to find beauty in ornament rather than in form."[19] Form and method defined Luccock's homiletical philosophy. Not so surprisingly, then, he posited architecture as the sermon's closest equivalent in structural logic and aesthetic aim: "The relationships between architecture and sermons," he wrote, "are many and significant."[20] In print, one sees clearly that "A Knock at Midnight" is nothing if not conventionally architectural, which is to say schematic, balanced, and connective, without ornament or excess, a grammarly interdiction against the anarchy of what Luccock called "formless sprawl," tempting to those like King "cursed with a facility for extemporaneous oratory."[21] Methodically, King followed Luccock's formula for organizing his topic, namely the social somnambulism of the church in the West and the hope of its imminent reawakening, into three refrains: "It is midnight within the social order," "It is midnight within the psychological order," and "It is also midnight within the moral order."[22] Though King proposed a "positive belief in the dawn" to cure the "staggering midnight" of the times—a synthetic judgment, following a familiarly Hegelian logic—the sermon's dialectical method, straightforwardly architectural, was not as plainly Hegelian as the night-and-day dichotomy implied by the midnight leitmotif might suggest.

As Keith D. Miller has shown so well, King's printed sermons strived to follow the orderliness and argumentative schema of liberal homiletical presentation metaphorically figured as ladder, key, jewel, Roman candle, classification, and mousetrap strategies by Luccock and other liberal preaching experts.[23] With its triptych of metaphorical midnights, and its ecclesial criticisms ("One [church] burns with emotionalism, and the other freezes with classism"[24]), "A Knock at Midnight" combined elements of Luccock's jewel and classification patterns. It was, thus, a sermon in search of its form when King included it in *Strength to Love*. But inasmuch as it was searching for a fitting form, Miller argues that it was also simultaneously set to certain academic theological ambitions, not the least of which was a proper theology "*best communicated in print.*"[25] Failing to inhere in conventional philosophical or theological modes of discursive production, King's sermons in *Strength to Love*—"A Knock at Midnight," to be sure—were left to create pastiche forms, the better to contain the problem of extemporaneity King had inherited from the black preaching tradition but which Luccock, and presumably Keighton, saw as insufferable.

Ultimately, the curious assortment of forms prescribed by *In the Minister's Workshop* and made to seem everyday in their mechanistic object-identifications tended only to standardize the preacher's printed "voice." Only the remembered sound of King's preaching—remembered by those who would read his text as a souvenir of that hearing—could save *Strength to Love* from serving as little more than "training sermons,"[26] as Lischer saw them. Whatever their historical value, Lischer depicted the sermons composing *Strength to Love* as but "the products of learning by imitation and preaching as rhetorical drill."[27] Not coincidentally, with the sermons in *Strength to Love* "effectively 'froze[n]'" by formal constraints, King "never produced another book of sermons."[28] It seems both the book itself as a print object and the anti-modern architectural fixation in Luccock's and Keighton's influence on King's sermonic writing instincts conspired against it.

Admittedly, the want of a second collection of literary sermons is scarcely proof of anything. But King's subsequent turning to historical memoir and to the long essay in his two books, *Why We Can't Wait* (1964) and *Where Do We Go from Here: Chaos or Community?* (1967), respectively, raises the prospect at least of his own disappointment by his sermons' failure *to achieve resonance* in print form. Against extemporaneity, improvisation, excess, and ornament—*against the modern gospel sound*, we might say—*Strength to Love* could only be called up to fix, correct, corral (to clear up, even if it cannot clear away) the an-archic exorbitances Luccock's architecturalism was calculated to discipline. Affecting a belief in the "essential rightness of order and outline" that Luccock promoted, in other words, King set *Strength to Love* to purge preaching of its ornamental flights, prone as such impulses are to the "blur[ring]" of "clear, hard beauty," Luccock warned.[29] Eventually, however, King would come to be habituated to, rather than eschew, this blurring as a practice in modern black preaching, an ethic and aesthetics of black preacherly performance which, not unlike the institutionally inflected conditions of composition, circulation, and performativity surrounding early gospel, aspired to a miscegenation of sound and print in the airy openness between the Ebenezer (Atlanta) sound in King's preaching and the sermon's generic identification in King's educated writing.

In its later hearing at Mt. Zion Baptist Church in Cincinnati in 1967, for instance, "A Knock at Midnight" was no longer a sermon in search of a form fit to its aim of also limning a "satisfying religious system," as Miller writes,[30] for the work of racial justice; not unlike its earlier hearing at Ebenezer (Chicago), it was in search of its essential sound. Whereas the printed sermon expressed King's lament of "two world wars hav[ing] been fought within a generation" in its first few sentences, when the sermon was reprised for the pulpit this line was omitted. In its place, more clearly in Cincinnati than Chicago, King nodded to a crisis in the Middle East, then his attention turned to "a futile, bloody, costly war taking place on Asian soil." He had scarcely started his sermon before the immediacy of the Vietnam War overwhelmed the historical memory of the two world wars, long since won, preoccupying the sermon's published text. "King wrestled with Vietnam's immense-gravitational pull on national politics," Taylor Branch would write in *At Canaan's Edge: America in the King Years, 1965–1968*, and "in fitful departures" from prepared text, he routinely yielded to that pull after 1964.³¹ Cincinnati was no exception. At Mt. Zion that impulse to depart from, and thus effectively to *blur*, extended swaths of the preaching manuscript was conspicuously in evidence.³²

Pitching piety and respectability to the wind, King altered several lengthy sections of "A Knock at Midnight" original to its publication. With the war in Vietnam growing thornier by the day and its official justification more clearly dishonest than it had previously pretended, King's live preaching took no part in the impertinence of tinkering with properly formed sermons while Rome, we might say, burned. Insisting in one place that American morality had "become a dirty shade of gray,"³³ he abandoned the sort of measured elocution *Strength to Love* was intended to convey to liberal audiences, opting for a stentorian defiance hardly ministerial in its bellicosity. Proposing that Luke's parable of the three loaves might be understood allegorically, King inveighed against white Americans who dismissively refused the "bread of love" to their black neighbors:

> The great problem of mankind today is still that there is too much hatred around. More than anything else, we've got to learn to love. In America, the white man must love the black man, and the black man must love the white man, because we are all tied together in a single garment of destiny. *And we can't keep having riots every summer in our cities, we can't keep having all of these problems all over our nation, our white brothers must understand that we're too poor, and the federal government has enough money to get rid of slums and poverty and get rid of these conditions that make for riots, there's no point in continuing to make up excuses, our white brothers have got to come to see* ONE THING: *We are* IN AMERICA *and we are* HERE TO STAY, *and we got to learn how to* LIVE *together.* WE AIN'T GOING NOWHERE!

As he goes off-script, a certain unruliness and refusal of the proper, both at the level of grammar and social cooperation, power King's prophetic rage, a propheticism Moten and others would surely agree attained "eloquent vulgarity."³⁴ "*WE AIN'T GOING NOWHERE!*" sonifies an an-archic double-negative defiance communicating not only an attitude or ethics of black outrage but the "means of nonviolent resistance" in itself against the well-oiled instruments of violence, domination, and mortal terror, direct and disguised, animating and ruling over the oppressive systems of this world. As Charles L.

Campbell argues in *The Word before the Powers: An Ethic of Preaching*, "The very act of preaching—the choice of *preaching as a means*—represent[s] a rejection of and alternative to the 'myth of redemptive violence.'"[35] Inasmuch as King identified himself, first and last, with the call and practice of preaching—"I am fundamentally a clergyman, a Baptist preacher. This is my being," he avowed in *Ebony* in 1965[36]—"A Knock at Midnight" enacted the very "*that* of preaching" to which Campbell set in sharp opposition preaching's "*what*" ("what we speak, the message we proclaim"[37]). More specifically, at Mt. Zion the infuriated sound of King's preaching performed an equal counter-coercion to those acts of brutality intended to silence blacks, women, the poor, queer persons, and all who dared resist, or defy, order(s). "WE AIN'T GOING NOWHERE!" King came preaching, the aural *that* (i.e., the loudness of speech—the means) somewhat surpassing the *what* (i.e., the refusal, the bodily resistance to fear and intimidation) in remonstrative intensity.

To summarize, King's preaching after *Strength to Love*, it's safe to say, was nothing if not out of order in both *that* by means of which "A Knock at Midnight" encouraged King's listeners and *what*, specifically, the sermon encouraged in them: steadfastness in struggle. Being out of order, which is to say being out *from* order, King's riffs on what was written down beforehand effectively blurred the lines on the page into vocal effects. I mean that, performatively speaking, King submitted the published text of "A Knock at Midnight" to a sort of "ceaseless worrying, an endless rub, a troubling pregnancy, an obsessive overpolishing that eventually blurs always and everywhere with undoing" not unlike that which Moten observed in *Black and Blur* in the contemporary art practice of Charles Gaines.[38]

In Gaines's *Librettos*, Moten explains, the artist superimposes excerpts from the score of Manuel de Falla's opera *La Vida Breve* over the text of an April 1967 speech by King's younger pan-Africanist counterpart in the black freedom struggle, Stokely Carmichael. More concretely, Gaines allows a space between Falla's score and Carmichael's script, "a palimpsestic interval" as "lateral fascination through which attention passes."[39] As Moten further explains, this intervening space in-between (which is out from the order that formally distinguishes the paper representation of music and speech) is like "an exploratory envoy of breathing":

> You send air [as it were], or you are sent as air through the individual "panel" or blurred unit while being sent through the three-dimensional blurred air of the space itself, the gallery operating normally as a devotional gathering of pilgrims circling inside a square, held periodically by stations that in this

case take the form of hung rectangles, roughly human in scale, relatively flat but standing forth, nevertheless, as an airy thickness. In a series of twelve panels, Carmichael's words, proximate to the wall, are covered by envelopes of plexiglass approximately eight inches thick, upon which is printed Falla's score.[40]

Gaines's visual blurring of Falla and Carmichael, foreground and background, score and text, music and speech, $sound_1$ and $sound_2$, gives the lie to their works' categorical difference as similarly prosthetic print objects—notative representations of sonic materialities. Gaines's *Librettos* is thus a fitting illustration of the relation of black musical print culture, like that which helped to found gospel, and the insurgent sounds of black speech and song.

King's blurring of the printed (pre-)text of "A Knock at Midnight" and the sound of the sermon as a religious oration, their duality roughly corresponding to Falla's score and Carmichael's improvised speech-making, set the in-between of black print and proclamation in rebellious relief. There the affective potential of the written sermon was realized in and by the blurred lines of its vocalization in public speech acts and performance habits. In this way King exemplified "the faithful preacher," and "A Knock at Midnight" the epitome-object of his task, in Campbell's general theory of Christian preaching. According to Campbell,

> The practice of preaching involves an *ethical performance*. . . . Some texts begin to deliver their full meaning only when they are performed. A play delivers its meaning only when it is performed by a company of actors. A musical score delivers its meaning when it is performed by a group of musicians. . . . The Christian interpretation of Scripture [specifically] is similar to the interpretation of *Macbeth* by a company of actors or the interpretation of "Take Five" by the Dave Brubeck quartet.
>
> The primary poles in the interpretation of Scriptures are not fully written texts. . . . Rather, the poles in biblical interpretation are *patterns of human action*. . . .
>
> The act of preaching plays a central role in the [Christian] church's interpretive performance of Scripture. . . . Specifically, preaching enacts a concrete ethical performance of Jesus' third way—the way of active, nonviolent resistance to and engagement with the principalities and powers of the world. . . .
>
> The faithful preacher does not remain silent [then] but witnesses boldly . . . exposing the deadly idolatrous ways of powers, and envisioning an alternative world—the new creation. Indeed, preachers may at times

seem assertive, even pushy; for Christian preaching is not a form of passivity but an engagement with the powers.[41]

Later, Campbell will invoke King directly as an exemplar of "assertive, even pushy" preaching, in the tradition of St. Paul, Jesus, and Mahatma Gandhi. He might have nominated the black preaching tradition itself as exemplary of the "concrete ethical performance of Jesus' third way" in between the Mosaic Law and, say, his Parousial voice "like the roar of many waters."[42] For the ethical force of preaching's witness to "the way of risky, nonviolent engagement with the powers" of oppression, as Campbell tends to say,[43] is significantly bound up with preaching's power to *intone* the new heaven and the new earth called up by the preaching imperative. In the United States, none has sounded the "otherwise possibilities for thought, for action, for being and becoming," as Ashon Crawley writes—for Campbell's "alternative world," in other words—so forcefully as its preaching blacks and their choric coproductionists.[44] And this, not for leisure but for the sake of life itself—black life and the biosustainability of the world.

"If You See My Savior": Black Dying and Its Discontents

The gospel instinct in King's pulpit blurring of "A Knock at Midnight" cannot be overstated. But it was more than the voice-and-vellum miscegeneity of early gospel that connected King's stylized, resistive preaching to the modern gospel sound overtaking the religious landscape of black Chicago when he stood at the Blackstone podium to preach "A Knock at Midnight" a fifth time.[45] In gospel blues, King also found a sympathetic tonal accompaniment agreeing in color and cadence with the elegiac air in his preaching manner. He was attuned, it seems, to gospel blues as a poetics of lament as much as he was to its mixed modes of composition and/as improvisation. Put another way, early gospel found in King, sometime after it seized Dorsey, another host, an *elocuting* instrument for its intonation in speech. That Dorsey's sound, in particular, should be dimly echoed in King's preaching ought not seem strange. For as LeRoi Jones (who was still to become Amiri Baraka) explained in *Blues People: Negro Music in White America*, blues was "primarily a verse form and secondarily a way of making music."[46] As a verse form—a poetics of precarity, if not of the black absurd—blues, Jones wrote in 1963, contains "as much social reference as any poetry," even if it is "*not*, nor was it ever intended to be, a strictly social phenomenon."[47] And yet "love, sex, tragedy in interpersonal relationships, death, travel, loneliness, etc., are all social phenomena. And perhaps these are the things which actually create a poetry, as things, or ideas: there can be no such thing as poetry (or blues) exclusive of the matter it proposes to be about."[48] Two Dorsey compositions, "If You See My Savior Tell Him That You Saw Me" (1926) and "Take My Hand, Precious Lord" (1932), index this blues-as-verse interpretation of early gospel reflecting and refracting the elegiac expressiveness of blackness in consequence of what Christina Sharpe has called "the fact of Black life as proximate to death."[49] In the *sound* of King's preaching, perhaps more than the *words* composing the veritable "score" from which said sound must inventively depart in order to realize itself as the sound of *King* preaching, the social phenomenality of Dorsey's music as an expressive index of the social life and discriminations of the city also resides. That is, what I have been calling "King's vibrato," those vocal exorbitances that sound "abobenea" (above and beneath) words, as I put it in chapter 3, nodding to poet Norman Pritchard, approaches a black lament of the modern experience that is as familiar as it is scandalous in civil and modern historical terms. In the pages that follow, I take up, briefly, the conditions informing the seeming *a*sociology of "If You See My Savior" before proceeding in the next section to dedicate more significant space to foregrounding the compositional background of Dorsey's "Precious Lord," that doleful anthem to black loss and the necropolitics of black subsistence "up South." What follows is less a close reading of the micro-phonics of King's preaching and public speech-making than the reader has seen in previous pages, in this chapter and earlier ones. Rather, my objective over the remainder of this chapter is to paint a picture of the lived conditions of black loss and lament that gospel blues sonifies in (veiled) words and mood, lending requiem tones to the timbre and environment of King's preaching in undifferentiated mourning and remonstrance.

"If You See My Savior, Tell Him That You Saw Me" was the first of many gospel hits penned by Dorsey. Written in 1926, "If You See My Savior" languished three years before it gained the notice of a wide audience. Dorsey was still plying his talents in secular blues when the shock of a dear young friend's sudden death moved him to write only his second religious song. As Dorsey recalled to Heilbut in *The Gospel Sound*, "If You See My Savior" came "out of a sad condition."[50] Newly married and twenty-seven years old, Dorsey himself had been suffering from a chronic and debilitating "unsteadiness" for more than a year when, abruptly one morning, a younger neighbor he'd come to grow fond of fell ill. By evening the fellow was dead.

News of the young neighbor's passing rattled Dorsey. It seemed to him to defy sense that he should suffer so long—"six to eight months," he recalled to Heilbut; "over a year," he narrated to Harris—"and this boy'd been ill not twenty-four hours and died."[51] Awash in feelings of guilt and gratitude all at once, Dorsey, mystified, was left to wrestle with the thought that his survival of death so close to his door (in two senses) might be owed to his divine election. His survival, in other words, seemed so much a sign to him. "From that day," Dorsey explained, "I took on new faith, consecrated myself fully to God and grew stronger and stronger physically, mentally and spiritually."[52] Yet for all the awakened feelings of vigor and piety Dorsey says he experienced "from that day," it was rather his first mournful and anxious reaction to the death upstairs that looks to have inspired "If You See My Savior." More plaintive than exulting, "If You See My Savior" was a blues dirge.

> I was standing by the bedside of a neighbor
> Who was bound to cross the Jordan's swelling tide
> And I asked him if he would do me a favor
> And kindly take this message to the other side
>
> If you see my Savior tell Him that you saw me
> Ah, and when you saw me I was on my way
> When you reach that golden city think about me
> And don't forget to tell the Savior what I said
>
> Though you have to make this journey on without me
> Oh, that's a debt that sooner or later must be paid
> Well, you may see some old friends who may ask about me
> Oh, tell them I am coming home someday.

In *The Rise of Gospel Blues: The Music of Thomas Andrew Dorsey in the Urban Church*, Dorsey scholar Michael Harris posited "If You See My Savior" as "an affirmation of life after death—an assurance the Christian could expect to hear over and over in scripturally based homilies."[53] I differ with Harris somewhat as I cannot see that Dorsey's song discloses anything quite so confident or assuring. The singer's appeal to his dying neighbor expresses rather a forlornness, a slow unfolding regret of the mournful condition of black life as perpetual loss. The "favor" of informing the Christian Savior "that you saw me" before crossing over "Jordan's swelling tide" comes near to voicing not an assurance so much as an anxious plea for *re*assurance that neither "the Savior" nor "old friends" will forget the one death has left behind lonesomely mourning. "When you reach the golden city, think about me," the singer implores his neighbor. Thus, it is his own (black) life he despairs of; the active passing of his neighbor is all but envied as the messenger-neighbor shares company with departed friends and the celestial Savior who has redeemed them.

Following the theme of Dorsey's first religious tune, "If I Don't Get There" (1922), which Harris correctly describes as portraying a "sense of the threat of not . . . getting 'there,' or to heaven,"[54] "If You See My Savior" conveyed not so much a certainty of life beyond death as the mere hope of it, a more modest yearning, in a glorious freedom from the sufferings of black life and loss. So mournful is the condition of black life in "If You See My Savior" that the sorrow of him whom death has left behind, separated from dearly departed friends, intimates an overwhelming death-in-life aloneness in Dorsey's verse that is its subject's sad lot. "If You See My Savior," then, so far from "an affirmation of life after death" or the "assurance" Harris imagines, is rather a plea to be remembered by those "mak[ing] this journey on without [him]."

"If You See My Savior," against all claims to the contrary, posits an experience of aloneness and unbelonging in time worse than death outside it. Out of this crucible, this unspeakable blues-burden, the lonesome singer dreams of flight to a new North, so to speak, much, much farther from (the white world) here. Regrettably, Dorsey would suffer this awful lonesomeness again more acutely not very long after "If You See My Savior." The hymn this direr torment would yield, however, bore not just Dorsey's loss, or black loss in the general sense, but black *mother-loss* in the specific sense that black maternal and infant mortality deeply burdened black people's strivings in the North. This problem, in particular, vexed the freedom dreams early gospel sounded in the blurs and breaks of words, form and practice far more profoundly than most scholarly reflection has considered. It is no surprise, then, that almost a hundred years later, the problem of black maternal and infant mortality hasn't been solved yet. "Take My Hand, Precious Lord" may have been composed by Thomas Dorsey's hand, but in a very real way it was the song of his wife, Nettie Dorsey. That it was also a known favorite of King, who often requested it of singers at religious services and civil rights rallies, suggests how profoundly the gospel sound broadly, and the Ebenezer sound in particular, relied on black women's laments, even as they tended to obscure the marked particularities of black women's issues and influence on gospel's social and aesthetic fields. This concern is the focus of what follows.

"Precious Lord": What Nettie Knew

There was a stirring, a movement of mud and dead leaves. She thought of the women at Chicken Little's funeral. The women who shrieked over the bier and at the lip of the open grave. What she had regarded since as unbecoming behavior seemed fitting now; they were screaming at the neck of God, his giant nape, the vast back-of-the-head that he had turned on them in death. But it seemed to her now that it was not a fist-shaking grief they were keening but rather a simple obligation to say something, do something, feel something about the dead. They could not let that heart-smashing event pass unrecorded, unidentified. It was poisonous, unnatural to let the dead go with a mere whimpering, a slight murmur, a rose bouquet of good tastes. . . . The body must move and throw itself about, the eyes must roll, the hands should have no peace, and the throat should release all the yearning, despair, and outrage that accompany the stupidity of loss.

Toni Morrison, *Sula* (1974)

Inspired by a second death more devastating than the one which moved Dorsey to write "If You See My Savior," Dorsey composed "Take My Hand, Precious Lord" (hereafter, "Precious Lord") on the equally unexpected death of his wife, Nettie, who was due to deliver their first child. Nettie Dorsey's pregnancy had been routine up to the time she went into labor in late August 1932. Dorsey himself was away in St. Louis, promoting his music and conducting a series of workshops teaching it to local church soloists, choruses, and music directors. When a male relative whom Dorsey had relied on to see after Nettie in his absence saw that she'd gone into labor and that her breathing was growing worrisomely strained, he saw her to a South Side hospital where they quickly learned "no beds were available."[55] Rather than seek admission at another hospital, Nettie preferred to return home and have her baby there with a doctor and nurse on hand. Hours later, Nettie was dead. She had expired during her delivery. She was just twenty-five years old. The newborn, Thomas Dorsey Jr., was to die too the very next day.

As he got word of Nettie's death while he was still in St. Louis, Dorsey's grief was unbearable. Looking back on it many years later, he remembered the tragedy poignantly:

> Anyways, I was in a revival, and my wife was to become a mother. I went away with the feeling that . . . ehh . . . she'd make a lovely, lovely mother when I'd come back . . . [Nettie was] well when I left home and they sent for me to come to the door. [A messenger] brought me a telegram. I took it and read it. Almost fell out. Says, "Hurry home! Your wife just died." And I don't

know how you would accept that. I couldn't accept it at all. And . . . ehh . . . a friend of mine put me in the car. And took me right home. I got home, jumped out and ran in, to see if it was really true. And one of the girls just started crying, said "Nettie just died. Nettie just died! NETTIE JUST DIED!" and fell in the floor. The baby was left alive, but in the next two days the baby died! Now what should I do then and there? And then they tried to tell me things that would soothe—be soothing to me. But none of it's *never* been soothing to me. From that day to this day.[56]

Captured on film in the 1982 George T. Nierenberg documentary *Say Amen, Somebody*, Dorsey's pain, recalled fifty years on, remained almost inexpressible, his weathered leathery voice rising and falling, his arms orchestral in gesticulative accompaniment. No words brought any comfort, he remembered, as friends "tried to tell me things that would soothe me."

To Dorsey, Nettie's unexpected death was a blues-woe deeper than any he'd known performing as Georgia Tom alongside Ma Rainey. Struggling to cope with the single greatest tragedy of his life, Dorsey sought consolation in a more devotional sound than had ever been heard in secular blues. "Precious Lord" was born of Dorsey's unremitting despair of death and of being left behind to lonesome life. Theatrically, Dorsey narrated the history of "Precious Lord" and its sudden, even soothing, irruption into his swelling grief before Nierenberg's camera.

Two fellas come by—I forget their names—they were friends of mine. And . . . ehh . . . they were telling me about it, and I says, "I don't know what to do, and I don't know how to do." And . . . ahh . . . —I just tried to make my little talk to the Lord, but it was wasting, I think. And . . . ehh . . . I called the Lord some—one thing, and one of the others said, "Noooo! That's not his name." Said, "Precious Lord!" I said that just sounds good. Got several amens on *Precious Lord*. And ladies and gentlemen, believe it or not, I started singing right then and there *Precious Lo-o-o-o-r-r-d-d / take my han-n-n-n-d / Le-e-e-e-a-a-e-e-a-a-d me o-o-o-o-u-u-o-o-n-n / And let me stan-n-d / I-I-I-I-I am tired / I am weak / I-I-I-I-I-I-I-I-I-I am worn.*[57]

If Dorsey's live telling of happenings fifty years after the fact seems not altogether fluent, we have only to turn to Harris for clarification of Dorsey's dialogue. As Harris explains, mere days after losing his wife and newborn son, Dorsey, still in self-evident mourning, had been at the piano fiddling at the keyboard when he "tried to make [his] little talk to the Lord." According to Harris, "Dorsey had no intention of composing at that moment."[58]

He had been only praying on the keys, it seems, searching after the Divine by way of unstructured sound. Yet the song came on forcefully as if from beyond the piano's playing.

Said another way, "Precious Lord" seems to have been always already in the flow of being written, composed as it was out of the brooding performance of what Crawley calls, discerningly, "nothing music"—that "ever-overflowing excessive nothingness" Dorsey called "wasting." Sometimes referred to as "'soft chording,' 'padding,' [or] 'talk music,'" Crawley explains, "Nothing music is the connective tissue, the backgrounded sound, of [black] church services heard before and after songs, while people are giving weekly announcements, before the preacher 'tunes up' and after the service ends. Ask a musician, 'what are you playing?' and—with a coy, shy smile—he/she will say, 'nothing.'"[59] "Nothing" is a particularly fitting reply to the question of what it is one has been heard playing, since the "playing" is (rather) a performance of anticipatory listening—a *listening-for*, to be exact. Accordingly,

> meaning is made through the inclined ear, through the anticipation, the materiality of nothing, the vibratory frequency of black thought, of the *more to come* that *has not yet arrived*. . . . And we hear this in the musician's virtuosity: they uphold, they carry, they anticipate, through the performance of "nothing" [but a searching listening]—it is not a song, it is not a melody; we might call it improvisation, though that implies a structure upon which he is building. With the playing of nothing music, there is a certain lack of attention, a sort of insouciance with which one plays, a holy nonchalance: being both fully engaged in the moment while concentration is otherwise than the music.[60]

Dorsey was not so much playing the piano, I mean to argue, when "Precious Lord" came to him as he was listening through it, trying "to make [his] little talk with the Lord" out of otherwise-than-words. What he was listening *to* (without knowing suppositionally what he was listening *for*), namely "the sound of the gift of [an] unconcealment,"[61] merely found him seeming to play at the piano. The whole thing must have mystified Dorsey too as the compositional history of "Precious Lord" was "nothing" he could clearly explain.[62]

If a certain incoherence obtains to Dorsey's on-camera remembrance of how "Precious Lord" came to be, it is surely owed to the effect of that similar searching of nothingness in between words Dorsey (un)voices as he "ahhh . . . just tried to make [his] little talk" on film. From within the elliptic space where "ehh" and "ahh" and ". . ." signpost nothing verbal—which is to say, the verbal nothing to Crawley's musical nothingness—Dorsey called

4.3   Thomas Dorsey. Still from Nierenberg, *Say Amen, Somebody* (1982).

up again what lay waiting as memory: namely, the unspeakable experience of black mourning. To be clear, the mournful condition of the experience of black life and death exceeds the mere mood intoned by "Precious Lord"; in "Precious Lord," mourning follows (black) memory. Memory is its mood's essential tinder.

Overcome by that which was to break in on nothing and compose itself as "Precious Lord," Dorsey, we might imagine, was afflicted by the haunting of *too much* memory—which is to wonder if he was so completely prepossessed with the fact of black dying coming again and again so near to him that the dread of it undid him at the piano, leaving him only (the very generativity of) "excessive nothingness." As Dorsey sat at the piano in the wake of Nettie's and the newborn's passing, "Precious Lord" materialized not out of thin air in the colloquial sense but out of the dense air of memory, the memory of "what happened," as James Baldwin would come to express it, reconstituted in and as the gospel sound. "Niggers," he wrote (clearly with an ironic edge),

> can sing gospel as no other people can because they aren't singing gospel—if you see what I mean. When a nigger quotes the Gospel, his is not quoting: he is telling you what happened to him today, and what is certainly going to happen to you tomorrow: it may be that it has already happened to you, and that you, poor soul, don't know it. In which case, *Lord have mercy!* Our suffering is our bridge to one another. Everyone must cross this bridge,

or die while he still lives—but this is not a political, still less, a popular apprehension. *Oh, there wasn't no room*, sang Crunch, *no room! at the inn!* He was not singing about a road in Egypt two thousand years ago, but about his mama and his daddy and himself, and those streets are just outside, brother, just outside every door, those streets which you and I both walk and which we are going to walk until we meet.[63]

Baldwin's 1979 novel *Just above My Head* demonstrates the author's acuity concerning the cold, disinherited condition of black American life few writers who have represented gospel have matched in either fiction or nonfiction. His limning of nineteen-year-old "Crunch" Hogan singing "*Oh, there wasn't no room . . . at the inn!*" indexes something other and more than material dispossession, however, and the sort of streetly (or otherwise outdoor) wandering common to black folks' blues verse. It reflects rejection as well, including the everyday denials experienced by black citizen-subjects turned away from and forced into "those streets [that] are just outside," as Baldwin says, by hotels, restaurants, retail establishments, public schools, white churches, movie houses, libraries, and—as Dorsey would recall, painfully—public hospitals.

According to the sad backstory to "Precious Lord" recounted by Michael Harris, the Dorseys had planned for Nettie to deliver "at a hospital."[64] On its face, the mention of this small detail by Harris is a rather banal one. But beneath it lay a complicated history of race and reproduction that suggests a tragic banality about Nettie and her newborn's death which, far from being benign, does not diminish but redoubles the weight and deepens the significance of their loss. This awful everyday of black women's reproductive experience, so critical to understanding the wider frame of what happened to Nettie Dorsey and child as well as the "bridge" Dorsey had to cross in "telling you what happened to him today, and what is certainly going to happen to you tomorrow," was as much an offense against black women's life chances in the 1930s as it remains in our time. Except for the testimony of Dorsey's gospel requiem, in fact, we might have little reason at all to remember that prior to the 1930s, American babies were born at home far more often than in hospitals. Not until that time did a movement to radically improve the hygienic conditions of hospital care, especially around women's and infants' health, render hospitals preferable to houses as birthing places for modern American women.[65] For most black women living in segregated Chicago, the cultural shift from childbirth as a domestic event to a clinical one set in the hospital's delivery room was at best incomplete. For women like Nettie Dorsey, the new obstetrics was stymied by a medical caste system in the city that restricted medical services for African Americans to a undersized corps of itinerant public health nurses, a few medical dispensaries, and two city hospitals: Cook County Hospital and Provident Hospital.

To put this in even balder terms, "many of Chicago's local health centers and neighborhood medical dispensaries either did not admit black patients at all or set aside a restricted number of hours for African Americans in order to keep them separated from their white clientele."[66] In the face of these discriminations, the 200,000 black Chicagoans who'd migrated there from points south between 1910 and 1930 were forced to seek hospitalization, when circumstances required it, in one of the only two public hospitals in Chicago open then to African American, immigrant, and indigent patients. In 1932, the year Nettie Dorsey died, Cook County Hospital was a twenty-one-year-old, three-thousand-bed complex set on the near West Side of Chicago. In contrast, Provident Hospital, founded in 1891 by the pioneering African American heart surgeon Daniel Hale Williams, was a significantly smaller institution. With just seventy-five beds, Provident occupied the corner of 36th and Dearborn on the city's black South Side.[67] Although documentary evidence is elusive, it seems likeliest that the delivery the Dorseys arranged for Nettie was to take place at Provident. Not only was it fewer than two miles away from the Dorsey home at 448 East 40th Street,[68] but in 1932, forty years after it opened, Provident "remained one of the premier black hospitals"[69] in the nation. Its patient population was ninety percent African American.

While these particulars about Provident Hospital recommend it as the Dorseys' chosen facility for Nettie's delivery, with just seventy-five beds Provident could hardly keep pace with the demand occasioned by the Great Relocation north. Though it aspired to become, as one historian put it, "a black medical mecca in Chicago," it could not have imagined in 1891 the unprecedented surge of black migrants who'd converge on the city, mecca-like, to overwhelm the founder's dream.[70] Already by the mid-1920s, according to one historian, Provident "had severely deteriorated under exorbitant pressures to meet virtually all of the health care needs of Chicago's black population."[71] If the Dorseys assumed that their prepaid arrangement for Nettie's delivery guaranteed a bed for Nettie at Provident when the time came, the young couple was tragically in error.

Whatever reasons Nettie Dorsey gave for preferring to return home for her delivery rather than seek a bed across town at Cook County, it was Jim Crow and its program of separate and unequal health care in the early hospital age that crippled Provident's mission to provide "proper care ... without regard to race, creed or color"[72] and doomed black women and infants to maternal and infant mortality rates in Chicago not at all different from those observed in the prehospital era. With the mortality rates of black mothers and children at the turn of the century exceeding those of white women and children by as much as 50 percent nationally—and rates in Chicago even higher than the national average—the problem of black women's precarious reproductive health was not new in 1932.[73] With little relief from so much dying between 1900 and 1930, modern gospel inherited at its beginning black women's hopes and fears about childbearing as affairs both of social justice and spiritual reckoning. In its brooding solemnity, Dorsey's "Precious Lord" expressly testified to this black maternal faith-in-despair born of the crisis in black women's health that saw Nettie Dorsey die in parturition. Contrary, then, to official assertions of black mismanagement and fiduciary irresponsibility thwarting the black hospital movement in Chicago, and also against the narrativizing of black women's reproductive health history in Chicago according to an anonymized "lack of high quality obstetrical care available to African Americans"[74] there, Dorsey and the broad sound of modern gospel bore witness to a deeper structural malpractice, which neither "Precious Lord" nor "No Room at the Inn" (invoked by Baldwin in *Just above My Head*) was ever *not* haunted by. Dorsey's song, especially, though composed by a black man out of the exorbitance of "nothing," did not look away from loss but leaned into the affective experience of it to become, effectively, a black women's sorrow song.

Given the longevity and scale of the problem of black maternal and infant mortality in Chicago in the early decades of the twentieth century, it should hardly have been surprising that when Dorsey and Frye introduced "Precious Lord" to the congregation at Ebenezer (Chicago) not many weeks after Nettie's passing, it was met by the corroborations of black women "shouting"—that is, erupting in vocal and physical intensities of mother-loss and sympathetic feeling. "The folk went wild," Dorsey recalled. "They broke up the church. Folk were shouting everywhere."[75] While he was not explicit in saying that everyone who was moved to a shouting feeling that historic Sunday morning was a woman, elsewhere Dorsey associated the enfleshed feeling of shouting with women almost uniquely. During blues sets on the road with Ma Rainey, "I seen women in the audience jump up, so touched," he once remembered, marveling at seeing them "jump up [out of their seats] like you shouting in church. I've seen that right in the theater. Whatever it is that touches them, they jump up and wring and shout" just as they'd do in church.[76] If men also shouted this way, Dorsey seemed not to notice their activity much. To him, the music hall and the church were the same ritual geography of black feeling and expressive freedom, and black women were its main actors.

Much later on, Dorsey's sense of the closer association of black women specifically with this indeterminate form of "social ecstasy" that is gospel shouting—indeterminate because, as Crawley points out, one never knows for sure whether this excitement is "falling out, fainting, swooning and loud vocalizations" or a frenzied dance—would be affirmed by Lisa Cain, a black woman folk artist.[77] In *Art of the Spirit: The Culture of the Rural South, Self-Taught Artist Lisa Cain*, Cain remembered her own childhood fascination with "women who fainted from shouting or had fallen out from grieving at a funeral."[78] She recalled how "the individual would get emotional, feel the spirit, throw back their arms, fling them around and people would rush to hold them. Men," she noted, "rarely shouted."[79] Although her 2011 art-memoir is set far from Chicago in Canton, Mississippi, Cain's shouting women are at least the kinfolk—mothers and grandmothers—of those gone to Chicago with the thousands of other working-class migrant women. Considering Chicago's black belt saw "Baptist, Holiness, [and] African Methodist Episcopal churches practically transported from Mississippi and [neighboring] Arkansas,"[80] though, Cain's shouting women may not only represent the Southern relatives of those Dorsey saw in the theater "jump[ing] up like you shouting in church"; Cain's shouting women may very well *be* those in Dorsey's narration—"touched" by the blues Saturday, and Sunday—"shouting everywhere." Alternately "grotesque," "awful," even "funny," as Du Bois famously wrote, and ranging in expression, he observed, "from the silent rapt countenance or the low murmur and moan to the mad abandon of physical fervor—the stamping, shrieking, and shouting, the rushing to and from and wild waving of arms, the weeping and laughing, the vision and the trance,"[81] this frenzied "shouting everywhere," as Dorsey put it, far from the din of unmeaning pandemonium, was rather the fulfillment of a liberative sociality or "social ecstasy," to quote Crawley. It would not be reductive to say that this sociality obtained according to historical black feminist impulses as "Precious Lord" gave poignant voice to black women's historical experience of mother-loss, and shouting black women sounded forth their lament and disruption of the anti-black order of urban development and modern reproductive health care at once.

To the extent that the ecstatic response to Dorsey and Frye answered back to the unique precarity of black women's lives under Jim Crow, both the expressive black church and the music hall realized a counterpublic of voluble dissent and creative, kinetic suffering. At Ebenezer, specifically, the shouting that "Precious Lord" triggered when it was introduced weeks after Nettie Dorsey was laid to rest was simultaneously a wailing and a "wild" noncooperation with the forces of racial exclusion, discrimination, violence, and other forms of injustice in the material world of black mother-loss. In the haunted/haunting vibrato-space of Ebenezer auditorium, designed in 1899 by the pioneering Jewish American architect Dankmar Adler for Reformed Isaiah Temple, "Precious Lord" amplified a black feminist—even black womanist[82]—structure of feeling so intensely and mystically experienced that it could be nothing other than "hapticality, or love."[83]

Moten and Stephano Harney have theorized hapticality as a vital black radical resource. Its teleology, "to gather dispossessed feelings in common to create a new feel," was one of the gifts of gospel to black striving. Overwriting form, style, technique, and verse to figure gospel as more a "vehicle for your feeling" and "a grasping of the heart"—Dorsey's expressions of the nature of gospel music's discrete ends[84]—than a closed system of aesthetic logic and devices, the haptical enables gospel's phenomenality as the sound of the insurgent feeling within the black modern itself. This insurgent *feeling* (which is also a grasping-after and a feeling-for) stirred up even as it was stirred by a fugitivity of hope and memory beyond Dorsey's design or understanding. His surprise at the overwhelming affective response to "Precious Lord" at its debut, and his wonder at "what they were shouting for; I was the one who should be shouting . . . or sorry," was almost certainly that of a *man* whose loss surely felt unique, not epidemic.[85] Backgrounded by the widely known story of the song's tragic, though not unusual, inspiration, "Precious Lord" was already keyed to a lower frequency of hearing than Dorsey realized when "right then and there" it came to him grieving at the piano. Like few gospel songs since, "Precious Lord" bore the irruptive, aural memory of an eternity of black mother-loss endured by black women in its mournful, moaning excesses.

More than one authority attributed what gospel enthusiasts have long recognized as the unsurpassed plangency of "Precious Lord" to the depth of Dorsey's suffering. "There's no sound that could equal 'Precious Lord,'" proclaimed Willie Mae Ford Smith, a Dorsey contemporary. "He wrote it when he was discouraged and his spirit was broken."[86] But it was likely *Nettie* Dorsey's brokenness *over and above* that of her husband's that the audience of black women at Ebenezer (Chicago) heard. The moaning sound of life struggling to stay or go—the sound of *Nettie's* suffering in the song, darkly mingling with the groans of those struggling to bear life as life is, black women, "tired . . . weak . . . and worn"[87]—their ears knew as much as their own bodies did the combinatory stress of pregnancy, parturition, and black women's unequal access to modern reproductive health-care delivery. The shouting feeling "Precious Lord" excited answered a hearing beyond the hymn that could not, in the final analysis, be other than the beyond where haptical experience comes into being. "Hapticality, the capacity to feel through others, for others to feel through you, for you to feel them feeling you . . . To feel others is unmediated, immediately social, amongst us, our thing, and even when we recompose religion, it comes from us, and even when we recompose race, we do it as race women and men. . . . Though refused sentiment, history and home, we feel (for) each other."[88]

To be sure, "Precious Lord" was a requiem to Dorsey's personal loss—a song written in Nettie's memory, and thus, from this vantage point, a song *for* her—but I am arguing here that gospel's greatest hit was conceived inside of Thomas Dorsey's grief by Nettie Dorsey's memory as an immaterial materiality of "overflowing excessive nothingness" (Crawley) irrupting musically on Thomas Dorsey's mourning and heard in the register of (as if it actually was) Nettie's voice: heard, that is, by the shouting black women at Ebenezer feeling one another feeling her as though they were feeling *Nettie* singing, praying, feeling *them* in the song's travailing tones and testimony. Recomposing Dorsey's broken spirit as their own, a hidden class of race women (to go along with Moten and Harney) reconstitutes race within the modern liberal project of American Protestantism. Shouting, they theatricalize a hermeneutics of African American religious faith many generations old, coloring the social conditions of modern gospel's protest black in sound and womanist in sensibility.

All of this, to put the matter still another way, is to argue moreover for a black feminist interpretation of the early history of modern gospel, one that subordinates Thomas Dorsey, "the father" of the genre, to Nettie Dorsey, the genre's ghostly "mother." Viewing it this way, and following a course already suggestively charted by Jerma A. Jackson in *Singing in My Soul: Black Gospel Music in a Secular Age*, one comes not only to discern more clearly how, in Jackson's words, "women became important innovators in solo gospel" and "helped shape the contours of gospel's solo tradition"[89] especially (which I'll pursue in the next chapter), but to appreciate how Nettie Dorsey's unanticipated (yet sadly predictable) death, how the elegiac narrativization of her parturient passing, and of Thomas Jr. short hours later, gave new birth to black religious music according to a vaguely Marian conceit. As

4.4   Nettie Dorsey and Thomas Dorsey Jr. Still from Nierenberg, *Say Amen, Somebody* (1982).

"Precious Lord" set about restaging Nettie Dorsey's death and rehearsing the mourning/moaning of her loss (to Thomas Dorsey, in one sense; to black motherhood, in another), the song's first hearing could not have helped calling up the visual poignancy of the Madonna and child in their final repose in death. However, against the shining maternity of the *Theotokos* ("bearer of God") in traditional Marian iconography, the aural mood of "Precious Lord" was haunted, brooding, and spectacularly funerary.

To say that "Precious Lord" is a haunted composition is not merely a figurative statement. By expressing its sound this way, I mean to refer to a descriptive analytical "language and . . . experiential modality," to quote Avery Gordon, for apprehending how "abusive systems of power make themselves and their impacts felt in everyday life, especially when they are supposed to be over and done with."[90] Said another way, I mean to invoke "haunting" in the sense Gordon has theorized, namely as "an animated state in which a repressed or unresolved social violence [makes] itself known, sometimes very directly, sometimes more obliquely."[91] Though it was as if it was Nettie singing that likely inspired the women to shouting on hearing "Precious Lord," it was not the audibility of Nettie's voice *per se* so much as the undifferentiated sound of her memory and the racial circumstances of her dying, blocks away from a full hospital, that trouble the song's rendering, as gospel historian Robert Marovich writes, with "feelings of loss, solitude, separation, indignation, poverty and illness" familiar to shouting black women in the age of Jim Crow.[92] Inasmuch as the specific haunting Gordon theorizes discloses "what's been concealed [as] very much alive and present, interfering precisely with those always incomplete forms of containment and repression ceaselessly directed toward us," then it is an insufferability toward the unspoken ongoingness of indifference to black maternal and infant mortality over time that simultaneously haunts "Precious Lord" and is resisted by it.[93] In other words, within, between, and around its worried lines a tenacious grief obtains,[94] resounding to the rafters in mother-loss, by which language, it should be clear now, I mean to evoke both the loss of black mothers to death in childbirth and black mothers' experience of loss as mothers of sons and daughters, born and prayed-to-be-born, to the already-ready hand of black death so proximate to black life.

"Pretty Music" and Black Feminist Elegy

"I want you to play it real pretty." Seconds before his assassin delivered the bullet that tore through his jaw and jugular vein, King leaned over the second-story balcony at the Lorraine Motel in Memphis to ask jazz saxophonist Ben Branch to play Dorsey's "Precious Lord" at a mass rally scheduled at Mason Temple Church of God in Christ later the same day. It was April 4, 1968, and King, who was in Memphis to lead a public demonstration supporting the city's striking sanitation workers, had inspired three thousand there the night before with a staggering address, "I've Been to the Mountaintop." Branch was well-known in Memphis. For much of the 1950s he was a bandleader in North Memphis, where his group, a house band called the Largos, played nightly at Currie's Club Tropicana.

Though he was a familiar name locally, Branch was in Memphis on this occasion from out of town. Like Dorsey many years earlier, he, too, had gone north to Chicago and resettled there. In Chicago, he assembled a volunteer band associated with Chicago's Operation Breadbasket. A department of the SCLC, Operation Breadbasket was officially dedicated to the economic empowerment of African American communities across the nation, though the greater part of its work was in Chicago.[95] Branch's Operation Breadbasket Band was the musical complement to Operation Breadbasket, performing at organizational rallies and demonstrations as a matter of course. Invited to support SCLC activities in Memphis, the Operation Breadbasket Band was two hours from their scheduled performance at Mason Temple when King called out over the wrought-iron railing of the Lorraine to make his appeal to Branch, who was standing with SCLC staff in the courtyard below.

King had heard Branch play "Precious Lord" two weeks earlier at an event in Chicago and was powerfully stirred by what he heard. That day he couldn't get enough of Branch or Dorsey's song, it seems.[96] According to Michael Honey, in Memphis King "told Branch how much he had enjoyed his version of 'Precious Lord' . . . and he asked to hear it again at that night's rally: 'I want you to play it real pretty.'"[97]

Given its solemn, supplicatory tones, few would consider "pretty" an aesthetic ideal for the highest performance hopes of "Precious Lord." Affectively, "pretty" lies distinctly outside of the tonal range of the chords and character of Dorsey's funereal blues-prayer which Johari Jabir has referred to as a "black anthem of lament."[98] That King should envision "pretty" as a performative possibility for Branch, or as a desirable affective end at all, might have seemed especially strange in light of the dark mood that had been settling upon his preaching in recent weeks. But having heard Branch's "Precious Lord" already, King surely understood "pretty" in a sense other than mere beauty and light. For "music that is merely pretty," one authority maintained, "is as meretricious . . . as talking that is merely pretty." An early twentieth-century liturgist, he offered the following illustration in evidence:

> One of my friends has told me the misery of his soul when he had preached what he thought a very vivid sermon on the day of judgment. He had described the sermon with much use of metaphor and poetical allusion, but counted it rather a fine sermon, altho [sic] it laid stress on the terrors of judgment. After the sermon the first person to come to him was an effusive woman, who took his hand and said, "O doctor, I want to thank you for that lovely sermon." Lovely sermon! . . . My friend said that the cheapness of his work that day appeared on the instant. She was right. He had preached a lovely sermon on the day of judgement. Music that is merely "lovely" is not music for service of worship.[99]

Whether King ever encountered Cleland Boyd McAfee or his writing for *The Homiletic Review* (as he might have done in seminary or, later, as a pastor) is less significant here than the way McAfee's reflection on the aesthetic purposiveness of sacred music brings some clarity on the meaning of King's request for "pretty" playing.

In "The Worshipful Element in Music," McAfee appealed to a class and performance of sacred music, "pretty" in its own right, that nevertheless exceeded the euphony of "pretty music" as "only that." Whereas the "merely 'lovely'" is "meretricious," McAfee insisted, "on the other hand, music without what most laymen call an element of loveliness, beauty, rhythm, is generally perilous in a service."[100] Whatever its adjudication by expert ears, whether an ineffectual execution of the musical presentation or an excellent one, "the music is there for the sake of the soul's uplift."[101] Given the success of "I've Been to the Mountaintop" one night earlier, surely King was not after a lesser experience. The kind of light or lively expression "pretty" conventionally implies was no more desired than "a lovely sermon." For "I've Been to the Mountaintop" was more terrible in its elocution than "pretty": *"Mine eyes have the seen the glory of the coming of the Lord!"* he had roared. Instead, the "pretty" in King's imagination—the "pretty" he had indeed *heard* Branch play in Chicago—exceeded the simply agreeable and cheery. This "pretty" reaches to "the highest in us," McAfee says, in order to "make [one] exult, sending through him the thrill of the roar of the sea, of the crash of the thunder, of the shriek of the wind along the valleys. Sometimes it may voice for him, in organ tones, thoughts that lie too deep for words, emotions that are ever voiceless, visions that are evanescent and undefined. Sometimes [one's] soul will be borne up by the prayer of the soloist or the full chord of the chorus. But always the music is there for the sake of the soul's uplift."[102]

What I am striving to make clear here, on the strength and limits doubly of McAfee's discriminations, is this: If the mesmeric hold "I've Been to the Mountaintop" had on the three thousand who had all but filled the Mason Temple auditorium effected what he hoped Branch might help him recapture at the coming rally—even if it only approached the haptical feeling he hoped Branch's playing would engender—then his "pretty" had to permit a greater range of expressive meanings to obtain to it than "loveliness, beauty, rhythm." Somewhere near the outer limit of pretty's signifying possibilities, it must have also necessarily included that which was capable of evoking "the roar of the sea . . . the crash of thunder . . . [and] the shriek of the wind." Both tonally and discursively, Branch thus stood to expand King's range beyond the horizon of worded expression by way of a saxophonic surrogacy King trusted to sound the intensities of a more copious "pretty" than the "merely lovely."

Almost as soon as King had finished making his appeal to Branch, his assassin, James Earl Ray, abruptly canceled everything. A couple of weeks on, in a memorial tribute to the murdered SCLC leader, Branch would fulfill King's request belatedly. Back in Chicago, Branch and the Operation Breadbasket Band, rechristened the SCLC Operation Breadbasket Orchestra and Choir, took over the South Side recording studio of Chess Records to honor King's life and public activism on vinyl. To "Precious Lord" Branch added eight more tracks—a miscellany of hymns, protest songs, and blues. *The Last Request: Ben Branch and the Operation Breadbasket Orchestra and Choir* took only two days to record. With vocal accompaniment by the standout Chicago pastor and gospel singer Rev. Clay Evans, Branch's nine-minute "Precious Lord," the project's opening track, covered Dorsey with a poignant expressiveness Branch knew to be what King himself had heard as he urged the jazzman to "play it pretty." With organ and piano especially prominent in sounding the ensemblic sociality so critical to jazz performativity, in addition to a felt resistance by Branch to conform to the prescriptive power Dorsey's now well-known lyrics might have easily enforced to produce a musical syntax and phrasing "proper" to "Precious Lord," Branch's performance—now slow, then swinging, now retarding again—foregrounded Dorsey's blues background. With heavy vibrato and marked slurring, the coarse grain of Evans's voice rising and falling with Branch's playing made gospel and blues more manifestly intimate than the religious moralists allowed. But it was Branch's styling of Dorsey's composition as a blues played according to King's express interest in a "pretty" performance that set it apart to haunting and, in spite of him, to black feminist elegy.

While Branch's grasp of King's notion of "pretty" is best discerned by lending a careful ear to the *Last Request* recording of "Precious Lord," we may also, by way of an audio prolegomenon to that task, turn to Little Stevie Wonder in our approach to a sharper listening of Branch's playing. Wonder had come onto the black music scene a few years earlier as a twelve-year-old prodigy with a precociously expansive, even King-like, conception of "pretty" already in view. Mere months before Wonder's Motown hit "Fingertips" reached number one on the *Billboard* Hot 100 in 1963, launching him into national prominence, he'd already released his first single, "I Call It Pretty Music But the Old People Call It the Blues." It struck an appropriately youthful first chord:

> I was sittin' in my classroom the otha' day
> Playing my harmonica in a mellow way
> A teacher seemed to have gathered 'round
> Trying to figure out what I was puttin' down
>
> I call it pretty music
> But the old people call it the blues
>
> They were looking at me sittin' there all alone
> Mumbling to each other in a real low tone

> I couldn't figure out what they were sayin'
> They couldn't understand what I was playin'
>
> I call it pretty music
> But the old people call it the blues
>
> Well I call it pretty music
> But the old people call it the blues
>
> I call it pretty music
> But the old people call it the blues.

However innocent the lyrics seemed, Wonder's performance of "I Call It Pretty Music" on Motown's Tamla label suggested a black aesthetic knowing deeper than expected of so young an artist. Written by Clarence Paul and Berry Gordy, Wonder's "I Call It Pretty Music" not only blurred pretty playing with (the terrible intensities of) the blues titularly, it prefigured the privilege of instrumental play over the sung text of "Precious Lord" in the Operation Breadbasket Orchestra and Choir performance. Little Stevie Wonder's own harmonica playing and singing put a performative and lyrical emphasis on the instrumental effects that bring "pretty music" into being over its verbal articulations. That is, just as Moten and Harney have argued concerning the primacy of the already-always-playing instrumentation in the Staple Singers' 1972 track "I'll Take You There," Wonder's *words* also call attention to nothing so much as his wunderkind *playing*. Write Moten and Harney analogously about "I'll Take You There": "If you listen to the Staple Singers' 'I'll Take You There,' it's got one little chorus, one four-line quatrain, and then the whole middle of the song is just Mavis Staples telling the band to start playing. . . . That's the heart of the song. Not the damn lyrics. It's just her saying, 'play,' and they're already playing."[103] In the same way, Wonder's *two* four-line quatrains (to the Staple Singers' one) in "They Call It Pretty Music" constituted its "little chorus" while his harmonica made up the "the whole middle of the song." Like that which is necessarily going on *already* when Mavis Staples enjoins the band to "play"—that informality of sound and sociality out of which the recognizability of music as such emerges—Wonder's first line also points up a music already playing, his own "pretty music" coming from the young talent himself "sittin' in the classroom . . . playing [his] harmonica in a mellow way." In between bars, Wonder's repeated exclamation, "Ain't that pretty?," a self-referential pointing to the harmonical heart of the song, ends his interjective excitement with the disfiguring sound of a melismatic blurring of (what sounds like) "man" (as in "Ain't that pretty, *ma-a-a-n*") and "now" (as in "Ain't that pretty, *n-o-o-ow*"). The result is an aural indecipherability of the melisma which, in any case, does not pass meaningless.

Relatedly, the verbal strand narrativizing Wonder's second verse repeats, in the tune's closing couplet, this resistance to word-bound meaning-making which Wonder's harmonica was already, in its insistent previousness, rebelling against:

> They were looking at me sitting there all alone
> Mumbling to each other in a real low tone
> I couldn't figure out what they were saying
> They couldn't understand what I was playing.

Between conventional speech and instrumental sound—which is to say, between "what they were saying" and "what I was playing"—lay a gap, the verse illustrates, where words cannot abide and understanding in the conventional sense is thus lost to it. On one side, that is, the history of black music's insufficient audition by professional critics and (white) audiences has left them all merely "mumbling to each other." On the other side of the musicohermeneutic gap sits the black artist (*"They were looking at me sitting there all alone"*) bewildered that black music, interanimated by sounds called up to supplant words too brittle to bear the weight of blackness on their own, could go so long misheard (*"They couldn't understand what I was playing"*).

Even as "I Call It Pretty Music But the Old People Call It the Blues" blurs words precisely to point to the extraverbal voicing of Wonder's performance of melisma-as-metalanguage and of black harmonical breath, the two being performativities of *vocal* deformation and *aerobic* intensity respectively, Wonder's debut worried normative time as well. Part two of "I Call It Pretty Music," recorded on the B-side of the two-sided single, repeats the blues melody and vocal refrain of part one but substitutes a slower, funereal solemnity for part one's bouncy swing time. Part two is part one's searching reprise, a slow, long-winded coda extended from part one as an exaggerated echo of its extraverbal and instrumental emphases. Although Ben Branch's "Precious Lord" was contained to a single track, it similarly consisted of two parts. Listening to it closely, one hears his slow and measured playing interrupted not too soon by an orchestral and choral swing time before finally retarding to a distended cadence refusing its properly musical, timely end. In this arrhythmic refusal, Branch recalls the automortological refusal of the proper end of King's life that, I argued in chapter 1, "The Drum Major

Instinct" performed a refusal, in other words, of the calendrical limits of April 4, 1968.

I want to think about this refusal by King and, in a restaged expression, Branch as a kind of (un)dying performativity prefigured in the first instance by the material memory of Nettie Dorsey in Thomas Dorsey's song. By this notion, "(un)dying performativity," I am aiming to signify both a refusal of death on anti-black terms and a looked-for passing-on, a shimmering transitoriness into an otherwise world where, it is said, the wicked shall cease from troubling. An encore of "Precious Lord" in Memphis was a key part of King's vision for this (un)dying and the future of the freedom movement.

As addendum to "I've Been to the Mountaintop," King's (un)dying address at the Mason Temple hours before his assassination, "Precious Lord" challenged death directly, first by an internal drive simultaneously toward and against finality, then by the improvisatory exigencies of gospel repetition and metrical (re)patterning. This ineradicable radicality is set so powerfully against the (dead) end of things that no distension of time or repetition of text is extraneous to its purpose. Rather, *every round goes higher, higher*. Every surplus, supplement, overflow of time or tone, text or technique, in other words, is purposive, each one extending the abeyance of a predictable end whose postponement it takes up and on as modulation, even as the law of the end it sets out to unsettle/overthrow has been in suspension already, deferred by the refusal of and within the previous repetition(s). Not entirely coincidentally, this ongoing "postponement" of the power of the dominant diatonic logics of musical study and performance to demand proper (i.e., regulated) ends shares a good deal in common with the rehabilitation of that erstwhile problem for classical and contemporary musical study, "feminine endings."[104]

In 1991, feminist musicologist Susan McClary called overdue critical attention to the sexual politics latent in classical and contemporary musicological history and discourse in her pathbreaking book *Feminine Endings: Music, Gender, and Sexuality*. Important as McClary's intervention in American and European musicology proved to be, an obstinate whiteness in its feminist aims, try as McClary might, impeded the work from meaningfully approaching how black women have inhabited the space of feminine endings in modern musical performance.[105] McClary may be rightly concerned with "repetitive, ornamental, [and] chromatic excess, and how normative procedures representing reason are erected around them to serve as protective frames" against women's imagined incorrigibility, but her valorization of the ways Madonna's "Open Your Heart" and "Like a Prayer" "subvert expected points of arrival" and create images of "open-ended . . . erotic energy" misses the everyday ways of trespass and extravagant poststructure that informed black women's musical performances long before Madonna's time.¹⁰⁶ While the postponements of ends that obtain to "Precious Lord" by way of repetition—that is, by way of an inspired *vamp* moving the music outward toward greater and greater degrees of fugitivity—share with McClary's Madonna a subverting of "expected points of arrival," namely endstops, in black cultural contexts like "Precious Lord" they also sound (out) the deeper depths of black maternal memory, experience, and dreamwork McClary might have been expected to look for on the inspiration of her reverence for an artist called Madonna.

The shining picture of maternity European Marianology has lent to the construction of white motherhood as blessed fecundity, however, overlooks black women's melancholic history of mother-loss which instead haunts the history of gospel blues on frequencies mostly inaudible to hearing conditioned by the narrativization of "Precious Lord," for instance, as mourning *Thomas* Dorsey's loss. Black women, I mean to say, challenging Harris *and* McClary somewhat, not only "made [but] broke narrative," too.¹⁰⁷ This is how black feminist theorist and poet Alexis Gumbs describes the effects of black women's extraordinary and everyday will to "defy . . . the oppressive interlocking set of narratives that entrap Black women every day," those structures of social and material life set on fearfully containing black feminist worlds, worlds whose proposed containment by "Heteropatriarchal capitalism? Colonialism? The Western idea of the individual life?"¹⁰⁸ was already hopeless before it was proposed.

Spill is Gumbs's chronotope for black women's willfulness in overflowing (and overturning) the schemes of racial and gender unfreedom against which overflow, excess, *spill* ongoingly (and implacably) press to a loosening, lightening, pliancy, porousness, breaking through and breakdown of capture/captivity/containment. "Black women have not been contained, even though our blood has been spilled over and over again (including internal bleeding)."¹⁰⁹ Gumbs's recent *Spill: Scenes of Black Feminist Fugitivity* represents this black feminist disposition toward the law of containment and proper ends poetically, elegizing the black-woman "desire to be free" that cannot in any case escape "the urgent impossible-to-ignore presence of the ongoing obstacles to [that] freedom."¹¹⁰ Each poem in *Spill* is (the making or unmaking of) a "scene." One verse, especially, evokes the inexorable hauntedness of "Precious Lord" by mother-loss, as the poet wonders:

was that her baby's skin? what water did. what waste. what fire did. what thrown-away machine. could not be. this could not be the smooth the kissed the cherished the Vaselined skin she would scald her life off for. was this the sweetest face she had sacrificed sleep and sense for? was this the child she brought here? and why?

she did not cry. she did not touch. it was too much. the texture of her loss.[111]

Inspired by a precise turn of phrase, "altered human tissue," in Hortense Spillers's classic "Mama's Baby, Papa's Maybe" essay, Gumbs proposes a new meaning for Spillers's words, a meaning other than, though continuous with, the sadism of slavery Spillers intended "altered human tissue" to conjure. As an improvisatory experiment in "tak[ing] specific phrases from particular essays" by Spillers "out of context," which she soon realized she "could never take . . . out of context"[112] or, for that matter, allow context to take, Gumbs put new language to another mutilation and dying, mourned and refused all at once by the haptic power of the sound of black mother-loss expressed in verse.

Grief's refusal ("she did not cry. she did not touch") of the melodrama of mourning long associated with black funeral rites is not identical with its denial in Gumbs. *How* mother-loss as child-loss sounds in Gumbs, if the sound itself isn't clearly heard, is according to, and suggested within, that crescendo of questions spilling grief from the page until, threatening madness ("was this the sweetest face she had sacrificed . . . sense for?"), grief is checked by a mother's bleak "why?" In answer, only the expressive economy of "too much" can begin to approach the excess of sounds and significations by which black mothering and black mourning come into aural entanglement with power and precarity. In Gumbs, just as surely as in the sociosonic hauntedness of "Precious Lord," black motherhood sounds in, and as, the remonstrative grief-tones (i.e., spilling voicings) of "too much" loss in black America.

Similarly, I submit, in the grain of King's voice, if rarely in his words, King bore the lament of a black maternal "too much" as well, not unlike Dorsey singing Nettie's song. Though his descent from three generations of male preachers before him surely formed the greater part of what he said from one preaching platform to the next, the Ebenezer (Atlanta) gospel as a theological orientation within the church's preaching tradition cannot alone account for the distinctiveness of that voice conveying said gospel as copastor from 1960 to 1968. Even his affection for Dorsey's "Precious Lord" suggests a deeper reservoir of influence than the male-centered lineages that frequently narrate great men's lives and make their greatness seem a natural inheritance. But as the black feminist telling of the roots of gospel music I have limned in this chapter has demonstrated, I hope, King's gospel modernism was a mixed inheritance, owing as much to the affective sounds of black mother-loss as to the performative blurring of print and preaching. Chapter 5 explores the deeper wells of women as aesthetic actors and cultural workers in the making of the black musical soundscape, North and South, within which King found his voice and vibrato in echoic outline.

5

Four Women

Alberta, Coretta, Mahalia, Aretha

Although it is certain that no living memory of King's April 4, 1968, assassination can silence the blast of James Earl Ray's Remington Gamemaster rifle, neither is the imagined sound (always already playing) of Thomas Dorsey's gospel elegy "Precious Lord" extricable from that crime and its ensuing chaos, or from King's career more generally. This is owed to not only the deepened pathos "Precious Lord" lends to the specific memory of King's (un)dying, or the hymn's soundtrack status in the modern African American imagination, but King's own widely known regard for it. That King often requested "Precious Lord" from musicians called upon to perform ahead of him at invited sermons and mass rallies suggests much about the allure and power of black maternal tonality, given the song's bitter inspiration in black mother-loss—as undertone, overtone, timbre, *vibrato*.[1] King was as familiar with such tones as he was with his own mother, Alberta, seated at the Wurlitzer organ inside Atlanta's Ebenezer Baptist Church. There, where anthems, cantatas, chorales, and other forms of musical respectability were apt to collide with the "ever-overflowing excessive nothingness" Alberta King's playing sounded below her husband's preaching, Mother King amplified "the vibratory frequency of black thought" internal to, but sometimes directing, Daddy King's speech.[2]

What I am proposing here, by way of Alberta King's musicianship, is a resonant black motherliness possessing King's public speech acts, continuous with the "pretty" playing and soulful singing that "Precious Lord" came to evoke so dependably. That the sign *motherliness* appears so graphically close to *motherline* is scarcely accidental to the genealogical point this observation serves: as LeRoi Jones (Amiri Baraka) wrote in *Blues People*, "Certain traditions that were usually given their impetus by the male members of an African community could, in the strange context of the slave and post-slave New World society, be developed equally by women, and in some cases even be brought to perfection by women."[3] King, of course, tended to view his preaching less liberally than that, taking it to have been formed out of a strict patrilineage of vocational precedence and influence: "This is my being and my heritage," he pronounced in 1965 in *Ebony*, "for I am . . . the son of a Baptist preacher, the grandson of a Baptist preacher and the great-grandson of a Baptist preacher."[4] This lineage represented "not only [King's] own bloodline but also the long line of witnesses" called "the Black Fathers" of the African American preaching tradition.[5] Although preaching scholar Richard Lischer, noting the politics of exclusion this patriarchal construction of black preaching history supported, made sure to include black women like Jarena Lee, Zilpha Elaw, and Julia Foote in the pantheon of pioneering black preachers, few other commentators have strayed from King's illiberal, sexist construction. I admit, therefore, that to argue for the grain of King's voice as inhering in black mother-tones seems a surprisingly radical proposition. Yet as clearly as King's theology was shaped by prophetic and pastoral models of black ecclesial leadership along patrifocal lines, so is a countergenealogy of *musical women*—singers and players of "pretty" strains of black sacred sound—traceable within the broad assemblage of material factors shaping the sacred culture of black moderns in America.

It is not enough, however, to simply *assert* that the sonic quality of King's remarkable, resonant preaching was owed extensively to women, strong as the claim is. More concretely, the period framing black women's keynote sound in the cultural production of black religious modernism, 1929 to 1974, begins and ends with a specific motherliness apart from which the particularity of King's acousmatic voice, as the representative soundmark of black prophetic testimony, could never have been "brought to perfection," as Baraka put it.[6] In January 1929, Alberta King delivered her second child—a son, Michael Luther, his father's namesake.[7] Forty-five years later, in 1974, Alberta was shot to death inside Ebenezer by a deranged visitor. Seated at the church's new Baldwin electric organ and playing Albert Malotte's "The Lord's Prayer,"[8] she was cut down, a most public mother-loss, by a fatal bullet to her head.

I take the overshadowed life and death of Alberta King as the marker of an alternate history of influence upon the platform performativities of speech, sound, and gesture that helped distinguish her son among black moderns as the voice of his people. Corresponding to all but the first twenty-five years of Alberta King's sixty-nine-year life, this period does not just contain the time of the son's coming-to-voice and -vibrato under black feminist tones of influence and, sometimes, performative coproduction, which I will discuss at length later. It also audaciously posits an extended era of what might be called, with a deep debt to the brilliance of Emily Lordi, *black feminist resonance*, a discrete phase in the arc of black modernism corresponding loosely with the late days of the Harlem Renaissance at one end, and the ascendancy of so-called urban contemporary gospel music at the other.[9] Not only Alberta King but Coretta King, Mahalia Jackson, and the young Aretha Franklin personify this period. Importantly, each woman maintained a musical relation to the preacher King and the broader culture of black political struggle that was sensitive and knowing. I take the happy fortuity of feminine endings obtaining to the given names of all four women not as the lucky accident of their common connection to King, but as a palimpsest and echo of deeply gendered cultural logics. In fact, we might think of the coincidence of the feminine endings obtaining to the names *Alberta*, *Coretta*, *Mahalia*, and *Aretha* as an aural inflection of the general feminine condition animating King's own resonant sound and the resonant sound of blackness itself in the modern era.

Alberta

One Christmas, my sisters and I each received the same book from my mother, *Songs of Zion*, a songbook from the African American church tradition.... Inside the front cover she wrote, "for my children, so that they might remember. Love, Mother."

I do remember. I remember her singing and I remember seeing her in the choir loft of her last church....

I did not need the *Songs of Zion* to assure these memories. I still hear her voice in my heart ... but sometimes it is my own song that emerges and I hear my daughter saying, you're singing Mom.

Karla FC Holloway, *BookMarks* (2006)

Martin Luther King Jr. was as a mere child when he first faced a public audience. As a "very young soloist,"[10] he stood close by his musician mother as she accompanied him on Ebenezer's mechanical tracker organ. According to Lischer, King's "Mother Dear" taught him hymns and songs like "I Want to Be More Like Jesus," which he performed at the drop of a hat or the passing of a plate. The minutes of the National Baptist Convention meeting at Mount Vernon Baptist in Newnan, Georgia, include the following note: "Master M. L. King, Jr., age five, accompanied by his mother, sang for the Convention and was given a rising vote of thanks."[11] Far from innocent performances for adult amusement, these childhood rites of public presentation, vividly recalled by Karla FC Holloway and Deborah E. McDowell decades after King, admitted "generations of [African American] youngsters . . . into public community life."[12] Not yet adolescents in many cases, they "flung their voices out to a congregation of family and teachers and friends who awaited this moment of their children's inauguration" into public (and emphatically middle-class) subjecthood, Holloway writes.[13] Although Holloway's *Codes of Conduct: Race, Ethics, and the Color of Our Character* (1995) and McDowell's *Leaving Pipe Shop: Memories of Kin* (1996) are reflections on the culture of public speech-making that aided African American children's extramural education in the undercommons of (white) civic space and cultivation, still a certain already-rhythm and loose meter are required of, and conditioned by, these bantam exercises. Holloway, for instance, recounted the recitative requirements on black children's public speech in her first oration of James Weldon Johnson's 1922 "The Creation":

> My mother taught me to pause for two counts after each word in the author's name. As I spoke, the sound of the n in Weldon and Johnson buzzed and hung suspended in the hot, still air of the church basement. She told me to pause (for three counts) after I recited the poem's title—"the [*to rhyme with 'me'*] Creation" [*one, two, three*]—and again after saying: "By James [*one, two*] Weldon [*one, two*] Johnson" [*one, two three*]. Then I was directed to step up to the microphone in concert with the sermon's first line: "And God *stepped* out onto space."[14]

McDowell remembered her tutoring similarly:

> Miss Harvey had been coaching me for weeks. "Remember now, President Lincoln was dedicating a cemetery. This was a solemn, lofty occasion. Don't go galloping through the words like you are on a racehorse. Start off slowly, somberly. Listen to me: 'Four score and seven years ago, our fathers.' See?" As instructed, I clasped my hands together just underneath my breast. "Speak from your diaphragm. Stand up a little straighter, and lift your shoulders. Be sure to enunciate 'continent,' 'dedicate,' 'consecrate,' 'tuh.' All right?"[15]

It is not hard discerning the resonant effects ritualized into the performance of black speech-making by Ms. Clapp and Miss Harvey in Holloway and McDowell. Not the counting itself but the pauses—Holloway's "*one, two, and three*"—ensure hollow space for written words' aporetic sonancy in and in excess of speech. The sustained, feminizing fermata of *n* trailing *Weldon* and *Johnson* lives in the clear-cut openness Holloway's mother insists she build for the poem's breathing as Holloway herself "step[s] up to the microphone," not only to mimic God's own approach to the creative task, but to dramatically underline the sonic materiality of that space (of God) where *n* buzzes ongoingly, overflowing what Lischer has called "the dead ends of language" for an indefinite time.[16]

Miss Harvey's directives to McDowell screen a similar impulse to black feminine end(ing)s in Lincoln's Gettysburg Address. Print does not easily permit its hearing. But "Be sure to enunciate 'continent,' 'dedicate,' 'consecrate,' 'tuh'" might be alternately represented as "Be sure to enunciate 'continent,' 'dedicate,' 'consecrate,' *tuh*," the italics a typographical hearing aid for those who might otherwise seek the strange word *tuh* in the text of Lincoln's speech. Although proper pronunciation was almost certainly its objective, in the school of dramatic recitation and literary learnedness that was Miss Harvey's boot camp ("Stand up a little straighter, and lift your shoulders"), to enunciate as she directed was to effectively contravene the bounds of the proper by overcorrection. *Tuh* is the extrasyllabic sound obtaining to feminine endings. "Continent"-*tuh*, "dedicate"-*tuh*, and "consecrate"-*tuh* aim at correct diction but, in the mouths of most, overshoot their objective. Technically *im*proper, then—inasmuch as *tuh* does not properly belong to the orthographical or phonetic design of any of the works in Miss Harvey's library of "Inspirational/Educational Readings" McDowell recalls—*tuh* is nonetheless heard among the affects of black acoulogical speech.[17] It is a learned overtone of black public speech, signifying in itself.

Like Holloway, McDowell, and many others nurtured in intimate, segregated black communities across the Jim Crow United States, King's voice, too, far from being the unique inheritance of the Black Fathers, was born of the fugitive futural cadences of the Black Mothers (the Alberta Kings, the Ms. Clapps, the Miss Harveys). In King's preaching and speech-making, I argue, he comes as near as any man to the realization of that "specific occasion" Spillers prophesied to, "to learn *who* the female is within itself [i.e., within its own gendered community], the infant child who bears life against the could-be fatal gamble, against the odds of pulverization and murder." This gamble, moreover, favors infant and maternal mortality *against* the lives of black mothers and sons. King's vibrato, echoing the expressive mother-tones Alberta labored to sound from the pipes of the Ebenezer organ, was always trembling at the edge of "'yes' to the 'female' within."[18]

Leaving aside Daddy King's officious and outspoken manner in private and public settings, the weight of *Mother* King's influence upon the younger King's preaching and oratory is not to be underestimated. The resonant power of the voice of the junior King, I aver, is owed appreciably to the gift of his mother's musicianship as an embodied response to deep listening. King's biographers have all but passed over the *maternal* claims on King's calling, overlooking entirely how "the 'mark' and the 'knowledge' of the mother upon the child," as Spillers has put it, surely imprinted on King musically. Instead, Alberta King's motherhood has largely been represented as significant only inasmuch as it is by her (or merely *through* her) that a direct vocational inheritance is passed down from great-grandfather to grandfather to father to son, a lineal trompe l'oeil that disappears the daughter from the line of sacerdotal descent as her husband, King Sr., takes her place. Likewise, that fiction of continuous paternity King himself constructed in his 1965 article for *Ebony*, "The Un-Christian Christian," hinged on the false impression of his *father's* descent from A. D. Williams (King's grandfather) and Willis Williams (King's great-grandfather) for its providential effect. In truth, it was Alberta King (née Alberta Williams) who connected the junior King to the first two generations of Baptist preachers in his *Ebony* account. But "because the rites and laws of inheritance rarely pertain to the female child," as Spillers explains, Alberta King has no obvious place in the narrative of the social reproduction of black preachers King was constructing.[19] It satisfied the junior King to remark from time to time only that his "Mother Dear" was a strong, if quiet, presence in the King household. Ever the illegitimate agent of her descendants' legacy to her son, she was usually relegated to a supporting role in King's public mentions of her, when he mentioned her at all.[20]

Both "mother and *mother-dispossessed*," as Spillers writes, which is not to say a mother *without* a mother but dispossessed *as a mother* of fatherhood's possessive rights, Alberta King was, in Spillers's logic, "out of the traditional symbolics of female gender" by being lineally in the way, so to speak; "*and it is our task to make a place for this different subject,*"[21] whose musicianship, ever (playing) in the background of King's pedigree, preaching and public speech-making, runs over with different possibilities. That there has been no effort whatsoever "to make a place" for her in King's development as a preacher or orator, either by cultural historians, preaching scholars, or dedicated biographers, seems owing to the formal biases of historiography, biography, and homiletics against mother rites and these fields' corollary fetishization of the patrilineal ideal. However desirable an account of Mother King's life may be to some, the genre of biography, for example, may offer too little space or opportunity for the place-making reckoning with Alberta King's musicianship her life as King's mother demands. It is conceivable, then, that this "different subject," out of line and in the way of gender's prevailing logic, could only be justly constituted by means more speculative than typological.

Composer-musician Dameun Strange's "Mother King," a conceptual Black opera in three acts ("Black Birth," "Black Resilience," and "Black Joy") with libretto based on poems by Vanessa Fuentes, is one such speculative effort.[22] Premiering at Public Functionary in Minneapolis in July 2017, the opera opens, Strange explains, on the day Alberta King is shot sitting at the Ebenezer organ. Conceptually, Alberta King exists in the opera "in between time and the [sic] timelessness, between heaven and earth, she is still flesh but is mostly spirit."[23] Approaching magical realism on stage, "Mother King" eschews traditional operatic conventions. Instead, as an operatic experiment, Strange's conceptualism and Fuentes's libretto summon the murdered Alberta King into the footlights as a *revenante* ("still flesh but mostly spirit"), offering her up, in her radical animateriality, as the physical form of black mother-loss itself. Although one would be hard-pressed to identify much of the subject's experiences of loss or lament in Fuentes's libretto—the text seems intent on expressing the joy of Mother King's metaphorical resurrection from forgottenness to the familial foreground of the (Williams-)King legacy—Strange's score, on the other hand, places loss squarely in its logic.

"If you listen closely," one "Mother King" critic noted, "you'll hear how [Strange] emphasizes notes and pulses in unexpected places."[24] Strange introduces these unexpected notes, which he calls "hiccups," as figures for the seeming accidents of black injury and loss that interrupt black life so faithfully as to become everyday. As Strange explains it,

> The connection to me is creating this world that seems normal but not normal. It seems real but not real. It has to do with the black experience in America overall, where there's these themes where you're trying to live your normal life but there's this thing that's thrown into your path that gives you a hiccup. Like you could be having a beautiful summer's day and then a nice guy who serves food to kids gets killed by a cop. That's that hiccup. You think of Mother King and the losses she had. Like the normal losses like you lose your mom. I lost my mom at 25. It seemed really early

but adults lose their moms. I was an adult. You lose your parents. They should go before you. But you think about Martin getting killed. Her kid went before her. I know that because my grandma lost both of her kids and she's still alive but my mom and my uncle are gone. So I know that from her experience. So Alberta lost her *second* son to a drowning accident just a couple of years before she was killed. So she had all this loss in her life—these interruptions that kept happening. That's the idea about having these skips and bounces and hiccups in the music. So it seems normal but these are the normal [events of] African American life in America. It's hard to go without these skips and hiccups and I think that people of color have them more than people of the dominant culture.[25]

Translated musically, Strange creates a skip-rhythm in the music, "as if there's a scratch in the record. And like there's a little hiccup."[26] Metrically this means an "extra 16th note and I want to accentuate that 16th note so you recognize that it's not just a normal pattern."[27] Or a normal experience of loss, "like you lose your mom." The general condition of blackness in America inheres in such abnormal degrees of (mother-) loss, Strange means, that new deformations of the normative forms of narrative representation (e.g., conventions in biography, history, homiletics, opera) are demanded of its excessive aspect.

Written into the "Mother King" score, the "interruptions that, that kept happening" can be heard at the beginning of the opera, as Mother King sits forward in a chair placed at center stage, passionately simulating the play of an invisible organ. These rhythmic hiccups early in the opera's orchestration foreshadow Alberta King's loss of not one but two sons (in 1968 and 1969), hinting at the depth of feeling that "all this loss in her life" must have inspired in her work at the "home I now make in/ Atlanta, for Ebenezer Baptist/ at the organ."[28] Undoubtedly, accompanying her son's singing was an early and consequential part of providing the "home I now make in/ Atlanta, for Ebenezer Baptist" with the sound I call "the Ebenezer sound," a sonification of brooding, atonal black feeling produced out of the sonic ecology of black hope, (mother-) loss, and lament in early- and mid-century Atlanta. For the music that was in King's preaching later on was hers. Just as the grief-tones of Strange's grandmother are remembered in the experimental "skips and bounces and hiccups" incorporated into "Mother King," so does the acoustemology of King's postpubescent preaching remember the musicality of Alberta King herself. I take "Mother King" to advance an implied interpretation of modern black cultural history and practice: namely, that in religious practice, musicality is black preaching's mother-tongue. And it is precisely the strain to say something to loss, to answer back to it what cannot be verbally said, that calls the mother-tongue to the sermon's side. "Mother King" upholds this interpretation lyrically.

Six characters comprise the operatic cast of "Mother King": three women (Alberta, Coretta, and Jennie) and three men, all preachers (AD, MLK Sr., and MLK Jr.). A fourth preacher, Willis Williams, is evoked but unseen on stage. AD is, therefore, the principal patriarch in the operatic present. While his voice is not too long silent, coming shortly after the extended "I AM (Alberta)" overture, when fictional AD (Williams) enters, his aria struggles to keep up the pretense of preaching as a strictly masculine production of that which Stephen Webb has called "the divine voice"[29]:

> Not when I was born, not until
> my someday-daughter's birth. Only plantation-work, the
> field, the
> house. But the music. Deep-in-the-
> buffalograss-music, music stitched tight by the
> quilt-makers. Music
> especially
> in my daddy's preaching, in his exquisite choice
> of words. That was always ours
> all the way back
>
> Emancipation Proclamation when I was two. Black
> codes kept me in mind in line, even while I
> collected glittering beetles
> even as I counted sky-high start (how my
> heart would break when night-clouds covered the notes of
> my lullabye). My infancy a stolen
> sideshow full of white-gloved sleight-of-hand, of shivering
> black fire, of
> inky ocean-sized grief.[30]

If AD took any pride in "[his] daddy's preaching" and "exquisite choice/ of words," he need only listen to Jennie's descanting. "Music is the gospel-truth" is her verse's last line.[31] Everywhere in "Mother King," in fact, preaching is carried along by a music it would be incorrect to call maternal, a "lullabye," as AD muses. Even the exquisiteness of his father's words is borne on the wings of "the music" from which black preaching, for MLK Sr.'s part, "source[s] strength."[32]

In "Mother King," the music—"deep-in-the- / buffalograss-music, music stitched tight by the / quilt-makers"—happens before and beyond the coming of the word/the Word into the world. Merely sketched in the score, its notes chart the sky as "glittering beetles" only the elect can read, fewer still transpose for organ or voice. Though long overshadowed by son, husband, father, and grandfather, Alberta King belonged to the elect. Against the daughter-disappearing biases of biography and modern historiography, the "Music / especially / in my daddy's preaching" did not mature in the son's in spite of her. It grew there because of her, in the vibrato-strains of his voice imitating, and thus aiming to capture, the tremulant power of the organ as Alberta King translated hope, loss, and lament through it. That is, while King and his father echoed the divine voice from the pulpit, Alberta King sacralized black life at the organ, baptizing loss and precarity in exorbitant sound and black feeling.

Coretta

While Alberta King gave Ebenezer its sound "black as music," as Fuentes writes,[33] it was Coretta King who made the musicianship of freedom-loving black women artists explicit as a political power in its own right. Though her early dreams of a career as a classical singer were sacrificed for a more traditional, if still public, life as wife and mother in a prominent clergy family, Coretta King's series of "freedom concerts" struck the near-perfect balance, in any case, between her competing desires to sing on the concert stage and "to serve," as she put it, on the front line of the American civil rights battle. More symbolically, they laid bare the political labor of black women's musical performance so often obscured in civil rights scenarios of charismatic black political leadership, as Erica Edwards pointed out in one especially compelling instance.[34] So far from mere accompaniment to the essential speechcraft of men in such scenarios, Coretta's musicianship, like that of Alberta King before her, worked to oppose the everyday acoustics of phoned-in death threats, earsplitting explosions, and the vile blasphemies of determined segregationists with a counteracoustics of hope and resistance as insurgent as any man's sermon or speech. My revaluation of Coretta King's musical participation in the civil rights movement follows from Emily Lordi's insistence upon "a critical practice" that understands inspired black women vocalists as "artists-at-work" rather than as romanticized muses for black men's expressive acts.[35] "We cannot simply highlight black women's contributions to male-dominated expressive traditions without developing new modes of reading those traditions—by considering, for instance, that the very notion of female 'influence' may limit women more than it empowers them."[36] I regard the freedom concerts as paradigms of the political labor of black women's musical performativity on the civil rights stage. A somewhat lesser spectacle than Marian Anderson's iconic 1939 Easter concert on the National Mall in Washington, the freedom concerts Coretta King gave between 1964 and 1968 made as clear as Anderson's performance did thirty years earlier that music was not the "complement" to political speech and action; it birthed and sustained the political before and beyond words and deeds.[37]

The idea for the freedom concerts was conceived sometime between 1962 and 1964. Modeled on the concert legacy of Paul Robeson—singer, actor, radical black internationalist—they brought together hymns, freedom songs, poetic selections, and original narration to tell "The Story of the Struggle from 1955 to 1965," as promotional materials announced. Coretta King explained in her memoirs that, like Robeson, "I would open my concerts by talking about the struggle, the movement. I would narrate and sing, alternating parts of the story with a song."[38] Years of experience as a performer and public speaker combined to effect a repertory of modern civil-rights soundmarks in the protest concert tradition, blurring not only resistance and respectability in the set list of arranged works but also the separate and unequal spheres of song and speech-making in public political life. This latter combination of song and speech "gave me a unique means of communicating these experiences in the freedom struggle," Coretta would write, "which I felt was more powerful and effective than either speaking or singing alone could be."[39] In terms of her effectiveness as a movement storyteller, she was more right than she likely knew.

Debuting November 14, 1964, at New York City's Town Hall, Coretta King's concerts were staged across the country in some twenty-five major cities, including Philadelphia, Chicago, Los Angeles, San Diego, and Boston. They raised more than fifty thousand dollars in support of the work and mission of the SCLC. Despite their success and the wide geography they covered in the name and interest of the SCLC, Coretta King's husband, who presided over the organization, eventually drew back from favoring them. It seemed the freedom concerts had "meant too much" to Coretta. When it appeared she "was enjoying it," she recollected, he balked.[40] "I thought I did very well. So did he, really. But, there were times when I would get the feeling that he was bothered, especially if it appeared that this meant too much to me. He maybe felt I was enjoying it, or that it was more satisfying doing that than the role of wife and mother. Then he would say something. He would express it in some way.... 'I think you're going to have to cut back on your travel schedule, and your engagements, because of the kids.'"[41] Boldly, Coretta's reply, countering his pretense to regard women's charge over domestic affairs as its own activism, put her music and his speech-making on even ground. "Can't you understand?" she claims to have answered. "You know I have an urge to serve just like you have."[42] Regrettably, his conservatism prevailed. Soon thereafter Coretta King was widowed, and any hope she may have held of reviving her concerts evidently died with her husband. Still, the disagreement was not moot. Coretta had insisted on the singer's consequence to political struggle and lamented that her "role has been so misunderstood by so many people."[43]

The widow who would enjoy symbolic standing as the doyenne of the civil rights movement seemed again to answer her late husband's inelegant chauvinism in 1972 in what Spillers would most certainly call an "unalterable and discrete moment of self-knowledge"[44]: namely, the instant Coretta King approved the details of the biographical data sheet issued by her staff at the growing Martin Luther King Jr. Center for Social Change. In one place, it read succinctly, "Profession: concert singer, Freedom Movement lecturer."[45] The two vocations, singer and lecturer, were all but one in her measure of what mattered in struggle. As the occasion also allowed, Coretta grew sure that her husband's efforts to limit her concert activity were, in sum, a projection of "his own feeling of not giving the kids the attention he felt *he* should have been giving them."[46] That Martin King's misogyny in this case was motivated by fatherly guilt is a persuasive speculation on Coretta King's part, an opinion not to be discounted. But equally plausible is the possibility of envy as its source feeling—which is to say, in words I am also borrowing from Spillers's "Interstices: A Small Drama of Words," that Martin King's misogyny might well have been born of his witness to the black female vocal performer as a figure of self-possessed female sexuality and the "sheer pleasure she takes in her own powers," since "enjoying it," to use Coretta's phrase again, seemed an offense to him: "He maybe felt I was enjoying it ... more ... than the role of wife and mother."[47] He maybe felt covetous, I conjecture, noticing Coretta sounding a depth of bodily self-knowledge and -indulgence that he could scarcely replicate, much less tolerate in view of that proprietorial drive that is intrinsic to the social relations of marriage and monogamy. To put this in more elaborate terms, I aver, quoting Spillers, that all of "the principal elements involved in the human drama" are "compressed in the singer into a living body, insinuating itself through a material scene."[48] In that scene, "the motor behavior, the changes in countenance, the vocal dynamics, the calibration of gesture and nuance in relationship to a formal object—the song itself—is [the] precise demonstration of the subject turning in fully conscious knowledge of her own resources toward her object."[49] Coretta King's freedom concerts were so many "material scenes" of a political performance of freedom going beyond the presumptions of a "male-centered, mysticized charismatic authority," as Edwards writes,[50] to know and control it. Thus, when "women's erotic power confronts the masculinist strictures of charismatic authority," those which guaranteed to the preacher King, more than anyone, the divine warrant to black charismatic leadership, Coretta's public ambitions had to be, in Edwards's appropriately sonic term, "squelched."[51] As a black woman singer, she had a conscious awareness of the resources of her body as the bases of political power and knowledge—an awareness that was not just a challenge to the charismatic scenario but a drama of wayward self-expression too beautiful to be countenanced.[52]

To be sure, Coretta King's classical training at the New England Conservatory of Music did not diminish her bodily sense on the stage. Although classical performance has tended to theatricalize what musicologist Suzanne G. Cusick refers to as "ritual[s] of obedience" to nineteenth-century transcripts of true womanhood—piety, purity, modesty, ascetic sexuality— these obedient acts and melodic protocols are predicated on an anterior freedom (at worst, an assumed profligacy) of women's bodies,[53] the ritual management of which has been part of the cultural work of traditional opera for centuries. Thus, the obedience opera has demanded of female performers necessarily involves a learned control over the vocalic body so subtle, so granular in its motor adjustments to correct pitch, timbre, faciality, and gesture, that attention is called precisely to the body (singing's *locus*)—where *dis*obedient impulses vie for vocalization and visibility against training. Even classical performance, then, notwithstanding its labor to forestall women's erotic knowing in "ritual[s] of obedience," might come too near to staging the private pleasures of women's bodily self-knowledge in public to comfort some and keep King, specifically, from feeling embarrassed or, worse still, threatened by Coretta's (black) feminist flirtations with the edge of *jouissance*.

Despite Coretta King's elite conservatory education, press reviews of her concerts were rarely serious in the artistic sense, so defining the extent of her performances' disobedience to properly gendered codes of musical conduct is tricky. While concert critics like the reviewer at *Newsweek* did not fail to note Coretta's "warm and expressive" voice, a well-worn cliché in white musical discourse on the timbral specificity of the black voice,[54] no one in the major press concerned themselves with the art of her performance. No one, I mean, gave any significant attention to what lay beyond strict vocalism, namely Coretta's "*attitude* toward her material, her audience, and, ultimately, her own ego-standing in the world as it is interpreted through form."[55] Spillers's redirection of the biographical focus common to musical criticism of black woman vocalists toward these concerns is especially urgent for black women in the European concert tradition. Historically, black women's relationship to the cultish ideals of nineteenth-century womanhood so frequently valorized in said tradition is a vexed one. Coretta King's conservatory background and concert dreams could not have escaped the racial politics of gender in concert performance. How the historical dialectic between the white European woman as feminine ideal and the African American or black woman as the paradigmatic figure of feminine lack was reflected in her singing might only be knowable by analogy to the experiences of other black women concert singers. Contemporaneous criticism of the freedom concerts was far too preoccupied with Coretta King's role in the life and work of her husband to have genuinely heard her.

If, as Spillers comments in "Interstices," "the singer is a good example of 'double consciousness' in action,"[56] then Cusick demonstrates this better than most. In her 1994 article "Gender and the Cultural Work of a Classical Music Performance," Cusick reflects on the two personae of the classical musical performer. Persona$_1$ reflects the performer's "extra-musical" life. Persona$_2$ dwells in the performance text as a "character" for whom persona$_1$ is "a medium," the one through whom this character is realized before an audience. According to Cusick, in the ideal performance, the subordination of persona$_1$ (biographical) to persona$_2$ (fictional) "might be so complete as to make the 'performance' disappear" into the ontology of the musical text/song. Building her case for the double consciousness of the operatic singer on the genius of dramatic soprano Jessye Norman, Cusick allows that

> Norman may be so completely transparent to me, seeming not to mediate, to inflect, to negotiate with the *persona* of the music. If Norman manages thus to disappear, totally replaced by [Robert] Schumann's conception of womanhood, I may well judge her a magician, a genius of interpretation exactly in proportion to her genius at disappearing. Or Norman may choose to "perform" a more overt, personal "interpretation," leaving me with a sense of her struggle to adjust her *persona* [i.e., persona$_1$] into Schumann's mold. And then I may well judge her a genius of interpretation exactly in

proportion to the traces of struggle which she leaves behind on her way to subordination. Either way, my pleasure in her performance and my sense of closure at the end of it partly derives from the public display of her temporary obedience to someone else's idea of who she should be."[57]

In Cusick, ironically, the critic is equal to the singer as a figure of double consciousness. For Cusick is gratified equally by what might be understood as Norman's "temporary obedience to someone else's idea of who she should be," on the one hand, and Norman's opposing "struggle to adjust her *persona*," on the other. But in the analogy I am drawing between Jessye Norman and Coretta King, the restrained pleasure the two singers share in "'perform[ing]' a more overt, personal 'interpretation'" of Schumann's Genoveva or Richard Wagner's Isolde, and the "traces of struggle" they betray adjusting persona's black womanhood to persona's white womanhood, risks disappearing from critical view. For Coretta King, persona was less often an operatic one than the larger European concert tradition and its aesthetics. Given her refined soprano voice and concert training, the freedom concerts, featuring mostly gentrified folk songs and concertized African American spirituals, were occasions for staging black womanly becoming as figures of modern political subjecthood in her own signifying body, on her own public terms.

By 1951, after four years at Antioch College in Yellow Springs, Ohio, Coretta King "was beginning to suspect that [she] had a warrior's spirit."[58] The first African American student at Antioch to major in elementary education, Coretta had publicly challenged the discriminatory policies of the Yellow Springs public school system, which had denied her a place among its teaching faculty as required to complete her teaching practicum at Antioch. In her posthumously published autobiography, *My Life, My Love, My Legacy*, she reasoned that her protest "fed [an] inward yearning."[59] An Antioch NAACP member, budding peace activist, and student delegate to the Progressive Party national convention in Philadelphia in 1948, Coretta "rather liked making waves," she confessed.[60] The prospect of breaking racial boundaries as a conservatory student inspired a similar feeling of relish: "In Yellow Springs, Ohio, I had challenged segregated teaching assignments. Now [in Boston] I saw myself adding color to the overwhelming white concert performing arts scene ... paving the way for other blacks. As I looked at my new experiences, I felt something exciting stirring within me. It felt good trying to make a

An Unusual Type of Concert!

SOUTHERN
CHRISTIAN
LEADERSHIP
CONFERENCE

Presents

Mrs. Coretta Scott King
(Mrs. Martin Luther King, Jr.)
— Soprano —

IN

A 'FREEDOM CONCERT'

A Moving, Sensitive Story

Of The

Freedom Struggle

Told In

Song And Narration

AT

NEW CIVIC THEATER
San Diego, California
Thursday, March 4, 1965   8:00 P.M.
Sponsored By
SAN DIEGO COUNCIL OF CHURCHES

Mrs. Coretta Scott King

MRS. Martin Luther King, Jr., wife of the internationally famous civil rights leader who recently was awarded the 1964 Nobel Peace Prize, tells a moving and beautiful story of the "Freedom Struggle" since the days of the Montgomery Bus Boycott up to the present. At the side of her husband since those early days, few persons know the full story better. Her telling of that story is done both in song and narration, presenting it with a unique rendering that has never been heard before.

A PRODUCT of Antioch College in Yellow Springs, Ohio, and the New England Conservatory of Music in Boston, Massachusetts, Mrs. King previously appeared in dozens of cities around the U. S. as well as in Europe, Africa and India before increased activity in the civil rights movement forced her limited appearances.

MRS. King made her concert debut in 1948 at the Second Baptist Church in Springfield, Ohio. She has since appeared in some 25 major cities across the United States from Los Angeles, California to Boston, Massachusetts. In 1959, while touring India with her husband, she was invited to sing for many groups in cities, towns and villages throughout India.

5.1   Coretta Scott King freedom concert flier, March 4, 1965. Southern Christian Leadership Conference records, Stuart A. Rose Manuscript, Archives, and Rare Book Library, Emory University. Courtesy of Southern Christian Leadership Conference.

difference."⁶¹ The good feeling of her earlier activism commingled with the pleasure of performance as a political act against the engulfing whiteness of institutional concert culture. While the Alabama-born daughter of a local black merchant and a church pianist was baptized into black and progressive political traditions as a student in Yellow Springs, in Boston Coretta King gained a newer, deeply personal understanding of the political challenge to the racial order: "I was gaining a sense of how *to create a life of meaning*."⁶² In view of the double consciousness of women singers in classical performance theorized by Cusick, this might suggest a growing facility to cultivate a stage persona that would aesthetically perform political labor.

While Martin King wished for his wife to give the greater part of her service to the freedom struggle at home as a traditional wife and mother, subordinating those mostly hidden labors to his resoundingly public acts as preacher and civil rights spokesman, Coretta King's freedom concerts afforded her another persona that not only matched his itinerant speechmaking in volume and visibility but answered back to the sexist constraints placed on her desire for a life of socially conscious public engagement like the one glimpsed at Antioch. Often, she "bit her tongue" as she struggled to adjust to his directives concerning the running of the house and her charge of their children. She told an interviewer, "I embraced the cause just as my husband did, and I would have done so anyway, had I not met Martin."⁶³ On stage, I maintain, Coretta King muddled the line between classical respectability and its resistance. Like Cusick's Jessye Norman leaving behind "traces of struggle . . . on her way to subordination," Coretta recreated herself in performance, becoming, in Spillers's words, "the primary subject of her own invention" behind the veil of idealized womanhood.⁶⁴

With no extant recordings of any of the roughly thirty freedom concerts Coretta King gave, we are left to wonder about a signifyin(g) intentionality beneath the production's opening song, given the domestic pressures placed on her by Martin King: Earl Robinson's 1943 "The House I Live In." With lyrics by Abel Meeropol, who also had Billie Holiday's "Strange Fruit" among his writing credits, "The House I Live In (That's America to Me)" had been a classic in American patriotic music for more than two decades when Coretta added it to the freedom concert program. Still, it was not an obvious choice for her since, for years, none of the song's popular recordings featured a female voice. It was not until 1962 that the reigning queen of gospel, Mahalia Jackson, lent her soulful contralto to "The House I Live In," including it on her obscure *Great Songs of Love and Faith* LP. In any case, Coretta King's more delicately tuned concert soprano must have made many wonder if there was anything personal to the domestic metaphor in the title, particularly those whose interest in the event was not so much musical as biographical. Promotional materials regularly advertised the freedom concerts as featuring "Mrs. Coretta Scott King (Mrs. Martin Luther King, Jr.)" (figure 5.1). Although we cannot know, absent an available archive, the extent to which Coretta King's performance betrayed any vocal or visual resistance to the suffocating—or at least limiting—straits of middle-class marriage and motherhood, this scarcely matters. As emphasized earlier, "we are interested in the singer's *attitude*,"[65] or her affective orientation toward a public self-display of black *womanliness*. What can we discern in other ways concerning the general disposition of the flesh in these performances, the audiences' attention to which was simultaneously invited and refused in the discursive play of the idea of *form*? Whereas the "sheer pleasure" the black woman singer enjoys in, and in theatricalizing, her *corporeal form* elicits the concertgoers' attention to her onstage "struggle" to become herself, the *musical form*, which is the generic or categorical tradition of the event, has in this case tended to thwart such attention by disappearing women's sexual bodies into the male-centered conventions of the European concert tradition. Thusly constrained, Coretta King's conception of what the freedom concerts signified was doubtless a capacious one, one that could only have included that born of the stifling expectations of marriage and motherhood laid to her by convention in the very house she lived in. The freedom concerts were not merely conceived and performed, then, *by* Coretta King; it seems clear they were conceived and undertaken *for* her as well. They were occasions, in other words, for Coretta's and other black women's extradomestic political performance, including the sexual affordances permitted by concert singing in the interstices.

To be clear, to refer to the affordances of Coretta King's singing as *sexual* is not to reduce the bodily enjoyment of singing to voluptuary or concupiscent longing but rather to suggest, after Spillers, the force of intensities inspiriting the black female singing body. The singer's sexuality, Spillers teaches us, "is precisely the physical expression of the highest self-regard" she takes in the autonomy she commands over her body's musical exercise.[66] Such self-regard on Coretta's part must have seemed to Martin King like so much *attitude* on public display—attitude of the sort she had learned, like so many black women coming of age in the Jim Crow South, in a proud corporeal dialect: "In the South, since black women were so disrespected by whites, our response was to push our shoulders back, keep our heads high, and walk with dignity, looking as if we had oil wells in our backyard. Moreover, I was not on a traditional career track for a black woman. As a budding concert singer, poise and decorum were tools of the art; unfortunately, they could be mistaken for stiffness or for trying to be a prima donna."[67] Far from enacting the "stiffness" of a vain theatricality, Coretta King's performance of "poise and decorum" acts out a counterpolitics of lithesome black feminist *airs*. Only, her black-woman airs have the hint of something more than corporeal clapback about them. They recall the sassy suggestiveness of the womanish persona animating Maya Angelou's anthemic "Still I Rise"; Angelou's claim of "oil wells / Pumping in my living room" is echoed in Coretta King's memory of black women indignantly answering the affronts of racist glares and epithets somatically,[68] "looking as if we had oil wells in our backyard." Whether or not the ostensible immodesty of Coretta King's "backyard" and Angelou's "living room" is common to both women's words ("backyard" and "living room" both seeming to strike a euphemistic tenor), the "oil wells" they mutually conjure signify libidinally all the same. For out of their depths of oil wells, the black gold *spills*. Not unlike this metaphorical veiling inescapably betraying its erotic object, "poise and decorum" obscured a sexual performance politics in Coretta King's concert ambitions. Small acts of black feminist resistance smuggled onto the stage *in her body* spilled in overflows of willful maladjustment to the gendered scripts handed her by training and tradition. But the stages Coretta King commanded weren't only the musical ones. In time, she would be forced by the circumstances of Martin King's assassination to forgo singing and take to the lectern instead.

Three weeks after Martin King's assassination, Coretta King took on her late husband's mantle and delivered a slow, metronomic address to a large crowd of anti-Vietnam protesters gathered in New York's Central Park.[69] Written from notes found in the pocket of the suit Martin King was wearing when he was shot, her speech was devoted mostly to a rehearsal of his controversial view of "the problem of racism and poverty here at home and militarism abroad as two sides of the same coin."[70] In the final minutes of "10 Commandments on Vietnam," however, Coretta King stepped out of her husband's shadow as the speech became, abruptly, hers. "I would like to now address myself to the women," she pronounced. "The woman power of this nation can be the power which makes us whole and heals the rotten community, now so shattered by war and poverty and racism. I have great faith in the power of women who will dedicate themselves whole-heartedly to the task of remaking our society. . . . I believe that the women of this nation and of the world are the best and last hope for a world of peace and brotherhood."[71] Far from simply standing in for her recently departed husband, Coretta gave a speech that explicitly feminized an untapped reserve of anti-war energy. Though it was no different in kind from the broad logics of the US peace movement, "the woman power" changed the face of the politics of peace a misguided and costly war in Vietnam had given rise to. Echoing portions of Martin King's "Beyond Vietnam: A Time to Break Silence" on the triple evils of war, poverty, and racism, her speech, though only fifteen minutes long, was nonetheless a singular black feminist contribution to the history of anti-war oratory and declamation in its intersecting of "the power of women" with the affairs of war and poverty and racism.

Viewed in this light, who can doubt that Coretta King also belongs to the tradition of black women intellectuals and cultural workers Brittney Cooper has cast explicitly as a discrete "school of thought" in *Beyond Respectability: The Intellectual Thought of Race Women*? And, on this view, what is to keep us from "tak[ing] . . . seriously" Coretta King's freedom concerts as black feminist cultural praxis, early unfoldings of her part in black women's public intellectualism and race leadership?[72] One need only note the common appeal in Coretta King's concerts and Central Park address in juxtaposition with Langston Hughes's 1922 poem "Mother to Son" to recognize her extending the black feminist intellectual tradition of "us[ing] Black female embodiment as the zero point of their theorizing" not only "the precarity of Black women's lives,"[73] as Cooper writes, but the disinherited condition of modern black life extending from it:

> Well, son, I'll tell you:
> Life for me ain't been no crystal stair.
> It's had tacks in it,
> And splinters,
> And boards torn up,
> And places with no carpet on the floor—
> Bare.
> But all the time
> I'se been a-climbin' on,
> And reachin' landin's,
> And turnin' corners,
> And sometimes goin' in the dark
> Where there ain't been no light.
> So boy, don't you turn back.
> Don't you set down on the steps

> 'Cause you finds it's kinder hard.
> Don't you fall now—
> For I'se still goin', honey,
> I'se still climbin',
> And life for me ain't been no crystal stair.[74]

Taken seriously, as Cooper demands, "Mother to Son" not only permitted Coretta King, a mother of four, to voice her own maternal counsel to "the sons and daughters of this generation and those yet unborn,"[75] but, positing her as the "zero point" of an urgent retheorizing of intellectual history and political genealogy, offered the female line, or the mother-rite passed on to the son, as a twisting, turning figure of scaffolded *ascent* in Coretta's hands. A tropological inversion of the *descent* of sons routinely figured in the shadow genealogy of black political speech and performance "Mother to Son" backgrounds in this interpretation, Hughes's "splinter[ed]," "torn up," and "bare" stairway, with its difficult "landin's," "corners," and recesses "where there ain't been no light," reimagines political and intellectual genealogy in Coretta King's voice. Whereas the father's line pretends to unbroken descent—"I am . . . the son of a Baptist preacher, the grandson of a Baptist preacher and the great-grandson of a Baptist preacher," for example—the mother's line is consistently "denied, *at the very same time* that it becomes the founding term of a human and social enactment" of (black) life. It trades the easy, crystal-stair logic of patrilinearity for a more complex trigonometry of consanguinity as Hughes's "stair," its broken climb and navigation, contrasts with the strict "vertical transfer of the bloodline, of a patronymic, of titles, and entitlements . . . from fathers to sons" that is patriarchy's preferred fiction.[76] Stairs "splinter[ed]" and "torn up" with "landin's" compelling breaks in the heritable flow, on the other hand, portray anarrangements of the patrilineal order for which the prevailing structures of American social, material, and juridical life have, in the late Cheryl Wall's words, "no category."[77]

"Mother to Son," however, doesn't just offer up a visual tropology for nonpatriarchal configurations of black filiation to enter thought. The poem also invites consideration of black feminist formulations of public thought and praxis in its narrative voice phonologically. Noting the "ungrammatical profundity" of the black mother whose persona she has sought to realize, Coretta King strained to overcome the measured and half-clipped tones of academic English ("reachin' land-*ings*," "still go-*ing*," "still climb-*ing*") the poem was composed to resist. Though it is possible that qualifying the mother's thought ("ungrammatical profundity") and her performance dialect disclosed an angst about black vernacular speech and the middle-brow politics of black people's "proper" public representation just beneath the surface, I prefer to read Coretta King's proleptic appraisal of the mother tongue in Hughes not as an apology for black speech habits but as a "worrying," in the sense taken up by Wall, of serious thought's basis in categorical grammars of power and knowledge. I read "ungrammatical profundity," in other words, as naming a mode of (un)thought inapprehensible to grammatical capture and intent upon its ongoing fugitivity as the condition of black (thought's) survival. More especially, it is that which takes flight away from and against the father's law and its compulsory reproduction of "correct" thought and speech, a notion that cannot be so much as dreamt apart from the necessarily "incorrect" sign of blackness as its conceptual ground of possibility.

More concretely illustrated, the recitative close of Coretta King's "10 Commandments on Vietnam" sounded out a radical resistance to the order of modern philosophical power/knowledge in her own performative voice. Worrying the line between performed dialect and the living musicality of black vernacular speech, phonologically Coretta stood between "correct" (mis)pronunciation, on the one hand—that is, as Hughes (mis)represented Negro dialect on the page—and the sonic memory of the one upon whom "ungrammatical profundity" was first conferred in its exact phrasing. Mother Pollard was an "elderly Negro woman . . . poverty-stricken and uneducated" whom Martin King had previously commended in a sermon titled "Antidotes for Fear" in *Strength to Love*. Described by him as "amazingly intelligent and possess[ing] a deep understanding of the meaning of the movement," Pollard memorably answered back to those in Montgomery who worried that the bus boycott there in 1957 could not endure to success, confessing, "My feets is tired, but my soul is rested.'"[78] Resurrecting her husband's locution in Central Park, Coretta was more than merely a surrogate at the lectern. Overlooking as many as 100,000,[79] she stood rather as a civil rights leader in her own right, a conductor on an underground railroad of black feminist thought and praxis tracking along blurred and reconfigured lines of educated speech and "Negro" dialect, poetic recitation, song, and concert musicianship. To hear Coretta King at the climax of her Central Park address intone "Bare" in Hughes as an insistently breathy "Bay-uhhhh" is to hear the voice of Mother Pollard, if not also Mother King, gaining ground. She is "*claiming* the monstrosity" of black speech and dark instrumental sound as a reservoir of aesthetic and intellectual resources from which to inspire and direct a new (dis)order of things,[80] passed from mothers to son—all the black mother figures helping shape Martin King's own sound included.

Mahalia

Early in 1958, under pressure by executives at Columbia Records, Mahalia Jackson was persuaded to record a song with venerated big-band leader and jazzman Duke Ellington. A sacred number, "Come Sunday" was rewritten with vocals from an orchestral suite Ellington had debuted to little notice fifteen years earlier. With a view toward "taking advantage of Jackson's seemingly unlimited vocal range and emotional capacity,"[81] Ellington would rework his *Black, Brown and Beige*, thematically foregrounding its "Come Sunday" section with shorter and longer variations on its sacred theme over four revised sections. But the song around which Ellington and collaborator Billy Strayhorn would fashion the album's titular "Black" movement unnerved the Baptist soloist from Chicago. For some time ahead of the February recording session, she struggled in rehearsal to bring even the most lugubrious meter to the unmetered meditation Ellington had in mind. Not even her longtime accompanist, Mildred Falls, could help much. Although expertly churning out blues chords, interpolating triplets, and energizing Jackson's singing with a bouncing swing rhythm, Falls was rather more adept at reinforcing the regulative structures of time and meter that Jackson disregarded at will. Twenty years Jackson's pianist, Falls "gave Mahalia the latitude she needed, the freedom to ad lib new lyrics, *break time*, [and] alter the melodic line."[82] More apt to shore up Jackson's timing with compensatory fixes to Jackson's misheard rhythms and broken meter than to leave her to Ellington's irregulative experimentation, Falls "just couldn't get with" what Duke was putting down.[83]

Improbable as it was, then, especially for one who derived so much of her musical and religious sense from the mood and feeling of the church, Jackson's singing of "Come Sunday" came off brilliantly in the studio. There on Sunset Boulevard, in a well-appointed Columbia Records hall dominated by Ellington and his orchestra, Jackson nervously surrendered to Ellington's vision for *Black, Brown and Beige*. Conceived as a "tone parallel" to the history of black people in America, "Come Sunday" deviated from "the traditional 4/4 jazz beat," venturing experimentally "into the realms of 5/4, 3/4, and free-floating tempos."[84] It seems the very thing her most severe critics bemoaned in Jackson, an "atrocious sense of timing,"[85] suited Jackson to Ellington's aesthetic in the final analysis. Though she strained to get lost in "Come Sunday" without the assurance of a metrical terra firma to return to from fugitive time (or the quick fix to a broken meter she grew to expect from Falls), with Ellington prodding her, Jackson broke through to a place in her singing that she had not altogether expected to—in an idiom, jazz, that she typically swore off. That she got there in spite of the strict management of studio-time pressuring her must have surprised Jackson most. But recognizing how tentatively she had been approaching "Come Sunday" in free form, Ellington had an intuition: "Mahalia, listen," he recalled saying. "[We] want to try something different. We're not going to play, and we're going to put the lights out, and I want you to sing 'Come Sunday' by yourself."[86] Off the clock, in the dark and unaccompanied, Jackson stole away while engineers tracked her crossing the sacred/secular divide on tape.

Who knows what exactly Ellington intended? Was this a simple exercise in reduced listening purposed to steer Jackson's attention back to the reassuring resonance of her own vocal instrument? Or did a deeper instinct stir him—one compelled to connect the singer to an affective experience of blackness better to inform her performance in the suite's first movement, "Black"? Whatever Ellington's motivation, "the tone parallel" Jackson realized as she sang alone blurred the lines of categorical difference between gospel and jazz;[87] church and nightclub and concert hall; sonance, song, and words; history and eschatology; mourning and mon'in' and jubilee. Effecting a hibernation to rival that in the "Prologue" to Ralph Ellison's *Invisible Man*, Jackson entered into "the 'Blackness of Blackness'" in that dark-filled studio redolent with tones and tempos indistinctly heard coming through the music's ongoingly preterit soundscape of possibility. Against all the pretensions of light in modern thought, I mean, it seems it was in the dark that the spirit dwelled. In the voice of the one Ellison elsewhere ordained "the high priestess in the religious ceremony of her church,"[88] "Come Sunday" called the spirit to the creative work of secular black modernism in Ellington from its dark, brooding, infinite anteriority. With only Ellington's sparse piano play (barely two measures) to encourage her, Jackson sang searchingly and exposed for more than five minutes:

> Lord, dear Lord of love,
> God almighty, God up above,
> Please look down and see my people through
>
> God, dear God of love,
> God almighty, God above,
> Please look down and see my people through

I believe the sun and moon will shine up in the sky
When the day is gray
I know it's just clouds passing by

He'll give peace and comfort
To every troubled mind
Come Sunday, oh come Sunday
That's the day

Often we'll feel weary
But he knows our every care
Go to him in secret
He will hear your every prayer

Lilies of the valley
They neither toil nor spin
And flowers bloom in spring
And birds sing

Up from dawn till sunset
Man work hard all the day
Come Sunday, oh come Sunday
That's the day.

Then, as if to accent the deeper plane of liminal sounds and spiritual experience penetrating to the very grain of her voice, Jackson moaned a few bars more at the song's end. It was not a coda per se she was offering but an extravagance of visceral feeling ordinary words were too weak to express, a vocal enactment of the "spill" of black womanly affect-as-philosophy Alexis Gumbs observes in so many associated scenes of black feminist fugitivity. The poetic voice(s) helping to convey "How We Know" in *Spill*, Gumbs's theory-in-verse, might just as well have been Jackson's. Navigating the dark anteriority of blackness out of which "Come Sunday" came into tuneful being, Gumbs, the poet, sings,

> i am before that. i am not born this morning . . . i am before that. present like dew and steam and like dreams without request. . . . i am before that. i am structure of bone. i am contour of clay. i am paradigm of play. i do not arrive. i stay. i am before that. . . . i am the drumbeat that dramatizes the heart. i am the whole point. i am your favorite part. i am not artifice. i am art.

> before black is bad and broken I am more ... i am the energy of birth that you took. i am every blackened letter pressing on the book. and before that.
>
> before god bless the child that's got her own. i am the moan. I am the touchstone ...
>
> ... deeper than down i am core. and before. i am more.[89]

Like Gumbs's speaker-singer, Jackson's few bars of extemporized moaning *after* the song's proper end, an affect that might rightly be regarded as Jackson's benedictory "postscript" to the structuring materiality of the jazz hymn's scoring on paper, intone the "before" and "more than" comprising undifferentiated sacred and secular soundways within which the possibility for "Come Sunday," being "present like dew and steam," existed ahead of time. To be sure, neither song nor singer was "born this morning," but so long "before that," black had not yet been "bad and broken." It was the creative condition, "the energy of birth" for whole worlds.

Jackson's moaning, in other words, added temporal space for the spirit's coming, whose hoped-for visitation commanded waiting, as Jackson knew from experience.[90] Her complaints about the draconian time limits placed on her by television appearances, studio sessions, and, at times, "a big orchestra" were lost to the irruptive power of the spirit to *break time* in the dark.[91] For she was not idly waiting in that extended time-space she'd carved out from the before and beyond of song. She was tarrying in it—which is to say, after Crawley, intensely "wait[ing] with fervent prayer and song" in the manner of some Pentecostals "for the experience of Spirit baptism";[92] a waiting inspired by an ardently felt abeyance of that which is, in time, to come.

But if moaning is a return to the condition of black time-space before words, then Jackson did not *decide* on tarrying as a modality for overcoming the imagined secularity of Ellington's jazz sensibilities so much as *she waded into it*, the worded refrain "Come Sunday" (heard as "Come, Sunday") being the repeated "prayer-words" Pentecostalist historian David Daniels has posited as charismatic aids to "cross[ing] spiritual thresholds."[93] For the religious enactment of tarrying, Crawley points out, "doesn't ... begin as much as it happens, as it eventuates, as it anoriginally opens."[94] The tarry service cannot be said to properly "begin," he explains, "because such a concept would presume that the work of the Spirit is in need of being convoked" rather than seeing the invocation of the spirit as more precisely evocative than convoking.[95] Thus did Jackson introduce herself into the

FOUR WOMEN   163

flow of an out-of-time black time-space in the dark where "Come Sunday" might finally resound. This space, however, was more than just an allowance for the spirit to have being in the studio outside of industry-time. As we shall see, it was an affordance demanded by the flesh as well, by that which Crawley has posited as the body's "sacred possibility."[96]

Short months after Jackson and Ellington's "Come Sunday" studio collaboration, they took their good feeling about what they'd achieved to Newport, Rhode Island, where Jackson was to make her first appearance at the celebrated jazz festival. In the audience that July 3 at Freebody(!) Park was Ellison, the music critic. Surprisingly, the *Invisible Man* author decried the "Come Sunday" experiment, panning it as "a most unfortunate marriage and an error of taste."[97] But for all that he found failing about "Come Sunday," Jackson's Sunday morning set at Mt. Zion AME Church in Newport was beatific, and Ellison did not fail to pay a votary's reverence to "Mahalia the high priestess" or, crucially, to observe "the frame within which she move[d]" as moved by an affording of the spirit—in this case, "a triumphal blending of popular dance movements with religious passion."[98] One might argue persuasively that Ellison noted Jackson's body ("the frame within which she move[d]") in "As the Spirit Moves Mahalia" because the "physical gusto" with which she approached her craft, as Heilbut remarked, underlined it.[99] But to greater and lesser degrees, the same might be said of most gospel artists. Attention to Jackson's physical mystique, specifically, had been a preoccupation of music writers—men, not surprisingly—from the first. Ellison's attention to the spirit alive in Jackson's "frame" was not a new or unique interest.[100]

Long before Ellison's "As the Spirit Moves Mahalia," few writers resisted commenting outright on Jackson's form. Few did not note in the early part of her rise to musical distinction that she was "a big, beautiful girl" with a prodigious voice.[101] Biographer Jules Schwerin recalled hearing Jackson live for the first time in White Plains, New York, in 1955. "In her pink, floor-length organza gown, her black beehive fall piled high atop her head," he wrote, "she swayed, rocked, handclapped, and shouted, pouring it on, snapping her fingers—*a monumental body of a woman (she is said to have once weighed over 250 pounds) with her skirt rippling around her legs.*"[102] Flirting with a mostly forgotten retention of nineteenth-century scientific racism, according to which "so-called 'ethnic' vocal timbre" presumed to reveal "something essential about the person's body,"[103] as Nina Sun Eidsheim has shown so perspicaciously, Schwerin's voyeurism was nothing out of the ordinary in Jackson's coverage. His fetishization of Jackson's "monumental body" reflected a widespread fascination with her dark and feeling flesh—a fascination so impious, despite the music, as to follow Schwerin nearly in his recollection's indecent spectatorial play at her ankles and calves in an orgiastic atmosphere of "moans and groans and shouts built to shivering climaxes."[104]

By contrast, when Ellison turned to Jackson's corporeal presence on stage in the closing lines of "As the Spirit Moves Mahalia," it was not the sensual fact of her flesh he noticed—at least not so evidently as others. Instead, he appeared to hold interest in her body's motor aspect, the spirited swing and bounce of a dark corporeal aliveness at once sacred, sexual, and salvific in its ontotheological anoriginality. Differently put, Ellison was rather engaged by what Heilbut would later describe as

> a power and self-assurance of her own . . . breaking all the rules, changing the melody and meter as the spirit dictated. . . . "Mahalia took people back to slavery times." She was unashamedly Southern, moaning and groaning like the down-home congregations, skipping and strutting like the Sanctified preachers. . . . Some churches exiled her for her rocking beat, others for her "snake hips." . . . "The girl always had a beautiful voice but she was known for her hollering and getting happy and lifting her dress." . . . When the spirit presumes, Mahalia lifts her robe an inch or two: "Mahalia always was the sexiest thing out there."[105]

On the Newport stage, Jackson was much less theatrical than the image Heilbut painted. Ellison therefore was not a witness to "'her hollering and getting happy and lifting her dress.'" Even as the "rhythmical drive"—Ellison's phrase—of Jackson's "Keep Your Hand on the Plow" and, later, "Didn't It Rain" pushed her to punctuated hand-clapping, Jackson kept her "frame" mostly restrained and close to the mic. But Ellison saw or sensed something more and less in Jackson's deportment on stage—the hint of unashamed Southernness, perhaps—that one simply could not *see* clearly on any stage that was not the church but which Ellison, the erstwhile musician and child of the black church tradition in Oklahoma City, could somehow *sense* all the same.

Not surprisingly, then, at her Sunday morning set at Mt. Zion, Ellison witnessed "the art of Mahalia Jackson" in its rightful place and heard "the full timbre of her sincerity . . . distinctly" as the prior performance of "Come Sunday,"[106] resounding in the unconscious of the Sunday event, was accorded another level of meaning implicitly. Looking back on the Jackson-Ellington performance of three nights earlier from the temporal vantage point of Sunday's service of worship, Jackson's refrain, "Come Sunday," could not have avoided sounding like a priestly summoning, or *adhan*,[107] of the festival faithful to (the sacred sociality of) church the Sabbath then ensuing.

Whether Ellison was among those he marked "the fortunate few who braved the Sunday-morning rain" to hear Jackson in her "proper setting" his principal biographer and personal correspondences have left unclear.[108] Present or absent, Ellison maintained a clear vision in his essay of the "living idea of the rich and moving art" that Jackson embodied. In evident contrast with the "banality" of her performance on the festival stage, in the church she succeeded in calling up "that vast fund of emotion with which Southern Negroes have charged the scenes and symbols of the Gospels."[109] There, where architecture, instrumentation (namely, piano and pipe organ), and the antiphonal liberties taken by her audience generated a lived acoustemology of gospel sound, Jackson's admirers were the more suggestible to her singing's ethereal mystique. As one reporter was careful to convey, "From all over the congregation came the sounds of 'Hallelujah' and 'Praise the Lord' in an exceptional manifestation of spiritual fervor as Mahalia sang."[110] No video footage of this display survives to confirm or challenge the accuracy or adequacy of its translation of sounds, as "Hallelujah" and "Praise the Lord" may be mere placeholders of black religious cliché for a vaster trove of outbursts and exclamations too elusive to capture in print. But a sequence of Eadweard Muybridge-style photographs of Jackson at Mt. Zion—photographer unknown—may yet help in not only seeing how the "frame in which she move[d]" *moved*, but how the congregation sounded the movement of the spirit in its midst in contradistinction to what it may or may not have said exclamatorily. Though the Newport festival's strict schedule and dozens of set lists did not allow for much tarrying, these images allow us to observe Jackson's doubly musical and motor commitment to the work of enlarging the time-space of the spirit.

Although the five images of Jackson from the iconic Michael Ochs Archive of musician photography are unattributed and belong to a stock image collection, there is little question the anonymous photographer was as serious about music and photography as Ochs when the latter figure created his archive in 1977. The images' evident seriality, and the broad sweep of chancel space they cover in their order, suggest a sophisticated photographic interest in Jackson's singing. The wide range of lateral movement Jackson measured across the chancel in her setting undoubtedly led many to perceive her vocal gestures as so analogously palpable, dark, and dense that they must have seemed picturable. Jackson's cameraman that day recorded her sound, then, as much as the sight of her in religious ceremony.

Behind the rhythmical drive of Falls at the piano, Jackson fervidly sang. The pictures testified to her "rich and moving" timbre, quoting Ellison again, by way of what Tina Campt calls "the haptic encounter that foregrounds the frequencies of images and how they move, touch, and connect us to *event* of the photo."[111] In other words, "for those who have eyes to hear,"[112] as acclaimed African American fine-art photographer Roy DeCarava put it, the pictures amplified the sound of the spirit in motion in, and in the surround of, Jackson's singing.

In the first of five frames (figure 5.2), Jackson stands near Falls, stage right, already singing, tarrying there in time for the break within which the spirit comes, overflowing meter, which it is Falls's task to establish before Jackson—and soon Falls with her—gets carried away by the spirit's surging. Before Jackson takes her first fugitive steps away from the ground of Falls's anchoring tempo, and the musical labor Falls has put to sonifying the tonal and rhythmical preconditions for Jackson's singing gets backgrounded in the second frame (figure 5.3), the spirit has started Jackson moving already. Moreover, considering that no gospel singer drifts *into* a corner—only *out* from one as the singer gets passionately *carried away*—in figure 5.3 Mahalia's right arm swings up and out as she leaves the heavily furnished corner looking as though she's bent on marching. With a visible vibrato-effect I want to claim as that of the subject's will rather than an accident in development or the photographer's wrong selection of shutter speed, Jackson resists her camerical cornering, the blur of her right limb answering the untiring clicking of that instrument with a markedly visual sign.

Moreover, in figure 5.4 it is Campt's "sensorial" strategy of "juxtapos[ing] the sonic, haptic, historical and affective backgrounds and foregrounds through and against which we view photographs" that lets us hear the driving rhythm of Falls's walking baseline, a bounce style common to ragtime and stride piano play,[113] in Jackson's would-be march to the middle of the chancel floor as she quits the corner to expand into the ametronomic time-space of gospel's supersensuous expression. A performance theory of black visual intonation is thus posited by Jackson's picture, one that filmmaker and theorist Arthur Jafa has been after in film and video. "How can we ... find a way Black movement in itself could carry, for example, the weight of sheer tonality in Black song?" Jafa asked an audience of black artists and scholars in 1998.[114] What he intended by "tonality in Black song" he did not wish to leave to misunderstanding: "I'm not talking about the lyrics" sung by an iconic black woman vocalist, he stressed. "I'm taking about *how she sang them*."[115] He then went on to clarify that his search was for black aesthetic equivalencies for

FOUR WOMEN   167

"vibrato, rhythmic patterns, slurred or bent notes, and other musical effects" in visual media,[116] *tone* not the least among those "other ... effects." "How do we make ... Black images vibrate in accordance with certain frequential values that exist in Black music? How can we analyze the tone, not the sequence of notes Coltrane hit *but the tone itself*, and synchronize Black visual movement with that? I mean, is this just a theoretical possibility, or is this actually something we can do?"[117] Jackson's concert at Mt. Zion might be looked to as an affirmation that there's "actually something we can do." "All joy and exultation and swing," as Ellison wrote,[118] Jackson gives both voice and view in these images to what a black body "can do" performatively to compel "Black images [to] vibrate in accordance with certain frequential values ... in Black music." As a student of the dialectical intermateriality of visual and sonic experience,[119] I maintain that these five images archived by Michael Ochs help picture the possibility of the sort of black visual audition Jafa has called for (and has since achieved, in works like *Dreams Are Colder Than Death* in 2013 and *Love Is the Message, The Message Is Death* in 2016). In them, weight, vibration, frequency, movement, and tone all sonify at the sensory and technical limit of photography as Jackson moves on down the line swinging, bouncing, clapping, and (surely) moaning sounds, seen and unseen. Still images straining to be moving pictures, each one is nevertheless an unframing of "the frame in which she moves" out from the reductive fictions of the flesh so many critics and music writers wrote her into.

To be clear, it is not the image-maker who steers this movement toward unframing or freeing the photograph of its conceit of pure visuality (which Campt's *Listening to Images*, for example, is keen to deconstruct); its proper agent is Jackson herself, alive and feeling in these frames. Her movement in this curation of images is, if not volitional, *decisional* in any event—willed but not foreclosed to what is unchoreographed.[120] For the motive drive reflected in the stop-motion seriality of gospel singing's photo-audition in these frames is not merely transversal—moving *across* dialectical space to its visible terminus—but also exilic, moving centrifugally *out from* her "proper" place under the common gaze toward an acousmatic subjecthood *somewhere* at the edge of sight (figure 5.6).

It is precisely "at the edge of sight" that photographer and critic Shawn Michelle Smith locates "the revelation of an unseen world that photography does not fully disclose, but makes us aware of it in its invisibility."[121] According to Smith, the blind spots of everyday seeing are reproduced in photographic representation, belying the professedly revelatory power of photography to profitably *see*. As much as those early pioneers in photographic theory, like British inventor William Henry Fox Talbot and the German Jewish philosopher Walter Benjamin, enthused over the medium's "enabling one to see more," Smith has lately added that photography also "simultaneously demonstrated how little is ordinarily visible, giving one the unnerving sense of living in a world only partially perceived."[122] Smith's *At the Edge of Sight: Photography and the Unseen* closely examines six nineteenth- and twentieth-century photographers/photographic theorists and "the optical unconscious" they have long been credited with laying bare before opened eyes. Astutely, Smith reveals their work to have only called attention to said unconscious "in its invisibility."[123] Nothing, at root, is disclosed that wasn't seen ahead of them.

Given the vast differences in racial representation, setting, event, and time period between Eadweard Muybridge's late nineteenth-century motion studies and photographs of Mahalia Jackson performing in a New England AME church, it may seem improbable that Smith's close reading of Muybridge and my concentration on Jackson yield nearly identical criticisms. We both posit the logic of "motion itself" as the subject of the series before us. But for the eighty years separating Muybridge's studies from Jackson's Mt. Zion concert, Jackson might have been one of Muybridge's motion-study models. Her pictures, like the ones Muybridge made which "arrest motion, freezing and making visible incremental gestures usually lost in the blur of continuous movement," belie their goal as, according to Smith, Muybridge's also do.[124] Like the Muybridge studies, they are "full of gaps and contradictions" that emerge when what the camera purports to capture, human locomotion, "slips out of view and remains invisible, caught between frames."[125] In the end, "movement is only inferred." It "remains unseen in the space between frames."[126] It is thus pointedly untrue, *pace* Benjamin, that photography "reveals the secret" of "what happens during the fraction of a second when a person steps out" walking.[127] Even walking, Smith explains, the weary traveler escapes visual hold. Hear Smith describe the illusion at the center of Muybridge's famous work:

> In one of the series "walking," a young woman identified as "Model 6" stands naked, perpendicular to the camera, her body in profile.... Long, wavy hair falls to the middle of her back. Her full white breasts and bottom stand out against the dark background marked with white lines. She is framed tightly, feet and head nearly touching the top and bottom of the image. With her left foot firmly planted on the wooden platform, she raises her right foot, extending her leg out in front of her body. In the next frame, her right leg

is fully stretched, foot flexed up, casting a shadow into view. She has lifted her body slightly and the curve of her left buttock has come into view. Her left arm swings out slightly in front of her hip. In the third frame, her right heel makes contact with the walkway, and her left heel lifts. She is suspended in the middle of the frame, her weight evenly balanced between outstretched legs. In the fourth frame she presses her right foot fully down on the wooden path. Her left foot flexes, toes still on the ground, and her left arm is no longer in sight. Her body arches back slightly as her left leg bends. Such slight shifts in the woman's position are traced over the course of twelve frames, and it appears that she has taken only two steps across the entire sequence.[128]

In ways both glaring and understated, Muybridge's "Model 6" is Jackson's photographic negative. Her plain nakedness opposes Jackson's long, darkly patterned dress. And whereas the Muybridge model's "full white breasts and bottom stand out against the dark background marked with white lines," Jackson's outline appears silhouetted against a luminous whiteness (figure 5.6). This dramatic inversion of darkness and light, however, is hardly the most important observation to be made in this apposition of Model 6 and Jackson. Rather, what is shared and continuous across the two studies—one nineteenth-century, the other twentieth—matters more to Jackson's aesthetics and influence on the times.

Consistently, in her delineation of Model 6's walking, Smith notes the "slight" adjustments of the model's body to an imagined way of walking suited to camerical expectation: "She . . . lifted her body *slightly*" while "her left arm swings out *slightly*." In a subsequent frame, "her body arches back *slightly*" to begin a second step. Though removed from the time and inspiration of 1958 Newport, Rhode Island, the subtlety of these *"slight* shifts" nonetheless accords with the comparably "slight" movements of Jackson's gesticulating limbs which the slower shutter speed of her picture-taker's less scientific equipment permits us to glimpse in three frames as faint blurs (figures 5.2, 5.3, and 5.4). Thus, even if Jackson does not succeed entirely in disappearing her body from the zealous eyeballing of an anonymous photographer intent upon capturing her (sound), and the final frame suggests her body's arrestation under the celestial white light of colonial fantasy, her hands transform the scene of audiovisual subjection into a scene of black feminist fugitivity all the same. Erin Manning calls this sort of unseen everyday *interstitial* movement of the body in and against the event "the minor gesture."[129]

Allied with Gilles Deleuze and Félix Guattari's metaphysics of minority, Manning calls critical attention to "the subtle shifts" and "nuanced rhythms of the minor" within major categories of knowledge and experience. What is called the major (sometimes, "the grand"), she explains, "is given the status it has not because it is where . . . transformative power lies, but because it is easier to identify major shifts than to catalogue the nuanced rhythms of the minor."[130] The minor—be it a chord, a key signature, or a neuromuscular impulse or event—insofar as it exists before and deep within the major, is, thus, always "out of time, untimely, rhythmically inventing its own pulse."[131] The minor therefore "exceeds the bounds of the event" it gives rise to, "touching on the ineffable quality of its more-than." As a mode of real or symbolic action, the minor gesture is often overlooked, regularly "go[ing] by unperceived."[132] Still, Manning assures us, "the minor gesture is everywhere, all the time."[133]

Thus, the shuddering of Jackson's hands (figures 5.2, 5.3), even her clapping (figure 5.4), are easily missed because they are minor gestures, in Manning's sense. Despite their intimations of motion—their minor movement, that is, within the event of the singing body's migration across the chancel space—their blurred visuality no more "captures" their motion photographically than Muybridge's studies, which, according to Smith, *do not* convey scientific accuracy despite the pretenses of method and apparatus purporting to their scientific transparency. Motion is deduced in Muybridge through comparative observation, one still frame to the next. In point of act, motion does not appear *in* Muybridge at all (as one may, for example, witness it today in images generated by Apple's Live Photo or Google's Motion Stills technology); instead, it is "deferred, remaining invisible in the dark space between photographs." Similarly, the quiet blur of happy hands only infers their movement in Jackson's singing. Somewhere in the gaps and fissures within which motion disappears from tracking, the minor gesture is secreted in "sites of dissonance" where, as Manning suggests, the chord, the key, or the gesticulatory action pursues a more improvisatory time-space than that regulating the major move or event.[134] Only, the quality of "more-than" hinted at in Jackson's minor gestures lies less lavishly in the visual beyond of sight missed by Muybridge than it does in the aural beyond of visual representation, like that evoked by DeCarava's dreaming of "eyes to hear."

By this shift of emphasis to the aural unconscious informing Jackson's minor gestures, I mean to call attention *away* from the photographic invisibility of Jackson's hand and arm motions, despite their clear analogy to the locomotive invisibilities of Muybridge's Model 6, and toward the "choreosonic" activity that "minor gesture" necessarily signifies in its dual motor and musical intermodality.[135] Jackson's performance of black feminist

5.2 Mahalia Jackson, Mt. Zion AME Church, Newport, RI, 1958. Michael Ochs Archive via Getty Images.

fugitivity, I am saying, was not reducible to, nor even principally driven by, her major or minor movement out from pornotropic capture under the photographic gaze. Rather, her hands and feet were moved by music out of time with the musical event and out of step with the spatial order of liturgical regulation in modern black Methodism. Drawn out from time and space into the time-space of the spirit, Jackson was thus opened up to remembrances of minor experience resisting and exceeding white frames of black life and loss, joy and suffering. Against such memories, her singing and shouting and "skipping and strutting" quit Newport that bright Sunday on the force of a sterling hope and black feminist dream. Dark and feeling and fleshly were they, as sacred and secular joined together in brilliant black choreosonic congress. That day, the visual record suggests, Mahalia Jackson soared.

Aretha

Four years on from Martin King's exequies in Atlanta, Coretta King flew into wintry Chicago for another funeral event there. The "Queen of Gospel," whose talent Martin King had extolled as coming "not once a century,

5.3 Mahalia Jackson, Mt. Zion AME Church, Newport, RI, 1958. Michael Ochs Archive via Getty Images.

5.4   Mahalia Jackson, Mt. Zion AME Church, Newport, RI, 1958. Michael Ochs Archive via Getty Images.

5.5   Mahalia Jackson, Mt. Zion AME Church, Newport, RI, 1958. Michael Ochs Archive via Getty Images.

5.6 Mahalia Jackson, Mt. Zion AME Church, Newport, RI, 1958. Michael Ochs Archive via Getty Images.

but once a millennium,"[136] had died of heart failure. Just sixty years old, Jackson—a warm friend to the Kings, a dependable onstage protest participant, and a member of the SCLC board of directors—lay embalmed "in a polished wooden coffin lined with pale blue, surrounded with bouquets of red roses, and . . . a garland of white orchids" on the stage of the Arie Crown Theater.[137] More than four thousand filled the seats before her. Out from that crowd of mourners, Coretta King, who had been engaged to pay tribute to Jackson, approached the stage on cue. Those left seated honored her presence with a standing ovation. Alongside the bier holding Jackson's remains, Coretta King stood at the unadorned wooden podium, remembering aloud "my dear friend, your friend, a friend to mankind, Mahalia Jackson, black, proud, beautiful, extraordinarily gifted as a singer and a performer, singing the songs of her people in her own unique way. She sang a universal language, for she expressed in her songs, which were deeply rooted in the black experience, the joys, the sorrows, the sufferings, the longings and aspirations—yes, the desire for freedom for her people."[138] Other speakers celebrated Jackson's life and career, too, but the *Christian Century*, it should be noted, mainline Protestantism's flagship organ in the United States since the nineteenth century, remembered no one so vividly as Coretta King in its coverage of the service, as this picture of her holding forth at Jackson's service intimates. On stage, in that ritual space Martin King had so singularly commanded, his widow held forth not as "Mrs. Martin Luther King, Jr." this time, but as an independent black feminist performer-activist, measured and imperial behind the microphone as her training in concert music urged.

If Coretta King's encomium for the world's greatest gospel singer put language to the radical potentiality of black women's musicianship to perform the "desire for freedom for [black] people," however, then Aretha Franklin, who followed Coretta King in appearance on the stage, returned the public expression of that radical potentiality to its (an)original, unmediated modality in the gospel elegy. What other song, then, but "Take My Hand, Precious Lord" could have conveyed the material sound of modern black loss and longing so pregnantly? Franklin's performance of the Dorsey classic, which brought the Jackson memorial to its formal end, was especially significant since no black singer was more closely associated with Dorsey's composition than Jackson. Although other black acts like the Soul Stirrers, Sister Rosetta Tharpe, and the Blind Boys of Alabama made notable recordings of "Precious Lord" before it became Jackson's in 1956, Jackson's recording had the machinery of one of the most powerful labels in the recording industry behind it. With Columbia Records' help, Jackson brought "Precious Lord" out from the black world of sacred sound and studio spaces, introducing it to the American and international mainstream. Its suitedness for Jackson's last rites must have seemed obvious to Franklin, as it was by the time of Jackson's death, and owing appreciably to the slow-moving funereality of her Columbia recording of it, already "the black national anthem of mourning."[139] But Franklin's *singing*, rather than the fact of the song alone, conveyed the performance past polite homage. Against the backdrop of Franklin's own live recording of "Precious Lord" in 1956, her appearance in Chicago would seem to dramatize, if not a competing assertion of responsibility for the song's anthemic ascendance, then the signifyin(g) of an emergent Detroit sound upon the motherliness/motherlines of Chicago's claims on gospel blues.[140] It is as if Franklin biographer David Ritz had in mind the scene at Arie Crown Theater when he posited Franklin's approach to the sacred song in 1956 as "signal[ing] a readiness—even an eagerness—*to stand beside the magnificent Mahalia, who performed it countless times.*"[141] Tall behind the podium, not many steps away from the closed full-couch of Jackson's floriated casket, Franklin realized a feminist ending like Susan McClary's *Feminine Endings* did not imagine.

Though just fourteen years old in 1956, Franklin was already enjoying a mounting reputation as a young virtuoso, the prodigy daughter of black Detroit's—soon to be black America's—most popular gospel preacher, Reverend C. L. Franklin. A doyen of black preaching, Reverend Franklin was so prodigious a talent at the lectern that by the time he arrived in Detroit in 1946 to take over as senior minister at New Bethel Baptist Church, admirers referred to him as "the man with the million-dollar voice." The antonomastic tag was no exaggeration. In 1953, chiefly on the strength of his success as a radio preacher, Chess Records, recording home to Muddy Waters, the Moonglows, Howlin' Wolf, and the early Ike Turner, began pressing live recordings of Reverend Franklin's sermons at New Bethel. Three years later, with his fame growing worldwide, sales of his sermons exceeded a half-million copies.[142] The talents of the younger Franklin gleamed in the light of her father's success. "Joining [Reverend Franklin's] Gospel Caravan tours as a highly talented teenager," Nina Öhman has pointed out, "was an important part of [young Aretha Franklin's] grooming process, and her participation . . . helped build the tour's popularity."[143] It was thus in his interest as much as hers—he was, after all, eager to further monetize his million-dollar allure—that Reverend Franklin consented to the debut of his daughter as a child recording artist at the apex of his own popular appeal. "Chess Records asked Daddy whether they could record me," Franklin would write in her autobiography decades on, "and he agreed."[144]

Yet for all the commercial interest in the younger Franklin's launch into notoriety as an independent gospel performer, the imagined capture of her voice on vinyl had greater historical than financial significance. Her first five recorded tracks, including "Precious Lord (Part One)" and "Precious Lord (Part Two)," recorded on tour with Reverend Franklin at the Oakland Arena, stood to augment more than her father's name, in other words; they would also bare/bear the trace of her *mother's* name, Barbara Siggers Franklin. Saying *her* name in this chapter not only moves her memory out of invisibility and maternal misnaming toward the just reparation due her in death—a too-belated acknowledgment of the awfulness of her loss of five children—but urges us to consider the daughter's singing at Oakland Arena under pressure of the fact of black mother-loss. Heard in this context, the precocity of Franklin's performance of "Precious Lord (Part One)" and "Precious Lord (Part Two)," so far from the father's proud display of the daughter's accelerated talent, paints a more doleful portrait of black-girl lament-in-mother-loss than anyone has been willing to imagine critically.

> The message is among the deepest and most beloved in all black gospel.... Barely a teenager, Aretha embraces the most grown-up of spiritual moments—the declaration of despair before the reality of death. "When my life is almost gone," she cries, "hear my cry." The cry for connection to the unseen source of creation is chilling. This is not a child singing, but a woman ... making her way through life's tragic maze. She stands in darkness. She sings, "As the night draws near and the day is past and gone, at the river I stand." The river is the Jordan and the river Styx, the river between life and death, sorrow and renewal. After the lyrics are sung a single time, they are no longer adequate to express the depth of her feelings. "Ain't no harm to moan," says Aretha, who wordlessly renders the melody. Her voice is ageless. Her art is fully formed and wholly realized. She is much more than a child prodigy or a surprisingly good singer. She is already a great artist.[145]

While Ritz's enthusiasm for fourteen-year-old Franklin's two-part performance of "Precious Lord" in Oakland focuses attentively on the prodigious talent "Precious Lord" requires of one as young as Franklin, he misses the tragic irony of travails inhering to black-girl precarity in migration-era

Detroit, Chicago, St. Louis, Philadelphia, Washington, DC, and New York—travails pertaining to sex, work, education, health, and family that, as Aimee Meredith Cox and Marcia Chatelain have shown, trouble the girl/woman distinction in black feminist studies.

With their attention focused on the lived experience and history of black girlhood in Detroit and Chicago, respectively, Cox and Chatelain both show how normative considerations of black girlhood in scholarly literature and public life tend toward a reflexive elision between prepubescence and adulthood. A black girl's childhood, "connected to the ideas of domesticity, motherhood and safety," as Cox writes,[146] is not infrequently compressed compared to that of other girls. The privileged protections of adolescence meant to effect a "proper" (i.e., middle-class) transition from childhood into adulthood are all but foreclosed to black girls. Black girls are always already "adults in the making," it would seem.[147] Ritz's marveling at the maturity of Franklin's performance then—namely, his wonder at her affect of "a woman . . . making her way through life's tragic maze," though she's "barely a teenager"—is its own marvel in a way. He could not have forecast how precisely his incredulous impressions would convey the troublesome liminality of young black female subjects so readily adulted from puberty into "ageless" postpubescence. In this sense, what else is to be expected from the black girl singer formed and fashioned in Detroit, but a womanish sound?[148]

Ritz's fanatical regard for Franklin's teenage singing, "fully formed and wholly realized" as the voice of "a woman," is, in my judgment, overdetermined. The "depth of feeling" he reveres in Franklin scarcely warrants zeal; the depth of knowing that inspires wordless feeling might instead warrant pity or dread or, perhaps, shame. For even though hope, anticipation, and disappointment may be the commonest amalgam of feelings in black girls' narratives of life and loss during the migration eras,[149] they tell half the story. The dreads, trepidations, and despairing parts of black girl being haven't words to adequately convey their provocations. Perhaps, then, the power of "Precious Lord" lies extensively in the broad sweep and reach of its witness to modern black womanly knowing and feeling.[150] Black girls' keen awareness of the banalization of violence against them, as Cox shows, and the "limited social lexicon that makes [said] violence . . . legible to the broad public" might have made the wordless moaning predictable, not to say inexorable.[151] Against the backdrop of structural and private precarities Aretha Franklin shared with other migration-era Detroiters—her race, age, and sex—it should not have surprised Ritz to hear the tremulant sound of lament inhabiting the black girl's darkly tuned voice.

Thus, Aretha Franklin's adolescent performance of "Precious Lord" in Oakland—the one full minute of moaning she sounded, especially—distilled the mid-century political yearnings of black girls and women for nonviolence, an overlooked aspect of their hopes. Though these yearnings were variously borne in educational, economic, racial, civic, and sexual avowals of desire, as Cox and Chatelain observe, Franklin's moaning gathered them into a common existential expression of suffering and want. This was no conscious act of black feminist representation, however. At fourteen, Aretha Franklin's travail was as intensely personal as it was historical. When Aretha was six, her mother, Barbara Siggers Franklin, an admired singer and pianist in her own right, separated from Reverend Franklin and returned to Buffalo, New York, where the Franklin family had lived in the years before their relocation to Detroit in 1948. Siggers Franklin left Detroit and the infamously philandering Reverend Franklin with the Franklin siblings' fourteen-year-old half-brother from a prior relationship, Vaughan, while Aretha and Erma, Cecil, and Carolyn—ten, eight, and four, respectively—remained in their father's custody in Detroit. The children visited their mother in Buffalo often. But at so great a distance, going "to see Mother all the time" did little to heal the trauma little Aretha Franklin experienced at her parents' split.[152] As Erma Franklin would later explain: "I think Mother's move impacted Aretha more than anyone. At the time I was barely four and less conscious of what was happening. Aretha was a severely shy and withdrawn child who was especially close to her mother. . . . Aretha and I shared a room, and after Mother left I saw her cry her eyes out for days at a time."[153] Still lamenting her mother's distance from Detroit, at ten Aretha would get news that Siggers Franklin had suffered a fatal heart attack in Buffalo and, at thirty-four, was dead. For weeks, young Aretha refused or was simply unable to speak. "She crawled into a shell and didn't come out until many years later."[154]

We might hesitate to trust Erma Franklin's four-year-old memory of events in Aretha's young life if it was not so clearly confirmed by others whose friendly and familial recollections of six-year-old Aretha Franklin as a "traumatized child" complement the older sister's. Perhaps most critically, Erma Franklin's picture of the six-year-old "cry[ing] her eyes out for days at a time" harmonizes with the mourning of black motherhood as the acoulogical pretext of "Take My Hand, Precious Lord," that dark intoning of haunted, haunting mother-loss that was (the sound of) Nettie Dorsey's dying *before* it was Thomas Dorsey's song. When fourteen-year-old Aretha Franklin sang "Hear my cry, hear my call," I am arguing, she was not so much her six- or ten-year-old self again "cry[ing] her eyes out" as she was already—to use Ritz's term—"ageless," her grief a re-sounding of the phantasmic sound of her mother's certain grief at thirty, when Siggers Franklin left Detroit, effectively disinherited from "'motherhood' as a . . . blood-rite/right."[155] Aretha Franklin's intoned "cry" ("Hear my cry, hear my call") and the overtones of anguish inhabiting its (dis)articulation are more than a child's motherless "cry for connection," to recall Ritz again. Hers is rather a cry *of* connection, a "call" to and from those disinherited others, black girls and mothers—and black girls *as* mothers—whose affective experience of black motherhood during the black migration periods was loss. Two years a mother at the time of the Oakland recording, Aretha Franklin raised a black motherly lament, sounding interference into the anti-black order of the material world of black mother-loss with mourning and moaning.

> Lead . . . lead . . . lead me on, to the light
> Oooh-oooh, take my hand, Precious Looooooord, and lead, yoooo-our child, on home
>
> When my . . . when my way, grooows drear, Preeeeci . . . Precious Lord, please linger near
> And oooh-oooh, when my . . . when my life is al-moooooost, almost gone
> Father . . . Father . . . Father hear my cryyyy, Lord, and oooh-oooh, hear my call
> And hold . . . hold my . . . my hand—Please suh, Jesus—lest I fall
> Oooh, take my hand, Preeeeci . . . Precious Lord, and leeeead meeeee, lead me home
>
> Mmmmmm, mmmmmm . . . mmm. Ain't no harm to moan
> Mmmmmm, mmmmmm . . . mmm.
> Mmmmmm, mmmmmmmmmmmmmmm . . . mmm,
> At . . . at . . . whooooa, at the river, Lord, oooh—oooh, here I stand
> Guide my . . . guide my feet, and oooh, hold my hand
> Ooooooooh, oooh, ooooh
> Precious Lord, take my ha . . . hand. And leeeead
> Yoooooour child ho-ome.[156]

Between the optimism of so many seeking their new northern "home" and the foreboding of "night draw[ing] near," the black girl singer achieved an improbable agreement of disconsolate and dissenting feeling in sonifying modern black maternal memory and melancholia. Unfortunately, the historical grief/regret of black mother-loss, the sound of which Franklin re-sounded at Oakland Arena in bewailing interjections (*"Ooooooooh, oooh, ooooh*") and unremitting moaning ("*Mmmmmm, mmmmmm*"), barely echoed in the hall at Arie Crown on the occasion of Mahalia Jackson's funeral. This, though, is no remark about acoustics; Franklin *did* echo in that sense. Instead, it speaks to a problem of popular resonance with an audience predisposed by the immediacy of Jackson's death before them to enter the haptic experience "Precious Lord" could easily provoke, proficiently and passionately sung.

Now twenty-nine, Aretha Franklin stood at the onstage podium at Chicago's Arie Crown Theater, vigorously singing. Short steps away from Mahalia Jackson's closed casket, she "worked the hymn higher and higher, with her voice bounding off the theater walls." She sang not altogether mournfully this time but "*as if to prevail against all the evil rumors*" about Reverend Franklin, seated on the stage behind her.[157] By 1972, his widely whispered reputation as an inveterate womanizer, a substance abuser, and a clandestine drug smuggler was an outrage upon the churchgoing public. If true, Franklin's performance of "Precious Lord" at Arie Crown wasn't simply her homage to the Queen of Gospel, not just the sign of her "readiness—even an eagerness—to stand beside the magnificent Mahalia" in the gospel tradition[158] (though that could have been far from her thinking).[159] Far more complicated than that, Franklin's Arie Crown performance was—*had to have been*—something else as well. But on this occasion and after, the father interfered to induce the mother's forgetting (again) in the public history and performance of "Precious Lord." I suggest that this forgetting of the mother is one more loss to the memory of Martin Luther King Jr. It erases the figure with whom future studies of King—of black modernism, of black political culture and intellectual history, of the phenomenology of black preaching and the cultural politics of public oratory—should be concerned. Indeed, it erases "the position of the unthought" of blackness to the modern(ist) American order, for it is she who "breaks in upon the imagination with a forcefulness that marks both a denial and an 'illegitimacy.'"[160] In her is the possibility of "gaining the insurgent ground of female social subject[s]" outside of authorized structures of verbal communication and the vocal arts to convey,[161] with exorbitant sound, a gospel (aesthetic) that may save us all yet.

III

Technologies of Freedom

6

King's Vibrato

Visual Oratory and the "Sound of the Photograph"

For twenty-five centuries, Western knowledge has tried to look upon the world. It has failed to understand that the world is not for the beholding. It is for hearing.
Jacques Attali, *Noise* (1985)

And as though the sound contained some force more impervious than the image of the scene of which it was the living connective tissue, I was pulled back to its immediacy.
Ralph Ellison, *Invisible Man* (1952)

I'm interested in the convergence of blackness and the irreducible sound of necessarily visual performance.
Fred Moten, *In the Break* (2003)

It is said that Frederick Douglass was the most photographed American of the nineteenth century. That this is true is not be doubted—and neither is the prodigious probability that Martin Luther King Jr. was Douglass's closest counterpart in the twentieth century. Unlike Douglass, though, King did not propose or consent to sit for the majority of the vast number of photographs of him still decorating the halls of American political memory. Modern photojournalism made King a different class of photographic subject. When novelist Charles Johnson commented in the introduction to *King: A Photobiography of Martin Luther King, Jr.* (2000) that King "permeates—in ways great and small, direct and indirect—every facet of our social and political world . . . his hypnotic voice and unique vision linger[ing] ghost-like, in the background of every conversation that touches upon race, [and] the state of black America,"[1] he did not have King's visual image specifically in mind as the agential source or medium of King's ubiquity. Johnson's remark was a simpler statement about King's intellectual and moral impact on American social and political life. Yet Johnson might just as easily have argued for the force of the pictures comprising *King* as enjoying a spectral property all their own. For, arguably, the popularization of King's visual likeness, equally in the mass media and in the material culture of black iconography in the United States, supports King's enduring, even "ghost-like," presence in the race consciousness of American moderns, even and especially after his 1968 assassination.

Benedict J. Fernandez's 1968 photographic image "Vendor in New York City, New York" (figure 6.1) hints at this surfeiting of King's photographic likeness as (street) art and black American icon. The image is not only a metapicture of the material reproduction of black (and white) image-making in public culture, but a portrait in a series of visually inflected mourning rites Sara Lewis has proposed to call "Martin Luther King, Jr.'s 'aesthetic funerals,'" those popular or vernacular acts initiated "after his death to visually unfurl images, ideas, [and] epic visions of African American culture, as if to secure the horizon line that felt suddenly in doubt."[2] To the extent that these popular practices of aesthetic funereality preserved picture-worthy "images, ideas, [and] epic visions" of King's legacy to public memory, then King's posthumous haunting of contemporary racial discourse in Johnson's introduction could not escape tracking in the optical unconscious. There, where Walter Benjamin posited the hiddenness of "entirely new structural formations of the [visible] subject" gone previously unrecognized to conscious reflection,[3] a spectral King lingers in the historical unthought of "every conversation that touches upon race, [and] the state of black America," as Johnson said.

But let us imagine that King's spectrality isn't at all reducible to the optical unconscious of the historical record as it is reflected in, say, political portraiture, family pictures, or, most critically for my purposes, everyday photojournalism. Might the spectral image of King at the root of Johnson's reflections haunt racial conversation precisely because the sensory ground of the optical is aural? In a way, "Martin Luther King, Jr.'s 'aesthetic funerals'" are remembrances of King's voice as it is recalled by the resounding aurality repressed in King's image. This chapter argues for sound as a neglected

6.1 Vendor in New York City, 1968. Photo by Benedict Fernandez.

consideration in photographic criticism by way of close attention to photographs of Martin Luther King Jr. captured at angles high and low in the visible act of preaching or speech-making. Each image in this photo-repertory of oratorical performance represses the phonic materiality of speech and antiphony clearly attending to the event in view. I examine King's career in pictures to demonstrate how photographs record not sound's frequential audibility in the optical unconscious obtaining between frames, but sound's reverberant memory. I refer to this subset of images in the material history of King's insurgent life and work as archives of black visual oratory.

Although mostly uncollected in the formal sense, the images that comprise this discrete archive are not especially obscure. Many of them are iconic and thus exist in plain sight, although they rarely function as much more than "epic visions" of modern African American history. A heightened circulation of these unconsciously aural photographs of King was recently evident in the weeks and months leading to the 2018 semicentenary anniversary of King's April 1968 assassination. In that period, it was near-impossible to avoid the dozens of picture books and magazines illustrating King's short life and career conspicuously displayed in bookstores and on newsstands everywhere. Dramatic photographs of King, black-suited or religiously vestmented, were as visible in grocery checkout lanes as they were in the special exhibits created by major museums and historical societies in his honor. These many and varied pictures of King holding forth cast King in an *amplified* light, one illuminating a power otherwise than the "unique vision" Johnson attributed to him; this light would reveal King's "hypnotic voice" to the camerical eye as well. To see the sound of King's voice under this light, however, requires hearing eyes—eyes of the sort Roy DeCarava honed while photographing jazz in the 1950s and early 1960s, and Arthur Jafa has since nurtured in experimental black film and video. For the sake of the black past and its archival afterlives, these photographs of King and the black vocalic event deserve to be heard.[4]

Perhaps more than any other thing pictures may be said to "want," to venture an answer to W. J. T. Mitchell's rich query,[5] photographs strain to be heard. Inasmuch as they are always already the precluded possibility of film or video, that is, and thus also a reflection of their most elemental lacks, sound and motion, they repress the force of the sonic in their very being. This, though, is not to say that photography is a disabled medium that cannot sound out its content. It can. As sound "does not simply persist at a different level with regard to what we see," according to Žižek, and "rather points toward a gap in the field of the visible, toward the dimension of what eludes our gaze,"[6] then the sound of the photograph is not *not-there* at all, but *there* so intimately as to dwell *in* and *with* the picture, hidden in a sensorial blind spot. With the slightest turn and tilt of the head, then, and a gaze more agile and searching than our gallery habits of pause and meander, we may see the sounds of pictures yet and hear with our eyes their lower frequencies more loudly amplified. Still, one may want to cover her eyes a time or two. The background sound of the King photograph is sometimes ominous.

Photography, Threat, and the Aural Unconscious: Washington, DC

I think we'd be fooling ourselves if we had an audience this large and didn't realize that there were some enemies present.
Malcolm X, "The Ballot or the Bullet" (1964)

The familiar prints of Martin Luther King Jr. annually aiding his national birthday commemorations serve a necessary memorial function—that is, they help us remember a crucial subject in the moral and social history of modern America. That photographs often enough have the opposite effect, however, is equally and coevally true. By way of their availability in limitless duplication, photographs also aid our forgetting as they formalize their contents' exclusions—those objects existing outside the visual frame—and, with each new copy, sediment the objects' forgottenness. Though occluded from view, these exclusions abide, in any case, within the unseen frame of the blind spot in the spectatorial field of vision. Out of sight, what photographs omit from their view is easily forgotten, but forgotten, to twist an old saying, ain't gone. "Disappearance," in other words, "is not absence," as Fred Moten reminds us.[7] Rather, photography is subtended by an "optical unconscious," a sense of the world "only partially perceived."[8] This optical unconscious, as Shawn Michelle Smith has written, carefully parsing Sigmund Freud, Benjamin, and Rosalind Krauss, holds "the revelation of an unseen world that photography does not fully disclose, but makes us aware of in its invisibility."[9]

Smith's *At the Edge of Sight: Photography and the Unseen* explores the revelatory limits of photographic vision—the "unseen" to Hartman and Wilderson's "position of the unthought"—superbly.[10] While the significance of Smith's study to photojournalism especially is not to be underestimated, I want to posit a corresponding and contrapuntal "aural unconscious" at photography's ground. By photography's "aural unconscious" I do not mean to imply a living subliminality inherent to the mechanical or digital processes of picture-making, as if camera, print, or production possessed a psychic life apart (though, on second thought, these processes very well may). Instead, I mean a metaphorical domain where the sounds formerly adhering to, or otherwise called up by, the photographic event—before the objective possibility of sensorial distinction from vision—are archived for those with ears to hear. Few photographic subjects call us back to the undifferentiated event as forcefully—or loudly—as Martin Luther King Jr. The picture of him atop the steps of the Lincoln Memorial in 1957 (figure 6.2) is a resounding case in point.

A Paul Schutzer photograph taken for *Life* magazine on the occasion of the third anniversary of the 1954 *Brown v. Board of Education* ruling portrays King speaking from the identical location where, six years on, "I Have a Dream" would inspire the nation. Demonstratively holding forth before an audience estimated at fifteen thousand, King's oration, "Give Us the Ballot," sang, the near-silhouette outline of his clerical robe situating him symbolically between judge and priest on the monument's steps. His would-be anonymity, the suggestion of a posterior view obscuring his face, and especially his black sleeves draped open at the ends of two widespread arms, also invite consideration of an apparitional subjectivity for King, whose death is not so much prefigured by the spectral intimation as, for us, already past. For the contemporary viewer, Schutzer's picture realizes a version of spirit photography ex post facto which, quite unlike a postmortem portrait (to which it might otherwise be compared, in this context), presumes to capture the likeness of one only partially lost to her survivors. Though dead, she remains ethereally alive. Interpreted this way, Schutzer's subject is less the historical personhood of King; it is more the afterlife of the sound of civil rights oratory and the unseen dangers posed to its insurgent possibilities.

Shot from an angle at which King could never see himself, Schutzer's photograph images the young preacher's mortal exposure to the threat of a panoptic power at once precise and covert enough to summarily silence him. The angle is predatory. Willed or inadvertent, it effects a simulation of the violent threat, affirming that Susan Sontag's theory of picture-taking was not overblown when she averred that the photographer commits "a sublimated murder" or "soft murder" in the act.[11] In Schutzer, one sees a vision of murder even less qualified than the "sublimated" and "soft" strains theorized by Sontag. The murder that is to come, when the twenty-eight-year-old has turned thirty-nine, we see lurking in *the look* the photograph also frames as it looks on its proper subject. Caught as he was in the crosshairs of countless

6.2 Rev. Dr. Martin Luther King Jr. at the Prayer Pilgrimage for Freedom, Lincoln Memorial, Washington, DC, 1957. Photo by Paul Schuzter.

cameras trained on him at podiums significant and small, it seems King was always already a dead man—silenced already—under the photojournalist's gaze. This is the message Schutzer's reimagined spirit photograph allows the serious student of the black visual archive looking back.

Said another way, I maintain that in the visual archive of King's career, the heuristic of Schutzer's *Life* photograph suggests the shadow-threat of King's coming assassination whenever he appears standing, unprotected, in the agora to prophesy against national sins. This is not the fantasy of death that Benedict Anderson showed "the magic of nationalism" as relying on for its affective power in transforming violent or accidental death into a luminous act of state sacrifice and sanctification.[12] It is the threat of a death that is terrible because it is afforded no meaning at all. It is tragically banal. And predictably premature. Symptomatically, the camerawork that casts King visually as an oratorical or sounding subject simultaneously conceals and enforces an amnesic disregard of the grave dangers of still photography's repressive designs on speech and sound. The menace of death in the optical unconscious of King's visual oratory is thus compulsively overlooked—because what is hidden from direct view, what the photographic act has precluded the curious from hearing, are the range of violent intimations pictures of King labor to bury and keep contained in the unconscious.

Considered from the distance of many decades, this archive of visual oratory misremembers, then, precisely what it purports to preserve to public history. The objects in it bear false witness to the photographic event they pretend to faithfully record with a romantic, rose-colored screen of abstracted moralisms; after King's murder, the work of photojournalism at midcentury could no longer paper over the clear and present danger of death. Undeniably, the viewfinder and rifle scope patterned an identical look on him, the common aim of which it could be said was the capture, dead or alive, of his insurgent voice. Only the relative intensities of their sonic levels of activity—the shutter's click as compared to the rifle's blast—separated the "soft" shooters from the viler treachery of the louder ones. To get to hear a photograph of King orating, therefore, is not only to be called back to the sound of public address in his unique voice, or to install oneself squarely within the borders of the social, natural, or mechanical soundscape surrounding him, but to turn one's sensitivities toward the aural conditions of threat that marked his speech-making from the first.

To be sure, photography's aural underside is not new to visual thought. Slavoj Žižek has maintained that "between the visual and auditory dimensions" lies an abiding "tension" productive of a reciprocity according to which voice and gaze each exist as the condition of the other's possibility.[13] To Žižek's thinking, voice functions "as the [Lacanian] *objet a* of the visual." "Voice does not simply persist at a different level with regard to what we see," he explained; "it rather points to a gap in the field of the visible. . . . Ultimately, *we hear things because we cannot see everything.*"[14] To the extent that photography distinguishes itself from film and video by its avowed commitment to pure visuality (to say nothing of the resolute stillness it relishes as another essential difference), it is consummately deaf to its own "voice"—to "the fleshless and boneless entity" that is "beyond the voice," as Mladen Dolar writes.[15] This *"silent sound, [or] soundless voice"* sensed aurally before it is ever auditory, Dolar calls thought's "object voice," after Lacan.[16] Dull of hearing its object voice, photography on the whole has been resigned to a conception of itself as voiceless when it is only mostly inaudible, conditioned by certain misapprehensions of not hearing itself speak audibly as film and video do. True enough, photography does not literally resonify its subject(s) like those other forms of media, but it can make us hear the "soundless voice" in the visual environment viewers see in its frames.

Photography's practiced oblivion to the object voice has likely made those of us who study visual culture hard of hearing, critically tone-deaf to the sounds photography-as-mnemonic-technology portrays.[17] Yet this near-deafness only encumbers hearing to the ear straining for reception. It doesn't forestall hearing at eye level. We need only consider the sensory affordances of the hard of hearing in everyday life to discern the difference between otological and ocular auralities. Brenda J. Brueggemann's "On (Almost) Passing," a first-person essay about living and working between hearing and deafness, is a useful aid in this. In attempting to pass for a hearing person as a young researcher of deaf student writing culture at Gallaudet University, Brueggemann "spent a good deal of time," her essay notes, "*watching*—an act for which I had, as a hard of hearing person, lifelong experience and impeccable credentials."[18] Not completely deaf, but not hearing enough on the other hand, Brueggemann went about watching compensatorily, "watching myself, watching the students I was doing case studies of, watching everything in the ethnographic scene of Gallaudet Deaf culture before me. I kept seeing myself in and through many of the students I worked with. . . . They were the mirror in my ears."[19] The epiphanic power of so much "watching" as an object aurality in Brueggemann ("*They were the mirror in my ears*") suggests an aural dimension to the insistence by photographic theorist Ariella Azoulay that "photographs [should be] *watched*, not looked at."[20] To surface the sound of the photograph, in other words, we have but to "watch" more attentively. The silent sound and the soundless voice of the visual archive of King performing public speech-making, like that captured by Schutzer, are there to be heard in the mirror in our ears.

Considering that so little has been contemplated about King's life and career in pictures relative to the aural unconscious in photographic practice and discourse, it seems safe to say that the "fullest possibility" of what King sounded like has yet to be heard or imagined, despite countless recordings by corporate and independent labels (e.g., Creed, Gordy, Atlantic, Dooto), and amateur audiophiles taping King's speeches from the crowd.[21] Pictures of King holding forth on the national mall in 1957, say, or inspiring jubilation at a mass rally in Memphis on the eve of his assassination in 1968 (figure 6.4), contain a repression of sounds both oratorical and environmental that have gone unheard in historical reflection. With amplification technology and public-address apparatus in plain view, these images depict nothing less than the phonic anteriority of (black) voice on their face, all this equipment standing in for a muted but still dynamic sonority prior to, and productive of, King's visual capture on camera.

More than coincidental details, the daises, polished-wood pulpits, and hard-metal microphones commonly staging King's public life in pictures hint at this repressed remainder buried behind (or somewhere very deep within) every image made of King preaching or performing speech-making. The amplification apparatus, especially, so wholly naturalized within the scene of speech and performance that it mostly passes unseen, has the effect of deafening the spectator's view to the sounds helping achieve the picture's robust visuality as an object of sight uniquely. Amplification may have redoubled the volume or intensified the tone of King's voice in real time in Washington and Memphis, but it also dampened the sounds of threat emitted by cameras, recorders, timers, and triggers only those of us "watching" are likely to hear under its loudness. It appears King himself was "watching" as he spoke in Memphis. Though the Promised Land may have been glimpsed there, its prospect did not diminish the sounds of terrors on the ground. Nowhere was King's faculty to hear into the scene surrounding him in greater evidence than in Memphis.

Watching and Waiting: Memphis

"I've looked over, and I've seen the Promised Land" brings to near-conclusion King's April 3, 1968, address at historic Mason Temple Church of God in Christ on the eve of his assassination. "It doesn't matter with me now," he preached. "'Cause I've been to the mountaintop. And I've looked over. And I s-e-e-e-e-n the Promised Land." An intensely cooperative production between speaker and audience, King's last address was electric. The energy his voice stirred among the hundreds who braved the inclement weather to hear him almost certainly equaled "the power and the glory" Baldwin said he "sometimes felt" as a child preacher

> when, in the middle of a sermon, I knew that I was somehow, by some miracle, really carrying, as they said, "the Word"—when the church and I were one. Their pain and their joy were mine, and mine were theirs—they surrendered their pain and joy to me, I surrendered mine to them—and their cries of "Amen!" and "Hallelujah!" and "Yes, Lord!" and "Praise His name!" and "Preach it, brother!" sustained and whipped on my solos until we all became equal.[22]

In "carrying, as they said, 'the Word,'" the young Baldwin seemed to approach a parturient experience preaching. The "miracle" of it lay in what Žižek refers to as "the spectral autonomy" of the word/Word from the body which "hollows him out, and in a sense speaks 'by itself,' through him."[23] Like young Baldwin, King bore words and sounds from the Mason Temple pulpit that many experienced not as *his* in the possessive sense, though they surely came "through him." His "heavy-chested 173 lbs.," in fact—the description *Time* magazine gave its 1963 Man of the Year[24]—seemed built for carrying (or nursing) the otherness of "I've Been to the Mountaintop" within (if not at) his breast, his preaching accruing a vague maternity to its production in this context that *Time*'s writers probably did not imagine. To say that King's very last public address, arguably his greatest, was brilliantly *delivered* at Mason Temple, then, is to imply unavoidably that the living, miscegenated sound of black hope, struggle, and resistance that came to be through him in that auratic place was no simple exercise of talent, but a strenuous act of creation out of the sound and sociality of black political yearning.

From Mason Temple's raised pulpit, King's voice thundered loud as the forbidding sky, threatening a storm, rumbling outdoors. Inside, his vibrato tones resounded to the rafters as "I've Been to the Mountaintop" acquired a "horrifying dimension of omnipresence and omnipotence," to repeat Žižek.[25] Rousing as the night was, though, "I've Been to the Mountaintop" almost didn't happen. King had come to Memphis for a third time in less than a month to shine a national light on a local labor struggle pitting the city government against 1,300 African American employees of the Memphis Department of Public Works. Their hazardous working conditions (recently killing two) and depressed wages and an official refusal by the mayor's office to accept their right to collective bargaining led the sanitation workers to a strike. In mid-March, as head of the SCLC, King flew to Memphis and addressed an overflow crowd of more than fifteen thousand in support of the local struggle. Ten days later, he returned to lead a march through downtown Memphis to City Hall. But the march took a violent turn. The death of sixteen-year-old Larry Payne, a black boy shot by Memphis police in the march melee, risked doing irreparable damage to the Memphis campaign. King's counselors advised against organizing a second march, but King was intent on proving that a nonviolent demonstration could succeed in Memphis. King's new anti-poverty crusade demanding jobs and economic justice in America was at stake.

Determined to redeem nonviolent direct-action protest, King arrived in Memphis again on April 3, more weary than unwavering this time. The trip from Atlanta had been taxing, to put it mildly. A bomb threat delayed King's flight inbound, and the forecast for the evening was foreboding. Still, King gave no thought to giving up plans for a mass rally hours later in anticipation of the next day's second-attempt march. Instead, he deputized his friend and staff lieutenant, Ralph Abernathy, to address the small crowd they expected in light of the gathering storm outside. King prepared to spend the night resting at the Lorraine Motel. But when word reached him there that more than three thousand sanitation workers and supporters had braved the weather to hear him, he had little choice but to make an appearance. In a short time, King arrived at Mason Temple. He entered the sanctuary to a standing ovation.

No longer on the hook for a political speech, Abernathy gave an introduction of King that was nearly twenty minutes long. Mounting Mason Temple's elevated rostrum, King began his address extemporaneously:

> I'm delighted to see each of you here tonight in spite of a storm warning. You reveal that you are determined (*Right*) to go on anyhow. (*Yeah, all right*) Something is happening in Memphis, something is happening in our world. And you know, if I were standing at the beginning of time with the possibility of taking a kind of general and panoramic view of the whole of human history up to now, and the Almighty said to me, "Martin Luther King, which age would you like to live in?" I would take my mental flight by Egypt (*Yeah*), and I would watch God's children in their magnificent trek from the dark dungeons of Egypt through, or rather, across the Red Sea, through the wilderness, on toward the Promised Land. And in spite of its magnificence, I wouldn't stop there. (*All right*)
>
> I would move on by Greece, and take my mind to Mount Olympus. And I would see Plato, Aristotle, Socrates, Euripides, and Aristophanes assembled around the Parthenon [*Applause*], and I would watch them around the Parthenon as they discussed the great and eternal issues of reality. But I wouldn't stop there. (*Oh yeah*)
>
> I would go on even to the great heyday of the Roman Empire (*Yes*), and I would see developments around there, through various emperors and leaders. But I wouldn't stop there. (*Keep on*)
>
> I would even come up to the day of the Renaissance and get a quick picture of all that the Renaissance did for the cultural and aesthetic life of man. But I wouldn't stop there. (*Yeah*)
>
> I would even go by the way that the man for whom I'm named had his habitat, and I would watch Martin Luther as he tacks his ninety-five theses on the door at the church of Wittenberg. But I wouldn't stop there. (*All right*) But I wouldn't stop there. (*Yeah*) [*Applause*]
>
> I would come on up even to 1863 and watch a vacillating president by the name of Abraham Lincoln finally come to the conclusion that he had to sign the Emancipation Proclamation. But I wouldn't stop there. (*Yeah*) [*Applause*][26]

King's survey of the great periods of Western civilization assumed a bird's-eye perspective much like the one he had standing behind the lectern.

Below him the excited assembly stood or sat gazing reverently upward at their oracle. All five feet six inches of the man must have seemed to hover sight-line high before the buzzing crowd as he assumed, in narration and physical standing, "a kind of general and panoramic view of the whole of human history *up to now*." This panoramic perspective was set against the panoptic power of the state and those lesser antagonists holding him in their camerical and ballistic sights since 1955. As much as he was in their view, they were, in effect, in his too.

In a way, it was the modernist design of the Mason Temple auditorium that created the conditions for an extemporaneous figuration of panoramic vision in King's measured opening ("if I were standing . . . with the possibility of taking a kind of general and panoramic view of the whole of human history"). The same is true of the speech's unrestrained, iconic closing ("I looked over and I *seeeen* the Promised Land!"). By this I mean that the mountaintop was not so much called up whole cloth out of King's capacious imagination as it was *inspired* by the vista of the glinting multitude seen from his perch on the preaching platform. As "no other church or hall available to King was close to the size of Mason Temple,"[27] it was uniquely suited to panorama. Its raised rostrum and lectern guaranteed the panoramic perspective structurally with a certain monumentality granted them by their elevation and prominently center-forward location in the main sanctuary. Put in design terms:

> The main seating area contains seating for approximately 5,000, arranged in rows of theater-type seating separated by aisles that radiate outward from the pulpit areas. . . .
>
> The raised rostrum for the Temple [sic] is placed nearly in the middle of the auditorium, with a full-width running balustrade of cast concrete to define its separation from the main seating area. The rostrum bows forward into the main seating area at center to accommodate the pulpit, with seating for Senior Bishops behind. Approximately 250 people may be seated in the immediate area of the pulpit.[28]

If, standing so tall and towering above his audience, King saw his supporters from this built mountaintop—saw their sociality below and around him—then he surely heard that sociality too. Between them—speaker and listeners—"a happy congruence" was realized, Keith Miller writes, as the audience "pushed him toward much greater eloquence than he normally achieved," a dynamic "possible only because of the close proximity of . . . fervent listeners to the speaker and . . . the wonderful acoustics of Mason Temple."[29]

As key as architecture was to the *visual/visible* inspiration and tropics enlivening "I've Been to the Mountaintop" to "much greater eloquence," it seems "H. Taylor," the figure credited for the 1945 Art Modern design of Mason Temple church, had an *acoustic* dream foremost in mind.[30] In "expanding the floor on both sides of the pulpit and . . . imaginatively wrapping a horseshoe-shaped balcony above the sides and back of the sanctuary,"[31] Taylor effected a worship space and experience at once compact and capacious. This meant that large numbers of people could be seated in relative proximity to the lectern, whereas the longitudinal orientation of many of the Gothic Revival sanctuaries popular in the United States since the turn of the century challenged clear hearing when larger crowds created a greater and greater distance between the pulpit and pews farthest away. As Miller noted, "King sometimes spoke in such sanctuaries," but "such audiences did not respond so dramatically to King, nor did he respond so dramatically to them."[32] Modern auditorium chairs furnished by the Americana Seating Company replaced traditional church pews in Mason Temple to seat more than pews typically permit and to arrange more seating "within a few score feet of the pulpit."[33] Miller is correct in this. Yet the proximity of so many to King in the Mason Temple pulpit was not all there was to the sonic ecology of the room where King made history in Memphis.

Just as the dozen or more microphones snaking their way up to the preaching lectern hinted at visually, Mason Temple was a densely wired environment in 1968. The modern auditorium conceived architecturally by Taylor and called for in 1940 by Bishop Charles H. Mason, the revered leader and founder of the Church of God in Christ, realized its modernity in sound to some extent. The whir of "four 48-inch ventilating fans" droning overhead may or may not have drowned out the mosquito-hiss of "45 four-light fluorescent fixtures on the ceiling of the main auditorium."[34] They were, in any case, among the several "electric modernisms"—new electrical technologies revolutionizing modern experience in the early and mid-twentieth century—that set Mason Temple apart.[35] Sound—namely, that low and continuous body of sound commonly introduced into the modern soundscape by a mechanization of production that R. Murray Schafer has figured as "the flat line in sound"[36]—was an essential feature of the temple's modern condition. With and against the low drone of electric modernism it boasted, King and congregation radiated an insurgent "hum" of their own, no less electric in affect. Their hum carried "the distinctive pitch of African American participant proclamation" theorized by Evans Crawford, the late Howard theologian.[37] At Mason Temple, the hum-pitch of black participant proclamation commingled with what church leaders boasted as "the finest public address system available at the time" to effect a haptic experience of black proclamation and protest.[38] This sounding, however, was no simple chorus of controlled antiphony voiced between speaker and audience. Instead it approached a fantasia of speech and feeling, call and response, tones and tempos, shouts, shrieks, silences, moans, cries, and other unregulated intensities betraying complicated, even shifting, modes of black oratory and audition. The acoustic ecology of Mason Temple—the peculiarities of architectural design, audience, and, finally, the weather—had everything to do with the affective electricity conducted through and by King's last stand in Memphis.

The Preacher King's Footing

With his attention turned to Puritan preaching practices in the early US republic, literary scholar Michael Warner, playing on a key category of interactional communications analysis known as "footing," refers to the complex performative dynamics of address and engaged audition in the Protestant preaching tradition as "the preacher's footing."[39] Warner's focus on the habitually unheard subtleties of sound and sociality in early Protestant preaching helps amplify pictures of King delivering "I've Been to the Mountaintop." While King's stature in the Mason Temple pulpit afforded him an apex view of the beloved community of peace and justice glimpsed in the flesh, his *footing*, on the other hand, charged the sonic environment inside Mason Temple with an electric feeling even as the weather outside theatricalized the moment. In Warner's words, audience "byplay . . . back-channel participation, turn-taking,"[40] and other barely audible testimonies to involved hearing buzzed under thunderclaps and whistling winds to intensify the ensemblic surround engendered by the sound-making registrations of congregational copresence alongside King. An extension of the exorbitances of speech and speech-making I call by the shorthand "King's vibrato," this noisiness, much as it goaded King to an ever greater eloquence, also remonstrated with King against the "total climate" of Southern terrors and racism that Christina Sharpe refers to, with an even terser shorthand, as "the weather."[41] In calling for scattered thunderstorms and "southerly winds 6 to 14 miles an hour,"[42] the Environmental Science Services Administration's April 3, 1968, meteorological forecast for Memphis and vicinity seemed to foretell a turbulence within the social milieu of the mid- and Deep South as well.

In the not-quite-figurative sense proposed by Sharpe, "the weather is the totality of our environments." It is "the total climate; and that climate is antiblack."⁴³ In Memphis, the jolting sound of open window shutters crashing closed by gusts of wind intruded upon the night's proceedings, startling King repeatedly with the sonic specter of gunfire or explosives. A Civil Defense siren warned of the approach of a tornado touching down thirty-five miles to the northeast. The tornado in small-town Atoka, which would kill two that evening, and the thunderstorms in Memphis repeated the violent antiblack weather that was everyday in the city in 1968.⁴⁴ Against the symbolism and sound of this gale-force fury, King and the whole congregation of sanitation workers and sympathizers around him answered back in phonic refusal of the climatic terms of order. Together, their sonant fantasia of talk, dark tones, and the lower frequencies of black political desire noised a magnificent counterclaim against the virulence of the weather in Memphis and other parts South that had been made to seem, like strong winds and torrential rain, manifestly natural. The ground rumbled protest at the sky as King and company sounded a competing vision: the righteous will to justice as the very "coming of the Lord."⁴⁵

Arm's Length: Oratory, Statuary, Photography

Everybody knows that when individuals in the presence of others respond to events, their glances, looks, and postural shifts carry all kinds of implications and meaning.
Erving Goffman, Forms of Talk (1981)

If "the preacher's footing," with its conceptual roots in Erving Goffman's 1981 sociolinguistic study *Forms of Talk*, seems a well-suited hermeneutic for bringing to light the social logic of what we might think of as the picturability of radical democratic audition and speech in the King archive, this is not to preclude Warner's image-idea from going beyond historical communications analysis (back) to render visual its suggestiveness. In other words, we might easily extend "the preacher's footing" in King's case from the habitually unheard subtleties of sound and sociality to the power of any number of images of King to elicit spectatorial hearing. Given the extraordinary design of the Mason Temple sanctuary, to contemplate the preacher's footing spectatorially in this precise setting is also, first of all, to notice the preacher's pose, physical stance, corporeal attitude, stature, and rise. To attend to the preacher's footing in *this* context, Warner's focus notwithstanding, is to observe King "cutting a figure" visually, a self-sculpted

6.3 Interior of Mason Temple Church of God in Christ, Memphis, TN, 1968. Memphis and Shelby County Room, Memphis Public Library Information Center. Photo by H. A. Hooks.

cast of black oratorical terribleness angrier than the weather and more halting than rifle fire.

Differently put, inasmuch as one may *hear* in the rhetorical or tonal changes of a speaker's voice a discernible shift in the social footing of said speaker relative to an audience, as Warner points out, one *sees* in photographs and video footage of King at Mason Temple the preacher-orator "cutting a proverbial figure," to borrow a trope from art historian Richard Powell.[46] In "cutting a figure," he "enters an entirely different realm" and, like the black subject in art, metamorphoses from physical body to metaphysical being.[47] King's pulpit footing is sure: a stiffening, statue muscularity born of a tensive excitement in the oratorical body and giving rise to a fiery physicality in his performance. A concentrated bodilyness, vaguely sculptural and seen over and over again in the photo archives of King's career, gave visual aid to the voicing of black insurgent hope and resistance. Although many photojournalists over the years seem to have found King's active preaching

6.4 Rev. Dr. Martin Luther King Jr. at Mason Temple Church of God in Christ, Memphis, TN, 1968. Photo by Vernon Matthews.

and speech-making photogenic (as if they, too, like DeCarava, were seeing a picturable sound), a somewhat earlier image of King at Mason Temple (figure 6.4), most likely made by staff photographer Vernon Matthews for Memphis daily *The Commercial Appeal*, exemplifies King's bodily reflex to gestural eloquence and oratorical self-fashioning in vivid profile.

"I've Been to the Mountaintop" was only King's last address at Mason Temple; it was not his first. Two weeks before his final, fateful appearance, he stood in front of thirteen thousand there openly declaring his resolve to support Memphis's striking sanitation workers and committing the SCLC's financial resources to their struggle.[48] His March 18, 1968, speech, "All Labor Has Dignity," was predictably poignant and intrepid. In his signature anaphoral style, King struck a ferocious tone:

> And so we assemble here tonight, and you have assembled for more than thirty days now to say, "We are tired. We are tired of being at the bottom. [*Yes*] We are tired of being trampled over by the iron feet of oppression. We are tired of our children having to attend overcrowded, inferior, quality-less schools. [*Applause*] We are tired of having to live in

dilapidated, substandard housing conditions [*Applause*] where we don't have wall-to-wall carpet but so often we end up with wall-to-wall rats and roaches. [*Applause and cheers*] We are tired. Of smothering in an airtight cage of poverty in the midst of an affluent society. We are tired of walking the streets in search for jobs that do not exist. [*Applause*] We are tired of working our hands off and laboring every day and not even making a wage adequate enough to get the basic necessities of life. [*Applause*] We are tired of our men being emasculated so that our wives and our daughters have to go out and work in the white lady's kitchen, [*Applause*] leaving us unable to be with our children and give them the time and the attention that they need. We are tired." [*Cheers*]

So, in Memphis we have begun. We are saying, "*Now is the time.*" Get the word across for everybody in power in this time in this town, that now is the time to make real the promises of democracy. Now is the time [*Applause*] to make an adequate income a reality for all of God's children. Now is the time [*Applause*] for city hall to take a position for that which is just and honest. Now is the time [*Applause*] for justice to roll down like water and righteousness like a mighty stream! *Now is the time.* [*Cheers*][49]

Overshadowed by the incantatory power of the Promised Land peroration of "I've Been to the Mountaintop" that was to come days later, "All Labor Has Dignity" has gone mostly neglected by King experts and movement historians.[50] As a result, King has been spared the severer critique of the manifestly middle-class and chauvinistic sensibilities betrayed by his speech; we who ardently oppose his legacy's violent misappropriation by corporate interests and erstwhile enemies prefer to emphasize the more radical strains in his oratory and preaching. The sad plight of black men "being emasculated" in consequence of "wives and . . . daughters hav[ing] to go out and work," leaving black children to their own unmothered care and social development, as well as King's later lament of the black worker's wages being too low to "take his wife out to dine," are certainly worth our pause inasmuch as these seem so much the symbolic strivings of bourgeois patriarchy and somewhat fly in the face of that racist and classist outrage against the city's indifference to black workers' occupational health and safety that brought him to Memphis in the first place. Critical as it is to call out the intransigent conservatisms that can, more often than we'd like to admit, adhere to insurgent black thought and praxis, I want to focus here on a conservatism of another type altogether: that inherent in the presumptions of typography and transcription to record the distributive, ensemblic sociality of black sound and performance in typescript. In other words, I am equally interested in what Moten paints as "the insistently unbridgeable gap separating the spoken word from any visual representation" and King's embodied gesturalism as a silent, if still somehow verbalizing, supplement to the "graphic-verbal presentation" of King and his congregation on the page.[51]

The printed text of "All Labor Has Dignity" is exemplary of the limitations of typographical and grammatical systematicity in representing King's transcribed speeches. Michael Honey's collection of previously unavailable King speeches taking up the labor question is a significant medium for seeing King's life and work in the broader light of American economic history and the prospect of a social revolution engendering economic transformation, including the relationship of American workers to their labor; but, like all efforts to transcribe an epiphenomenon, "All Labor Has Dignity" can only hint at the listening experience afforded by tape. In his "Editor's Note," after offering a meticulous outline of the editorial protocols observed in producing "what we think are the most accurate and complete versions of [King's] speeches" on labor, Honey himself owns that, for all his "careful listening to audio versions" of the collected speeches, "reading and hearing King's speeches are two different experiences."[52] For the most part, Honey's texts of King's labor orations prioritize the typed version of those speeches as King originally wrote them, leaving the attentive editor to log King's departures from his manuscripts in the collection's appendix.[53] Earlier in this book, I likened King's relationship to his lectern manuscripts to that existing between the early gospel composers and the print matter of the gospel score. I did so to explain the inevitability of these variances between the original typed text and what a careful researcher like Honey hears on tape. Honey's confidence in assembling "the most accurate and complete versions of [King's] speeches" on labor is, thus, a confession also, an implied acknowledgment that "the *most* accurate and complete" transcription of King's thoughts on the labor question (which may not have been actually spoken, only written) is a fundamentally comparative judgment and, realistically, the best one can aspire to. The hope of a singularly "accurate and complete" inscription of King's speech-making is always already a dashed one, therefore—as impossible as an "accurate and complete" performance of "Take My Hand, Precious Lord" or other gospel standard. To black modernist sensibilities, improvisation was de rigueur.[54]

Just as a proper editing of King's speeches is ineffectual to authoritatively accommodate King's improvisations to the page, so too are the typographical features available to the transcriptionist of the public speech event to faithfully convey "how King's inflections and the crowds' responses make his speeches come alive."[55] This Honey readily admits. "For [this] reason we include with this book audio from two of King's speeches."[56] Despite this avowal of the inherent disability of print to give a faithful representation of the paralingual expressivities of the speech-making event, the effort to reproduce what he has heard in the audio record is a strong one on Honey's part. Although parentheses surround text "that existed in the original document,"[57] for example, Honey marshals them to also enclose the reactive and proactive interjections of King's audience symbolically. At best, the aural interpolations on the sonic event are acknowledged as part of the sonic event, but "(Yes)," "(Applause)," and "(Cheers)," for example, no more convey the aurality of the audience's exuberance than the original text does King's inflections. They are merely signifiers of *the idea* of sound in the general sense, visual proxies for a general sonic supplement graphically unrepresentable (except, perhaps, by poetic suggestion). Try as anyone might, King's speeches at Mason Temple lie "beyond transcription," following Moten, in their exorbitant sonancy.[58] In Matthews's photograph, a not-so-subtle display of oratorical theater on King's part gestures to the very pitch and timbre of sounds that typescript words and their glyphic auxiliaries are generally impotent to approach. In Matthews, that is, King's inflections achieve aurality visually in the physical gesture of *adlocutio*.

Matthews's capture of visual oratory for Memphis's *Commercial Appeal* readers (figure 6.4) represents the sound of the photograph in and as a vigorous platform physicality. King's outstretched arm corporealizes that "radical movement" Moten discusses, which "rend[s] . . . the opposition of aurality and spatiality," thus raising "the question of the gestural" as an aural potentiality as well.[59] Seen from Moten's vantage point, gesture as "that which matches or even exceeds verbal assertion through spacing, position, or . . . visual-graphic architectonics" is the visual trace of an aural unconscious subtending Matthews's image.[60] Since spoken words "are never independent of gesture," nor is gesture "given priority over the words-as-sound," Moten avows, King's declamatory gesturing in Matthews would seem the very picture of the deadened sound of transcribed typographical speech come back to life again, "radically reconnected to their essential sonic performance by eccentric physical action."[61] The gesture, then, belongs equally as much to the sound of the photograph, to the "hum" of black haptic sociality, as to the optical unconscious of the picture where the gesture's invisibility to the viewer *as a gesture*, not a pose, is installed.

While the "eccentric physical action" Moten imagines as bringing words back to their sonic remembering appears to stress the lingual, labial, or, more broadly, oral physical distortion—a trill, a glissando, a *vibrato* disarticulating words as "mere vessel[s] of meaning"—I want to posit the gesturalism secreted in the pose of *adlocutio* as King's "eccentric" action.[62] Pictured in a chancel-space crowded with strike leaders, security detail, local clergy, and reporters, King extended his right arm in front of him in what Matthews and the other photojournalists present must have regarded as a gesture classical enough to "speak for itself" with art-literate readers. To wit, the rising arc of King's arm extended head-high over the lectern repeated a likeness and form idealized in ancient Roman statuary—specifically, the figure classicist Glenys Davies maintains "was understood to represent the elite of Roman society performing their most prized activity: oratory."[63]

According to Davies, orators of old depended on a keen awareness of corporeality and physical complements to vocal communication—facial expressions, arm and hand gestures, and footing, among them—to achieve effective *pronuntiatio* and *actio*, expression and delivery. Indeed, "effective use of body language and gesture," Davies asserts, "could be said to count . . . as one of [the orators'] professional skills."[64] Perhaps nothing signifies the gestural accompaniment in classical oratorical performance more concretely than classical-era togate statuary and its convention for depicting the model Roman citizen as a public orator. Within the statuary arts, the paradigmatic representation of the gesturalism of classical oratory is *The Orator*, a life-size bronze togate currently housed in the National Archaeological Museum in Florence. Likely created in the late second century, *The Orator* is distinguished by what Davies observes as its "most immediately noticeable feature," which is "the commanding gesture of the right arm, raised at the shoulder and held out in front of him with the open-palmed hand on a level with his head."[65] In this reaching gesture, a "rhetorical thrust" obtains.[66] Matthews's photograph mimics the gestural aesthetic of "the Orator"—arm extended, mouth agape, hand unfurling a heightened intensity of speech. With dramatic visual force, the commanding expressiveness of King's outstretched hand, like his reaching arm, points at that in *the camera's* field of vision (as if breaking the photograph's fourth wall), which Lacan posited as "the threshold of the visible world."[67] This time-space is almost touched (or, as Spillers might say, "handed"[68]) by King at the left-most limit of the frame, where visuality is cut off from the beyond of the sonic field his hand appears determined to (re)join.

Whereas the photographer of visual oratory may aspire to render the sound he sees monumental, frozen in historical time, the photograph itself, I want to argue, aspires not to monumentality but to motion, to gestural freedom from the essential stillness of its own ontology. It thus aspires to sound as a re-sounding of auralities both formal and fugitive. This desire to gestural freedom is the inheritance of visual oratory, which follows the form of statues like *The Orator*. Dozens of public statues honoring King—such as those that stand in Austin, Texas; Binghamton, New York; Milwaukee, Wisconsin; Roanoke, Virginia; Long Beach, California; Houston, Texas; Atlanta, Georgia; and Westminster, England—cast King in this classical vocabulary. They install King's memory in the African American pantheon as a speaking subject above all else—*a voice* intent upon sound as it labors against the "power that paralyses" in modern images, as Giorgio Agamben has put it.[69] Like the photograph, the statue is subject to "a kind of *ligatio*," Agamben explains, "whose spell needs to be broken" if the inherent "*dynamis*" of the gesture is to be unbound. In "Notes on Gesture," he writes, "It is as if, from the whole history of art, a mute invocation were raised towards the freeing of the image in the gesture. This much is expressed in those Greek legends about statues breaking the fetters that contain them and beginning to move."[70] However, it seems to me that it is not motion for its own sake that is the end of the togate statue's will to "break free"; rather, it makes this "mute invocation" for the sake of sound.

It is not clear if Agamben is ascribing this silent supplication to "the whole history of art" ("It is as if, *from the whole history of art*, a mute invocation were raised") or to the form of the sculptural subjects "breaking the fetters that contain them" in Greek legend. But he is keen to recognize, in any case, a negative aurality in the visual conditions of gesture obtaining to still images and statues. He is keen to note sound adjourned from the precise time-space where invocation is listened for, where it is seemingly mute. And yet despite this aural sensitivity to the visual work that would be free to move, Agamben's sense of the muteness of visual art form mistakes *his own conditioned hardness of hearing* for the disability of statuary to project sound. Unlike Žižek, for example, Agamben does not appear to *see* the sound of the visual. He misses, owing to a ruse of the unmoving materiality of sculpture, the sonic activity at "the lower ranges of intensities generated by images" and image-objects "assumed to be mute," as Tina Campt has taught us. "While it may seem an inherent contradiction in terms," Campt writes, "sound need not be heard [with the ear] to be perceived. Sound can be listened to, and, in equally powerful ways, sound can be felt: it both touches and moves people."[71] This haptic capacity for sound in the visual object, which Agamben evidently overlooks in imagining the invocatory representation in "Notes on Gesture" as "mute" rather than muted, was not lost to Matthews. The "felt sound" of the photograph, expressed on the lower frequencies of perception ("below 20 Hz"[72]), may well escape the one who sees only the pose of the orator/*The Orator* in it. The one attuned to the gesture, by contrast—that is, to the still image liberated from its "mythical fixity" in the appearance of an unblurred pose—cannot fail to discern the motion from within which Matthews extracted the frozen moment in view. On tape, King amplified the haptic sound of the motor gesture, as if to corroborate its inaudible hapticality "in and as vibration,"[73] in a low, groaning vibrato-speak. He made his physical gesturing at Mason Temple "visible," in other words, with his "gesturing" voice.

The Vibrato Problem

While the jeremiadic content of "All Labor Has Dignity," "I've Been to the Mountaintop," and dozens more of King's remembered speeches and sermons constitutes the major part of the dream-wish of still images to be heard, King's vibrato is the "minor gesture" moving the major speeches below verbal discourse. That fugitive "force" set loose within the authorized structure of thought, category, or event, "unmooring its structural integrity, problematizing its normative standards,"[74] the "minor gesture," Erin Manning explains, is the "continual variation on experience. . . . Its rhythms are not controlled by a preexisting structure, but open to flux. . . . It thus gets cast aside, overlooked, and forgotten in the interplay of major chords. . . . It does not have the full force of a preexisting status, of a given structure, of a predetermined metric, to keep it alive. It is out of time, untimely, rhythmically inventing its own pulse."[75] The context for Manning's theorization of the minor gesture is disability studies, particularly the political and new epistemological potentialities within autistic perception and motor diversity (i.e., new ways of understanding how bodies move, often by way of a discrete gesturalism, in and through spaces designed to support major or neurotypical acts and bodily experience). But the vibrato seems as much a minor gesture in King's speech-making vocally as it is in the bodily excitements of autistic enthusiasm similarly "attuned to, and in excess of, the articulation of words."[76] Not surprisingly, Manning scarcely approaches the minor gesture in nonmusicological terms. The minor gesture, for instance, is coterminous with the "minor key" in Manning.[77] Alternately rhythmic and arrhythmic, it provokes "a shift in [the] tone" of major norms and their presumptions.[78] Generative of "resonance" here and "dissonance" there, the minor gesture "is the force that makes the lines tremble" in everyday experience.[79]

Musically, of course, the vibrato "makes the cultural field tremulous" in a baldly literal way.[80] Not unlike the physicality of autistic perception in Manning (though perhaps not fungible intensities either), the vibrato, too, stands to open up "the everyday to degrees and shades of experience that resist [major] formations [of normative being-in-the-world] long enough to allow us to see the potential of worlds in the making."[81] As all minor gestures do, the vibrato accomplishes this also by moving "the nonconscious toward the conscious, mak[ing] felt the unsayable in the said, bring[ing] into resonance field effects otherwise backgrounded in experience."[82] Alive in the aural unconscious, the minor *vocal* gesture carries the major along without credit, "work[ing] the major from within,"[83] haunting it with the tremulous suggestion of an imminent inbreaking or an outbreak of radical possibility already roiling.

As a musical gesture, the vibrato has rarely been approached as anything other than a kind of irreducible stylistic adornment to plain, monochromatic expressions of musicality. Almost entirely neglected in its phenomenological aspect, it has gotten only the merest attention as an aesthetic distinctive in modern musicological literature—with two very notable, closely connected exceptions. In 1932 and 1936, the University of Iowa published two volumes—one in each of the two years—of scholarly research on the vibrato under the general title *University of Iowa Studies: Studies in the Psychology of Music*. Both volumes were edited by Carl E. Seashore, head of the Department of Psychology and dean of Iowa's Graduate School. Seashore's two volumes gave the lie to the vibrato's self-evident and irreducible function in music theory and practice. Writes Seashore in the introduction to volume one, subtitled *The Vibrato*:

> The subject is somewhat unique in the literature of the psychology of music in that, although it is one of the central problems in music both in theory and practice and is one of the most fascinating and profitable psychological approaches to the study of expression of emotion, the field remained practically untouched by experiment until the problem was taken up in our laboratory. It is also a somewhat unique situation that for a decade or more we have been able to coordinate a continuous series of experiments within this field as to cover it systematically, establishing adequate techniques for measurements, outlining a fundamental series of hypotheses, and progressively organizing data in a cumulative way.[84]

True to form given modernism's vital commitments to scientific and technological transformation and discourse, Professor Seashore's approach to the vibrato within the psychology of music was intensely empirical. As "a problem for the laboratory," the vibrato passed through "experiments," "measurements," and "hypotheses" in Seashore's study, subjecting it to modern scientific investigation based upon the Iowa School's supposition that the vibrato, like all "expressions of emotions," was an affective response to scientific realities, and thus predictably scientific in itself. But while this empirical approach to the psychologization of the vibrato as a vocal and instrumental practice was surely a modernist phenomenon—Seashore praised the new audiometers, tonoscopes, phonophotographic cameras, and piano cameras to the high heavens—it is the scientific construction of the vibrato as a problem for modernity that commands the greater space here where I explore the urgency of science to objectivize and subsume "vibrato" beneath its banner in the interwar years. For the question of "what the vibrato is and should be," as Seashore wrote in 1932, not only drove a search for "objective and verifiable definitions, analyses and principles" aimed at the establishment of "a scientific foundation for esthetic [sic] theory" and a "means of remedial and artistic training in the art of control of the vibrato,"[85] but in casting what we might call "the vibrato problem" this way, Seashore also betrayed extra-aesthetic interests. The "art of control of the vibrato," he insisted, "takes the [vibrato] problem from the realm of the hazy, misleading lingo of cults which have prevailed in [the] musical field, and simplifies, clarifies, and places the phenomenon under control."[86] Thus, insofar as the vibrato tacitly announces and sounds aloud a certain fugitive potential for speech and meaning beyond scientific legibility or "control," it is no wonder that Seashore and his Iowa colleague, Milton Metfessel, included attention to "primitive peoples, such as the uneducated Negro or the Indian" and "Negro vibratos," respectively, in their individual investigations for *University of Iowa Studies: Studies in the Psychology of Music*.[87] As a matter of insufficient "training," the vibrato problem, it seems, was continuous with the so-called Negro problem in America. The vibrato, too, needed tutoring in its freedoms.

From as early as the postbellum period through the modern civil rights era, the rhetorical shorthand of "the Negro problem" has strained to name an imagined defect in black character and culture responsible for the race's inability to properly assimilate into the American social body, black people being childishly fickle in their being or unformed in their racial development or, many claimed, inherently capricious. In a November 1884 article for *Atlantic Monthly*, Harvard scientist Nathanial S. Shaler concluded that consistent with his "animal nature," the Negro's "emotions are easily aroused through the stimulus of music or motion, and the tide of life that then fills him is free and unrestrained."[88] This vim that "fills him" might be "charming" in one respect, Shaler acknowledges, but it is "discontinuous" and "generally arises from the lack of consecutive will."[89] Later, Shaler suggested that the effort "to combine these millions of the African people in a social order to which inheritance has not accustomed them" was a concern for the sciences as much as for governance and legislation.[90] Although Shaler's 1890 "Science and the African Problem" called for a "systematic scientific effort" that posited a more capacious notion of science than its reducibility to the physical and life sciences, Shaler was nevertheless clear that "the class of work which the negro problem makes necessary" necessitated the proficiencies of "those who have been so disciplined by scientific methods that they can keep in its moderately safe ways."[91] He advocated for "a broad statistical view" by "all who are at once interested in the problem and can give anything better than words towards its solution."[92] Against the political motives mere words warn of, Shaler appealed to the empirical protocols of a patently modern anthropology for "the prospect of any happy solution of the [Negro] problem."[93] "It hardly need be said," he maintained, "that this study should be based upon a careful application of anthropometry to the peoples in both regions. Difficult as such an extensive work would be, it is quite within the limits of accomplishment, and would give more results than a 'polar expedition,' at a relatively trifling expense. Even a careful study of the crania secured in the two regions would, if the inquiry rested on a sufficiently large basis, give a beginning for the discussion."[94]

Going further, Shaler added, "The anthropological inquiry should not end with the study of the physical system [however]; it should be extended to the mental parts as well. It would be interesting to know, as we well might expect to from this investigation, whether the brain of the American African is larger than that of his African prototypes."[95] Crucially, he saw meticulous scientific observation as a control against, and clear contrast to, the excesses of primitives set free from white rule. Sexual wantonness and marital perfidy were particular worries of Shaler, signs of "the old waywardness" atavistically returned to the Negro in freedom. Against this troublesome fixation by Negro problem-solvers seeking a science of white supremacy and black social control, Shaler did not fail to wonder, anticipating the Iowa researchers, whether the Negro problem might in any case generate the lucky fortune of a (white) science of (black) musicality—as though the musicality of blacks was the likeliest attribute among the many undeveloped ones Shaler offered that stood to be improved by the (white) power of science. Shaler reckoned.

> There are reasons for believing that the negroes can readily be cultivated in certain departments of thought in which the emotions lend aid to labor; as, for instance, in music. There is hardly any doubt that they have a keener sense of rhythm than whites of the same intellectual grade—perhaps than of any grade whatever. The musical faculty is, perhaps, of all the so-called artistic powers, the easiest to measure in a precise way. Statistics could easily be gathered which would show whether or no [sic] this was a true racial capacity. The ability to determine the differences which are necessary to success in music can be ascertained with extreme accuracy and with tolerable ease. Yet I am not sure that any basis for comparison between the powers of the whites and of the blacks has ever been secured.[96]

A half-century on from "The Negro Problem" and "Science and the African Problem," Seashore and Metfessel followed Shaler's lead faithfully. Like Shaler, they were after a scienticity of black musical thought-practice and "racial capacity."

In his contribution to the 1936 volume, "The Vibrato in Voice and Instrument," Seashore repeated Metfessel's 1932 "The Vibrato in Artistic Voices" in his turn away from the universal to a particular concern with the vibrato among "Primitive peoples, such as the uneducated Negro or the Indian."[97] Just as Metfessel lingered over the Negro vibrato in a section of "The Vibrato in Artistic Voices" called "The Vibrato of Children and Untrained Adults," Seashore devoted significant space to closely analyzing the vibrato's affect in the black singing voice. Evidently, neither Seashore nor Metfessel could think "the vibrato problem" apart from "the Negro problem." Though they understood the vibrato to be "a vibrant palpitating thrill in the voice . . . an interesting, warming vocal quality . . . and a legitimate emotional wave present in freely flowing voices," they both worried for the vibrato's debasement into "a dangerous vice to be shunned, a vicious wavering . . . and a vulgarity."[98] Their common fear recapitulated Shaler's apprehensions concerning "the negro nature, charming in many respects," but also "weak" in keeping under check the sexual impulses, which he said "mark the limits between savage and civilized man."[99] We might even say that, to Seashore and Metfessel, the particular figure of "the uneducated Negro" was compelling because the vibrato in the Negro voice was the sound of the Negro problem itself, sounding the Negro problem not only as a social problem for the country

TABLE II
VIBRATO

I. Factors	II. Laws of vibrato, e.g.:
1. Pitch (Freq.)	1. Quality of emotion
(1) Absolute pitch	2. Musical feeling (talent)
(2) Extent oscillation	3. Æsthetic effect
(3) Rate oscillation	4. Spontaneity
(4) Form oscillation	5. Age
(5) Regularity	6. Training
(6) Duration of tone	7. Emotion real or feigned
2. Intensity	8. Criteria of worth
(1) Absolute intensity	9. Emotional stability
(2) Extent oscillation	10. Voice of instrument
(3) Rate oscillation	11. Personal traits
(4) Form oscillation	12. Primitive music
(5) Regularity	
(6) Duration of tone	

6.5 "Table II shows what factors we should have to deal with and the practical situations with reference to which we should desire to work out its laws, bearing in mind that the vibrato is a periodic pitch-intensity fluctuation of the voice or instrument." From Metfessel, *Phonophotography in Folk Music*, 10.

but as a "problem for thought," too, to repeat Nahum Chandler. In worrying the lines that normally isolate speech acts from musical expression and verbalization from mere vocality, the Negro vibrato as a challenge to the proper organizing of knowledge thus worried the Manichean logic of the modern racial idea itself. Seashore's readiness to propose an "art of control of the vibrato" betrayed then a prescriptive inclination on his part toward not just "what the vibrato is" but toward what it "should be" according to "esthetic norms."[100] Although unsaid, his will to set the terms of what the vibrato "should be" could only have been his anxious reaction to a prior worry about the deforming, irregulative, fugitive drive that he supposed constitutional to the "primitive" and "uneducated" black. Against this impulse in the incorrect, even vulgar, display of the Negro's vibrato, nothing less than a modern science and taxonomy would do to recapture the vibrato's "legitimate" vitality and regulate it (figure 6.5).

Importantly, in their scientizing attempt to tame the vibrato in black speech and song, Seashore and Metfessel called on two modern photographic technologies. By rigging a modified portable moving-picture camera together with a timing device and a small mirror all housed in a suitcase, Metfessel devised a "phono-photographic method" for recording voices in the field in such a way that he made possible the picture-taking of sound waves created by black vernacular singers and speakers: the machine, in other words, translated phonophotographic data into frequency charts. Metfessel's portable sound photography camera, or "phono-photograph camera," captured "the most delicate variations in pitch, variations which are often too subtle for the human ear to perceive," by graphical recording of sung or spoken sound on superspeed moving picture film.[101] The phonophotograph camera, we are told, "gives a picture of exactly what a voice or a musical instrument does."[102] Metfessel promoted his phonophotographic method as an alternative to conventional musical notation practices. Unlike the traditional notational system, the phonophotographic method permitted early ethnomusicology a new capacity for representing the "elusive facts" of black sound inhering in the "queer pranks of [Negro] voices,"[103] as he put it. The "subtle embellishment[s] of grace-notes, turns and quavers, and the delightful little upward break in the voice" as well as the "turns, twists, and intonations not represented by any musical term" demanded analysis, Metfessel maintained.[104] A scientific modernist, he refused that bewilderment of others in their conclusion that specific subtleties of black voice were finally "indescribable" extraverbal fugitivities from established musicological knowledge and classification.[105] Phonophotography, he believed, answered the problem of the black voice.

Although Metfessel did not disagree with his contemporaries who held that any reliable analysis of black voice and speech depended on the researcher's direct hearing of the black sounds, he nevertheless proposed that the visual supplementarity of phonophotography afforded more sophisticated scrutiny of the continuum of vocal sounds obtaining between plain black talk and the sibylline tones of black musicality.[106] By way of the phonophotographic method, researchers might double as seers of sound, he reasoned, including and especially seers of the fluctuating pitch and intensity that brought vibrato into being. Together Metfessel and Seashore produced a series of phonophotographic pictures to demonstrate the technology's promise for the capture of black voices for science. Working in North Carolina and Virginia in the fall of 1925, Metfessel and Seashore marshaled their new device specifically to the visual charting of black song, black laughter, and the black field hand's holler. Their studies materialized the vibrato by etching sound waves themselves onto paper. The vibrato was thus made a property of the photograph as the new science and its jury-rigged technology recast the tensions of the Negro problem (i.e., those obtaining to integration, black

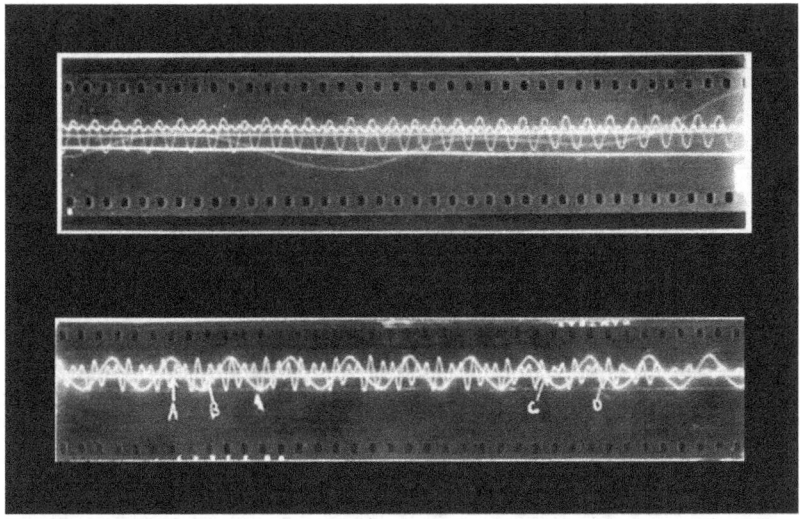

6.6 An example of Milton Metfessel's vocal phonophotography, circa 1920. Feaster, "Pictures of Sound" (2011), 0:30:24.

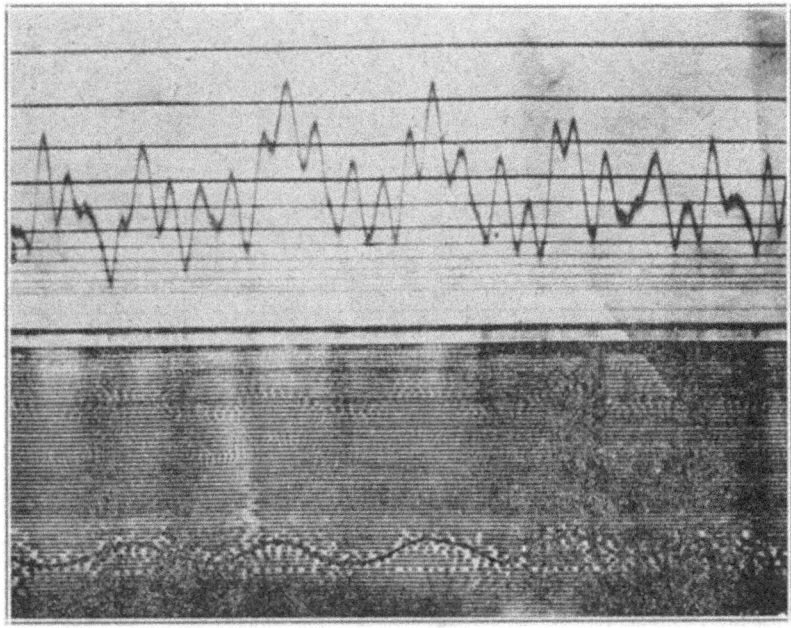

6.7 Phonophotogram: upper curve measures vibrato intensity; lower curve measures pitch. Tiffen, "Phonophotograph Apparatus," 119.

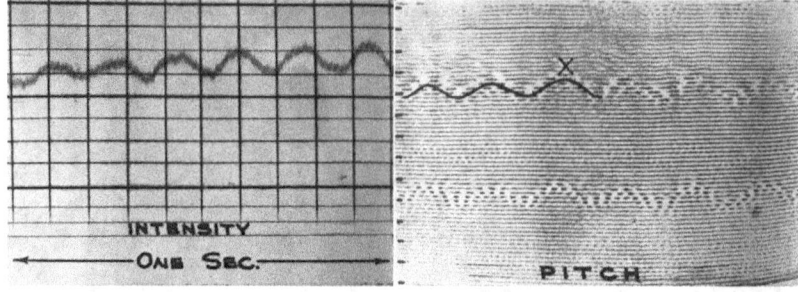

6.8 Magnified phonophotogram measuring the intensity and pitch range of a black singer's vocal vibrato. Seashore, "Vibrato in Voice and Instrument," 14.

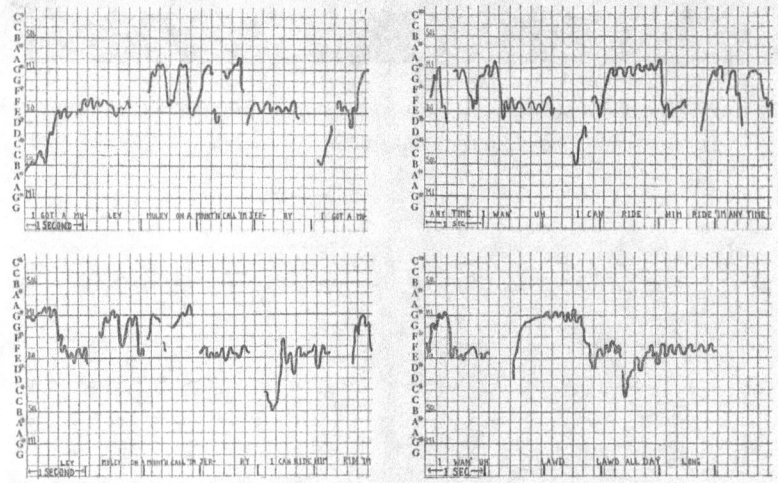

6.9 Scientific musical pattern score, "I Got a Muley." The pattern should be read from left, top to bottom, and then right, top to bottom. Odum and Johnson, *Negro Workaday Songs*, 258–59.

enfranchisement, and equal rights) as those between the law of the regulative as sounded by a "good vibrato," on the one hand, and the lawlessness of the irregulative "and/or anti- and ante-regulative," as Moten reminds us, on the other.[107] Indeed, one needn't strain to hear in their formulation of the "good vibrato" one enjoying "freedom from irregularity" in the extent of pitch or intensity, an echo of the "good Negro."[108] In a certain sense, the Negro *is* the vibrato.

For all his middle-class credentials and social formation, Martin Luther King Jr. was not a "good Negro." His voice was against it.

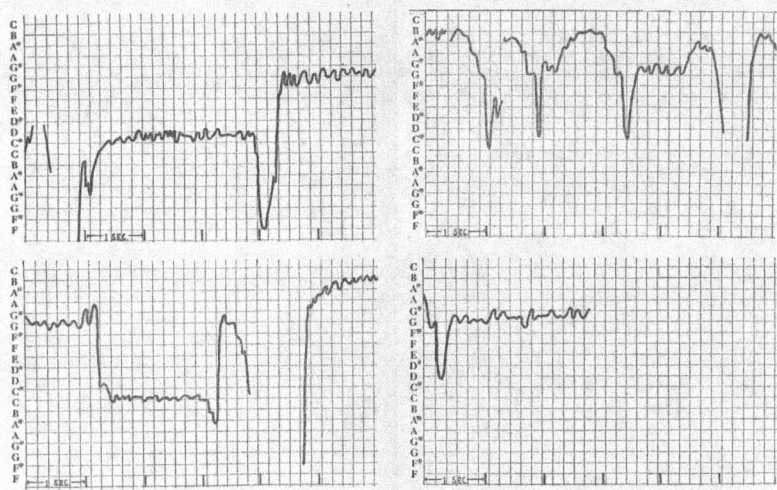

6.10 Scientific musical pattern score, cornfield holler. The pattern should be read from left, top to bottom, and then right, top to bottom. Odum and Johnson, *Negro Workaday Songs*, 260–61.

Mouthing Freedom

Seashore and Metfessel's black-voiced phonophotograms and "pattern scores" (which translate phonophotographic data into frequency charts) haunt later sound imagings of King holding forth at Mason Temple. A recent digital imaging of "All Labor Has Dignity," for example (figure 6.12), reveals the vibrato as a dependable dynamic in King's preaching and speech-making. More than that, it visualizes King's vibrato as a visitational re-sounding of the black workaday world of horse and mule and pick and shovel "choir[ing] an echo to swell through time," as a young poet lately put it.[109] Attuned to the diacritical cries, calls, and songs of slavery's aural past and its early afterlife in the tenant-farmed fields of the Jim Crow South, the spectrograph picture of King's vibrato, I mean to argue, is nothing other than a recording of the resistive, profligate, an-archic commitments of black song and speech saved within the vibrato-memory of the black preaching voice. Like those untutored types whose vibrato habits Seashore and Metfessel judged to be uneven, irregular, and uncultured, King gave away a "primitive" impulse— perhaps, an inheritance—in the vibrato-speak of "All Labor Has Dignity." If the opinion of Seashore and Metfessel is to be trusted concerning the erratic quality of the undulated tones of black vernacular singing, then

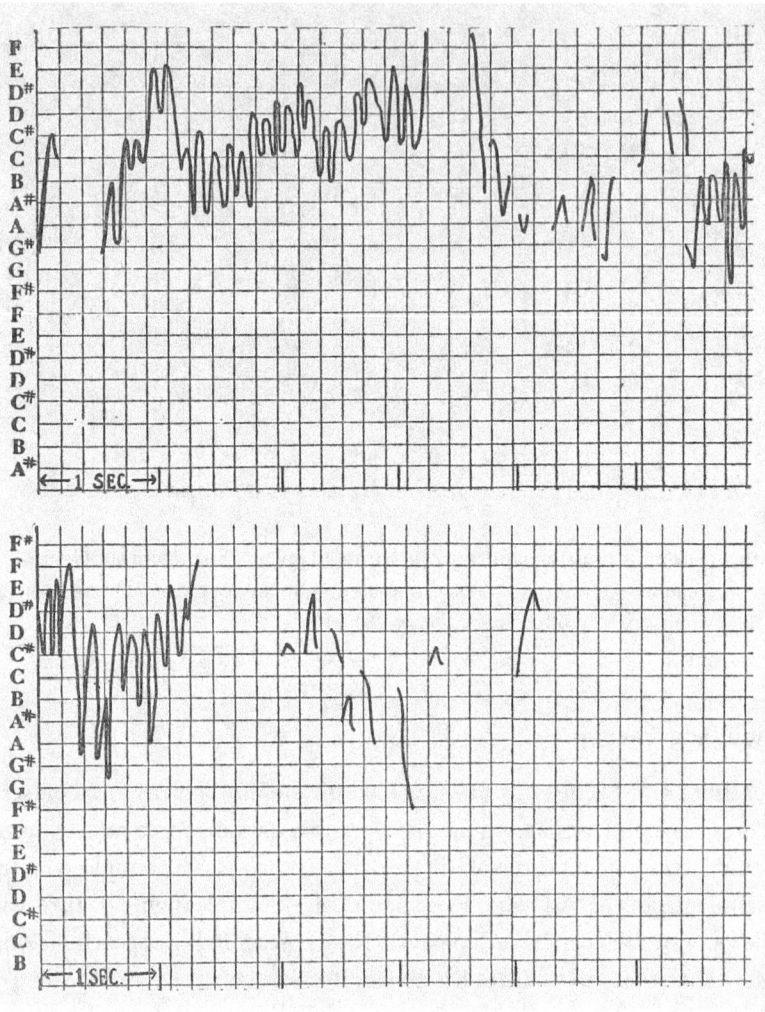

6.11 Scientific musical pattern score, Negro laughter. Odum and Johnson, *Negro Workaday Songs*, 262.

those irregular fluctuations, always worrying the purer tones of reductive, transactional speech, would seem to have sounded an echo, forty years on, of black labor's own radical vocalic aesthetics. King's identification with the black laborer in this way—the Memphis sanitation worker being representative—may go some way to explain the C+ and C grades given him in public speaking at Crozer Theological Seminary. For all its emphasis on vocal control in speech-making, Donald C. Bryant and Karl R. Wallace's

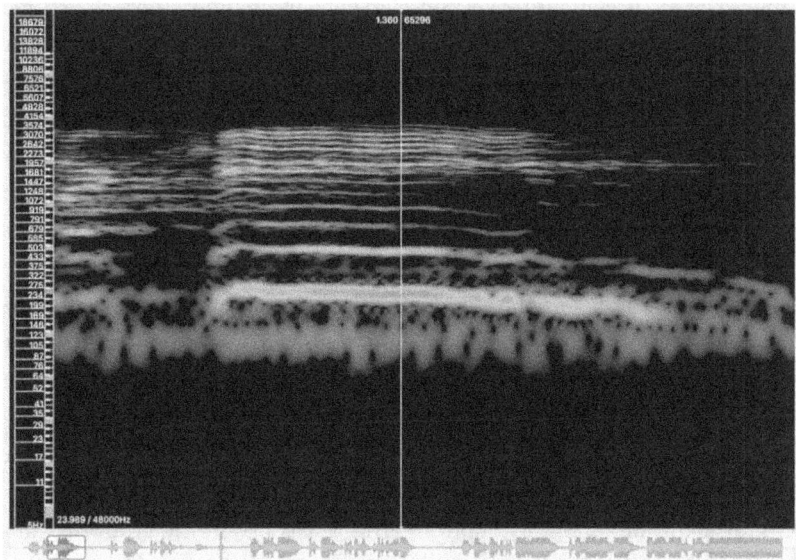

6.12 Smaart® Tools Spectrograph image of King's vibrato when he spoke the phrase "Bull Connor *came* with his dogs" at the American Federation of State, County, and Municipal Employees (AFSCME) mass meeting during the Memphis Sanitation Workers' Strike, March 18, 1968 (King, *"All Labor Has Dignity"*). Author-created image.

Fundamentals of Public Speaking (1947), Crozer's preferred handbook, simply could not overcome the restless swells of vibrato-memory stored in the performative pitch and timbre of King's tremulant platform voice.

Metfessel and Seashore's schematizing of black vibrato did not rely solely on Metfessel's inventive phonophotographic equipment, however. To some extent, the vibrato's subjection to the hegemony of scientific vision was also enabled by the technological modernism of film, as "moving pictures of the singers, their faces, their bodily movements, their emotional expressions, and whatever reactions the camera may reveal" pretended visual confirmation of the ethno-musical argument.[110] In fact, according to Howard Odum and Guy Johnson, Seashore and Metfessel filmed nearly every subject in their study whose voice was pictured by a phonophotogram. Although their phonophotograms may be thought of as another sort of moving picture, Seashore and Metfessel's film recordings aimed to show, in lieu of the sounds of blackness imagistically reflected by the phonophotograms, the social setting, physical gesturing, and labial enactments of the vibrato event. Not unlike the pictures made by Vernon Matthews in Memphis more than three decades later, both phonophotograms and film recordings appear to insist upon sight's sensual and epistemic superiority even as the mechanical capture of sound remains the goal. Consistently, by appealing to moving pictures as sources of data, Metfessel in particular sought visual corroboration of empirical conclusions supposed to have been drawn from the phonophotographic record; he strained to fit observations concerning metronomic time and the regularity of rhythms to the exactitudes of his science. Where the filmic evidence might suggest the subjects' singing to "a slightly different sense of time," as the narrator of Ralph Ellison's *Invisible Man* was later to put it,[111] Metfessel nonetheless believed he saw singers keeping regular time by other means, such as by their hands and feet. In this way, pictures, moving and still, served to subjugate sound to science with visual checks on black sound's capacity, if not penchant, for temporal overflow—or what Alexis Gumbs calls, more simply, "spill." Perhaps it is not ironic at all that appealing to these pictures helped Metfessel set the location of "bar[s]" (his word) he would impose onto scientific scores of black vernacular singing to effectively "capture" (my word) and tame black timing. Where black song isn't "quite on the beat. Sometimes [it's] ahead and sometimes behind," as Ellison's storyteller explains, phonophotographs of black singing, on the other hand, were looked to for cues about the systematic or scientific potential of "pitches, words and measures" otherwise delinquent to (white) technical explanation.[112]

Among the strategies Metfessel used to mine visual records for sonic data was a crude (and wholly unreliable) form of facial recognition which, far from pretending to identify the singer, imagined that it could know the habits of black singing by a visual focus on the singer's mouth. In observing, for instance, that a certain tenor "did not pronounce the [r] by our standard" but "brought together" his lips to sound "more nearly like [w]," Metfessel noted "an indication of the trouble the colored man encounters with English consonants."[113] Dedicated as he was to the modernist sciences, Metfessel noted what he had no real option but to see, for science's sake, an enunciatory deficit in the black singer. That black reading of black soundings Houston Baker associated with "deformation of mastery" in his excellent *Modernism and the Harlem Renaissance* was not imaginable to Metfessel. Where Metfessel saw only an Africanist defect in the verbal efforts of "the colored man" to properly articulate stiff English phonemes, Baker later posited a radically different black cultural expressive strategy that, far from seeking to convey black cultural sensibility through "recog-

6.13 Milton Metfessel's visual study of a black singer's mouth purporting to give "scientific" evidence of the intrinsic artlessness of black vocal style. Metfessel understands the visible distortions of the singer's mouth to reflect Black singers' innate predilection to grossly mispronounce standard English forms. In Metfessel, *Phonophotography in Folk Music*, 50.

nizably standard forms" of social scientific grammars, enacted a linguistic guerrilla strategy instead.[114] A "resonantly and continuously productive set of [black aesthetic] tactics, strategies, and syllables," the deformation of mastery emerged, Baker says, from "an unashamed and bold dedication . . . to rendering the actual folk voice in its simple, performative eloquence."[115] Quite apart from the Negro tenor in Metfessel having trouble with English consonants, Baker allows that black song and speech conspired to *create* trouble, disfiguring normative pronunciation and grammars "as active, outgoing resistance and response to oppressive ignorance and silencing."[116] With a keener (or, perhaps, less fearful) ear tuned to his own phonophotograms, Metfessel might have seen this troublesome potentiality for what it was and predicted, on the social force of it, that a figure like King—with lush vibrato expressiveness—was sure to come.

If Baker was particularly astute to call attention to one of the signal discursive strategies of African American speech and expressive culture, we have in political theorist Davide Panagia an aid to parsing the further micro-politics of the filmic and still visualizations of black orality by Metfessel and Seashore. In a second illustration from Metfessel, for example, he observed "a wide extent of lip movement" in another singer's song-making; "his wide open mouth quite fits into the general expression of the song" the scientists were recording on a phonophotogram.[117] Panagia's musings in political philosophy on the mouth as "a complex organ" and "an organ of political reflection" do not let us pass over Metfessel's oral asides without critical pause.[118] Specifically, in *The Political Life of Sensation*, Panagia focuses on "the centrality of the mouth" as "at once an organ of transmission for the mind's ideas and an organ of consumption for the body's sustenance."[119] These two functions are incongruous, Panagia argues. The mouth as an organ for communication is altogether independent and separate from its function in eating. Consequently, as interests Panagia, political philosophy "cannot account for the confusion of associating the mouth both with the divinity of the mind and the baseness of the digestive tract" in its logics. He calls the mouth then "just such an ambivalent confound."[120] The ambivalence of this "mouth-confound" is also recursive, though. To the extent that the mouth is the privileged organ of political articulation, that is, Panagia shows (by way of Deleuze's "body-without-organs") that it also carries with it a disarticulating potential. While the visual picture of his singer's "wide open mouth" is, for Metfessel, scientific proof on its own of a minstrel mispronunciation of standard English phonemes, the arrogance of that view obfuscates the complex ways the singer may artfully mouth subtleties consistent with the ludic play of the minstrel mask itself. Whatever primitivistic or minstrel strain Metfessel and Seashore were aiming to emphasize by their individual publishing of the same six filmic stills of North Carolina cornfield descant in two separately authored studies on the vibrato (figure 6.13), they did not fail in any case to situate the singer within the visual iconography of (the possibility of) black insurgent oralism.[121] Visually, their cornfield singer sits somewhere between the stomatic enormity of Billy Kersands's complex minstrel mimicry in the 1870s and 1880s and the full-mouthed faciality of Martin Luther King's Chicago Coliseum New Politics Convention nearly a century later (figure 6.14).[122] Fernandez's photograph of King holding forth at the October 1967 convention and Matthews's slightly later ones belong

6.14 Rev. Dr. Martin Luther King Jr., New Politics Convention, Chicago, IL, 1967. Photo by Benedict J. Fernandez.

to the subarchive of preaching pictures of King that we might call, after Kyla Wazana Tompkins, "orificial."[123]

To pay closer attention to the open mouths of the black moderns represented in the photographs shown in figures 6.13 and 6.14—King, the pulpiteer, and the unnamed North Carolina field worker—is to catch a glimpse into that dark creative abyss "blacker than a hundred midnights / Down in a cypress swamp," a chamber through which escapes the vibratory swell of what Emily Lordi calls "black resonance." It is to identify a visual analog for what Baker has referred to as the dark, tropic invisibility of the "black hole" of Afro-American literature, which Stephen Henderson had nominated a "mascon," or a massive concentration of Black experiential energy.[124] But it is also to challenge the privilege afforded the eye in photographic transactions—as well as in "human affairs, politics, and life more generally," as Panagia avers—such that the gaze is countered not by a look returned or refused,[125] but by a pregnancy of sound so stark that, despite its mechanical repression, we stand to witness its (re)birth by the camera, having developed phonophotographic sensitivities of our own.

In this way, in the secondary archive of black visual orality, the preacher and the laborer are the same, as "the no D," King assured the March 18,

KING'S VIBRATO   223

1968, Memphis crowd, "is as significant as the PhD, and the man who has been to no-house, is as significant as the man who has been to *Mo*-house [Morehouse]."[126] King's *words* at Mason Temple expressed faith in a coalition liberalism that would unite the political and social demands of black Americans with those of organized labor, making him mouth the assumptive logic of the dream of the Gramscian worker to reconfigure the civil society.[127] King's *sound*, on the other hand—and not just his pronunciation of Morehouse as *Mo*-house but his worrying of vocal pitch over the full stretch of his speech-making time at Mason Temple that March—was that of the slave. He sounded "the subject-effect of an ensemble of direct relations of force" before and after emancipation, expressing a dream Du Bois called the "open revolt of slaves—refusal to work."[128] King's vibrato contained the insurgent call and consent of thirteen hundred municipal garbage collectors to the "open revolt" of a general strike in Memphis.

The Heroic Slave

Given the violent materialist circumstances of King's March 1968 visits to Memphis—a strike of the city's African American public works employees on the event of two workers crushed to death by an improperly maintained and malfunctioning garbage truck—it should not be surprising that a materialist politics also obtained to the sound of King's vibrato in Memphis. The extent of the neglect of this consideration in King studies seems the greater surprise. His vibrato was haunted not only by the physical work-related deaths of Echol Cole and Robert Walker but by the social death of the slave whose enduring place in the death-bound position King's vibrato was a (re)visitation upon. Spilling wordless protest, it sounded the slave's demand for a reparation that could be realized only by a revolution, a radical transformation of the modern racial and class order.

In his 2003 "Gramsci's Black Marx: Whither the Slave in Civil Society," Frank Wilderson reminded us that the worker and the slave are distinct subject positions in the modern civil state. The dream of the worker, figured as unraced and exploited by the capitalist order, is opposed to the hegemony by a differential relation to "rational/symbolic (the wage) power."[129] The slave, by contrast, figured black and disposable, is opposed to the hegemony by an "unwaged relation," a "relation of terror," and "direct relations of force."[130] By virtue of its existence outside the logic of the civil state—the violence of slavery is the precondition of the emergence of the modern civil state the worker seeks fairer relations in—the subject position of the slave precludes a fully coherent articulation of emancipatory demands within the existing terms of political/economic order (as in wages, so-called benefits, and time off). Rather, it is through the extraverbal exorbitances of black vocality, where Moten (conjuring Charles Lloyd and Cecil Taylor) reminds us "words don't go,"[131] that the slave-subject intones these demands nondiscursively—and, as it were, more exactly. The worker has words—which is to say, a scientific discourse—from which to derive a counterlogic appropriate to her antagonism toward production's exploitations. The slave, on the other hand, is always already bereft of words fit to her injustices; the black subject position, sui generis in the history of the Western world, lies always already outside the assumptive logic of labor as ideology and politics. For the slave, then, words (alone) won't do. Thus, King's *performativity*—not his politics, properly speaking—is the ground on which claims of his radicalism find solidity.

Properly speaking, King's politics were as often liberal as they were radical. Inside of a single speech, for instance, King cast both a liberal vision of a reformed civil society and a radically materialist one wherein the end of the exploitative and deadly dynamics of work was not just imagined but hailed into history. As it was out-and-out "criminal," he charged in "All Labor Has Dignity," "to have people working on a full-time basis and a full-time job getting part-time income," King declared the rally's intention "to demand that Memphis . . . do something about the conditions that our brothers face as they work day in and day out for the well-being" of the civil society.[132] This goal, it seems, was fundamentally corrective—the liberal, Gramscian demand of workers. A few minutes later, however, King concluded his address with a more radical vision than is suited to "function[ing] in the mainstream of the economic life of our nation."[133]

> If we are going to get equality, if we are going to get adequate wages, we are going to have to struggle for it. . . . You may have to escalate the struggle a bit. If they keep refusing, and they will not recognize the union, . . . I tell you what you ought to do, and you are together here enough to do it: in a few days you ought to get together and just have a general work stoppage in the city of Memphis. And you let that day come, and not a Negro in this city will go to any job downtown. When no domestic service will go to anybody's house or anybody's kitchen. When black students will not go to anybody's school and black teachers.[134]

If the audible agreement of King with his audience that Evans Crawford called "the hum" was evident early in his address, then his more radical vision of a general strike in its later part raised the pitch and intensity of that "hum" to an exuberant roar. On its face, though, King's not-so-modest proposal was not especially pragmatic. Even with the financial support of the SCLC behind the garbage collectors' strike, a broader work stoppage risked "no-house" becoming a more serious pun on the threat of economic dispossession to the city's black residents than it was originally calculated to signify in its rhyme-play on "*Mo*-house." Too, his call for a walkout of black students and teachers from Memphis public schools betokened a surgical disruption of the state ideological apparatus; such a protest would strike at an education system whose statist functioning helped socialize the worker and the slave into the economic order, risking the removal of those warehoused in classrooms to carceral captivity much sooner. Still, "All Labor Has Dignity" was met with jubilation. More than what he said, it seems King's insurgent sound—that willful tonality excessive of word-bound political discourse—set the assembly shouting euphorically and brought (non)sense to the sudden *end* of words where the speech proper left off, still ongoing.

Despite certain representational limits, a phonophotogram of the cut created by King's precipitous closing might have amplified "All Labor Has Dignity" in ways foreclosed by more orthodox transcription practices, which are mostly anemic in their efficacy to reproduce black voices. Such a technology would most assuredly have represented King's voice retarding and building volume in his closing lines such that the *aural* transcription of the revolutionary idea for a general revolt might appear in a deformation of conventional transcription like this:

> ... an'
> just.
> haaave ...
> a GEN-eral WORK-stoppage
> in the city of Memphis.
> AN' YOU LET THAT DAY COME.—

This trial is, of course, a failure too, inasmuch as it, like the phonophotogram, cannot sound aloud what its words and print manipulations merely point toward. Unluckily, the sound this text refers to, inevitably faltering in its poetic approach to the aural, lies as much in the surround and background of the lexical units composing its versificatory facade. And yet the hope of hearing King here is the only avenue into what Moten calls, in his essay of the same name, a "knowledge of freedom" being shared between pulpit and pew at the Mason Temple mass rally.

By this, I mean that one hopes to hear not any single subject speaking so much as the "voicing and revoicing of [the] ensemble" that is always already King *improvising*.[135] Without preamble, a certain "something out-from-outside," as Moten puts it, irrupts upon the orational event, "something unbound by ... relation or nonrelation," something—if I may appeal to Moten's rich prose again—"situated at an opening onto the site of the intersection of the knowledge of language (as prayer, curse, narrative [*récit* or recitation]) and the knowledge of freedom (as both a negative function of the experience of oppression and the trace of what Noam Chomsky calls an 'innate endowment that serves to bridge the gap between experience and knowledge')."[136] For those with ears to hear it, or eyes to perceive the trace of it harboring inside King's caverned mouth, the ensemble of voicings and re-voicings sounding the knowledge of freedom reached an eschatological pitch: "AN' YOU LET THAT DAY COME—" repeated the found rhythm and modulating "out-from-outside" timbre that lifted the better-known "I Have a Dream" speech to flight five years earlier. The brooding echo of "THAT DAY," in particular, which King called upon to "COME" not in later linear time but in the unbound atemporality of the kairotic now ("*No-o-o-w* is the time" he urged again and again), cued the listening chorus to a vision as sweeping as the dream envisaged on the steps of the Lincoln Memorial. Summoned by the repeated word-charms of black fantastic thought, "one day" and "that day," King's unrestrained closing (hardly a finish) carried his Memphis audience back to Washington so as to recall the radical vision "*that day* when all God's children, black men and white men, Jews and Gentiles, Protestants and Catholics, will join hands and sing in the words of the old Negro spiritual, 'Free at last, free at last, Great God a-mighty, we're free at last.'"[137] By dint of a subtle preacherly affect, King mediated, and the people wildly ratified, a modern eschatology, vivid as the Johannine revelation, born in the slave's unforgettable knowledge of freedom.

Between King's liberal economic ends and the radical means of the slave to realize them insurgently, then, lies that "strife" which Jared Sexton, echoing and straining against Moten, has observed as a conflict "between 'radicalism (here understood as the performance of a general critique of the proper) ... and a 'normative striving against the grain of the very radicalism from which the desire for norms is derived.'"[138] This is the ambivalence that attaches to the radical King, the visual archive of his living speech-making being a vivid framing of the vexed politics of affect and oratorical desire in the black tradition. As the speaking subject of photographs in the sprawling archive of his life and work in the United States and abroad, King mediates the gap between visuality and aurality as modalities of black political subjecthood and representation. He mediates, in other words, between looking and—you might say—mouthing, between the worker and the slave, between experience and the knowledge of freedom, between the material mundane and the eidetic to-come. Thus mediating, his radicalism and liberalism alike are impossible strivings except insofar as they may be imagined to coexist, precariously, in the otherwise-than-impossible figure of the radical democrat that Cornel West commends in the editor's introduction to *The Radical King*. If not impossible, then, such a figure is hauntological at the least—forcefully present but outside of and beyond the political order of things. In the camera's viewfinder, King, heroic slave as radical democrat, could only be always already dead to the terms of our liberal democratic order.

In sight, then—as well as in the sound the sight of him seems always to be after—King's March 18, 1968, Memphis address was an ensemblic prefiguring of "I've Been to the Mountaintop." Photographs of the former event, by Vernon Matthews and others, set the stage visually for King's more ceremonial memorialization in granite on the nation's capital decades later. Differently put, King's visual oratory, specifically that subarchive of standing platform images which want nothing more desperately than *to be heard*, does not fail to replicate the pose of the petrified orator materialized in stone just off the Tidal Basin between the Potomac and the Washington Channel. There, too, King appears to "cut a figure," as Powell says, enacting (or cast as appearing to enact) the *eloquentia corporis* (body eloquence) of *adlocutio*, the classical gesture of the orator-as-ideal-citizen. But if what pictures want, in their quiddity as pictures, is "to be invited to speak," as Mitchell has proposed, then what is the desire of the more specific picture of the *black* orator not only gesturing but, as the poet disclosed, "mouthing . . . subtleties"?[139] What could it be but that which is, by Mitchell's logic, the dream-wish of speech (though not often enough of the speaker): namely, tunefulness and the end of words. Vernon Matthews's photograph of King holding forth on the dais at Mason Temple Church of God in Christ two weeks before King's assassination pictures just that, in the break between King's irrepressible affect and Matthews's documentarian intention. There, words are exhausted into wordlessness as blackness *sounds* the knowledge of freedom out of time, out of turn, out of tune with subjection.

7

Dream Variations
"I Have a Dream" and the Sonic Politics of Race and Place

Almost universally, "I Have a Dream" stands out as one of the greatest speeches by an American in the twentieth century. To be sure, it is among the most recognizable orations in English in the modern era. Today, nearly sixty years after its ringing elocution in the shadow of Abraham Lincoln seated in Georgia marble behind him, King's oration on the National Mall in Washington continues to attract scholarly and popular notice. Drew Hansen's 2003 *The Dream: Martin Luther King, Jr., and the Speech That Inspired a Nation* and Eric Sundquist's 2009 *King's Dream* both revisit King's iconic speech in Washington as a watershed event. More recently, Clarence B. Jones and Stuart Connelly's 2011 *Behind the Dream: The Making of the Speech That Transformed a Nation* and Gary Younge's 2013 *The Speech: The Story behind Martin Luther King Jr.'s Dream* have attempted to return critical attention to what was arguably, for African Americans, the most consequential performance of public speech-making in US history.

More recent still, W. Jason Miller's 2015 *Origins of the Dream: Hughes's Poetry and King's Rhetoric* links King's most iconic trope, the dream, to a cycle of similarly themed poems by Langston Hughes, "that black bard of Harlem,"[1] including Hughes's "I Dream a World," "Dream Deferred," and "Dream Variations." Miller, of course, is not the first to observe the intimacies between King's oneiric metaphor and Hughes's, but *Origins* goes to extraordinary lengths to demonstrate "how Hughes's poetry became a measurable inflection in the voice of Martin Luther King."[2] Miller's concern is to help students of King's life and oratory "understand the fullest resonance of King's metaphors."[3] Despite the visual associations inhering to dreams, the vocalic and sonic allusions in Miller's argument point to a property in King's 1962–63 cycle of dream speeches that sets them apart as emphatically acoustic performances of black emancipatory possibility. This chapter posits the development of "I Have a Dream" over three addresses in North Carolina, Michigan, and Washington, DC, obtained within the sonic ecology of modern black speech-making afforded by the "resonant," "room," and "outdoors"[4] geographies where King held forth in Rocky Mount, Detroit, and Washington. These successive settings, moreover, occasioned ongoing improvisations on the oneiric theme, with each improvisation constituting an approach to a new, or otherwise, mode of hearing black power and possibility in familiar black tones.

Put more methodically, I am interested in attending to the acoustic and timbral effects, specifically, of wood, flesh, and water—the primary matter by which the ensemblic sounds of "I Have a Dream" were conducted in their resonant, room, and outdoor settings—as well as modern engineering and amplification technologies on the performative and auditory culture of black speech-making. I explore the radical democratic politics of these effects under, first, Jim Crow, then industrial modernity, and, finally, US democratic liberalism. To take one example of this bio-material emphasis in the acoustemology of King: a 2003 Rocky Mount initiative to install a monument to King's 1962 visit to the city, the first time he would set "I Have a Dream" to a refrain, was resisted by black residents. It was King's *voice*, I maintain, not the fact of his visit, that black Rocky Mount wished to recall. Their memory of King's speech-making in the hardwood environment of a high school gymnasium was decidedly aural; to be properly remembered, the dreamer had somehow to be more vividly *heard* than *seen* if he was to stand for modern black struggle and aspiration. But how does one give form to voice as public memory? What does black audition look like as a public art installation—and may a sculptural likeness of King ever be productive of his aural memorability?

Prelude to a Dream: Rocky Mount, North Carolina

The second Tuesday of June 2003 was a clear eighty-eight degrees in northeast North Carolina. Against the backdrop of such pleasant weather, who could have anticipated how stifling the day would become? African American residents on the northeast side of downtown chafed at what was supposed to be a material symbol of a new racial accord in the largely rural railroad and tobacco town. A seven-foot cast figure of King had been commissioned by the majority-white city council to commemorate the event of the civil rights leader's 1962 address at the local Booker T. Washington High School. When it was unveiled, however, artist Erik Blome's bronze likeness of King—by one account "a tightly bound composition" with its subject "wearing a Brooks Brothers suit and wing tips"—was not very warmly received.[5] Who could have guessed how deeply Blome's sculpture would discompose the very community it was expected to flatter? It was not the sartorial extravagances in which Blome cast King that displeased the black residents looking on at the statue's installation, however. Rather, Blome's design did not deliver on what black residents expected to see somewhat higher up: a familiar face. "That ain't Dr. King," pronounced a local preacher who once marched with King. "The lips, the eyes, the head, the mustache, the cheeks. It don't favor him," he insisted.[6] Reverend Elbert Lee's assessment was very nearly universal among local black viewers. Hot debate ensued as, according to public arts historian Renée Ater, "various constituencies fought over Blome's depiction of King, particularly his facial features."[7] Try as he might, Blome's defense of his likeness of King won him no fans in Rocky Mount. "Artwork is not a body cast. . . . It's a person's interpretation," he condescended to point out.[8]

Despite the national attention the debate drew and widespread sympathy in the press for Blome, black criticism of Blome's work was not philistine, as Blome and others complained. Rather, to abstract "the lips, the eyes, the head, the mustache, the cheeks" of King, rendering him an interpretation of the sculptor's view of him, was to risk something far more costly than the public shaming Blome invited when he deprecated the position of "the people of Rocky Mount" for their "different mentality to, say, what you might find in a city where they are used to art."[9] In framing black intransigence on the question of whether Blome's nonrealistic "interpretation" of King was suitable in art-critical discourse, Blome and his defenders betrayed a dullness of the liberal imagination to connect African American desire for a realistic likeness of King to mortuarial feeling. They missed entirely the sense of memorial obligation in that feeling to the reconstructed integrity of the face and neck of one whose assassination—a grisly, disfiguring liquidation by rifle fire on the Lorraine Motel balcony in Memphis—remains as plain upon the screen of black cultural memory as the March on Washington, Selma, the Montgomery bus boycott, or, again, King's speech in Rocky Mount.

What if the black citizens of Rocky Mount, far from being ill-adapted to modernist tastes in their demand for a more faithful likeness of King in the new park downtown, understood realism as a restorative artistic gesture critical to black memory in the age of necropolitics? What if the leisure presumed by the conceits of sculpture was denied the sculptor whose work was more urgently reparative, inasmuch as its end is visually embalmatory and purposed to reproduce the living image of the disfigured dead for public viewing?[10] What if we think of restorative justice not only in penal contexts, but as an aesthetic counterdemand and visual reparation for the racial state's everyday violence against insurgent expressions of black social life? Might African American insistence upon "an exact likeness of King's facial expression" approach, in affective and aesthetic terms, a form of care—"care in the wake," to invoke Christina Sharpe's formulation?[11] This care would constitute itself, in part, in a "vigilance" against institutional *mis*-remembrances of the dead,[12] those disfigured a second time by the violence of artists, publics, and politicians who cannot be trusted to take proper care in their memorializing.

For four years, Rocky Mount's black community kept up the fight for the integrity of King's facial/racial memory. The reparative, embalmatory motive I theorize as having fueled that struggle, while preoccupied with the look of more than one of King's facial features ("the lips, the eyes, the head, the mustache, the cheeks"), could not have failed to corroborate Davide Panagia on the mouth, specifically, as "a complex organ" and "an organ of political reflection."[13] It was, after all, the appearance of King's "quiet" in Blome's vision that offended so many. Blome had explained that he "wanted to show a different side of Dr. King that was *quieter, calmer, and pondering*. I wanted to show [him] as I admired him repeatedly in a photograph that I have pinned to my wall and admired for years."[14] But this "interpretation" was hardly the one the black citizens of Rocky Mount believed was restorative. As local resident Kimberle Evans put it, "If [King] was quiet, we wouldn't be here doing a statue of him in the first place."[15] Evans's comment speaks wryly to Blome's ignorance of a significant source of sensorial affect lost in the facial, and especially oral, abstracted features of his statue: aurality. Considering that it was King's speech ("And so my friends of Rocky Mount, I have a dream tonight") and the *sound* of its reverberations in the Booker T. Washington gym that the statuary was commissioned to commemorate, Blome's design effectively worked against the preservation of King's memory in Rocky Mount. Differently said, if a significant aspect of the inspiration for Rocky Mount's Martin Luther King Jr. Park, and for the commissioning of a memorial statue of King, was the city's desire to memorialize King's speech almost forty years earlier, then one might wonder if Blome's "quieter, calmer, pondering" King was not visually opposed to the memory of King's visit. So far from quiet or calm, this visit was experienced and remembered in black life and legend as a spectacularly sonic—indeed, "noisy"—event.

"Please Do Not Erase": Tape, Temporality, and Black Audition

Before 1999, when plans for Martin Luther King Jr. Park became part of the public record, Booker T. Washington was far and away the most iconic black figure in Rocky Mount public history. In 1910, Washington visited Rocky Mount on a tour of North Carolina, one of eleven major stops he made throughout the state. Speaking inside a tobacco warehouse, which was then the largest structure in town available for a mass gathering, Washington addressed a crowd of four thousand, holding forth before a racially mixed audience for two hours.[16] Although Washington was "far from universally popular in the white community,"[17] one historian reminds us, his speech won over many elites. One of them was Thomas H. Battle. Battle was a prominent white lawyer, local politician, and onetime chairman of the Rocky Mount Board of Education, whose politics of paternalism in racial affairs were sympathetically intoned by Washington. Not only his national fame, but very probably the local memory of his speech-making in Rocky Mount, too—"Just splendid, full of eloquence, wit and wisdom combined with the plainest and most wholesome advice," Battle enthused—inspired officials in Rocky Mount to name its first dedicated high school for African American students for "the Wizard of Tuskegee" in 1927.[18] It was in this facility that King delivered "Facing the Challenge of a New Age," the precursor speech to "I Have a Dream." But for an expected crowd of more than 1,500, King might have delivered his fifty-five-minute oration in the building's well-appointed but smaller auditorium, its seats being too few for the assembly. That King should have had to address the supporters of the Rocky Mount Voters and Improvement League in the school gym was unfortunate since, for sound, the auditorium was said to be "of incalculable value."[19] Still, it seems event organizers made do. A photograph of the event attributed to J. B. Harren, a local NACCP leader, intimates as much. Whereas the raised rostrum at Mason Temple, crowded with hard-metal microphones leaned in to catch King's cantillated speech, educed the sound of the photograph as oratorical, here the foregrounded visibility of the magnetic recording

7.1 Rev. Dr. Martin Luther King Jr. at Booker T. Washington High School, Rocky Mount, NC, 1962. Photograph by J. B. Harren. In Markovitch, "Dawn of the Dream," n.p.

technology lining the front edge of the gym's improvised dais posits the image's extravisual remainder not as sound this time, but as sound's assumptive priority: audition. It is not in what he *said* in Rocky Mount but in what his audience of black Tar Heels *heard* the night King came to Rocky Mount that the public memory of his visit consists. And what that audience heard, both what was said and that which was not speech, was captured on tape—not sculpture—*embalmed*.

In chapter 1, I appealed to Jonathan Sterne's history of early sound recording, *The Audible Past: Cultural Origins of Sound Reproduction*, in order to show how phonography's beginning was bound up with funereal desires and designs. I showed how the April 9, 1968, playback of King's sermon "The Drum Major Instinct," recorded on tape at Ebenezer Baptist Church (Atlanta) a few weeks earlier, extended a tradition of phonographic self-eulogy almost as old as sound recording technology itself. As Sterne points out, "there [were] many cases reported in the early phonograph industry press" of clergymen who, with the aid of phonography, preached their own funeral sermons.[20] More to the point, though, "the practical and imagined possibilities of recording's permanence," Sterne reminds us, "existed as part of a longer history and larger culture of preservation,"[21] including, especially, the preservation of food from spoilage and dead bodies from rapid decomposition. The phonograph was thus marshaled to one key preservationist end; namely, in language Thomas Edison himself used to promote his invention, the material capture of "the sayings, the voices, and the last words of the dying member of the family—as of great men."[22] Or, as Andrea Bohlman and Peter McMurray put it, the "*embalming [of] the voice[s] of the dead for future generations.*"[23]

Clearly phonography is not tape, but Bohlman and McMurray decry the habit of sound historians to subordinate tape to "the phonographic regime" they see dominating sound studies. They offer that tape, with its own discrete media logics, may well overlap with, even if it does not replicate or logically continue, the media logics of phonography. As such, tape may repeat the embalmatory function of phonographic technology vis-à-vis the voices of "great," if still yet mortal, "men"—but according to an alternate, even countervailing, dialectics. Ironic as it may sound, the telos of tape is not immemoriality but evanescence, an extended or abrupt erosion of memory into history's ether. For while "tape has emerged as one of the most stable archival media," as Bohlman and McMurray write (its function approaching the promise of permanence in phonography), tape's "erasability and reusability," on the other hand, undermine the pretense to permanent preservation in the social life of phonographic sound recording. "That 'erase' function" in tape recording, they assert, "is no drag-and-drop, digital flick of the wrist, but the very same operation as 'record'—creation and destruction are different only by sonic context."[24] Every new recording on the same tape is thus not a sedimentation of sounds past, as if a record of sound history was available in it, but an erosion of said record, with only the longer recordings or the projected distortions of aging or exposed tape leaving traces of "destruction" behind. All of this is to suggest that, *like* phonography, the found tape recording of King's Rocky Mount speech, forgotten in an attic for thirty-eight years then lost in a local government building for another twelve, made the gymnasium sounds of King's address seem alive again—or embalmed, at least—with its 2013 rediscovery forty years after his death. But *unlike* phonography, which pretends to perfect, unfading preservation, the restored reel-to-reel hinted at the eroded sounds poised to be sooner or later forgotten by the tape's age and/or autophagy.

In "Facing the Challenge of a New Age," a speech King had previously delivered in Atlanta, Montgomery, and Buffalo before its Rocky Mount revival, the rising star of the national civil rights struggle granted the crowd packed into the school gym an early glimpse of "I Have a Dream." I mean to reference not only intonations of the "I have a dream" refrain in "Facing the Challenge of a New Age," but the germ of tonal and vibratory force discernible in the earlier speech that is today reflexively identified with "I Have a Dream." Furthermore, the evanescent, degradative materiality of tape affords King's Rocky Mount recording a hearing by attentive ears that is simultaneously *historical* (of a given time) and *historicist* (concerned with the nature of history itself). A label attached to the King reel, reading "Dr. Martin Luther King's Speech November 27, 1962, Please Do Not Erase,"[25] orients the audition it invites toward a particular kind of listening—modern, directed, object-based. But suppose those who willed to listen to "Dr. Martin Luther King's Speech November 27, 1962" were, rather, oriented toward the time and place of the broader soundscape surrounding the particularity of "Dr. Martin Luther King's Speech" alone? Then a more general sensitivity to the "technically mediated *sonic* processuality of what is otherwise called history," as one media theorist writes, is called for, a sensitivity which we can call historicist.[26]

However critical it is to hear King's recorded voice distinctly proclaim the dream of a world where "my little daughter and my two sons will grow up ... not conscious of the color of their skin but only conscious of the fact that they are members of the human race,"[27] the historicity of "Facing the Challenge of a New Age" lies as much in the tuning and timbre of the scene on tape as it does in the distinctive content of King's civil rights oratory. In other words, the "material history" of King in Rocky Mount—the found tape recording—informs a generative "history of listening," as Brian Kane has put it,[28] that we might think of as *black audition*. Black audition is the name I give to an embodied mode of *listening-to* that is, at root, an encultured *listening-for*, practiced by those who live, as Jared Sexton has put it, in "the slow time of [black] captivity" as "captive[s] of an everyday, social incarceration" and await the break, the opening up of fugitive possibility.[29] None dare miss the sound of the call of freedom—or, defensively, the threat of anti-black violence fermenting. As I suggested in chapter 6, King himself exhibited this latter alertness as a sweeping, panoramic watchfulness on the night of April 3, 1968, when he approached the podium in Memphis. But this *listening-for*, which is also a *listening-against* the sound of that jeopardy lying in wait for death-bound subjects, is not just a defensive sentience toward dangers seen and unseen. It is a searching listening, an aural looking- and waiting-for: an interruption in the racial terms of order animated by a freedom drive that, according to Moten, "accompanies largely unthought positions and appositions."[30] Black audition is the grounds for an acoustemology of freedom attentive to hearing as an aestheticopolitical value, an impulse on the order of that "ethical listening" practice musicologist Nina Sun Eidsheim has outlined as affectively "multisensory, highly responsive, and physical."[31] In *Sensing Sound: Singing and Listening as Vibrational Practice*, Eidsheim argues that ethical listening "include[s] an active contribution to the material circumstances surrounding that which is sensed."[32] She continues: "As a material entity, I partake in the material propagation that I understand as hearing or listening. If I considered my sonic experience from the perspective of its participant and cocreator, aspects of it that previously seemed liminal might in fact reveal themselves to be ordering and distinguishing properties of the experience."[33] Deeply indebted to Eidsheim, I argue that black audition, far from being realized anatomically in or by the cochlea, is, rather, a "total-body activity," an experience of sound as a material effect on the listening black body by vibrational excitements "moving and being moved" within the aural environment.[34] It perceives the thick event of the sonic scene (or audition milieu) as clearly as the sound object around which the scene tends to accrue social or aesthetic meaning.

Although Eidsheim's theory of listening is not languaged as a theory of *black* listening, her radical reformulation of sound as "merely a trope" and listening as "the multisensorial and full-bodied participation of [a sound's] receiving body" is nevertheless an especially heuristic theory for expounding black audition.[35] Careful to follow the "wider scholarship on vibration," in particular, Eidsheim makes it clear that listening is experienced bodily within a vibrational field. The listening body "does not vibrate as a single mass,"[36] however. "Indeed, beyond the ear, different parts of the human body have their own natural frequencies. As a consequence, individual body parts resonate with the overall vibration—resonance that leads to amplification or attenuation of various vibrations in particular areas of the body."[37] As we shall see, this anatomized complex of vibratory excitements experienced in the body is a distinctive feature of black audition. The taped recording of King in Rocky Mount does not fail to disclose this, drawing attention to black audition by way of an automatic, interjective vocalization of vibratory resonance: a giddy laugh let go twice in the background by a lone man in the crowd. An element in the evanescent or eroded audiality of taped sound and nearly forgotten to local history, this "loud and prolonged cackling laugh," Miller has noted, is thought to have issued from one Reverend D. L. Blakey, then pastor of St. John AME Zion Church in Rocky Mount.[38] Blakey's outbursts of delight with King's speech-making, I submit, are impulse reactions to the resonant conditions the voice, environment, and listening body produce in frequential, vibratory synchronicity. His laughing constitutes a fugitive affect insofar as it escapes its called-for repression under the etiquettical terms of public oratorical listening. Except for Blakey's loudness imposing itself on a listening directed toward "Dr. Martin Luther King's Speech," what Ashon Crawley has dubbed the "vibratory frequency of black thought" in King's speech-making might well be eroded from our hearing.[39] But Blakey inclines us to listen for how black sounds are heard—inclines us, that is, to "listen to listening,"[40] in Eidsheim's formulation, insofar as tape's embalming power allows.

Reverend Blakey's Laugh

When "Facing the Challenge of a New Age" was recovered uncatalogued from the Braswell Memorial Library in Rocky Mount,[41] the discovery was especially remarkable because, as Miller would point out, it included King's first use of the iconic refrain (though not the phrase) "I have a dream." In "Facing the Challenge of a New Age," King in fact employed refrains from *two* prior speeches, according to Miller. "Not only does the [Rocky Mount] speech end with a version of the 'I have a dream' sequence," he observes, "but that sequence is immediately preceded by the 'How long? Not long' set piece that he made famous when he used it in his address at the end of the march from Selma to Montgomery in March 1965."[42] Critical as these observations are about the rhetorical pastiche of the Rocky Mount speech, Miller's transcription of the found audiotape is an equally vital aid to hearing the unworded aspects of the speech's delivery that are coconstitutive of the thick event of address and audition. Miller's annotations dutifully flag many of the noisy, sometimes shrill, excesses captured by the original recordist. "Someone can be heard responding 'Yes,'" Miller notes in one place.[43] "A laugh can be heard here,"[44] in another. "This moment marks what is clearly the loudest ovation of the entire address," Miller emphasizes at the end of King's "I have a dream" sequence.[45] Logged by Miller as footnotes in the speech's transcription, each such reference corresponds to a sonic referent in the recording. But what passes in Miller's annotations as so much talk-back, applause, and "hum"[46] are also cues to an entry into "listen[ing] to listening." One cue, Reverend Blakey's laugh, exemplifies the vibratory possibility of black audition and its affordances for a keener understanding of black sound and sociality as a radical irruption on the regulative rhythms of segregation.

Twice noted by Miller, Reverend Blakey's first laugh—not much more than a chortle—is modest, a small breach of the glottis which otherwise keeps listening's physical excitements silent within the body. Spilling into hearing as a sudden escape of vibrational force through the body's vocal folds, it irrupts on the scene in the middle of King's "How long? Not long" run. King's self-reply, "Not long," to his own rhetorical query, "How long?," evidently amused Blakey:

> I know some of you, and suddenly all over, we get weary. I know that. And somebody is asking here tonight, *how long* will it take to solve this problem? *How long* will prejudice blind the visions of men, darken their understanding, and drive bright-eyed wisdom from her sacred throne? Somebody's asking tonight, *when* will wounded justice be lifted from this dust of shame to reign supreme among the children of men? *When* will the radiant star of hope be plunged against the nocturnal bosom of this lonely night (48:04), plucked from weary souls the manacles of fear and the chains of death. *How long* somebody's asking will justice be crucified, and truth be buried? *How long* will we have to struggle in order to get those rights which are basic, God-given rights deep down in the Constitution of this nation? (48:30). And I can only say to you tonight: *not long*.[47]

King's assurance that racial justice was "not long" in coming to America didn't just resonate figuratively with those who had gathered hoping to hear exactly that. Aurally, King's utterance of "long" also emanated a low, tonal microphonic hum, faint beneath the sound of his voice, in the very space of sound Blakey's laugh was to cut in on a half second later. By the sound of it, the whole gymful of admirers was moved even as they were also *being moved somatically* by the vibrational effects of King's canting oratory. Reverend Blakey's laugh was at once the sign and confirmation of this movement.

If the laugh heard in the break of "How long? Not long" attests to this double effect of inspiration and vibration—dually moved and being moved—then a *second* Blakey laugh redoubled the vibrational intensities in the room.[48] In his speech's final flourish, King declaimed the opening verse of Francis Samuel Smith's "My Country, 'Tis of Thee," intoning a new civic hope of black American belonging. Specifically, it was King's anaphoral continuation of the imperative ending of Smith's verse, "Let freedom ring," that stirred his listeners:

Let freedom ring.
That must become true all over America if this is to be a great nation. Yes,
Let it ring from the prodigious hilltops of New Hampshire,
Let it ring from the mighty mountains of New York,
Let it ring from the heightening Alleghenies of Pennsylvania,
Let it ring from the snowcapped Rockies of Colorado,
Let it ring from the curvaceous slopes of California.
But not only that, from every mountainside let freedom ring.[49]

It is at this point on the tape recording that Blakey's second laugh spills over into sustained, irrepressible glee. The vibrational practice that is, in Eidsheim, listening in the mode of "receptive engagement" reveals its animateriality in this outflow of laughter from Blakey's listening body, which goes past the limits of polite audition that might have been expected of him seated alongside King on the dais.[50] But this is no contemptuous or mocking interruption of King breaking out of Blakey. It is rather like the suggestion of an insurgent black hilarity: at once a childlike enjoyment of the haptic power the material practice of black audition affords, and a grown-up seriocomic assertion of laughter's radical refusal of what a smart young poet referred to as "a world insistent on your pain."[51] This letting-go isn't like Blakey's first laugh, however. As it did before, it combines vocal sound and hearing in the voiced reaction of the neck or abdomen or larynx to vibrational amplitudes and frequencies interanimating the listening body; but at the moment of laughter, it blurs speaker and listener(s) into a few extended seconds of overlapping intermaterialities of vibration and overflow. This, too, would seem intrinsic to black audition.

Not altogether unrelated to the insurgent sound of Reverend Blakey's laugh, poet Allison Pitinii Davis, in a verse titled "The Function of Humor in the Neighborhood," portrays laughter as a rebellious affect—"something you'd be shot for," the poet warns, "in the shtetl."[52] To laugh is to deliberately "*choke on history*."[53] Notwithstanding the Jewish backdrop of this ironic inversion, wherein laughter supplants lament in the scene of racial subjection, nothing is more deadly serious than the sense of humor black laughter renders bodily by way of intermaterial vibrationality. While Blakey's discordant noise-making may have vexed the object-oriented hearing of those focused on hearing King's address undistracted, ironically his interference may well have kept the wider event of black oratory and audition on track, critically disrupting the impulse of others—the people and the press—to reduce black oration minimalistically to speech and the practice of black speech-making to theatricalized oration. As the noise of Reverend Blakey's laugh spills out into the space of speech-making as the sound of black audition (to us who have learned to "listen to listening," in black settings), it announces its part in the general poiesis of otherwise worlds of black freedom and flourishing that King saw coming into being.

As often as King appealed to the trope of dreaming in both early and late speeches, he also evoked mountains as a doubly visual and acoustic leitmotif. For example, in the previous chapter I argued that the trope of the mountaintop on which turned the climax of King's appropriation of Moses's farewell to ancient Israel was not so much called up whole cloth out of his biblically suffused imagination as it was inspired by his vista from the elevated preaching platform at the Mason Temple church. In Rocky Mount, King's anaphoral extension of Francis Samuel Smith invoked a litany of mountaintop references for conveying a picture of the echoic (re)soundings of freedom all over. In calling for *the sound* of freedom everywhere, however, "Let freedom ring," modally worrying the line between hortative and imperative grammars,[54] also effectively called the freedom-dream itself into being as a sonic effect. Redolent of speech's creative modality in Genesis 1:3, King canted the creative power *fiat lux*—literally, "let light be made"—as he obscured the difference between creator and deliverer. In the acoustic environment that is the school gymnasium—where, often enough, high ceilings and hard surfaces realize an actual echo chamber of variable reverberation times and intensities—King echoed the divine voice of creation, I would argue, which he himself heard echoed in the "Let freedom ring" hortative.[55]

Although the unadorned spokenness of the "ring" that moved Blakey to a "loud and prolonged cackling laugh" failed to have a ringing effect on tape—as "Not long" had a humming effect in the speech's previous sequence—a more elusive reverberation conducted by the acoustic architecture of high ceilings and hard surfaces must have traveled at least as far as Blakey's listening body, just steps removed from King at the podium. If the gym had been a church or a chapel, we might say that Blakey's "cackling" laugh was "the effect of an angel affecting the auditory nerves, as an apparition does the optic nerve or retina," after John Wesley.[56] But the secularist has at hand the logic of what acousticians refer to as "early lateral reflections" and "auditory source width," early and late reverberative intensities that reach the body "out of phase," to understand the subvocalic circulations of sound in the idiosyncratic acoustic space closest to the dream-stirred speaker.[57] In whatever discourse their accounting-for is most profitably made, the issues of echo and reverberation, whether sonant or soundless, are inseparable from the acoustic conditions of the physical setting where they come into vibrational being. Thus, a different sound obtains between deliveries of the same speech sequence orated at Booker T. Washington High School in Rocky Mount and, seven months later, Detroit's newly erected municipal arena. The distinctive acoustic and recording conditions of Cobo Hall marked King's June 1963 improvisation on "Facing the Challenge of a New Age," the precursor to his iconic Washington, DC, oration two months later, with an unrestrained dialogic sound of civic performativity that was not so much absent in Rocky Mount as distilled into a history-choking laugh.

"A Dream That Came True": Detroit

Detroit's Cobo Hall was conceived in the aftermath of World War II. As architectural historian William B. Keller wrote, "Postwar planning theory invited radical change in the fabric of cities; action on a large scale was both dynamic and liberating."[58] Tied to federal allocations designed for the renewal of America's business and commercial districts, large-scale downtown development projects were launched in significant municipalities all over the country. "City planners sought to build downtown by developing large entities on top of the existing street grid," Keller adds. In this period, the civic arena entered onto the urban environment "because public policy included it in the investment formulas directed toward the rehabilitation of the central business district[s]" of major cities.[59] In Detroit, a ten-block site at the foot of Woodward Avenue on the Detroit River was selected for arena construction. Designed by father and son Eliel and Eero Saarinen and named for Albert Cobo, mayor of Detroit from 1950 to 1957, the circular, roofed Cobo Hall was the focal point of a complex of opposingly rectilinear, and somewhat lesser, exhibition buildings built out from it. The Saarinens envisioned this modernist "superblock organization of rectilinear forms around one dominant curvilinear form" as a contrast to the gridwork of the city's streets and aging industrial sites already set for urban clearance and renewal.[60] Built handsomely of green slate, gray granite, and aluminum- and-glass panels separated by white marble pilasters, the Cobo Hall exterior projected a postwar modernist design worthy of the MIT Chapel, the US Embassy in London, Washington Dulles International Airport, the Gateway Arch in St. Louis, and other notable Saarinen structures.

Inside Cobo Hall (figure 7.2), sleek marble surfaces, multihued concrete walls, and tile and teakwood floors helped effect a bright and exceptionally capacious interior. Three tiers of theater-styled seats, ascending eighty-four feet to the hall's suspended ceiling, lined the U-shaped perimeter of the arena's auditorium with capacity for almost ten thousand. Overlooking 21,600 square feet of open, adaptable floor space at the center of the hall, Cobo's seating bowl opened onto the arena stage at one end. A portable structure measuring fifty-six by forty by four feet, the stage was set below a cascade of decorative panels which, "appear[ing] to float," were nonetheless fixed in their place so as to provide "a proscenium-like focal point for stage shows and a surface for projection of color effects."[61] More impressively, the view of the stage was wholly unobstructed. As no pillars or other visual impediments were present to interfere with the audience's sight lines, both floor and stage were in clear view of every seat in the hall. To city leaders, the completion of Saarinens's futurist design of Cobo Hall in 1960 was, in more ways than one, "a dream that came true."

I have not referred to this formulation of official feeling toward Cobo's completion in oneiric terms to exploit an available cliché ("a dream come true"). Rather, the phrase "a dream that came true" plays on the will of the City of Detroit to do so. Headed by Detroit's Department Report and Information Committee, a 1963 promotional campaign boasted of Cobo Hall's "part [in] the effort to make Detroit an unsurpassed convention and tourist center."[62] Across two full-color pages, their brochure boldly declared, "COBO HALL, a dream that came true." That very year, in June, King traveled to Michigan for the Detroit Walk to Freedom, a mass rally of 125,000 organized by the Reverends C. L. Franklin and Albert Cleage and the Detroit Council for Human Rights. At the end of the march, from the Cobo Hall stage, King offered a second variation on the Langston Hughes leitmotif enlivening the near-ending of "Facing the Challenge of a New Age." Before a crowd significantly larger than the Rocky Mount assembly, King shared a dream of his own, "a dream deeply rooted in the American dream," that, despite the proud completion of Cobo Hall, was not yet. Whether it was purely coincidental that the "dream that came to be" in Detroit was also the site of the freedom-dream that was not yet—and not a speedy appropriation, barely concealed, of King's moving speech-making there to commercial ends—is difficult to say. What is clearer is that *King* connected with the realized dream of Cobo Hall at the level of an acoustical aesthetics of what Paul Carter calls "in-between sounds" inspired by practices of radical democratic listening the Saarinens, I'd venture to say, never heard coming.[63]

In *The Sound in Between: Voice, Space, Performance*, Carter theorizes "in-between sounds" as ambiguous sounds that obtain in "representing what

7.2   Interior of Cobo Hall, Detroit, MI.

cannot be said" in the dialogic encounter between two languages.[64] More precisely, Carter points up a "dialogic vitality" animating the "sound in-between." He narratively relates the dynamics of this cross-lingual (mis) communications act:

> The sound in-between: listening to an unfamiliar language it is a constant experience. Unable to distinguish significant words and phrases or grasp the nuances of different stress patterns, naturally we tend to respond to those sounds that are recognizable and, eager to make contact, we repeat them. For their part our interlocutors are equally puzzled: for what we say back to them, our echoic syllables or proto-words, have no meaning in *their* tongue. What approximates to a lexical unit in our language is, in their tone, most likely only a phoneme, a verbal building-block without any import of its own.[65]

In the "temporary meeting place" where, Carter argues, sound in-between happens across linguistic systems, I see a spatiosonant analog for the cut, where the exorbitances of speech and hearing abide in black speech-making and oratorical performance as what Erving Goffman has called "forms of talk."[66] In the cut across the ritualized divide between listener and speaker, the "echoic syllables and proto-words" left where dialogic interpretation fails betray the stranger speaking and the platform speaker in the same way. Despite the sincerest effort to communicate, the stranger who parrots what they have heard but has not understood threatens the very connection desperately sought, as "a temporary rapport" gives way to "a mutual suspicion."[67] Similarly, the podium speaker learns that monologue is a misnomer for the dynamic action involved in what passes reductively as "holding forth" or "delivering a speech" or—worst of all—"public speaking," all pretending to the possibility of disinterested public discourse and apolitical audition.

But more than the sheer fact of in-between sounds left in the wake of an originary desire, "partly historical, partly performative,"[68] to move toward the other with and by way of sound (e.g., a whimper, a word, a sentence, a song, a knock—each "a symbolic means to a human end"[69]), I mean to underline an aesthetic as well, what Goffman calls a "production format" and Carter characterizes above as "echoic." From Cobo's minimalist stage, King sounded his Freedom Rally address into the yawning spatiality separating platform and people, the one from the thousands whose listening bodies, packed into arena seating ceiling high or standing tall on their feet over every inch of the arena floor, painted the walls and carpeted the ground. Both King's own cadenced speech-making, then, and the sounds and rhythms generated in the interchange demand close hearing since, together, address and audition approach an aesthetics of radical democratic relationality. To borrow from Eidsheim, this "spatial-relational and acoustic"[70] aesthetics of voice, vibration, and (black) political desire can rightly be styled *echoic* (after Carter) since King's audience may be heard promiscuously and improvisationally echoing his most resonating (affectively relatable) and resonant (acoustically resounding) lines on tape. King speaks in kind, echoing not so much his listeners' words echoing his, but the in-between sounds generated in their ongoing recursive exchange. Standing on a small wooden box behind a modest podium made too tall by a tangled grove of microphones, King lifted his voice as well. With no less calculation, he pitched it high above the podium's wood and metal structure into the lofty interspace of echoic sound, both worded and wordless, "passing back and forth between [normative] meaning and nonmeaning" in radical dialogical fashion.[71]

"Spaces may amplify and project the voice but they enlarge extraneous noise too," Carter writes in *The Sound In Between*.[72] For all the pride taken by city leaders in the direct, unobstructed sight lines from seat to stage in Cobo Hall, the arena's open-bowl, high-ceiling design generated an uninterrupted flow of sound waves between stage and spectator. Thus, the visual focus on the individual speaker and "the smooth contours of speech" vocalized by one as fluent as King could scarcely censor the "shadowland of turbulent rhythms, puns and vocalic ambiguities" in the open arena-space all bearing witness by way of echoic syllables and proto-words to the dialogical dream.[73] Above and beneath Cobo's floor and ceiling, respectively, an oceanic field of overlapping vibrations emerged so full and resounding that the space itself became performative, a third voice "eager to enter into conversation, to carve out a position from which to speak,"[74] as Carter imagined it. In Carter's theory of architectural acoustics, this third voice is "the dialogical voice."[75] In theatrical terms, the dialogical voice "emerges when the actors achieve a rhythm, when they pitch the voice back and forth and find their tempo collectively."[76] In this way, the sounds which enlivened Cobo Hall on June 23, 1963, did not simply reference the rally and the one-and-a-half-mile Detroit Walk to Freedom immediately preceding it as historical events unfolding in real time but called attention to the arena itself as a *performance space* of radical democratic dialogue.

Although Carter does not explicitly characterize the dialogical voice in radical democratic terms, by which I mean terms suggestive of the will and potential of ordinary people (*demos*) for intensified political agency in the unfinished project of democracy,[77] the dialogic in-between voice is animated by a similarly pluralist and future-facing drive. *The Sound In Between*'s primal scene of "listening to an unfamiliar language," in fact, repeats the paradigmatic colonial encounter, "the first contact between peoples of different races," as Carter portrays it.[78] Inasmuch as "the paradigm of European arrival and occupation is the admiral who, even before dropping anchor, wafts his hand round the breadth of the bay and promptly possesses it with a name,"[79] the dialogical voice speaks a tertiary tone of resistance to the pieties of the colonizing subject. Moreover, this voice rejects the imperative to imagine its own history within an imposed framework of historical thought and narration that may be dignifying in one respect—in its counterhistory of the colonial encounter—but not finally liberatory. Instead, the dialogical voice insists on a "third, in-between history, the frankly speculative and open-ended account of the differences and misunderstandings that dogged human relations, and which . . . remain unresolved."[80] King's Detroit Freedom Rally address and audition echoed inside Cobo dialogically, according to an-archic rhythms and a radical democratic drive in the face of forgotten and unrealized freedoms.

In its in-betweenness, the dialogic sound holding space between King at the Cobo podium and the human surround of his listeners is not, to quote Carter, "a natural sound," or even "a fully linguistic one" for that matter.[81] In its ambiguity, it "hover[s] on the border between human and nonhuman sounds."[82] It is what one hears on tape as so much prattling, chatter, and

Crawfordian "hum" beneath and above the rhetorical reach of the civil rights spokesman toward a freedom of in-between speech, liberated from the lectern to sound the echoic open space of radical (black) democratic hope. The echoic character of this acoustic will-to-freedom, this intensifying revolution drive in the convention hall, undoubtedly drew on the overflowing sociality generated by the march beforehand as it disclosed "flashes of people's aspirations and frustrations," as Robin D. G. Kelley put it—these "*imprecise public voicings*, and signs of crisis"—carrying on in the arena like an additional track beneath King's speaking.[83] Like Reverend Blakey's laugh, King's speech-making distilled the anarrangement of these (black) sounds and political sensibilities into one pregnant with the many.

The Great March to Freedom: MLK and the Motown Sound

In Detroit, King revisited the dream he had proclaimed in Rocky Mount, North Carolina, eight months earlier. With characteristic deliberateness, he began his appreciably shorter thirty-six minutes with a protocolary acknowledgment of the platform presence of the most popular preacher in black America at the time, "my good friend, the Reverend C. L. Franklin." A universally recognized recording artist in black America with seventy-five recordings, including *The Eagle Stirreth in Her Nest* (1953), and a national radio broadcast to his credit, Franklin was also a leading light in the civil rights struggle in Detroit. His seat on the Cobo dais, therefore, was far more substantive than symbolic of his celebrity. His presence alongside King was appropriate to his equal profile with King's, the interplay of faith, black consciousness, and civil rights activism being common to the Detroit and Atlanta preacher alike. But the universal familiarity of Franklin's own "million-dollar voice" in the Motor City and over black radio across the country would lend the event a deeper, keener sonicity. Certainly, Berry Gordy, founder and president of Motown Records, thought of the affair at Cobo in profitably sonic terms. King had agreed months earlier to allow Motown to record and distribute his Freedom Rally speech, for a four-hundred-dollar advance and forty cents per copy sold. Though it's doubtful Gordy's vision of King as the next spoken-word recording star required Franklin, Franklin's visibility as president of the Detroit Council on Human Rights (DCHR) almost surely reminded Gordy and King both of the earnings potential of King's work. On the Chess and Battle labels, Franklin had already amassed a small fortune from his recording royalties.[84] King, on the other hand, was cash-strapped. Gordy, one of the most important curators of black sounds in the twentieth century, perceived something valuable—and salable—in the "I have a dream" refrain that could possibly change that.

Whereas King's speech in Rocky Mount closed with the same "Let freedom ring" refrain he would employ later in Washington, DC, to bring "I Have a Dream" to its ringing finish, in Detroit the "I have a dream" set piece furnished his address its peroration. King had honed his words for a national stage. In place of local references like "Sasser County, Georgia," and "Rocky Mountain, North Carolina,"[85] King called up "Georgia and Mississippi and Alabama" as synecdoche for the segregated South generally. Mention of Emmett Till and Medgar Evers (recently assassinated), tragic symbols of the depths of racial hate in the country, did much the same here to cast King's Detroit speech as a national address. One line, though, would challenge King's reformulation of that closing sequence. "I have a dream," he pronounced as he took in the crowd, "that one day right here in Detroit, Negroes will be able to buy a house or rent a house anywhere that their money will carry them and they will be able to get a job." King's allusions to the problems of black unemployment, wage discrimination, and a program of urban renewal in Detroit resulting in the dislocation of tens of thousands of black citizens from the city's Black Bottom and Paradise Valley districts exposed Detroit's postwar renaissance as a progressivist facade.[86] And yet for all its local specificity, Detroit's issues also reflected the general conditions and concerns of millions of African Americans gone North away from Southern hardships. By 1963, in fact, Detroit had emerged as one of America's most significant cities, a model city in the view of many. With dreams of a future of social and economic prosperity, the hope of which was symbolized in brick and mortar by Cobo Hall, Detroit was transforming into a progressive—sometimes radical—political and cultural hub in 1963.[87] It was also becoming a singular black acoustic community with a unique musicosonic style and sensibility that soon would come to be known everywhere as "the Motown sound."

Undeniably, the vocal talents of Motown's early artists—Stevie Wonder, the Miracles, Martha and the Vandellas, Mary Wells, and the Four Tops among them—were extraordinary. And Gordy's determined marketing efforts did not fail to extend Motown's modern Detroit sound to wider and wider black and, soon enough, white audiences. But the particularity of "the Motown sound" also lay in Detroit's distinction as the industrial Disneyland of the United States, the city one historian called "modernity's great tool room, its vast industrial complex the envy of the world."[88] Although many have argued, as Suzanne E. Smith points out in *Dancing in the Street: Motown and the Cultural Politics of Detroit*, that the Motown phenomenon "could have happened anywhere, or at least in any city with a large and vital African American population," such arguments, she avers, downplay "community life, urban geography, economic structures [and] race relations" in Motown's rise to black musical and cultural prominence.[89] Instead, they "tend to emphasize [Gordy's] individual ambition."[90] I follow Smith, though, in maintaining that the Motown sound in 1963 was inseparable from Detroit's cultural, political, and historical distinctiveness as a newly industrial city and terminus for myriad African Americans fleeing the South. More specifically, the Motown sound, far from springing uniquely from Gordy's musical and entrepreneurial imagination, also materialized out of the soundscapes of Detroit's black cultural and labor histories. In a way, the Motown sound preceded Motown itself.

As early as 1914, when Henry Ford vowed that none of the workers at his Ford Motor Company would earn less than five dollars a day and "Negroes came hundreds of miles to line up outside his employment offices,"[91] as LeRoi Jones (Amiri Baraka) commented in *Blues People: Negro Music in White America*, the blues found a home in Detroit with them. As Ford and other automakers drew more and more African Americans out of the rural South to the assembly lines of the early automotive industry, and the blues offered those thousands of early black auto workers "a creative outlet from assembly-line work," as Smith writes,[92] the music inevitably evolved in relation to (the soundscape of) Detroit's modernizing technologies. One Detroit bluesman, a Chrysler worker known as Bobo Jenkins, hinted at precisely this musical and machinic confluence: "That whirlin' machinery gives me the beat. It's like hearin' a band play all day long. Any song I ever wrote that's any good has come to me standin' on that line."[93] Motown, of course, did not record traditional blues; it fashioned "the Sound of Young America" instead, as its company slogan proclaimed. Still, Motown capitalized on Detroit's industrial ethos and the automobile industry's emerging technologies to distill the unique sound, derived from blues roots, that came to be rhythm and blues.

Whereas Suzanne Smith emphasizes Motown's Fordist operations with Gordy declaring his vision for Motown as " a place where a kid off the street could walk in one door an unknown and come out another a recording artist—a star,"[94] I, on the other hand, want to highlight the relationship between the Motown sound and Detroit's new automotive technologies to point to the influence of technology in general (e.g., new media technologies, innovations in manufacturing, building and design technologies) on the distinctive timbre of modern black sound in Motown's Detroit. More particularly, I want to underline the point, expressed best by Smith, that "while Motown artists could have performed at the rally" at Cobo Hall in June 1963, "the company chose instead to record King's compelling arguments."[95] As Motown's studio "was one of the best equipped in the city to preserve King's speech with the highest degree of audio fidelity,"[96] the opportunity presented by King's Cobo Hall appearance was too significant and commercially salable (if C. L. Franklin was any index) to leave to the popular press to record in writing only. Just as automation abruptly modernized automotive manufacturing in the 1950s, in other words, new audio technologies helped establish the Motown sound not a decade later, revolutionizing black musical style, performance, and commercial appeal for which reportage was simply no substitute.

In 2019 Dante Fumo and Joel Handley set out to uncover the exact acoustic grammar Gordy and his sound engineers employed in the small upfitted recording studio on West Grand Boulevard a few short miles from Cobo. In their article for Reverb.com, "What Makes Motown Sound Like Motown," Fumo and Handley discerned that Motown's recording operations were distinguished in three categories: "All-Star Talent," "Expert Engineering," and "A Well-Equipped Studio."[97] As talent goes, Motown's house band, the Funk Brothers, was a superior group and vital to Motown's musical success long-term, Fumo and Handley maintain. Too, Motown's engineers were wizards at control boards, innovating and experimenting to elevate the Motown sound above industry formulas. Vital as talent and engineering were, however, Motown's modernism inhered most fundamentally in its high-tech recording investments. As a matter of priority, Fumo and Handley explain, "Motown kept up with the cutting-edge of recording technology, from their custom-built direct box and Motown EQ to the latest and greatest from Pultec, Langevin, and Fairchild."[98] Above all the cutting-edge devices Motown had on hand in its cramped Hitsville USA studio, though, was a low-tech echo chamber, "one of the most iconic elements of the Motown sound," which lent the music dimensionality.[99]

As Fumo and Handley describe it, "a speaker and a microphone sat permanently wired up in the attic of Hitsville, which had been drywalled and coated with shellac but otherwise untreated. During mixing, engineers would pipe certain tracks through the speaker, record the reverberation with the microphone, and blend it into the mix to add a sense of space."[100] Too indistinct for the average ear to consciously take in, this echoic effect, generated overhead in the studio's attic space, repeated, if it did not prefigure, the acoustic conditions of the spatiosonant in-between found at Cobo. If the Motown echo chamber "add[ed] a sense of space" to the recording and, with other subtle distortion techniques, increased degrees of tonal coloring, then the spatiosonant in-between where King's voice mixed with the acoustic feedback of the listening bodies lining the hall's interior behaved as an echo chamber all its own, an effect accomplished by the drummed roof of the public arena commonplace in municipal design after World War II.[101] There, in the ovate hollow of auditorium space where the thousands sat or stood in the surround and reverberating outbreaks of antiphonal applause joined King's voice, the echoic effect approached that which the Hitsville echo chamber helped generate in the percussive intro of the Supremes' "Where Did Our Love Go?," for example. The extemporaneous hand-clapping at Cobo, like the foot-tamping that styled the Supremes' intro and lasting pulse, acted resistively to transform the narrowly verbal representation of (black) meaning into an ensemblic in-between sound of radical democratic desire. More promiscuously expressed than the mensural beat in "Where Did Our Love Go?," the arrhythmic, reformative applause in the break of speech and space could only have been engineered on the ground, since the stage, Carter writes, "is almost by definition a site cleared for speech."[102] Little there offers resistance to the univocal representation of meaning the radical democratic impulse necessarily contests. Those who packed Cobo Hall offered applause, marked new time, accented thought, and punctuated the in-between space according to an alternate grammar of speech and communication from that which organized the modern industrial regime and its veiled racial logics. Gordy captured the resistive sounds on *The Great March to Freedom*.

The echoic undercurrents of King's address at Cobo Hall, Gordy's LP suggests to close listeners, were more than an architectural effect alone, the converging and interlocking articulations of political speech and public demonstration under Cobo's drum roof. They also issued from the mimetic repetition of "significant words and phrases" central to Carter's theory of in-between sound as "a new cross-cultural *argot*."[103] In this case, the eager repetition of "I have a dream" and its adjunct, "one day," by some audience members confirmed the coproduction of black speech performance by a black acoustic community disposed to polyphonically re-sound the black speaker's voice. At Cobo, King's liberal integrationist voice was given back to him vaguely "changed,"[104] in other words. The acoustic echo his audience realized at Cobo, alternately reverberatory and mimetic, modally speaking, did not so much antiphonally *answer* as *augment* King's voice and vision with a bustle-hum of voices all their own. Theirs were not separate from his but rather within it. In this way, King's Detroit address, though soon overshadowed by the "I Have a Dream" oration in Washington, DC, weeks later, disclosed how critical the politics of place, space, and audition were to King's second, seamless performance of dreaming freedom.

King's Cobo Hall speech was released by Motown's subsidiary, Gordy Records, on August 28, 1963. Calculated by Gordy to capitalize on the immense publicity already surrounding the March on Washington, his promotional strategy to release Motown's first spoken-word album, whose title cleverly played on the upcoming Washington demonstration, on the very day of the carefully planned national event, was not entirely to King's liking. According to black music historian Brian Ward, King was "clearly piqued" at Gordy.[105] Perhaps serendipitously, Gordy had also formally designated a portion of the previously untitled address "I Have a Dream." While King resented Gordy for exploiting the timing and title of *The Great March to Freedom*, placing *The Great March* in direct competition with a planned March on Washington album to benefit the tapped-out SCLC, Gordy's alertness to the propulsive rhetorical power of the "I have a dream" refrain, business acumen notwithstanding, may suggest the degree to which sometime songwriter Gordy discerned its aural harmony with Detroit's nascent Motown sound. For the Motown sound of black migration, industrial modernization, urban renewal, and black disinheritance that animated the Freedom Rally in Detroit was as unique as the voice of the dreamer. Therefore, a second album, one that Gordy envisioned for the *Washington* speech engineered and sold by Motown as well, was not, from a purely acoulogical point of view, an irrational proposition. In matters of place, space, and audition, after all, the sonic ecology of Washington, DC, was a world apart from Detroit. Acoustically, the outdoor mall was as unlike the room design of the postwar auditorium in Detroit as the Detroit auditorium was unlike the school gym in Rocky Mount eliciting laughter as one of its resonant effects.

Dream and Variation: Washington, DC

Early in *The Soundscape: Our Sonic Environment and the Tuning of the World*, R. Murray Schafer introduces "the main themes of a soundscape by distinguishing between what we call *keynote sounds, signals* and *soundmarks*."[106] Setting aside "signals" and "soundmarks," I have implicitly argued that the Motown sound, insofar as it is a general name for a historical intonation of black cultural and labor history in early industrial Detroit, was the "keynote sound" informing King's Freedom Rally address. A "keynote sound," Schafer explains, establishes "the anchor or fundamental tone" of a sonic experience, "and although the material may modulate around it, often obscuring its importance, it is in reference to this point that everything else takes on its special meaning." More than that, "keynote sounds do not have to be listened to consciously," Shafer writes, for though only "overheard," they "cannot be overlooked."[107] In visual terms, keynote sounds constitute the "ground" to the sound object's "figure"; the form the figure takes depends vitally upon the ground, which is anterior to its definition in and as form. All of this is to say, in the final analysis, that if the space in between blackness and modernization generated a keynote sound differentiating Detroit's Cobo Hall from Rocky Mount in terms of tone, resonance, and audition, then the keynote sound in Washington, DC, was more manifestly *amplitudinal* than both, given its out-of-doors airing.

While much has been written about King's August 28, 1963, "I Have a Dream" address on the National Mall, including significant monographs dedicated to its thought and composition by Hansen (2003), Sundquist (2009), C. B. Jones and Connelly (2011), and W. J. Miller (2015), I want to turn attention away from the formalist concerns of intellectual genealogy, rhetorical strategy, oratorical conceits, and structural logics that preoccupy those works. My concern is the aural force of "I Have a Dream"—its power to incite radical democratic listening. To boil down the success of King's speech to its most celebrated rhetorical and performative aspects—its power of poetic expression, anaphoric facility, citational eclecticism, and unselfconscious philosophizing—risks neglecting that essential property of black oration or vocal art that is, as I have shown, audition. As Jones, King's onetime lawyer, was compelled to concede, "If you read the text of the speech, while you might be impressed and moved by certain parts of it, you would probably think it was a good speech, but not necessarily a profound or powerful speech. . . . What made the speech an extraordinary speech was a combination of factors. One of the most important was that this was a speech at a gathering of . . . the largest group of people assembled anywhere in the country at any time in the history of the United States for any purpose, [only?] twenty-five percent of whom were white."[108] As a collaborator with King and with a second King associate, Stanley Levinson, on the written composition of King's speech, Jones recognized that King's improvisatory departure from the written script short minutes in was as much *called for* by the listening body/bodies of "the largest group of people assembled anywhere in the country at any time" as it was by King's extemporaneous divining of an opening onto a higher plane of historical feeling.[109] Another observer's report that the dream cadenza "set off reverberations" (in) between King and the listening crowd may have been aimed at conveying the haptical power of King's oratory only metaphorically,[110] but the metaphor potentially marshaled was too perfect for figurative ends. King's speech not only elicited audible applause and reinforcement, it *literally* reverberated across the full breadth of bodily, environmental, and spatial materialities within range of King's brilliant vibrato voice.

Somewhat more discerning than other commentators of the categoric leap King realized by extemporizing "I have a dream" in Washington, Jones maintained that "naturally, letters spilled across the page cannot even begin to re-create the power of that moment.... In a very real sense, the [end of the] speech is truly meant to be heard."[111] If the March on Washington's other featured speakers—nearly ten of them, all men—saw only an immense crowd on the Mall as they addressed their onlookers, King at least recognized that he was not addressing a crowd so much as an *audience*. The distinction lay in a sense of the greater raucousness of the crowd over the subtler self-consciousness of the audience as a listening body, if yet a voluble one. "I think [the march is] really, really—ah—really a very good thing," said one reflective marcher to a WRVR (NY) radio host covering the event, but "it wasn't quite as enthusiastic as I thought it would be."[112] The Rochester woman seemed to have expected a crowd, not an audience: "It seems to me that, ah, there would have been more rallying and everything like that."[113]

Had he heard the woman's remark, Bayard Rustin, the march's organizer and operations director, would have been very gratified, ironically. Determined to mitigate against any potential for acts of violence that could undercut the commitment of the march and its organizational sponsors to nonviolent direct action, Rustin hatched an astute plan that, devised though it was to manage the crowd on the Mall, helped create the condition of possibility for King's speech to "reverberate" later. To ensure order, Rustin concluded that "people needed to hear the program clearly."[114] He insisted on a superior sound system at ten times the average cost for large Mall events. The day before the march, American Amplifier and Television (AAT), a Lanham, Maryland, outfit boasting two presidential inaugurations, assembled Rustin's preferred sound system at the march site. A nineteen-thousand-dollar rental, the system delivered one square mile of clear sound from the Lincoln Memorial to the Washington Monument as Rustin, who would countenance no compromises in this, required. Rustin called the installation of AAT's loudspeakers "a classic resolution" to the problem of crowd control. To "keep a crowd from becoming something else," Rustin averred, you must "transform it into an *audience*."[115] By the time King approached the podium at the end of the march program, the loudspeakers had not only effectively transformed the march from a rambunctious political rally into a stage-based performance of open-air political theater but also helped establish the boundaries of a black listening lab. Here, in the auditory in-between of monument and memorial, nine outsized electrostatic speakers and several more "horn-type speakers to reach clear back to the Washington Monument" commingled with 250,000 listening bodies and nearly 340,000 square feet of water filling the reflecting pool in front of the Lincoln Memorial to create an amplitude for the carrying (on) of sound over and beyond the limits of time and other measures of political respectability.[116]

Loud Speakers and Forced Listening

Originally, the March on Washington was planned at the Capitol, not the Lincoln Memorial. The Eighty-eighth Congress was in session there, and march organizers believed a gathering in front of the Capitol would put pressure on the nation's lawmakers to pass a civil rights bill under consideration. Organizers had been resolute about the demonstration site for months, even when President John F. Kennedy cautioned that a march in front of the Capitol risked antagonizing lawmakers by creating, as he put it, "an atmosphere of intimidation."[117] Later, however, United Auto Workers president Walter Reuther convinced event leaders that the Lincoln Memorial, only somewhat removed from the Capitol, was a superior site for the march's aims. The Lincoln Memorial, he reasoned, had the advantage of a deeper historical symbolism exactly one hundred years after Lincoln's Emancipation Proclamation. Nor would the change of venue diminish the spectacle power of the civil rights showdown organizers were aiming to bring about. The blaring public address system Rustin had seen to, though surely not powerful enough to deliver *two* square miles of sound all the way to the Capitol, still allowed acousmatic acts of "aural aggression"[118] against legislative inaction on a civil rights bill and, at another level entirely, the ongoing background noise of Southern sonic terrorism to black civil life. Against the vicious aurality of aggravated canines, homespun explosives, and hate-filled invectives, orator and audience set King's "I Have a Dream" into flight well beyond the real and symbolic limits of Lincoln's architectural and historical shadow. This it excited by way of the loudspeakers hidden in plain sight of all.

To be clear, the *flight* of "I Have a Dream" past proper political speech and beyond the imagined perimeter of the Mall alludes to more than a dazzling display of eloquent speech. It also signifies sound's transversal will—its motile ontology—which is to say, its fugitive principle. To set a speech to flight oratorically is to free it from the pretense of words anchoring intelligibility and meaning *in place*. In flight, oration surrenders words to the winds of excess(es) that help words as sound carry, trespassing the spatial bounds of permitted protest. So while march organizers were committed to realizing a peaceful demonstration, "orderly, but not subservient . . . non-violent but not timid . . . outspoken, but not raucous,"[119] their carefully scripted "Statement by the Heads of the Ten Organizations Calling for Discipline in Connection with the Washington March of August 28, 1963," made it no less clear that they were equally devoted to "the marvelous new militancy" King commended in Detroit. That militancy, despite the urgency of peaceable conduct by the gathered march participants, was not abandoned in Detroit, in other words. It was alive in Washington, too. It expressed itself in the unthought of aural flight aimed east toward the Capitol and, symbolically speaking, everywhere beyond it. The "not subservient . . . not timid . . . outspoken" voice of black emancipatory hope and resistance approached the brilliance of black song as it sounded out from the steps of the Lincoln Memorial. Not surprisingly, black music, as Frank Wilderson reminded us, "has always known, and not been afraid to acknowledge, just how high the stakes of Black thought are."[120]

For all the oratory represented on the march program—King, A. Philip Randolph, John Lewis, Whitney Young, and Rabbi Joachim Prinz, among others—the program was not without musical distinction. In 1963 Mahalia Jackson was an international icon. She was, far and away, the greatest living gospel singer in the world. No stranger to the ritual drama of Washington pomp and protest, Jackson had previously performed on the Mall in 1957 at the Prayer Pilgrimage for Freedom and at John F. Kennedy's inaugural ball (alongside Nat King Cole, Harry Belafonte, Ella Fitzgerald, and Tony Curtis). At the March on Washington she joined Marian Anderson and "Mrs. Medgar Evers" as the only women to have an official role on the stage, Evers the only speaker.[121] Although Jackson's performance did not immediately precede King, it set the stage for him, nevertheless. A. Philip Randolph introduced Jackson with scant words: "We will now listen to another great singer, Ms. Mahalia Jackson. She will sing at the request of Dr. Martin Luther King, 'I've Been Buked and I've Been Scorned.' Ms. Mahalia Jackson." In deep contralto tones, Jackson commanded her vast audience. Unhurried, she seemed not to worry for time, indifferent to Rustin's obsessive timekeeping. Jackson followed the slow piano and organ prelude precisely, her voice seeming to extend their play:

> I been buked, and I been scorned
> I been buked, Lord, and I been scorned
> I been buked, Lord, and I been scorned
> Yes, I been talked about, sure as you born
>
> T'ain't but a'one thing I done wrong
> T'ain't but a'one thing I done wrong
> T'aint but a'one thing I done wrong, Lord
> You know I stayed in the valley, Lord, too long
>
> You know, I'm gonna tell my Lord when I get home
> You know, I'm gonna tell my Lord when I get home
> Yeah, I'm gonna tell my, my Lord when I, yeah, I get home
> How you been mistreating me so long.

The singer's intention to "tell my Lord" the many cruelties endured stirred the marchers audibly. But more than the will to justice Jackson's words expressed ("*I'm gonna tell my Lord . . . / How you been mistreating me so long*"), she electrified the Mall with her clearly defiant growl: and by growl, I mean at once the specific affect that betrayed "I've Been Buked and I've Been Scorned" as an insurgent's testimony and the growl as a heuristic trope for the historical voice and aesthetics of radical blackness. For it gave a sound to the new militancy King praised as "marvelous," growling back at Birmingham and the vicious K-9 tactics Sheriff Eugene "Bull" Connor infamously marshaled to terrorize young civil rights marchers there just months before. In that moment, Jackson's voice, to follow an argument of Moten's about Baraka's poem "Black Dada Nihilismus," distilled the ancestral sound, became "metavoice, shadowed and deepened by mourning, moaning, growl."[122]

Soon enough, Jackson had transformed the largest public demonstration in American history into a revival meeting. Deeply affected by her performance of the generally improvised spiritual, the Mall erupted with a thunderous applause when it appeared she had fulfilled her mission and was done. But her congregants were imploring her for more. From one point of view, she obliged; from another, she had not come to the end their applause supposed, but to a vamp. As Braxton Shelley teaches us, a vamp is a "musical module" in gospel performativity characterized by repetition and intensification.[123]

According to Shelley, the gospel vamp is that musical unit of "escalatory techniques," vocal and instrumental, which implicitly "announce a [new] heightened phase of liturgical activity,"[124] not a denouement. Cast in the light of sound's tropic flight in air, vamps are, as another musicologist put it, "holding patterns—stalls in the rhythmic and melodic unfolding of a song" that engender "a relentless build-up" and, over a protracted term, release.[125] Confirmation that Jackson had come to just such a place in her performance was not long in coming. Defying the bar line's control of the performance, Jackson postponed her song's logical finish with a moaning that not only led to another vamp and verse but extended her apportioned time on the stage. In Jackson's voice, "I've Been Buked and I've Been Scorned" sounded (out) the deeper depths of black feminist memory, experience, and dreamwork that had until then gotten such short shrift on the program.

> Mmmmmmm
> I been buked and I been scorned
> Oh yeah, I been buked, Lord, and I been scorned
> Oh Lord, and I been talked about sure as you born. Hallelujah!

Sure as you born. Against the backdrop of black maternal and infant mortality attendant to the rise of gospel blues in Chicago, which I discussed in chapter 4, "sure as you born" was hardly an apolitical phrase in Jackson's mouth. Perhaps only a black woman from Chicago could have shouted "Hallelujah!" on singing (or hearing) a line so seemingly mundane (and frequently ironic) as this, but few people who cared to hear it could miss how deep and knowing the singer's woe was.

There, in the shadow of Lincoln, on the event of emancipation's centennial, Jackson sang too the travail of the enslaved who first sang "I've Been Buked and I've Been Scorned," calling into the present a continuous and apposite slave past. As she yielded to the gospel impulse toward and against finality, Jackson effectively stole time for ancestral witnessing, in the religious sense, to the indignities of black life and struggle the Washington march was intent on redressing. In her voice another unseen but listening audience, the many-thousands-gone, both anticipated and seconded what King had yet to say but was coming: "One hundred years later, the Negro still is not free. One hundred years later, the life of the Negro is still sadly crippled by the manacles of segregation and the chains of discrimination. One hundred years later, the Negro lives on a lonely island of poverty in the midst of a vast ocean of material prosperity. One hundred years later, the Negro is still languished in the corners of American society and finds himself an exile in his own land. And so we've come here today to dramatize a shameful condition."[126]

In solemn vibrato tones overflowing metrical time and predictability with unexpected glissandos, ad-libbing, feminine endings, and visceral shouts, Jackson delivered the unrepresentable sound of the slave past as a living and ongoing presence King's words alone would have been handicapped to fully convey. Even more, Jackson's particular talent for locating sounds and broken sentences in the place where words do not go fit her specially to the translational task. Deferring the listened-for finish of her singing even longer, Jackson began yet another verse where "Hallelujah!" was thought to have punctuated the previous one's emphatic end.[127] When it seemed she was through, in other words, she positively wasn't.

> Stand by me, Lord, stand by me
> Stand by me, Lord, stand by me
> Stand byyyyyy, Lord, me
> Lord I can't stand this old storm
> Lord if you leave, Lord if you leave your child
> I cannot make it alone.

Then came another torrent of cheers and applause. The ovation made known that Jackson was anything but "alone" in the racial storm. The Lord, it seems, was standing by in the press of listening bodies packing the Mall, their fervor re-sounding the judgment of the Divine against racialized oppression in a thunderous, exultant roar. Jackson's *singing* of "I've Been Buked" may have ended, but the *song*, alternately sorrowful and growling, was set to carry on.[128]

Indeed, *carry on* is precisely the end Jackson hoped the growling marvelousness of "I've Been Buked and I've Been Scorned" and her encore performance, "How I Got Over," would accomplish. In her 1969 autobiography, *Movin' On Up*, Jackson recalled the March on Washington contentedly:

> As I sang the words I heard a great murmur come rolling back to me from the multitude below and I sensed that I had reached out and touched a chord....
>
> Flags were waving and people were shouting. It looked as if we had the whole city rocking. I hadn't planned to start a revival meeting but for the moment the joy overflowed throughout the great rally.
>
> *They later said my singing seemed to bounce off the golden dome of the Capitol far down the mall and I've always hoped it reached inside where some of those Congressmen were sitting!*[129]

What else could Jackson have wished for "those Congressmen" on the Hill to hear but the gravelly threat of heavenly retribution for racial abuses suffered by their legislative neglects? Their hearing Jackson's forewarning, though, her express oath to tell how long "you been mistreating me," depended pragmatically on *how far* her voice traveled. The facts of Rustin's preparations notwithstanding, Hansen maintains in *The Dream: Martin Luther King and the Speech That Inspired a Nation* that because so many had gathered on the Mall, "the loudspeakers could not carry the program across the entire crowd."[130] One wonders if the American Amplifier and Television loudspeakers Rustin insisted on, which boasted a wattage high enough to amplify the march's platform proceedings across one square mile, were less true to their claim than the company advertised. Or, if Hansen's account simply mistakes speaker clarity for sound's carriage in open air. In either case, the disagreement between AAT's audiometric boast and Hansen's re-creation of the aural experience hardly matters. Jackson's voice "overflowed ... the great rally" all the same.

Though Jackson's singing could not have directly reached the Capitol dome two miles away, Hansen notes that not a few people in the crowd "carried transistor radios, creating an echo effect with the loudspeakers."[131] Between the AAT loudspeakers and the echoic extension in time and dispersion her voice gained by the radiophonic boost from the crowd, Jackson's growl "reached out and touched a chord," resonating powerfully with the insurgent instincts of many—like the irascible John Lewis and the similarly strident, proto-pessimist leadership of the Student Nonviolent Coordinating Committee (SNCC). Waves of haptic feeling passed over and through the packed hold of the Mall's west end as the listening bodies of two hundred thousand, shoulder to shoulder near the loudspeakers, communicated their audition in—Jackson's words—"a great murmur." Drawing demonstrators into tight-packed pockets of resistive flesh, touching and being touched, the scaffolds of loudspeakers raised several feet overhead and diffusing the air with palpable musical vibrations kept the marchers, but not their growl, from breaking out of the Mall's hold, as if by a magnetic gospel sociality.

Whatever the source of the loudspeakers' power to synchronously convey and constrain the unruly impulses of insurgent listening, the sonic field created by the vibrating intermaterialities of voice, speaker components, and listening flesh exceeded the Mall's structural and landscape symmetries. As "the sonorous outweighs form," in other words, and "enlarges it," in the words of Jean-Luc Nancy, it also lends it "amplitude, ... density, and a vibration or ... undulation whose outline never does anything but approach."[132] This formulation of sound's indeterminate movement, only ever "approach[ing]," contrasts sharply with the strict linearity, symmetry, and axial logic that lay beneath Pierre Charles L'Enfant's historic 1791 blueprint for the Mall itself. The growl heard and felt on the Mall in 1963 not only enlarged the Mall, in a manner of speaking, but gave the sense of *exceeding* the one-square mile of promised speaker dispersion insofar as Jackson's singing—and, soon enough, King's oratory—"seemed to bounce off the golden dome of the Capitol far down the mall," to recall Jackson's reflections. No matter that Jackson's distance from the Capitol precluded her voice from reaching its brilliant dome in strict acoustical terms, it is "the way in which we *perceive* [the field of sound's] amplitude" that grants audition power.[133] Jackson's sense of the level of loudness she achieved—what professional acousticians would call the "headroom" the AAT loudspeakers *seemed* to have allowed— undoubtedly aided the effect of her voice's flight "reach[ing] inside where some of those Congressmen were sitting." The vocalic power of resistance the queen of gospel demonstrated in the minutes before King took the stage established the tone for the kind of convocation the people had been waiting for all day ("It seems to me . . . there would have been more rallying and everything like that"). None could hear Jackson's lead more clearly than King, I shall argue, but others heard her too giving the Mall "amplitude, . . . density, and a vibration."

Moving Speech

On the program, Jackson was followed briefly by Rabbi Joachim Prinz, president of the German American Jewish Congress, whose own religious sensibilities were likely piqued by the sustained cantorial tones of Jackson's spiritual. In fact, we might take his first words on reaching the podium, "I wish I could sing," to index that identification and express a very serious dream-wish for vocalic power equal to Jackson's performance of the unimaginable radicality of slave religion. With a reputation of his own as a charismatic and politically outspoken rabbi who had arrived in the United States from Hitler's Germany in 1937, Prinz was a force in American Jewry. In short order, he had, on the strength of his oratory and liturgical partnership with celebrated cantor Abraham Shapiro, resurrected one of the country's historic synagogues, Temple B'nai Abraham in Newark, New Jersey, from certain demise. An independent congregation severely hobbled by the Great Depression, Temple B'nai Abraham needed a rabbi like Prinz desperately. A preacher of considerable talent without notes, Prinz was practiced in the art of *moving speech* (here flight, growl, echo, and vibrato affects) as it was heard and experienced within the two-thousand-seat oval edifice where, from 1939 to 1976, his voice filled a sanctuary made modern by a soaring domed ceiling and an unobstructed view of the preaching stage from every temple seat. It was not surprising, then, given the acoustical suggestiveness of these architectural details, that in his prepared text for the Washington program, Prinz appealed to sound as a moral, and thus inescapably political, category:

> When I was the rabbi of the Jewish community in Berlin under the Hitler regime, I learned many things. The most important thing that I learned in my life and under those tragic circumstances is that bigotry and hatred are not the most urgent problems. The most urgent, the most disgraceful, the most shameful and the most tragic problem is silence.... America must not remain silent, not merely black America, but all of America. It must speak up and act.... And not for the sake of the Negro. Not for the sake of a black community. But for the sake of the image, the dream, the idea, and the aspiration of America itself.[134]

As much as Prinz meant for America to literally "speak up" against racial subjection, "speak[ing] up" nonetheless understated his intention. Relying on a phrasal distillation of a range of resistive forms of talk, he might have invoked his fellow refugee from Nazi Germany, Hannah Arendt. In *The Human Condition*, published five years earlier, Arendt posited the realm of human togetherness, which she christened "the space of appearance... where I appear to others as others appear to me," as coconstituted by the indivisible duality of "speech and action."[135] Prinz repeated Arendt, insisting America "must speak up and act" if the American future was to be realized. In Arendt, as likely in Prinz, this duality, acting and speaking, was a double-sided singularity, a Möbiusian "*sharing* of words and deeds."[136] To "speak up and act" as Prinz exhorted was to call the public to what Arendt refers to as a "life of public political matters," or to a common *vita activa*, a term and tradition deriving its meaning from the sonic metaphoricity of the Greek *askholia* (or unquiet activities) "defined from the viewpoint of the absolute quiet of contemplation."[137] From this point of view, "the image, the dream, the idea, and the aspiration of America itself," all of which for Prinz portended an American space of appearance, could not abide those Prinz called in his rally remarks "silent onlookers." Such hopes demanded engagement with what one keen Arendt critic portrayed as "the embodied and distinctly 'un-quiet' experience of words that are spoken out loud and heard together with others."[138] On the worldwide stage, interpolated between Jackson and

King, the rabbi, riffing on Arendt, called the assembly out from the aspirational space of *appearance*, where looking is liberal concession, into the auditive space of *amplitude*, where loudness is the ultimate liberatory force.

After an intervening introduction by labor leader A. Philip Randolph, who pronounced King "the moral leader of our nation," King followed Prinz at the podium. His iconic address was, by every report, electric. For decades since, historians, critics, rhetoricians, and popular commentators have searched for an analysis adequate to King's performance. Hansen's study of King's delivery that day is representative of that now half-century effort: "King began his speech at the march with an almost exaggerated slowness. He drew out the vowel at the end of nearly every word in his opening (the 'e' sound in 'happy,' the 'o' in 'you') until it almost filled the space before the next word in the sentence. . . . Throughout the speech, King returned to the deliberate tone of his opening. He drew out many of his long vowels (the 'a' in 'chains,' the 'i' in 'island'). He paused before and after phrases of particular importance."[139] Like so many others, Hansen took the distinctiveness of King's oratory to be a matter of style. King's tone was, thus, "deliberate"; his cadence and elocution doubly so, overreaching their regulative limits. Sensing movement in King's delivery, Hansen yielded to the musical impressions "I Have a Dream" left on its hearers. But even if one attributed Hansen's perception of King's unique "sensitivity to meter" to a simple poetic aptitude that needn't be musical in a strict sense, there is no mistaking that Hansen had something definitively musical in mind when he extended his description of King's performance as possessing "an inner swing."[140] He could not have heard the building rhythms of "I Have a Dream" more clearly.

Still, Hansen struggled to represent King's sound on the page. In *The Dream*, he gave the speech a poetic appearance, its prose lines arrhythmically broken into lyrical fragments spaced intuitively over the capacious whiteness of the page:

> But one hundred years later
>   the Negro
>   still
>   is not free.
>
> This note was a promise that all men—
>   yes,
>   black men as well as white men—
>   would be guaranteed the inalienable rights of life,

>   liberty,
>   and the pursuit of happiness . . .
>
> I have a dream
>   that one day
>
> *Yeah!*
>   this nation will rise up
>   and will live out the true meaning of its creed:
>   We hold these truths to be self-evident,
>   that all men are created equal.
>   *Yeah!* [applause]¹⁴¹

Suggestive as this is, transforming the conventional prose presentation of a printed speech into poetic form can only hint at the historical sound of the speech. It cannot relate how the speech *sounded* historically since, as I have written elsewhere, one of writing's handicaps is its inability to properly archive sound.¹⁴² Not even the capitalization strategies Hansen employed to represent the "slightly iambic tetrameter" he strained to name as the beat of King's delivery ("in-VIG-orating AUT-umn of FREE-dom and e-QUAL-ity"¹⁴³) could effect the mimetic sound of King's speech-making, the marks on the page "glaringly mute in comparison," to steal a phrase.¹⁴⁴ If Hansen and others had hoped to achieve King's impersonation by means of typography or poetic display, the effort would be in vain. Too much of what set "I Have a Dream" to higher affective heights in Washington than those reached in Rocky Mount and Detroit was impervious to graphic capture. Capitalization, for instance, might adequately reflect the idea of amplitude on the page, but the mere suggestion of King's loudness does little on its own to convey the resonant power of that loud growl of blackness he repeats, after Jackson, in the prophetic tradition conjured by his voice.

That King's "I Have a Dream" address departed from the prepared text he, with Jones's and Levinson's help, composed for the occasion is today common knowledge. The subtle shifts in his footing, however, are not. King was just seven paragraphs into his prepared text, for example, when he paused an instant and then, in Hansen's words, "began to improvise."¹⁴⁵ Whether or not he was stirred to digress from the planned speech at Jackson's urging, or by the strong pull of Jackson's inspired extemporaneity, or by Prinz—perhaps at his urging to all to "speak up," or his fleeting allusion to "the dream . . . of America itself"—King's improvisation was a surprise, fugitive from time, space, and the limits of liberal protest. Not unlike Jackson's "I've Been Buked and I've Been Scorned," the second half of "I Have a Dream" unfolded in a "louder register" than the one King established in the first part.[146] Where Jackson growled, King became a *loud speaker* all his own, pitching his voice to a shuddering volume by means of the power of the AAT public address system, a naturally theatrical vibrato-effect in his voice, and—lying directly before the stage, though glassy and nearly invisible—the amplifying properties of the Lincoln Memorial Reflecting Pool stretching east straightway into the open air in-between.

Say It Loud: Water, Reflection, Amplification

In this chapter, I discussed the importance of the Mall's public address system, especially its loudspeaker technology, to the proto-politics of the March on Washington. In two previous chapters (chapters 2 and 6) I dedicated significant space to theorizing the organological and vocal vibrato as an amplification of, and trope for, the deformational practices of what Alexander Weheliye has termed "sonic blackness" in and under modernity. Not the least of these influences on King's loud speaking in Washington, the water element in the center of the Mall didn't merely reflect light, as the image of the sky shimmering on its surface pretended to, but lent unassuming force to the day's most significant sounds as well, "I Have a Dream" chiefest among them. Ironically, King called attention to the dramatic potentiality of this hydrophysical force shortly before leaving the script of his prepared speech. Not a few observers have noted a shift in King's delivery as he began to ventriloquize biblical Amos: "We will not be satisfied, until justice rolls down like waters and righteousness like a mighty stream," King prophesied. A vibrato underlined "rolls" and "waters," as if to simulate the sound of "justice . . . like waters" running unrestrained. However placid the Reflecting Pool appeared, it could not but also receive this stream of fugitive sounds cascading into the auditory in-between above it from the stage, loudspeakers, and ground framing the great water feature on four sides. If sound traveling over water undergoes amplification, as elementary physics teaches us, and that effect is somewhat increased if the water remains serene, then the Reflecting Pool, 2029 feet long and 167 feet wide, contributed to the dynamic power of the March on Washington's effusive soundscape.

The 6,750,000 US gallons of water that lay calmly rippling in the August breeze are thus not to be wholly ignored when considering the March on Washington as a major event in the history of modern sound, nor in the regular effort of critics to grasp the transportive properties of "I Have a

Dream" as an oratorical marvel. As Douglass Kahn reminds us, "there has been a longstanding association of water and sound in observational acoustics from antiquity though Chaucer to Helmholtz and beyond."[147] Quoting Wagner, Kahn's *Noise, Water, Meat: A History of Sound in the Arts* outlines the figuration of what he calls "discursive water" in European and American music theory thusly: "If rhythm and melody are the shores on which music touches and fertilizes the two continents of the arts that share its origins, then sound is its liquid, innate element: . . . the immeasurable extent of this liquid is the sea of harmony. The eye recognizes only the surface of this sea: only the depths of the ear understand its depths."[148] To Wagner, sound approached liquescence in its innateness, coming to form in and as music only when rhythm and melody met with its flows, imposing structure upon that pelagic boundlessness cast speciously as "the sea of harmony." Inasmuch as Wagner conceived of music as an interpolation of rhythmic and melodic sense (thus, as an enlightenment) upon an endless sea of sound (or, from another orientation altogether, upon the darkness on the face of the deep), we can map his theory of music back onto the Reflecting Pool as a concretization of sound always already "in-between," to recall Carter, disciplined and held in check by the shorelines of its created limits.

From behind the microphone in front of the Reflecting Pool, King saw only the clouds, treetops, and Washington Monument in the pool if, consciously, he looked upon it at all. But what he *heard* was significantly more. The pool added a reflective supplement to the loudness of the loudspeakers, making the Mall a resonant chamber of bodily audition and King's dream a haptical, feeling-through-others experience. Kahn's contention that "with enough amplification any performance space could be turned into a resonant chamber, much like a body of a very large instrument in which humans are played" affirms this reading of the speech's dually amplitudinal and amplificatory effect on its audience(s) on and off the Mall.[149] This is not an empirical claim I am making so much as a perceptual or *acoustemological* one, to call up Steven Feld's term—a positing of "the dynamism of sound's physical energy" within and upon the social field.[150] This consideration of the March on Washington as an occasion for loudly speaking up and over the limits imposed by time, space, and words by the event's planners and its requisite permits *is* supported by one key empirical detail, however— namely, that "the human voice is always raised outdoors": "If one takes a portable tape recorder from an indoor room outdoors, talking constantly at the same distance from the microphone, the playback volume will register an increase. This results from the higher ambient noise as well as the fact that with decreased reverberation more vocal energy is required to give the sound the same apparent volume."[151] Whatever his other affects—and there were more—King spoke loudly on the Mall. In a way, it was natural to. Outdoor speech-making demanded it. Or, again, King's speaking was loud on the Mall, amplified by loudspeakers and somewhat loudened by a water feature functionally abetting the tonal, temporal, and spatial overflow of the sound of "I Have a Dream." But let us not reduce loudness to volume only. Let us also figure loudness as the affect of all sound sounded together within a given frame or field (or "sea") it is intent upon breaching. It is like noise, then, in its will to overreach and thus deform the limits of liberal political discourse. To "speak up" for "the image, the dream, the idea, and the aspiration of America itself," as Rabbi Prinz urged, is necessarily to speak loudly. It is to noise the beyond of speech where the dream, "I wish I could sing," seems more politically significant than innocently amusing. Perhaps none ever came so close to "speaking up" in this way, as to approach Prinz's longing to also sing, as King did dreaming freedom in Lincoln's uncertain shadow.[152]

The Reflecting Pool almost certainly supported the physical audibility of this timbral shift away from speech (or "the signing voice," to invoke the late Lindon Barrett) toward song (or Barrett's "singing voice"[153]), marking the improvisatory moment in King's delivery. King intoned his own thoroughly practiced set piece, "I have a dream," after the manner of, in Aldon Nielsen's titular phrase, "black chant," a cantorial timbre that "in order to be heard as chant" must have "present[ed] itself . . . as the at least vaguely familiar, the already heard" to those assembled along the Reflecting Pool's perimeter.[154] As an auxiliary technology, the pool helpfully conducted King's cantorial sound over the Mall, the water's sonancy bridging the 167 feet between the pool's north and south sides with an amplified descanting insurgent as black song. More fluid in its conduction than the loudspeaker with its engineered diffusion of amplitudinal energy, the Reflecting Pool also conveyed a less lawful loudness, carrying the *people's* voice as well, noisy over crosscurrents of sound and listening. Historian Taylor Branch recorded one instance of the reflection of the people's voice across the water. Near the end of the scripted portion of his speech, King decried the injustice of segregated public accommodations that kept "our bodies, heavy with the fatigue of travel" from "lodging in the motels of the highways and the hotels of the cities." On these words, according to Branch, "a shout went up from a pocket of the crowd so distant that the sound did not reach King for a second or two."[155] The Reflecting Pool's water could only have amplified this shout, I submit, not merely helping him to hear it audibly, but carrying it along as a call to

King to improvise—to *preach*, in other words—as the overspilling loudness of the faraway shouting finally reached the speaker a syncopated "second or two" later. Around the Reflecting Pool's edges, hundreds of listening bodies cosigned King's dream, their bodily surround as much a black aural experience and, by degrees, vibrational practice as a visual spectacle of black democratic assembly.[156]

Let Freedom Swing

The last of the day's featured speakers, King was already three minutes beyond his allotted eight at the microphone when he turned to the combined "I have a dream"/ "Let freedom ring" sequence closing "I Have a Dream." By then, King and crowd had settled into a loud dialogism of din and discourse. Regular rounds of ovation—din—only "interrupted" King, *pace* Branch, insofar as interruption means an interpellated breaking in onto the flow of speech and speech-making.[157] For din is also discourse, Édouard Glissant has taught us. And its loudness, which seems so much the root of its interruptive aspect, is not at all insignificant as it bears "the apparently meaningless texture of . . . noise," Glissant writes, but is as "essential to speech" as it is to speech-making.[158] What must have come to unhearing ears as "nothing but a shout," in Glissant's words, or just "a shout [that] went up from a pocket of the crowd," in Branch's, not only directed meaning by means of pitch intensity and other subtle excesses that camouflaged black intentionality in disallowed settings but distended time as it also did timing. King's eloquence, the rhythms of his dreaming on the National Mall, found expression in syncopated relationalities. His genius was not his own property; it was coproduced by amplified punctuations of ensemblic black noise to which his hearing and theirs seemed especially sensitive.

Nothing so much as the sound of a common appreciation of King's sentiment followed the first declaration of what the dream was. The audience applauded wildly and cheered on hearing that King was dreaming of the day when "this nation will rise up and live out the true meaning of its creed"—namely, that to which the Declaration of Independence swore: "We hold these truths to be self-evident, that all men are created equal." Now twelve minutes in, King might have dropped the mic there and, given the economy by which the creedal sentence effectively précised the moral of the previous eleven minutes, his speech would have ended well. But King went on, transforming that which in formal rhetorical analysis is appropriately called his "I have a dream" *sequence* into what might be more fruitfully contemplated in a musicoliturgical frame as a *litany*, an antiphonal recitation-prayer, civic in its telos, which is to say of, for, and by the people as a political unit.

> I have a dream that one day on the red hills of Georgia, the sons of former slaves and the sons of former slave owners will be able to sit down together at the table of brotherhood.
>
> I have a dream that one day even the state of Mississippi, a state sweltering with the heat of injustice, sweltering with the heat of oppression, will be transformed into an oasis of freedom and justice.
>
> I have a dream that my four little children will one day live in a nation where they will not be judged by the color of their skin but by the content of their character.
>
> I have a *dream* today!
>
> I have a dream that one day, down in Alabama, with its vicious racists, with its governor having his lips dripping with the words of "interposition" and "nullification"—one day right there in Alabama little black boys and black girls will be able to join hands with little white boys and white girls as sisters and brothers.
>
> I have a *dream* today!
>
> I have a dream that one day every valley shall be exalted, and every hill and mountain shall be made low, the rough places will be made plain, and the crooked places will be made straight; and the glory of the Lord shall be revealed and all flesh shall see it together.[159]

At the top, King's excursus was measured, its pace ponderous. More than that, his cadence was metrical. In technical terms, "I have a dream," the litanic refrain that would lend King's speech to permanent cultural memory, maintained a consistent choriambic rhythm over three incantatory iterations. The fourth, abruptly, breached the choriambic meter, overwhelming its versical limit to introduce a rhythmic exorbitance ("I have a dream *to-day!*"). Enjambment and caesural play syncopated King's peroration. Released from metrical control of choriambic repetition, the ensuing reiteration of "I have a dream" opening the fifth stanza in the litanic cycle was rhythmically merged with its verb complement, "that one day, down in Alabama, with its vicious racists. . . ." King's alternative phrasing, "I have a dream that one day [*pause*] down in Alabama [*pause*]," backgrounded the litanic refrain somewhat; the phrasal apposition of "down in Alabama" and "with its governor having his lips dripping with the words of 'interposition' and 'nullification'" together approached that dynamic rhythm and (over) flow called *swing* in jazz discourse. Slowly, a quarter-million listening bodies responded to the cadential change. Exuberantly, they joined King in the breaks his syncopations allowed, until the oration turned ensemblic and the leader, swinging now, improvised in and across the breaks, his flow turning fugitive and their shouts straining to keep pace. Quoting extensively from Isaiah 40, King collected "every hill and mountain," all the "rough places" and "crooked places" of America into a single staccato run of eschatological vision *heard*, unmeasured, "together" in a breathless bravura of enjambed jeremiad-speech.

"And this will be the day," King had to declare twice. The break was shorter than he supposed, and the amplified ensemble of sounds below him drowned him out on the first attempt. Soon King was dreaming song: "This will be the day when all of God's children will be able to sing with new meaning, *My country, 'tis of thee, sweet land of liberty, of thee I sing. Land where my fathers died, land of the Pilgrims' pride, From every mountainside, let freedom ring!*" On the steps of the Lincoln Memorial, no one could fail to hear Marian Anderson in 1939 also "projecting her voice out beyond the Reflecting Pool," as Gayle Wald wrote.[160] There, where King stood twenty-four years later orating Samuel Francis Smith's patriotic hymn, Anderson made her own operatic claim to the country that, owing to her color, had denied her access to the stage at Constitution Hall.

Finding an alternate stage outdoors at the Lincoln Memorial, which she gained with help from Eleanor Roosevelt, Anderson famously opened her Easter concert singing Smith's hymn. Almost immediately, Anderson's concert on the Mall and her symbolic victory over America's racial parochialism achieved iconic standing. Not least because Anderson was also on the Mall to sing in 1963, the acoustic memory of her 1939 performance was irrepressible in King's recitation—for she, too, had been loud upon the monument steps, her voice amplified "out beyond the Reflecting Pool." King may have been speaking in Lincoln's shadow ("a great American, in whose symbolic shadow we stand, today"), but the oration of "My Country, 'Tis of Thee" put him very nearly in Anderson's shoes that day. As she had done in 1939, King lifted his voice, even as it was being lifted, and enjoined the whole nation, from "the prodigious hilltops of New Hampshire" to "every hill and molehill in Mississippi," to lend *their* sound, too, to freedom's eschaton.

But King did not sing quite as Anderson had, who voiced "My country, 'tis of thee / Sweet land of liberty / Of thee *we* sing" to open her Washington concert so many years earlier. Instead, he intoned speech, *swinging the anaphoric litany to clamorous crescendo*—"*From every mountainside, let freedom ring!"*—before calling *"all* of God's children, black men and white men, Jews and Gentiles, Protestants and Catholics" to a second, still louder crescendo: *"Free at last! Free at last! Thank God Almighty, we are free at last!"* Like Anderson's singing, his preaching and speech-making were moving "envoicement[s]" of black democratic struggle. His voice, like hers, "filled space," as Wald put it.[161] His voice, like hers, like Jackson's, overflowed its bounds, teaching 250,000 listening bodies—and the world—what it sounds like, finally, *to be heard.*

Said one unnamed woman in the crowd, thinking, perhaps of the Eighty-eighth Congress a stone's throw away, and of the urgency of the legislation the whole march was clamoring for: "Who would open, ah, who would open your door for one, for one voice? But if, ah, thousands of people go, they can be heard without opening the windows."[162] Thus did Kennedy's civil rights bill make its way to Congress a second time in 1963. On paper, it arrived at the House of Representatives in June, but it was not until August that its demands were manifestly heard "without opening a window."

Epilogue
"It's *Moanin'* Time"
Black Grief and the End of Words

> For we know that the whole creation groaneth and travaileth in pain together until now. And not only they, but ourselves also, which have the first fruits of the Spirit, even we ourselves groan within ourselves, waiting for the adoption, to wit, the redemption of our body. . . . Likewise the Spirit also helpeth our infirmities: for we know not what we should pray for as we ought: but the Spirit itself maketh intercession for us with groanings which cannot be uttered.
> **Romans 8:22–23, 26** (King James Version)

> The first thing you hear is McCoy Tyner's fingers sounding a tremulous minor chord, hovering at the lower end of the piano's register. It's an ominous chord, horror movie shit; hearing it you can't help but see still water suddenly disturbed by something moving beneath it, threatening to surface. Then the sound of John Coltrane's saxophone writhes on top: mournful, melismatic, menacing. Serpentine. It winds its way toward a theme but always stops just short, repeatedly approaching something like coherence only to turn away at the last moment. It's a maddening pattern. Coltrane's playing assumes the qualities of the human voice, sounding almost like a wail or moan, mourning violence that is looming, that is past, that is atmospheric, that will happen again and again and again.
> **Ismail Muhammad,** "On John Coltrane's 'Alabama'" (2020)

No doubt, years from now, readers of Ismail Muhammad's piece "On John Coltrane's 'Alabama,'" a June 2020 blog post for the *Paris Review*, will still relish the lyrical descriptiveness of Muhammad's vision of Coltrane's playing—"mournful, melismatic, menacing"—as a distinct achievement in style. But one hopes the *Paris Review* set will not soon forget the occasion of Muhammad's piece: the death of George Floyd in Minneapolis, May 25, 2020. The video spectacle of Floyd's asphyxiation death under Derek Chauvin's unyielding knee, viewed across the world, was not only the painful provocation that prompted Muhammad's closer listening to Coltrane, and a finer writing about that listening, but the very grief-source of the rhetorical style separating "On John Coltrane's 'Alabama'" from other reflections on Coltrane. To return to Muhammad years from now and not remember Floyd's death or the new era of racial reckoning many believe was born in its wake would be, in fact, to fail to have ever read Muhammad at all. It is to fail, that is, to have heard Muhammad's textual groanings with and after Coltrane "sounding almost like a wail or moan" as the black writer mourns both the "violence that is looming, that is past, that is atmospheric, that will happen again and again and again" and the limitation of words to reconcile the history of black democratic hope to the maddening fact of death-bound blackness in this white world. What is a black writer to do or say when this trouble which has been our changing same exhausts words of their potency to indict white power or defiantly exult in black life? When there is no recourse for writing, in other words, but to listen for expressive possibilities in locutions/locations beyond words that witness to the ongoingness of black loss and the ineffable depths of lament?

To be called to the work of writing in times as violent as ours is almost a cruelty. "Violence has a way of making a mockery of words," Richard Lischer attests. "After Auschwitz, Hiroshima, Vietnam, Cambodia, Rwanda, all the words sound hollow. What does one say after a televised beheading?" he asks, bemused.[1] While *The End of Words: The Language of Reconciliation in a Culture of Violence* is concerned chiefly with what Lischer perceives as a growing cultural skepticism toward proclamations of divine justice (such as King's faith in the bend of the moral arc of the universe toward just ends) in the face of indescribable human horrors, we may extend his work's world geographies to include domestic intensities in Ferguson, Baltimore, Charleston, Baton Rouge, and Minneapolis—if not also Memphis in 1968. This further unfolding of the map of man's inhumanity toward man is no more a leap in the black American mind than that tropic reflex which has clung to biblical Israel as a type and shadow of the New World experience of black people since the early nineteenth century. The case made by Lischer, a distinguished preaching professor and King scholar, for the particular dilemma faced by the modern pulpiteer in the age of mass violence (a quandary long since confronted by the black divine at the dais) belongs no less to the "poet," he reminds us—the seeing, feeling writer "whose stock and trade is words and nothing else."² As video lays siege to the power of language to illuminate the world picture, poets, like preachers, are left to brood over the diminished vitality of words to answer or assuage the shock and trauma of "a televised beheading" or a femicidal police raid on a black woman's apartment in Louisville heard on tape or an execution by chokehold caught on camera. Muhammad attests to this: "It has been hard for me to know what to say regarding George Floyd's murder, or the uprisings that it has sparked. Sometimes I feel as if there is nothing new to say or write, or nothing that I can say or write that I have not already said and written."³ Overcome by the picture of Floyd dying on video "in broad daylight, in full view of citizens," Muhammad looks to Coltrane at the end of words.

In Coltrane's playing lies the beyond of words for mourning and worldmaking where words fade and miscarry. "On John Coltrane's 'Alabama'" is thus far from being a mere stylization of black musical thought; it is its own "Alabama"-inspired requiem *for* and *against* the "again and again and again" of failing words before the spectacle violence of black subjecthood and the death-bound condition within the racial state. Against the triumph of video in a spectacle society, words strain to matter.

One Lord, One Faith, One Baptism is the 1987 live gospel album of the Queen Mother of Soul, Aretha Franklin. Recorded for Arista Records at New Bethel Baptist Church in Detroit, *One Lord, One Faith, One Baptism* hoped to repeat the revival style of her double-platinum Grammy-winning gospel classic, *Amazing Grace*, twenty years earlier. For all its effort, though, the response to Franklin's *One Lord* album was mostly underwhelming. Even today, few besides Franklin's most earnest devotees and gospel music enthusiasts have encountered it. Among those who do remember it, it is recalled at the popular level not so much for Franklin's vocals as for the opening track of side 3 on *One Lord*'s vinyl edition, a soaring sermonic interlude by Rev. Jesse Jackson climbing to ecstatic eloquence on the epistrophic power of his felicitous theme: "*It's morning time!* Church, get ready. It's morning time! From slave ship to championship—it's morning time! From the outhouse, to the state house, to the court house, to the White House—it's morning time! Don't you turn back—it's morning time! *Its morning time! It's morning time!*"⁴

Despite Jackson's heralding of the inbreaking of "morning time" here, to hear him on the *One Lord, One Faith, Once Baptism* LP is to wonder if he is in fact intoning "*moanin'*" in place of "morning." Though the internal logic of Jackson's peroration suggests "morning" as the better-suited of the two hearings of his speech, one is never sure that Jackson did not intend "*moanin'* time" or, at least, "*mourning* time" where Arista's assumptive choice of "morning" impertinently overcorrects for an imagined deficit in Jackson's native South Carolina dialect. For while "moanin'" may seem to resist his sermon's internal logic narratively, in aesthetic and historical terms it accords well with the live *gospel* event *One Lord, One Faith, One Baptism* occasioned inasmuch as "the essence of the gospel style is a wordless moan," Anthony Heilbut argues, and the very sound of the condition of black life heard "again and again and again" over many generations.[5]

This is not to take Jackson's "*moanin'* time" or even Coltrane's "wail or moan" to express the sound or condition of black mourning as mournful only, however. Jackson's "Speech by Rev. Jesse Jackson [July 27]" sounds rather more remonstrating than despairing, a fervent "refusal of articulateness or articulation," like Coltrane's playing, "a refusal of a tidy Freudian mourning."[6] To declare "*moanin'* time" in repeated epistrophe, in other words, is not so much to call for moanin' to start (since black grief goes on and on and on) as it is to repeat, and to keep on repeating, the continuous time of black moanin'. It seems "the work of grieving never ends."[7] While this sense of an infinite present enlivening Jackson's preaching recommends *One Lord, One Faith, One Baptism* as an audio companion piece to Coltrane's "Alabama," the "Speech by Rev. Jesse Jackson [July 27]" should not go unnoticed as a fitting prolegomenon, on the other hand, to Franklin's performance of "Ave Maria" on the *One Lord* album, as Jackson's "*moanin'*" bears on the tremulant sound in Franklin's singing of Franz Schubert one also hears, as Muhammad observed, listening to "Alabama" today.

Despite the extended history of its various high-church musical settings, "Ave Maria" was made distinctly low July 27, 1987, by Franklin's dark, throaty, intermittently unmetered performance live at New Bethel Baptist. Her rendition's climactic closing stanza placed the pipe organ in her body, pulling out all the stops of her solemn, searching holler:

> Pray, oh pray, oh pray for us
> For us, wretched sinners
> Now and at the hour of our death
> Our death.
> [*moan*]

Franklin's "Pray, oh pray, oh pray for us / . . . / Now" may have echoed Jackson's felt urgency—*It's moanin' time*—but it also *anticipated* George Floyd's dying prayer thirty years in the future. "Momma! Momma!" Floyd cried out as his life was leaving him. The discernible re-sounding of Franklin's invocation, "Mother, hear a suppliant child" sung at the top of the hymn, in Floyd's cry to his late mother (which one journalist referred to as Floyd's own "sacred invocation"[8]) obscures past and present as differentiated temporalities, helping reconstitute Schubert's lyric, "Now and the moment of our death," within a single temporal frame. In the wake of black life and death (to evoke Christina Sharpe), "Now and the moment of our death" exist in, and as, the same undifferentiated field. This, it seems, only the specific, sacred, and (un)sung labors of motherhood console in us, labors few but Franklin could convey so soulfully. In a different form, Lezley McSpadden might warrant consideration as Franklin's equal in this work all the same.

In 2014, McSpadden lost her eighteen-year-old son, Michael Brown, to police homicide in Ferguson, Missouri. In 2016, prompted by the death of Alton Sterling in Baton Rouge, Louisiana—also at the hands of local police— McSpadden penned a poignant op-ed for the *New York Times*. Though not indifferent to public expressions of prayerful support, her piece did not shy away from shining an exasperated light on the poverty of public condolence in the face of black mother-loss:

> Someone asked me what I would say to Mr. Sterling's family, if I had the chance. To tell the truth, I wouldn't know what to say. When Michael was killed, people tried to talk to me, but I was in shock; I didn't know how to respond. I know enough now to advise well-meaning people to pause before offering kind words. So many told me, "I am so sorry for your loss." After a while, all the "sorrys" bled together, and at the end of it, nothing changed.

She went on:

> When their children are killed, mothers are expected to say something. To help keep the peace. To help make change. But what can I possibly say? I just know we need to do something. We are taught to be peaceful, but we aren't at peace. I have to wake up and go to sleep with this pain every day. Ain't no peace. If we mothers can't change where this is heading for these families—to public hearings, protests, un-asked-for martyrdom, or worse, to nothing at all—what can we do?[9]

At the end of words, McSpadden obliged us all to ask, what can anyone possibly say to these crimes? In a single, hopeful sentence, dimly hidden between forceful but despairing lines, McSpadden's appeal, no less urgent today than it was in 2016, suggests a proxy for the weakness of words to "do something": "Let Mr. Sterling's family members grieve," she proposes. It is by allowing Sterling's family space enough to "grieve with the people in their lives who knew him" that McSpadden imagines the possibility of their relief from the shocking cell-phone and, sometimes, body-camera footage they will never be able to escape. "Death isn't pretty for anyone, but what these families now face is the horror of seeing their loved one die over and over, in public, in such a violent way. They face the helplessness of having strangers judge their loved one not on who he was or what he meant to his family but on a few seconds of video."[10] That black mothers have been at once faithful witnesses, committed crusaders, and the most impassioned mourners of black death is, in one respect, worthy of the widest veneration. But it seems unjust, just the same, that the weight of this witness to black death ("over and over") should fall so heavily on black women. For McSpadden, Sybrina Fulton, Wanda Johnson, Samaria Rice, and Valerie Castile—as indeed for the mother of Alton Sterling—"a few seconds of video" means a lifetime of traumatic memory.

"We don't need the video. We don't," a black woman colleague of mine insisted on word of George Floyd's death. She was also remembering, painfully, her own first cousin's similar dying, also on tape. He had gotten no national press, but she and her family knew very well how resistant to closure open wounds are made by network and internet rehearsals of such violent losses as theirs. Their experience was no uncommon exasperation at the unending spectacle of black death for public consumption. "We don't need the video." Rather, Coltrane's "Alabama," Jackson's "Speech by Rev. Jesse Jackson [July 27]," and Franklin's version of "Ave Maria" together posit lamentation as actual need—not just as a psychic and emotional allowance but as an effectual counterpolitics, a challenge to the visual powers of racial tyranny that promises to "do something," as McSpadden implored us, about police brutality directed at the sons and daughters of black mothers.

Short months before McSpadden's opinion piece, writer Claudia Rankine addressed the insurgent power of black lament in the pages of the *New York Times Magazine*. Her portrait of Mamie Till-Mobley and Till-Mobley's resolve to make America turn its gaze on the murdered, misshapen body of her son, Emmett Till, cast a politics of black mourning in historical relief. "Insisting we look with her upon the dead," Till-Mobley "reframed mourning."[11] Through tears, indignation, and a series of postmortem photographs of her lynched child, Till-Mobley refused mourning's ritualized respectability. Instead, her intent to counter black death with its visual protest in mourning "was a new kind of logic," Rankine wrote. What might easily have been a more familiar ritual of mother-loss set within the veil of mid-century black church funeralism, Emmett Till's grisly photographs metamorphosed into "a mode of intervention and interruption that might itself be assimilated into the category of public annoyance." With a handful of pictures, Till-Mobley stirred grief to spectacular grievance. The pictures were not simply a visual witness to the actual and moral crime of Till's murder, however; they bore a phonic substance, too. As Fred Moten has helped us discern, "There is a sound that seemingly is not there in [the Till pictures], which this performance is about."[12] If one can bear to look on them long enough, looking gives way to "the complex musics of the photograph. This is the sound before the photograph."[13] This is "black mo'nin'" heard at the scene of suffering.[14]

The history of heard and "visible" black lament today—seen as often in the streets, on playing fields, and in athletic arenas as in funeral chapels and churches—would seem as modern as Mamie Till-Mobley, then. But it is as ancient as the Hebrew scriptures, too. Like the tradition of scriptural lament explored by theologian Walter Brueggemann, black mourning, for as long as black people have mourned (in/for) the New World, which is as long as there have been black people in the New World, doesn't only bemoan the condition of black life with hollers, shouts, shrieks, and wordless groans but, in *doing something*, also "partakes of something of a claim filed in court in order to ensure that the question of justice is formally articulated."[15] Black lament is not disinterested, in other words, but aims to shift the racial calculus, "redress[ing] the distribution of power," as Brueggemann might say,[16] between the strong and the weak. To put this another way, black mourning is a sit-in against black loss, a public objection refusing bargaining. Moanin' (or "mo'nin'") is the keynote sound of black lament (which sound Geneva Reed-Veal, mother to Sandra Bland, strained to keep suppressed while she stood center stage with eight other black mothers mourning their children's deaths at the 2016 Democratic National Convention in Philadelphia). As much an aesthetics of black sound as "an inappropriable ecstatics"of performance or impulse, moanin' carries the force of creation in its groaning-*for*, which is to say its longing-*after*, which is also inevitably its stretching-*toward*, a future glory, a new world brighter than words, which "shrieks, hums, hollers, shouts and moans,"[17] so far from being nonreferential, more nearly approach. Hear Moten:

> At my Aunt Mary's funeral (she was my favorite aunt but I was scared to look at her face in the photograph I couldn't help but look at that they made of her at the funeral home), Ms. Rosie Lee Seals rose up in church,

out from the program, and said, "Sister Mary Payne told me that if she died she wanted me to give a *deep moan* at her funeral." And, at that moment, in her Las Vegas-from-Louisiana accent . . . burying my auntie with music at morning time, where moaning renders mourning wordless (the augmentation and reduction of or to our releasing more than what is bound up in the presence of the word) and voice is dissonanced and multiplied by metavoice, Sister Rosie Lee Seals mo'ned. New word, new world.[18]

To be clear, Moten's Sister Rosie Lee pretends to no heavenly utopianism, no unreachable unreality. Her moanin', as Moten avows, is "a religious and political formulation"[19] that may be called eschatological in its convictions and pressing concern for a black bodily redemption worthy of the hope of the apostle above and obtaining, at last, *in the flesh*. Black moanin' is the sound of that doubly religious and political travail which, divining the coming light of mo(u)rning, calls a new world wordlessly into being. In ton(gu)es strange and wild to those dull of hearing, Sister Rosie Lee's moanin' sounds the wordless sound of the redeeming of black flesh—"a *deep moan*"—faithfully observing her part in the program, aiding Aunt Mary's crossing "with groanings which cannot be uttered."

At the end of words, at the end of life, in the end, black moanin' matters deeply. Against the immediacy of the visual record of black death already always bound up with the hegemony of racialized vision subtending antiblack thought and violence, black moanin' is a cultural resource we may do well to recover. Marshaled toward new expectations of love, life, and flourishing, black moanin' recalls to cultural memory the maligned, maimed, and murdered ones for their witness to the material and moral violence against black flourishing in the making of whiteness in the West. Emmett Till to George Floyd and Breonna Taylor, may they be spoken and written of again and again and again. Until justice rolls down like waters, as a certain man said, and righteousness like an ever-flowing stream.

NOTES

Introduction

1. Spillers, "Moving on Down the Line," 252.
2. Southern Christian Leadership Conference, "Proposal for an Audio History," 2.
3. SCLC, "Proposal for an Audio History," 1.
4. SCLC, "Proposal for an Audio History," 1.
5. SCLC, "Proposal for an Audio History," 2.
6. SCLC, "Proposal for an Audio History" ("Rider A"), n.p. Emphasis added.
7. SCLC, "Proposal for an Audio History," 4. Emphasis added.
8. Sundquist, *King's Dream*, 56–57.
9. Lischer, *Preacher King*, 119.
10. Barthes, "Grain of the Voice," 181.
11. Barthes, "Grain of the Voice," 188.
12. Barthes, "Grain of the Voice," 181–82.
13. Attali, *Noise*, 3.
14. M. M. Smith, "Introduction," ix. For a review of the vital work more recently undertaken on behalf of "historical soundscape studies" and "aural history," see Keeling and Kun, "Introduction."
15. Smith, "Introduction," ix.
16. I have in mind, for example, W. E. B. Du Bois's "Of the Sorrow Songs" in *The Souls of Black Folk*; Zora Neale Hurston's *The Sanctified Church*, especially the "Characteristics of Negro Expression" and "The Sanctified Church" sections of that work; Ralph Ellison's "Living with Music" and other essays from part 2 of *Shadow and Act* titled "The Sound and the Mainstream"; *Blues People* by LeRoi Jones (Amiri Baraka); and Frantz Fanon's neglected "This Is the Voice of Algeria" from *A Dying Colonialism*.
17. Schafer, *Soundscape*, 9–10.
18. Benjamin, "Theses on the Philosophy of History," 257.
19. Schafer, *Soundscape*, 10.
20. Schafer, *Soundscape*, 10.

21 Lischer, *Preacher King*, 5.
22 Lischer, *Preacher King*, 5.
23 Brown, "Language of Soul," 234.
24 Brown, "Language of the Soul," 234.
25 Lischer, *Preacher King*, 133.
26 Lischer, *Preacher King*, 66, 130.
27 Take, for instance, this trial:

> Through our airplanes, we've dwarfed *dis*-tance
> and placed time [*t-i-i-i-ahm*] in chains. (134)

Or see Lischer's observation of King's reflex to "pronounce the word *Lord* in such a way as to demonstrate the Almighty's majesty: *Law-ah-aw-awd* is a glissando" in perhaps more than one of King's sermons (Lischer, *Preacher King*, 134).

28 Lischer, *Preacher King*, 134–35.
29 Moten, *In the Break*, 42.
30 Moten, *In the Break*, 42.
31 Moten, *In the Break*, 175; Lischer, *Preacher King*, 135.
32 Throughout this book I use *an-archic* in the sense of being against *archē*—i.e., structure—not to be confused with the more common *anarchic*, indicating an intent to overthrow government.
33 In a 1993 C-SPAN discussion of his biography of Du Bois, David Levering Lewis spoke of Du Bois's "dry voice, very precise with . . . a lot of whistling towards the end." Lewis attributed Du Bois's whistling to "bad dentures." The accidental effect of Du Bois's whistle does not diminish its bearing on black sonority and diacritical noise, however. It cannot but recall the history of the shrill sound associated with Emmett Till's murder in 1955 and Otis Redding's "(Sittin' on) The Dock of the Bay" in 1968. See D. L. Lewis, "W. E. B. Du Bois."
34 Brown, "Language of Soul," 234.
35 Baker, *Modernism and the Harlem Renaissance*, xiv.
36 Kahn, *Noise, Water, Meat*, 4.
37 Baker, *Modernism and the Harlem Renaissance*, xvi.
38 Kahn, *Noise, Water, Meat*, 5.
39 Kahn, *Noise, Water, Meat*, 5.
40 Kahn, *Noise, Water, Meat*, 5.
41 Kahn, *Noise, Water, Meat*, 9.
42 Murphet, Groth, and Hone, *Sounding Modernism*, 1.
43 Weheliye, *Phonographies*, 47.

Chapter 1. Dying Words

1 "To prevent the church from [more] overcrowding," one account offered, "the doors were locked. There was a visible police presence." Said another observer, "People were lined up [in front of the church] like a human carpet." Burns, "Funeral." See, too, her *Burial for a King*.
2 Burns, "Mourning and Message," 5.
3 "Martin Luther King, Jr. Funeral Services."

4 "Martin Luther King, Jr. Funeral Services."
5 In his remarks before reading select passages from "The Death of Evil upon the Seashore" and "A Tough Mind and a Tender Heart," Abernathy hinted at a natural assumption that he would take over the leadership of the SCLC over which King presided for so long and, thus, fill King's shoes: "I ate my last meal last Thursday noon and I am seeking to fast in an effort to purify my soul. And I will not eat bread or meat. I will continue to fast until I am thoroughly satisfied and convinced that I am ready for the task which is at hand. I solicit your prayers." Although Abernathy was King's closest confidant, Abernathy's pious preparation for "the task which is at hand" must have seemed presumptuous to many. For oratorically, and therefore in terms of his potential for mass appeal, Abernathy was light years from being able to master King's charismatic persona. Still, Abernathy's egotism might have been expected. In their introduction to Jacques Derrida's collection of funeral orations and essays, *The Work of Mourning*, Pascale-Anne Brault and Michael Naas remind us, following Derrida, that "there is always in mourning the danger of narcissism . . . the 'egotistical' and no doubt 'irrepressible' tendency to bemoan the friend's death in order to take pity upon oneself." Derrida himself spoke of the temptation to "narcissistic remembrance" in his tribute to Jean-François Lyotard, whom Derrida, not unlike Abernathy eulogizing King, counted among "all those I like to call my best friends." In his memorial expressions for Lyotard, Derrida disavowed "homage in form of personal testimony, which always tends toward reappropriation and always risks giving in to an indecent way of saying 'we,' or worse, 'me.'" Derrida, *Work of Mourning*, 7, 225.
6 "Martin Luther King, Jr. Funeral Services." See, too, "Funeral Service for Dr. Martin Luther King, Jr., April 9, 1968, Ebenezer Baptist Church."

Given the plural form of "Sermon Excerpts" (rather than "Sermon Excerpt"), it is possible, I admit, that Abernathy had not mistaken his responsibility and had indeed been instructed to read a number of extracts from King's *Strength to Love*. Video footage of the memorial service's final minutes, however, clearly show Abernathy's puzzlement and apparent obliviousness to Coretta King's plan to have her husband's recorded voice included in the memorial liturgy. I read Abernathy's puzzlement as a sign of his prior assumption that *his* voice, not King's, would symbolically close out the service. Too, Abernathy had not been involved in what Coretta would later describe as the "debate about the eulogy" and "who would preach it," apparently. Those who were—Christine King Farris, Edythe Scott Bagley (Coretta King's sister), and King's secretary, Dora McDonald—judged finally that "no one could do it better than Martin himself had months before, at Ebenezer." (C. King, *My Life, My Love, My Legacy*, 168.) Perhaps, though, nothing has persuaded me of the self-importance with which Abernathy undertook his officiating duties as much as Burns's record of his behavior in the minutes *before* the memorial service:

> Police officers estimated that thirty thousand people crammed into the few blocks in front of the church. It was nearly impossible to move, and people were already tired and getting frustrated. . . . [Several observers saw] Ralph

> Abernathy come out of the church and try to rouse the crowd's spirits. The new SCLC president clambered up onto the roof of a black hearse.
> "My friends, this is Ralph Abernathy," the minister called. . . .
> What is he doing? . . .
> Abernathy called again. "My friends, my friends—"
> "Hey, get off my hearse!" yelled a funeral-home employee.
> "Who is your leader now? I am!" Abernathy shouted again, "Who's your leader now? I am!"
> He tried several times to get a cheer going, but the crowd mostly ignored him. Reporter Paul Hemphill, standing nearby, watched as the hearse's driver grabbed at Abernathy's calves and ankles, attempting to pull him from the top of the car.
> Charles Black [a volunteer and bystander] stared at the scene. I can't believe this. Why is he doing this? Why right now?
> After a while, Abernathy went back inside as the onlookers moved a little closer to the church.

Burns, *Burial for a King*, 142. See, too, C. S. King, *My Life, My Love, My Legacy*, 168.

7   Abernathy, *And the Walls Came Tumbling Down*, 461.
8   Burns, *Burial*, 150.
9   Baldwin, *No Name in the Street*, 155.
10 Sterne, *Audible Past*, 303.
11 Sterne, *Audible Past*, 304.
12 Sterne, *Audible Past*, 290. The recording was an excerpt from King's sermon, "The Drum Major Instinct," preached weeks earlier at Ebenezer.
13 Sterne, *Audible Past*, 290.
14 For more on canning, embalming, and John Philip Sousa, see Sterne, *Audible Past*, 292–334.
15 T. H. Kane, "Last Acts," 5.
16 Burns, *Burial*, 143.
17 Keith D. Miller opens his book *Voice of Deliverance* with an introduction to Reverend J. H. Edwards, "a postal worker and occasional preacher" at Ebenezer. Edwards oversaw the Rising Sons Sunday School class for second and third grade boys at Ebenezer where young "ML" was under Edwards's tutelage as a boy. Years later, Edwards served on the ordaining council that examined King and approved his elevation to ordained ministry. Faithful as Edwards was to Ebenezer and the King family since well before the elder King became senior pastor (assuming the mantle from his father-in-law, Reverend A. D. Williams, in 1931), he and his wife were "unable to fight their way into their beloved church." In "miss[ing] the funeral of the best third grade pupil in the Rising Sons class," Edwards was representative of many everyday others who, in spite of their close connections to Ebenezer and the King family, were shut out. Some who did gain entrance were relegated to seating in the choir loft and remote corners of the building. K. D. Miller, *Voice of Deliverance*, 1–2.
18 J. Wallace Hamilton originally preached his "Drum Major Instincts" on March 6, 1949. In 1952 Hamilton revised the original sermon and published the

redacted version in his book of twelve sermons, *Ride the Wild Horses*. It was the redacted sermon King appears to have relied upon (occasionally misspeaking and substituting the word *impulse*, from *Ride*'s subtitle, where *instinct* is called for). See K. D. Miller, *Voice of Deliverance*, 216n7, 8.

19 M. L. King, "Drum Major Instinct," 179–80.
20 M. L. King, "Drum Major Instinct," 172.
21 Lischer, *Preacher King*, 221.
22 Much more has been written about Mays, Thurman, and Rustin as influences on King's religious and social thought than about Gurley's importance to King's Ebenezer gospel. Mary Gurley was "one of the most well-known soloists in the Ebenezer choir, and a former leader of the Scripto Pen strike" (Burns, *Burial*, 149). The Scripto Pen strike occurred over a two-month period late in 1964. Scripto, then the largest manufacturer of writing instruments in the world, employed close to one thousand people in 1964, more than eight hundred of whom were production and maintenance workers. Among production and maintenance workers, black women constituted 75 percent of the work force. King and the SCLC supported the Atlanta strikers, helping the 250 strikers successfully win concessions from Scripto's management on Christmas Eve 1964.
23 On "religious black internationalism" see Azaransky, *Worldwide Struggle*.
24 K. D. Miller, *Voice of Deliverance*, 2.
25 M. L. King, "Drum Major Instinct," 185.
26 M. L. King, "Drum Major Instinct," 185.
27 Film footage of the funeral shows A. D. King, seated alongside Coretta King, on the edge of coming apart under the sound of King's preaching. "Dr. King's Funeral Service."
28 Baldwin, "Notes of a Native Son," 80.
29 Holloway, *Codes of Conduct*, 140.
30 Holloway, *Codes of Conduct*, 140. While I maintain that "too few" have given serious reflection to the precarious lives of black children, I note the exceptional work of scholars like Aimee Meredith Cox and Marcia Chatelain (whom I take up in a later chapter) for their critical histories of black girlhood, specifically. Holloway's absorbing reflections on the Atlanta child murders have their fictional, but not less illuminating, counterparts in James Baldwin's *The Evidence of Things Not Seen*, Toni Cade Bambara's *These Bones Are Not My Child*, and Tayari Jones's *Leaving Atlanta*.
31 Holloway, *Codes of Conduct*, 139.
32 Baldwin, "Notes of a Native Son," 80.
33 Burns, *Burial*, 150.
34 Burns, "Funeral."
35 Derrida, *Speech and Phenomena*, 16.
36 Derrida, *Speech and Phenomena*, 35.
37 Derrida, *Speech and Phenomena*, 16.
38 Burns, "Funeral."
39 Moten, *In the Break*, 1.
40 Moten, "The Case of Blackness," 182.

41 "Stolen life" belongs to Moten. "Stolen life" refers to "a fugitive movement" in and out of the prevailing, and necessarily constraining, social logic of (something like) the good, the responsible, the lawful, the proper. "Neither simple interdiction nor bare transgression," it is a "para-ontological disruption" ("The Case of Blackness," 179). King's recorded voice exists para-ontologically, at once inside and outside of the ritual life-closure of the funeral event.

42 Chion, qtd. in B. Kane, *Sound Unseen*, 4.

43 B. Kane, *Sound Unseen*, 24.

44 B. Kane, *Sound Unseen*, 8.

45 Although "the acousmatic situation" is a vital hermeneutic for Brian Kane, his own reading of Chion recalls instances of Chion using the phrase, though without the tropological power Kane intends it to carry in *Sound Unseen*. Whereas Chion's *Guide des Objets Sonores* (*Guide to Sound Objects*) regards the acousmatic situation as a positively generative intervention in Schaeffer ("The acousmatic situation changes the way we hear"), Kane's view of the acousmatic situation is more critical. Schaeffer's habit of approaching the acousmatic voice as, in effect, "phantasmagoric" leads Schaeffer, Kane argues, to too easily abstract the acousmatic sound's materiality (that is, its relative density) and mode of production into ahistorical myth-making. From Kane's point of view, "the acousmatic situation is precarious" (25). Chion, quoted in B. Kane, *Sound Unseen*, 4.

46 B. Kane, *Sound Unseen*, 25.

47 B. Kane, *Sound Unseen*, 9.

48 According to Brian Kane, Schaeffer traced the acousmatic experience back to Pythagoras, pointing out that "etymologically, the term 'acousmatic' refers to a group of Pythagorean disciples known as the *akousmatikoi*—literally the 'listeners' or 'auditors'—who, as legend has recorded it, heard the philosopher lecture from behind a curtain or veil" (B. Kane, *Sound Unseen*, 4–5). The point of Pythagoras's veil was to heighten his students' listening by depriving them of a visual through which they were apt to presumptively narrativize what they heard rather than attend to their teachers' words more nakedly. See B. Kane, *Sound Unseen*, 45–72, for an argument against a history of facile readings of Schaeffer on the Pythagorean veil that has gone universally unchallenged, in effect diminishing, rather than enriching, sound studies since Schaeffer.

49 B. Kane, *Sound Unseen*, 7.

50 "Ensemblic" belongs to Moten. I take him to be referring, coincidentally, to a performative synchronicity (which is not the same as a performative uniformity) and to a constellated musical (or otherwise expressive) subjectivity almost always approaching improvisation. In Moten, generally speaking, the "ensemble" is the figure for "a field of convergence" (*In the Break*, 255n1).

51 Lischer, in *The Preacher King*, helpfully distinguishes King's sermons from his civil religious addresses: "A sermon is a cultic performance of a biblical text among people who identify themselves as Christians. . . . A public speech serves its own political agenda, but a sermon must follow the Bible's leading" (8). Importantly King held these two forms, far from being entirely distinct forms, in complex tension. In short, King was "a black preacher and a social reformer.

He knew the vocabulary and spoke the language of both professions" (5). Let us assume that "I've Been to the Mountaintop," delivered from Mason Temple Church of God in Christ on the eve of King's murder, is best understood as a civil address, though one clearly "cast . . . in the light of biblical events and characters" (4). Whether he was delivering sermon or speech, that King was "always preaching" is the starting point of *The Preacher King*, so vital to this project.

52 Lischer, *Preacher King*, 177.
53 See, for starters, Lischer's index and the long list of devices offered under the main entry, "Style." Lischer, *Preacher King*.
54 Brault and Naas in Derrida, *Work of Mourning*, 37, 23.
55 Derrida, *Work of Mourning*, 192.
56 Derrida, *Specters of Marx*, 1, 6.
57 Derrida, *Specters of Marx*, 2.
58 Burns, "Mourning and Message," 1.
59 Derrida, *Specters of Marx*, 5.
60 Derrida, *Specters of Marx*, 5.
61 Derrida, *Specters of Marx*, 7.
62 Moten, *In the Break*, 41.
63 Lischer, *Preacher King*, 11.
64 Derrida, *Specters of Marx*, 120.
65 Derrida, *Specters of Marx*, 9.
66 Shakespeare, *Hamlet*, 26–27.
67 Derrida, *Specters of Marx*, 124.
68 Derrida, *Specters of Marx*, 64.
69 Derrida, *Specters of Marx*, 64.
70 In the final pages of *Where Do We Go from Here*, King invoked "the revolutionary spirit" of Marxism:

> These are revolutionary times. All over the globe men are revolting against old systems of exploitation and oppression. . . . The shirtless and barefoot people of the earth are rising up as never before. . . . We in the West must support these revolutions. It is a sad fact that, because of comfort, complacency, a morbid fear of Communism and our proneness to adjust to injustice, the Western nations that initiated so much of the revolutionary spirit of the modern world have now become the arch antirevolutionaries. This has driven many to feel that only Marxism has the revolutionary spirit. Communism is a judgment on our failure to make democracy real and to follow through on the revolutions that we initiated. Our only hope today lies in our ability to recapture the revolutionary spirit and go out into a sometimes hostile world declaring eternal opposition to poverty, racism and militarism. (200–201)

Here and elsewhere in King, the revolutionary spirit of the modern liberation struggle expresses itself coextensively with the specters of Marx and Marxism. M. L. King, *Where Do We Go from Here*.

71 Derrida, *Specters of Marx*, 126, 128–29.
72 Hughes, "Drum."
73 See Burns "Mourning and Message," 14, for an account of the governor's panic.

Chapter 2. Swinging the God Box

Abbreviations

IM   Ralph Ellison, *Invisible Man* (New York: Vintage Books, 1995).

TDS   Ralph Ellison, *Three Days before the Shooting . . .* , eds. John F. Callahan and Adam Bradley (New York: Modern Library, 2010).

1. Baker, *Modernism and the Harlem Renaissance*, 64, 93.
2. T. H. Jones, "Ebenezer Baptist Church," 13.
3. T. H. Jones, "Ebenezer Baptist Church," 11.
4. Fulton County Deed Book 152, qtd. in T. H. Jones, "Ebenezer Baptist Church," 11–12.
5. T. H. Jones, "Ebenezer Baptist Church," 13.
6. In the 1890s "the Late Gothic Revival began to challenge the hegemony of evangelical auditorium churches" popularized during the Second Great Awakening, "and in the early twentieth century it swept through the Protestant denominations." Kilde, *When Church Became Theatre*, 205.
7. Sterne, *Audible Past*, 2.
8. Kilde, *When Church Became Theatre*, 11.
9. Kilde, *When Church Became Theatre*, 12.
10. Kilde, *When Church Became Theatre*, 20.
11. Kilde, *When Church Became Theatre*, 6.
12. Kilde, *When Church Became Theatre*, 6.
13. Thompson, *Soundscape of Modernity*, 10.
14. Thompson, *Soundscape of Modernity*, 1.
15. See Corbin, *Village Bells*.
16. T. H. Jones, "Ebenezer Baptist Church," 38. John Brown was an English organ builder who plied his trade in Wilmington, Delaware, after immigrating to the United States from London in 1885. He showcased several of his organs at the 1895 Atlanta Exposition. Since the organ and pulpit set were excluded from the sale of the former Fifth Baptist when Ebenezer acquired it circa 1913, it is likely that the John Brown organ was acquired sometime between 1900 (moved from McGruder Street) and 1922 (upon the move to Auburn Avenue and Jackson Street). See Holy Trinity Archives Committee, "History of the Organs at Holy Trinity Episcopal Church, Gainesville, Florida," for another local history of a John Brown organ acquisition.
17. Ridgeway, *Atlanta's Ebenezer Baptist Church*, 23.
18. "Ebenezer Baptist Church Has New Pipe Organ."
19. Landon, *Behold the Mighty Wurlitzer*, 6.
20. Landon, *Behold the Mighty Wurlitzer*, 4, 5.
21. Landon, *Behold the Mighty Wurlitzer*, 4–5, 5, 96.
22. In technical terms, the Wurlitzer afforded what expert players understand as "higher pressures for reeds, the derivation of more than one stop from a rank of pipes, the decline of upperwork, console gadgetry, and orchestral effects." Ochse, *History of the Organ in the United States*, 338.
23. T. H. Jones, "Ebenezer Baptist Church," 41.
24. The sign, "a somewhat unique feature in outside signage of churches in Atlanta," according to Ridgeway (*Atlanta's Ebenezer Baptist Church*, 41), was installed in 1956.

25 Du Bois, *Souls of Black Folk*, 213.
26 Virginia Foundation for the Humanities, "First Baptist Church, Roanoke." On building improvement efforts, see "Church History," First Baptist Church–Gainsboro.
27 First Baptist's distinction as "the oldest Baptist Church in the city of Roanoke" is self-reported. It dates its founding at 1867. A second "First Baptist," white—First Baptist Church of Roanoke—dates its founding at 1875, though it maintains its own originality as a Baptist congregation in Roanoke. First Baptist-Gainsboro, "History"), https://fbcgrke.org/fbc/history-page1/. On the support of Andrew Carnegie toward the pipe organ purchase, see "Along the Color Line," 219.
28 "Church History."
29 From the Civil War to the Depression, especially, many established black churches—Methodist, Baptist, Episcopal, and Presbyterian, most notably—were finely furnished with pipe organs made in Europe and the United States. According to Wayne A. Barr, Rev. Absalom Jones's African Episcopal Church of St. Thomas in Philadelphia was the first among the many black churches to boast a pipe organ, while St. Philip's Protestant (then "African") Episcopal Church in New York City, led by Rev. Peter Williams Jr., soon followed.

Although I was unable to identify any scholarly history of the pipe organ in black religious and educational practice, specifically, a rough estimation of the breadth and variety of African American churches and chapels where pipe organs were installed since 1900 can be made by a careful search of the OHS (Organ Historical Society) Pipe Organ Database. Though the database is an incomplete catalogue of organ installations in all US churches and auditoriums, its thousands of entries compose what is the most comprehensive archive of organs built in the United States, in any case. Important keyword searches include *African* and *Church of God in Christ* as terms specific to black denominations whose member churches have had pipe organs built for them. Keywords *Baptist* or *Presbyterian*, on the other hand, are unable to distinguish African American congregations from white ones. Still, a sizable number of African American churches within these denominations are also included in the OHS database. They are knowable by a prior familiarity with the historic composition of specific local congregations or by cross-reference with local city directories which historically disaggregated the city's "Colored" churches from the "White" ones.
30 Lordi, *Black Resonance*, 6.
31 Ellison, "Living with Music," 13. Avery Chapel AME was one of the earliest black churches to be organized in Ellison's Oklahoma City hometown. In a 1976 interview with Rob Wilburn titled "Ralph Ellison's Territorial Vantage," Ellison recalled that this church, to which he had been dragged by his mother as a kid, "had an organ, and an orchestra" (17). The Ira Aldridge Theater in Oklahoma City was a nine-hundred-seat vaudeville and movie house co-owned by Zelia Breaux, an important Oklahoma City music educator and an abiding influence on Ellison. In his autobiography, *Good Morning Blues*, Oklahoma City great Count Basie remembered playing a "piano with a funny little organ attachment"

(10) during an early residency at the Aldridge. But it was his playing of "the organ," Basie writes, and not some piano "with a funny little organ attachment" that drew at least one fan, a local named Crip, to the Aldridge to hear Basie in his element. By the time Basie was playing in Oklahoma City, Ellison was already miles away, a student at Tuskegee Institute in Tuskegee, Alabama. There Ellison routinely heard music issuing from a 1922 Henry Pilcher pipe organ (rebuilt in 1938) at mandatory chapel services. The annual Founder's Day ceremony which loosely informs the vespers event in chapter 5 of *Invisible Man* was undoubtedly among the most memorable of these services. The pipe organ figures significantly in the Founder's Day scene. Ellison, "Ralph Ellison's Territorial Vantage," 17; Basie, *Good Morning Blues*, 10, 11; "OHS Pipe Organ Database."

32 Baker, *Critical Memory*, 31.
33 Baker, *Critical Memory*, 32, 33.
34 Baker, *Critical Memory*, 35.
35 Ellison, *Invisible Man*, 111. Subsequent citations will be to this edition and pagination indicated parenthetically in the body of the text.
36 Baker, *Critical Memory*, 26.
37 Seltzer, *Bodies and Machines*, 3.
38 Rampersad, *Ralph Ellison*, 318.
39 Ellison, "Living with Music," 7.
40 Spillers, "Mama's Baby, Papa's Maybe," 206.
41 Spillers, "Mama's Baby, Papa's Maybe," 206.
42 Spillers, "Mama's Baby, Papa's Maybe," 204.
43 Spillers, "Mama's Baby, Papa's Maybe," 203.
44 Spillers, "Mama's Baby, Papa's Maybe," 205.
45 Spillers, "Mama's Baby, Papa's Maybe," 206.
46 Spillers, "'Permanent Obliquity of an In(pha)llibly Straight,'" 236.
47 Dunbar, "Sympathy."
48 Ellison, *Three Days*, 866. Subsequent references are to this edition and pagination will be indicated parenthetically in the body of the text.
49 Bradley, *Ralph Ellison in Progress*, 46.
50 This is Bradley and Callahan's sequence title, not Ellison's. It is an editorial addition to the text.
51 Ellison, "Song of Innocence," 30–40. Reprinted in Ellison, *Three Days*, 1073–84.
52 Crawley, "That There Might Be Black Thought," 136.
53 Arnold, "Master Organ Is Dedicated at Ebenezer."
54 Basie, *Good Morning Blues*, 95.
55 Van Rijn, *Roosevelt's Blues*, 37. In 1945, on FDR's death, a *Life* photographer captured a grieving Jackson on accordion. The photograph of Jackson playing "Going Home" as Roosevelt's funeral train departed Warm Springs has since gained a near-iconic status.
56 Arnold, *Atlanta Daily World*, 1, 5.
57 In 1939, the United States had not yet entered the second world war, though the tide of public opinion was surely shifting from an avowed neutrality to

greater sympathy toward, and cooperation with, the British and the French. The bombing Jackson's playing simulated, then, did not simulate American bombs falling in Europe, though it seems, in retrospect, that Jackson had predicted (even "heard" in advance) the United States' eventual engagements.

58 Arnold, "Master Organ Is Dedicated at Ebenezer," 5.
59 Ultimately, (Rev.) Taschereau A[r]nold became "World Religious Editor" at the *Atlanta Daily World* newspaper. In 1940, however, he was a thirty-three-year-old "preacher," according to the federal census.
60 Recordings of "Rough and Rocky Road" are rare. However, a version of "(There's a) Rough and Rocky Road" by the Stars of Harmony is included on *The History of Rhythm and Blues, 1942–1952*. A second recording by the Mello-Tones is included on *Forever Mello-Tones*. It began, "*It's* a rough and rocky road. . . ." In both recordings the opening refrain is succeeded by several improvisations on a new refrain (leading Arnold to mistake the refrain for the song's title): "You have to *pray* sometime, before you get to heaven," "You have to *cry* sometime, before you get to heaven," and "You have to *moan* sometime, before you get to heaven" are all representative variations of the new stanzas to follow the song's opening, title-bearing verse.
61 B. Jones, "It's a Rough and Rocky Road Before You Get to Heaven." For a sketch of Jones's inspired life and works, see Stone and Harold, "Bessie Jones."
62 "Ebenezer Choir Scores at Gala 'GWTW' Ball."
63 Harris, *Rise of Gospel Blues*, 188.
64 Moten, *In the Break*, 255n1; Arnold, *Atlanta Daily World*, 5.
65 Baker, *Turning South Again*, 33.
66 Baker, *Turning South*, 34.
67 Crawley, *Blackpentecostal Breath*, 38, 34.
68 Crawley, "That There Might Be Black Thought," 123. Emphasis added.
69 Schafer, *The Soundscape*, 9.
70 Drake and Cayton, *Black Metropolis*, 673–74.
71 In his still-vital 1963 *Blues People*, LeRoi Jones (Amiri Baraka) sketches the inherent class conflict of a mixed-type church and the double voice of the middle ground it seeks in compromise, thusly: "(My own church in Newark, New Jersey, a Baptist church, has almost no resemblance to the older, more traditional Negro Christian churches. The music, for instance, is usually limited to the less emotional white church music, and the choir usually sings Bach or Handel during Christmas and Easter. In response to some of its older 'country' members, the church, which is headed by a minister who is the most respected Negro in Newark, has to import gospel groups, or singers having a more traditional 'Negro church' sound.)" L. Jones, *Blues People*, 58.
72 Lischer, *Preacher King*, 21. Emphasis added.
73 Lischer, *Preacher King*, 21: "A few top-echelon people, like C. A. Scott, editor of black Atlanta's *Daily World*, and Jesse Blayton, president of Citizens Bank . . . rounded out the little world at the corner of Jackson Street and Auburn Avenue."
74 Lischer, *Preacher King*, 49.
75 Lischer, *Preacher King*, 45.

76 Lischer is clear, though, that Benjamin Mays, president of Morehouse College, was King's preferred model of Christian faith, race consciousness, parish preaching, and public speaking.
77 Lischer, *Preacher King*, 17.
78 Lischer, *Preacher King*, 17.
79 Baldwin, "On Language, Race, and the Black Writer," 140.

Chapter 3. The Cantor King

1 Lischer, *Preacher King*, 221.
2 Lischer, *Preacher King*, 221.
3 Big Bethel AME Church, Friendship Baptist Church, First Congregational Church, Cascade United Methodist Church, Wheat Street Baptist Church, and Providence Missionary Baptist Church were the earliest African American churches in Atlanta.
4 Harris, *Rise of Gospel Blues*, xx.
5 Harris, *Rise of Gospel Blues*, xx. Emphasis added.
6 Harris, *Rise of Gospel Blues*, xix.
7 Harris, *Rise of Gospel Blues*, xx.
8 Harris, *Rise of Gospel Blues*, xx.
9 King had been a forceful voice for fair housing, economic justice, and integrated schooling in Chicago since 1965 and had preached from the most influential black pulpits in Chicago since 1956. To advance a Chicago Campaign by the SCLC, King also lived and worked in Chicago during 1966.
10 Moten, "Black Kant."
11 Moten, "Black Kant."
12 Moten, "Black Kant."
13 Moten, "Knowledge of Freedom," 270. Although Moten does not refer to the incantatory explicitly in "Knowledge of Freedom," Kant's *Critique of Judgment* is explored here as in the Kelly Writers House lecture.
14 Moten, "Black Kant."
15 Moten, "Black Kant."
16 Moten, "Black Kant."
17 Moten, "Black Kant."
18 In fact, King had preached this sermon several more times in 1960, under the title "A Man Who Was a Fool." His 1967 sermon at Mt. Pisgah, which included some of the elements of "A Knock at Midnight," also lately preached in Chicago, was the second time King preached the sermon in Chicago. According to Clayborne Carson, King had delivered the sermon "at Chicago's Sunday Evening Club on 29 January 1961, and the preaching journal *The Pulpit* published this version in its June 1961 issue (pp. 4–6). King later included a version of this sermon in *Strength to Love*. Carson, *Papers of Martin Luther King, Jr.*, 413n2.
19 M. L. King, "'Why Jesus Called a Man a Fool.'"
20 Street, *Memory of Sound*, 96–97.

21 Street, *Memory of Sound*, 97.
22 Street, *Memory of Sound*, 96.
23 Street, *Memory of Sound*, 96.
24 Beranek and Kopec, "Wallace C. Sabine, Acoustical Consultant," 4.
25 Wallace Sabine had a superior professional reputation when Alschuler contracted with him to consult on the design of Sinai's new temple. Sabine had made his mark consulting in the design and construction of Symphony Hall and the New England Conservatory of Music in Boston, St. Paul's Cathedral in Detroit, the Century Theater in New York, and the Hall of the House of Representatives in Washington, DC. In Sabine, Alschuler had come to an acoustical expert of the first order.
26 Beranek and Kopec, "Wallace C. Sabine," 4.
27 Beranek and Kopec, "Wallace C. Sabine," 4.
28 Beranek and Kopec, "Wallace C. Sabine," 6.
29 Gookin, *Chicago Literary Club*, 97.
30 Beranek and Kopec, "Wallace C. Sabine," 6, 4.
31 Beranek and Kopec, "Wallace C. Sabine," 6, 7.
32 Beranek and Kopec, "Wallace C. Sabine," 6.
33 Beranek and Kopec, "Wallace C. Sabine," 5.
34 Beranek and Kopec, "Wallace C. Sabine," 4.
35 Beranek and Kopec, "Wallace C. Sabine," 6.
36 M. L. King, "Why Jesus Called a Man a Fool." Emphasis added.
37 Turner, "Musicality of Black Preaching," 196, 203, emphasis added; M. L. King, "Why Jesus Called a Man a Fool."
38 Roberson qtd. in Nielsen, *Black Chant*, 30.
39 J. Johnson, "O Black and Unknown Bards," 115.
40 Schwartz, "Emil Gustave Hirsch," 236.
41 From the 1885 Pittsburgh Platform of American Reform Judaism in Meyer, *Response to Modernity*, 388.
42 Brinkmann, *Sundays at Sinai*, 8, 4.
43 Brinkmann, *Sundays at Sinai*, 4.
44 Brinkmann, *Sundays at Sinai*, 6. Emphasis added.
45 Rabbi Edgar F. Magnin was a contemporary of Hirsch. In an oral history, he remembered that Hirsch "was a radical reformer. In those days there was a revolution. He had no Torah for a while in his temple in Chicago. Then, later on he restored it." A firebrand in the early years of his tenure, Hirsch was, however, not without his conservatisms in later years. See Chall, "Rabbi Edgar F. Magnin," 38.
46 Brinkmann, *Sundays at Sinai*, 132.
47 Brinkmann, *Sundays at Sinai*, 132.
48 "The Institutional Church." Likely, the distinction "greatest living American Hebrew" had been given on the strength of Hirsch's public commitment to the ideals of moral destiny and social justice in the cause against racial prejudice. At a luncheon meeting of the Republican Club of New York in 1911, Hirsch shared a panel with W. E. B. Du Bois, calling into question all scientific claims to racial

difference. That same year Hirsch made a fast friend in Booker T. Washington, joining Julius Rosenwald (of Sears, Roebuck and Company prominence and a Sinai member) on a trip to visit Washington's Tuskegee Institute. Rosenwald, of course, would give handsomely to Tuskegee in the years to come, enough, in fact, to endow Tuskegee and, at Washington's urging, to erect six "Rosenwald schools" for the education of black children in Alabama, a number that would grow to exceed five thousand by 1932. At Washington's death, Hirsch published a brief tribute to the Tuskegee leader in the *Chicago Defender*. In it, he pronounced Washington to have been "appointed by Providence" and "one of the greatest sons of America." Earlier, the outspoken Hirsch represented Sinai's broad commitment to social action when he signed on to a public condemnation of racist elements in Springfield, Illinois, that had provoked ugly violence there days before. According to Brinkmann, "After a brutal riot in Springfield in 1908 on the eve of the Lincoln centennial, Hirsch joined the signers of a declaration calling for ending racial inequality and discrimination. Jane Addams, W. E. B. Du Bois, Rabbi Stephen S. Wise, and the preacher of the Chicago Ethical Culture Society, William Salter also signed the declaration. This call led to the founding of the National Association for the Advancement of Colored People" (*Sundays at Sinai*, 231).

Although Hirsch would not have a significant role in the NAACP, his commitment to anti-racism on behalf of Sinai Congregation was sure and well beyond the merely rhetorical. For Hirsch's flattery of Washington, see "The Institutional Church," 5.

49 Brinkmann, *Sundays at Sinai*, 134. To unpack this further, Robert V. Friedenberg, in "*Hear O Israel*," offers the following outline of Reform thought:

> The western European orientation of Reform Jews provided them with beliefs in liberty, equality, fraternity, and democracy. They were firm believers in the political messianism, which proclaimed the imminent brotherhood of all men. . . . Reformers tended to reject the need for a national homeland. Reform prayer books eliminated references to Galuth, or exile from Palestine, as well as the restoration of world Jewry to Israel and the rebuilding of the Temple in Jerusalem. Prayers calling for a return to Zion were also eliminated. The Reform movement rejected the belief that Jews were homeless or in need of a homeland. . . . Jews, the Reform movement suggested, were more at home in the dynamic young democracy that was America than they could be anywhere else in the world. (93)

50 Hirsch, "Concordance of Judaism and Americanism," 13, 14.
51 Hirsch, "Concordance of Judaism and Americanism," 14–15. Emphasis added.
52 Friedenberg, "*Hear O Israel*," 106.
53 Friedenberg, "*Hear O Israel*," 106.
54 Friedenberg, "*Hear O Israel*," 106.
55 Friedenberg, "*Hear O Israel*," 64.
56 Friedenberg, "*Hear O Israel*," 74.
57 According to Friedenberg, "Prior to the rise of German Reform Judaism, the primary function of the rabbi was to serve as an authority on Jewish law and as a teacher. The functions of preacher and pastor were not part of the

rabbi's duties. The typical rabbi spoke only twice a year, almost exclusively on a talmudic subject" (*"Hear O Israel,"* 20). Reform preaching, then, evolved with, and was evidently shaped by, Wise's oratorical innovations. I am borrowing "new measures" from Ted A. Smith, who refers to "a loose collection of practices hammered out in different ways by different preachers over the course of many years" of nineteenth-century preaching practices. T. A. Smith, *New Measures*, 4–5.

58 Friedenberg, *"Hear O Israel,"* 75.
59 Friedenberg, *"Hear O Israel,"* 131.
60 Friedenberg, *Listening and Voice*, 119.
61 "Chicago, Illinois. Sinai Temple. Casavant Frères Ltée. (Opus 454, 1911) 3 manuals. 67 ranks." Compare Ebenezer's more modest Hillgreen-Lane and Co. organ with its "Two manuals. 14 stops. 27 registers. 14 ranks." "Atlanta, Georgia. Ebenezer Baptist Church. Hillgreen, Lane and Co. (Opus 1191, 1955) 2 manuals. 14 ranks."
62 Ihde, *Listening and Voice*, 176. Emphasis added.
63 Crawford, *Hum*, 68.
64 Barthes, "Grain of the Voice," 185.
65 Crawford, *Hum*, 71.
66 Operatic in resemblance, the Sinai/Mt. Pisgah sanctuary, with its exalted ceiling and perimeter balconies, was clearly built for hearing. The preaching stage attracted listening visually by way of the background spectacle of a magnificent organ chamber. Framed by identical left and right pipe façades, ceiling-high, signposting the worship event's aural imperative, King's preaching in the built break between facades (with organ chamber and pipes backgrounding him) gave a visual cue to the pneumatic tonality of him who would that day effect a performativity preacherly and cantorial at one and the same time.
67 Schmidt, *Hearing Things*, 74.
68 Schmidt, *Hearing Things*, 35.
69 Schmidt, *Hearing Things*, 57.
70 Schmidt, *Hearing Things*, 53. Emphasis added.
71 M. L. King, "'Why Jesus Called a Man a Fool,'" n.p. Emphasis added. Reproduced here as transcribed.
72 Although this excerpt from "Why Jesus Called a Man a Fool" does not appear in Washington's collection *Conversations with God*, the volume does collect another prayer of King's, "A Pastoral Prayer" (1956). Notwithstanding Washington's omission of the prayer excerpted from "Why Jesus Called a Man a Fool"—he appears to have preferred direct prayers over indirect or mediated ones for his collection—*Conversations* is a rich, exhaustive, and invaluable resource. Washington's introduction is especially compelling. Washington, *Conversations with God*.
73 Schmidt, *Hearing Things*, 58.
74 M. L. King, "'Why Jesus Called a Man a Fool,'" n.p.
75 Schmidt, *Hearing Things*, 61.
76 Schmidt, *Hearing Things*, 65.
77 Schmidt, *Hearing Things*, 65.
78 Schmidt, *Hearing Things*, 65.

Chapter 4. King's Gospel Modernism

Part of this chapter was previously published in *Religions* 10, no. 4 (April 23, 2019): 285, under the title "'Precious Lord': Black Mother-Loss and the Roots of Modern Gospel." The special issue, "Between Self and Spirit: Mapping the Geographies of Black Women's Spirituality," was edited by Carol Henderson. I thank the Multidisciplinary Digital Publishing Institute (MDPI) for permission to reproduce those pages here.

1. L. Jones, *Blues People*, xii.
2. Darden, *Nothing but Love*, 90.
3. Darden, *Nothing but Love*, 88.
4. Heilbut, variously qtd. in Darden, *Nothing but Love*, 113.
5. Baker, *Modernism and the Harlem Renaissance*, 15.
6. Heilbut, *Gospel Sound*, 25.
7. Heilbut, *Gospel Sound*, 26.
8. Heilbut, *Gospel Sound*, 29.
9. Harris, *Rise of Gospel Blues*, 242.
10. Boyer, "'Take My Hand, Precious Lord, Lead Me On,'" 143.
11. Boyer and Yearwood, *Golden Age of Gospel*, 61.
12. Morris, "'I'll Be a Servant for the Lord,'" 333. Interpolations Reagon's.
13. Boyer, "'Take My Hand,'" 146. According to Boyer, the gapped scale was a favorite one of Dorsey, "for," in Boyer's analysis, "he set fifty-three of the songs" to it (149).
14. Moten, *Black and Blur*, 2.
15. Moten, *Black and Blur*, 2.
16. On notational experimentalism in the 1950s, see, for instance, Price, *Resonance*, 80–81.
17. Crawford, *Hum*, 52.
18. Crawford, *Hum*, 69.
19. Luccock, *In the Minister's Workshop*, 118.
20. Luccock, *In the Minister's Workshop*, 118.
21. Luccock, *In the Minister's Workshop*, 119.
22. M. L. King, "Knock at Midnight," 58, 59; Luccock, *In the Minister's Workshop*, 123.
23. See K. Miller, *Voice of Deliverance*, 123.
24. M. L. King, "Knock at Midnight," 64.
25. K. Miller, *Voice of Deliverance*, 117. Emphasis added.
26. Lischer, *Preacher King*, 111.
27. Lischer, *Preacher King*, 111.
28. Lischer, *Preacher King*, 111.
29. Luccock, *In the Minister's Workshop*, 118.
30. K. Miller, *Voice of Deliverance*, 117.
31. Branch, *At Canaan's Edge*, 413.
32. King's manuscripts were sometimes present and sometimes absent during the preaching event. In nearly all cases, however, a manuscript preceded preaching. In her autobiography, Coretta King recalled "helping him prepare his sermons.... He would start his preparation around Monday. By Saturday he would have a sermon written out, word for word, and he would memorize it."

When the manuscript was not physically before him, it was mnemonically "present" all the same. By 1967, King had preached "A Knock at Midnight" enough (in Atlanta in 1962, and in New York and Cincinnati [a first time] in 1964) that it is unlikely he had a paper manuscript in hand when he delivered it. See C. King and Reynolds, *My Life, My Love, My Legacy*, 54.
33 For reasons likely having to do with diction, King appears to have preferred "sullen" to "dirty" in *Strength to Love*.
34 Moten, *Black and Blur*, 161. I also have in mind Brittney Cooper's similar idiom, "eloquent rage," which lends her 2018 book its title.
35 Campbell, *Word before the Powers*, 75. Emphasis added.
36 "I am many things to many people; Civil Rights leader, agitator, trouble-maker and orator, but in the quiet recesses of my heart, I am fundamentally a clergyman, a Baptist preacher. This is my being and my heritage for I am also the son of a Baptist preacher, the grandson of a Baptist preacher and the great-grandson of a Baptist preacher. The Church is my life and I have given my life to the Church." M. L. King, "Un-Christian Christian," 77.
37 Campbell, *Word before the Powers*, 70.
38 Moten, *Black and Blur*, 246.
39 Moten, *Black and Blur*, 247.
40 Moten, *Black and Blur*, 247–48.
41 Campbell, *Word before the Powers*, 79–80.
42 Revelation 1:15 (English Standard Version).
43 Campbell, *Word before the Powers*, 81.
44 Crawley, *Blackpentecostal Breath*, 7.
45 King first preached this sermon in September 1958 for the Youth Sunday Services of the Women's Convention Auxiliary National Baptist Convention. The sermon drew significantly on D. T. Niles's "Evangelism," a 1954 address to the World Council of Churches, later to be published by Niles as "Summons at Midnight" Carson et al., *Papers of Martin Luther King, Jr., Volume VI*, 347. After 1958, King preached "A Knock at Midnight" several more times, including at Atlanta's West Hunter Baptist Church in 1962 on the occasion of Ralph Abernathy's installation as senior pastor there; at Riverside Church in New York in August 1964; and at Cincinnati's Revelation Baptist Church in September 1964, where Rev. Fred Shuttlesworth, cofounder of the SCLC, presided as senior minister.
46 L. Jones, *Blues People*, 50.
47 L. Jones, *Blues People*, 50.
48 L. Jones, *Blues People*, 50.
49 Sharpe, *In the Wake*, 17.
50 Heilbut, *Gospel Sound*, 62.
51 Heilbut, *Gospel Sound*, 62; Harris, *The Rise of Gospel Blues*, 96; Heilbut, *Gospel Sound*, 62.
52 Dorsey, qtd. in Harris, *Rise of Gospel Blues*, 96.
53 Harris, *Rise of Gospel Blues*, 168.
54 Harris, *Rise of Gospel Blues*, 220.
55 Harris, *Rise of Gospel Blues*, 217.
56 Nierenberg, *Say Amen, Somebody*.

57 Nierenberg, *Say Amen, Somebody*.
58 Harris, *Rise of Gospel Blues*, 228.
59 Crawley, "That There Might Be Black Thought," 123, 136.
60 Crawley, "That There Might Be Black Thought," 136.
61 Crawley, "That There Might Be Black Thought," 136.
62 Though Dorsey's memory of the genesis of "Precious Lord" has the sense of an ex nihilo creation, Harris informs us that "Precious Lord" owes a significant debt melodically to George Nelson Allen's 1852 hymn "Must Jesus Bear the Cross Alone," although "Dorsey seems to have begun playing 'Must Jesus' in an improvisatory mode, adding his ornamentation to Allen's song. By doing so he was already assuming compositional control . . . through his familiar blues 'trills' and 'turns.'" Harris, *Rise of Gospel Blues*, 237.
63 Baldwin, *Just above My Head*, 113.
64 Harris, *Rise of Gospel Blues*, 217.
65 Curry, "Birthing Practices."
66 Curry, *Modern Mothers in the Heartland*, 36.
67 Matthews, "Provident Hospital—Then and Now," 211.
68 State of Illinois, "NETTIE DORSEY."
69 Gamble, *Making a Place for Ourselves*, 133.
70 Gamble, *Making a Place for Ourselves*, 132.
71 Curry, *Modern Mothers in the Heartland*, 147.
72 Between 1910 and 1920, to take one measure, the black population of Chicago grew by 148.5 percent as compared to the more modest 21 percent increase in the white population during the same period. The number of black migrants moving into Chicago's South Side was far too large for Provident, the region's only majority black hospital, to provide for the South Side's public health and medical care. A 1946 report of the US Public Health Service allowed that in the intervening years between World War I and World War II the racial health-care gap "had not been significantly reduced" at all (Curry, *Modern Mothers in the Heartland*, 147).
73 Curry, *Modern Mothers in the Heartland*, 55.
74 Curry, *Modern Mothers in the Heartland*, 55.
75 Harris, *Rise of Gospel Blues*, 241.
76 Harris, *Rise of Gospel Blues*, 96. Emphasis added.
77 Crawley, *Blackpentecostal Breath*, 99, 98.
78 Cain, *Art of the Spirit*, 14.
79 Cain, *Art of the Spirit*, 14.
80 Wilkerson, *Warmth of Other Suns*, 269.
81 Du Bois, *Souls of Black Folk*, 212.
82 "Womanist" insofar as the range of black women's shouting acts issue from, and are reflective of, a complex of Afro-Protestant religious sensibilities that understand faith as in keeping with a panoply of social and intellectual commitments including, especially, anti-racism, anti-sexism, black feminist thought, black women's health, biblical and ecclesial inclusiveness, and economic justice. Black womanist theologian Emilie Townes approached this womanist sociality I aver as obtaining to black women's shouting in a 2006 verse, "They Came Because of the Wailing":

>   they came because of the wailing
>   the wailing of so many voices
>   who had a strong song
>   but were choking from the lack of air
>   they came because of the weeping
>   the weeping of so many tears
>   that came so freely
>   on hot but determined faces
>   they came because of the hoping
>   the hoping of the beating heart
>   the fighting spirit
>   the mother wit tongues
>   the dancing mind
>   the world in their eyes
>   they came because they had no choice
>   to form a we
>   that is many women strong
>   and growing. (Townes, "They Came Because of the Wailing," 251)

83 Harney and Moten, *Undercommons*, 97.
84 Harney and Moten, *Undercommons*, 97; Dorsey, qtd. in Harris, *Rise of Gospel Blues*, 125.
85 Dorsey, qtd. in Harris, *Rise of Gospel Blues*, 241.
86 St. Louis gospel figure Willie Mae Ford Smith, qtd. in Broughton, *Black Gospel*, 50.
87 Dorsey's lyrics follow:

>   Precious Lord, take my hand
>   Lead me on, let me stand
>   I am tired, I am weak, I am worn
>   Through the storm, through the night
>   Lead me on to the light
>   Take my hand precious Lord, lead me home
>
>   When my way grows drear precious Lord linger near
>   When my life is almost gone
>   Hear my cry, hear my call
>   Hold my hand lest I fall
>   Take my hand precious Lord, lead me home
>
>   When the darkness appears and the night draws near
>   And the day is almost gone
>   At the river I stand
>   Guide my feet, hold my hand
>   Take my hand precious Lord, lead me home
>
>   Precious Lord, take my hand
>   Lead me on, let me stand
>   I am tired, I am weak, I am worn

> Through the storm, through the night
> Lead me on to the light
> Take my hand precious Lord, lead me home.

88 Harney and Moten, *Undercommons*, 98.
89 Jackson, *Singing in my Soul*, 4.
90 Gordon, *Ghostly Matters*, xvi.
91 Gordon, *Ghostly Matters*, xvi.
92 Marovich, *City Called Heaven*, 105.
93 Gordon, *Ghostly Matters*, xvi.
94 Even today, "Precious Lord," Broughton writes, "cries out to be sung with all the dramatic phrasing and curlicues that characterize the emotive gospel performance," one writer proclaimed. See Broughton, *Black Gospel*, 50.
95 Years after King's assassination, a rift between King's successor at the SCLC, Rev. Ralph Abernathy, and the organization's point man in Chicago, Rev. Jesse Jackson, led to a formal split. Jackson formed Operation PUSH (People United to Save Humanity). Operation Breadbasket, severely crippled by the split, survived only a few years afterward.
96 Branch recalled, "Boy, he had me play that song. I guess I played it about, I don't know, a good 35 minutes. Over and over and over and over. Boy, yeah. He had stood up over me. He kept asking me, 'Keep on playing, boy. Play it again, boy.'" "On Anniversary of MLK's Death, the Sax, the Story behind His Last Words."
97 Honey, *Going down Jericho Road*, 433.
98 Johari Jabir, personal email to the author, June 12, 2018.
99 McAfee, "Worshipful Element in Music," 358. *The Homiletic Review* was a monthly organ devoted to "current religious thought, sermonic literature, and . . . practical issues."
100 McAfee, "Worshipful Element in Music," 359.
101 McAfee, "Worshipful Element in Music," 358.
102 McAfee, "Worshipful Element in Music," 358.
103 Harney and Moten, *Undercommons*, 129.
104 Generally, feminine endings are a matter of cadence and tone in traditional music theory. More specifically, McClary explains, feminine endings threaten the musical order. Writes McClary, "Apel defines 'feminine endings' as those in which the final sonority is postponed beyond the downbeat. But we could also describe such events in terms of *excess*—a feminine ending then becomes one that refuses the hegemonic control of the barline." McClary, *Feminine Endings*, 11.
105 This is not to deny the limited space *Feminine Endings* dedicates to Jessye Norman and Aretha Franklin.
106 McClary, *Feminine Endings*, 81, 162, 162.
107 Gumbs, *Spill*, xii.
108 KMT, "We Stay in Love with Our Freedom."
109 KMT, "We Stay in Love with Our Freedom."
110 KMT, "We Stay in Love with Our Freedom."
111 Gumbs, *Spill*, 9.
112 Gumbs, *Spill*, xii.

Notes to Chapter 5. Four Women

1. Crawford, *Hum*, 69.
2. Crawley, *Blackpentecostal Breath*, 136.
3. L. Jones, *Blues People*, 56.
4. M. L. King, "Un-Christian Christian," 77.
5. Lischer, *Preacher King*, 28.
6. "Keynote sound" and "soundmark," recall, are R. Murray Schafer's terms. "In soundscape studies," he writes, "keynote sounds are those which are heard by a particular society continuously or frequently enough to form a background against which other sounds are perceived.... Often keynote sounds are not consciously perceived, but they act as conditioning agents in the perception of other sound signals" (*Soundscape*, 272). Relatedly, "soundmark" is a term "derived from *landmark* to refer to a community sound which is unique or possesses qualities which make it specially regarded or noticed by people in that community" (274).
7. In 1934, after a trip to the Baptist World Alliance in Berlin, home of the Protestant reformer Martin Luther, King Sr. would change his first name to "Martin" and rechristen his son "Martin Luther King, Jr." This is according to Richard Lischer. For a more complicated version of King Sr.'s name change, see Garrow, *Bearing the Cross*, 636n20.
8. Accounts vary. Either A. King had just started to play Malotte (from a prelude "nothing music") or had just finished playing Malotte with "nothing" left to play. On "nothing music," see Crawley, "That There Might Be Black Thought," 125–50.
9. One might also view this history as ending with the calculated commercialization of black music to crossover (read: white) audiences, a manipulation that Nelson George famously refers to as "the death of rhythm and blues." See George, *Death of Rhythm and Blues*. For a theorization of black feminist resonance, see Lordi, *Black Resonance*.
10. Garrow, *Bearing the Cross*, 34.
11. Lischer, *Preacher King*, 26.
12. Holloway, *Codes of Conduct*, 79. See, too, McDowell, *Leaving Pipe Shop*, 67, 102–8.
13. Holloway, *Codes of Conduct*, 79.
14. Holloway, *Codes of Conduct*, 80.
15. McDowell, *Leaving Pipe Shop*, 103.
16. Lischer, *End of Words*, ix.
17. McDowell, *Leaving Pipe Shop*, 67.
18. Spillers, "Mama's Baby, Papa's Maybe," 228.
19. "The 'mark'": Spillers, "Mama's Baby, Papa's Maybe," 227; "because the rites": Spillers, "Mama's Baby, Papa's Maybe," 204.
20. On King's image of his mother see Garrow, *Bearing the Cross*, 34, and Lischer, *Preacher King*, 25–26. It is regrettable that "Mother Dear" cannot be heard here, since the spelling of that address and its pronunciation might be rather far apart—that is, in many black linguistic communities, what is properly "Mother Dear" is heard rather like the portmanteau "Madea" or "Muh-dear." It is unclear whether others' recollections of King addressing his mother "Mother Dear" echo King faithfully or seek to decode his speech into standard written form.

21 Spillers, "Mama's Baby, Papa's Maybe," 228. Emphasis added.
22 "*Mother King* by Dameun Strange."
23 "Dameun Strange Interview on *Mother King*."
24 Rosenbaum, "Strange Music of Mother King."
25 Rosenbaum, "Strange Music of Mother King," unedited transcript. Excerpt from Nancy Rosenbaum email to the author, August 18, 2018.
26 Rosenbaum, "Strange Music of Mother King."
27 Rosenbaum, "Strange Music of Mother King."
28 Fuentes, "I AM (Alberta)." While the year of Alberta King's official start as organist at Ebenezer is unknown, her musical leadership is noted in a 1939 *Atlanta Daily World* article about "the 60-voice choir of Ebenezer Baptist Church" and its participation in a staged performance of *Gone with the Wind*. See Ridgeway, *Atlanta's Ebenezer Baptist Church*, 26. Since we also know of her accompaniment of five-year-old Martin Jr. in 1934 (presumably), we can surmise a formal connection to the music department at Ebenezer at least as early as the mid-1930s. In 1931, Martin Luther King Sr. assumed the pastorate of Ebenezer after the death of A. D. Williams, Alberta's father. It is not improbable that Alberta's playing at Ebenezer began during her father's tenure as pastor in the 1920s.
29 See Webb, *Divine Voice*, 14.
30 Fuentes, "Forever Free (AD)."
31 Fuentes, "Jesus Leads Me All the Way (Jennie)."
32 Fuentes, "Preacher King (MLK Sr.)."
33 Fuentes, "I AM (Alberta)."
34 Here I am referring to Edwards's reflections on contemporary recording artist Erykah Badu's performance at the 2005 Million Man March. See Edwards, *Charisma and the Fictions of Black Leadership*, ix–xv. See also Edwards's chapters 1, 3, and 6 for further discussion of gender politics and the "charismatic scenario . . . of black political modernity" (xx).
35 Lordi, *Black Resonance*, 3.
36 Lordi, *Black Resonance*, 3.
37 Lordi, *Black Resonance*, 23.
38 C. S. King and Reynolds, *My Life, My Love, My Legacy*, 98.
39 C. S. King, *My Life with Martin Luther King, Jr.*, 248.
40 Leiffermann, "Profession," 56.
41 Leiffermann, "Profession," 56.
42 Leiffermann, "Profession," 52, 56.
43 Leiffermann, "Profession," 42.
44 Spillers, "Interstices," 165.
45 Leiffermann, "Profession," 42.
46 Leiffermann, "Profession," 56. Emphasis added.
47 Spillers, "Interstices," 167; Leiffermann, "Profession," 56.
48 Spillers, "Interstices," 165.
49 Spillers, "Interstices," 165.
50 Edwards, *Charisma and the Fictions of Black Leadership*, 79.
51 Edwards, *Charisma and the Fictions of Black Leadership*, 77.

52 With "wayward self-expression" I have in mind Saidiya Hartman's *Wayward Lives, Beautiful Experiments*.
53 Cusick, "Gender and the Cultural Work of a Classical Music Performance," 81.
54 "'Come by Here, My Lord.'" For excellent studies of the history and theory of the racialization of timbre in American concert singing, see Nina Sun Eidsheim's "Voice as a Technology of Selfhood" and *The Race of Sound*.
55 Spillers, "Interstices," 166. As early as 1959, the classical influence upon Coretta King's freedom concerts was clear. Her July 10 program, "Coretta Scott King: Soprano," at the Dayton Art Institute, though not officially one of the freedom concerts, included selections by Johannes Brahms, Franz Schubert, Domenico Scarlatti, and Giuseppe Verdi preceding arranged African American spiritual and Jamaican and calypso folk songs. Although the later freedom concerts mostly excluded classical works as such, Coretta's selections remained "classical" in voice, arrangement, and public promotion. "'Coretta Scott King: Soprano' Program."
56 Spillers, "Interstices," 165.
57 Cusick, "Gender and the Cultural Work of a Classical Music Performance," 82–83.
58 C. S. King and Reynolds, *My Life, My Love, My Legacy*, 33.
59 C. S. King and Reynolds, *My Life, My Love, My Legacy*, 27.
60 C. S. King and Reynolds, *My Life, My Love, My Legacy*, 27.
61 C. S. King and Reynolds, *My Life, My Love, My Legacy*, 33.
62 C. S. King and Reynolds, *My Life, My Love, My Legacy*, 33. Emphasis added.
63 Leiffermann, "Profession," 43.
64 Leiffermann, "Profession"; Spillers, "Interstices," 167.
65 Spillers, "Interstices," 166.
66 Spillers, "Interstices," 167.
67 C. S. King and Reynolds, *My Life, My Love, My Legacy*, 39.
68 Angelou, "Still I Rise," 41. The first two stanzas of Angelou's poem read:

> You may write me down in history
> With your bitter, twisted lies,
> You may trod me in the very dirt
> But still, like dust, I'll rise.
>
> Does my sassiness upset you?
> Why are you beset with gloom?
> 'Cause I walk like I've got oil wells
> Pumping in my living room.

69 C. S. King, "10 Commandments on Vietnam."
70 C. S. King, "10 Commandments on Vietnam."
71 C. S. King, "10 Commandments on Vietnam."
72 Cooper, *Beyond Respectability*, 27. Cooper's preface rightly insists academics "trust" black women intellectuals the way most of us "have been trained *to trust*" that white males of all varieties are capable of 'deep thought'" (2). In a word, this means that we "take Black women seriously" (2).
73 Cooper, *Beyond Respectability*, 9.
74 Hughes, "Mother to Son."

75 "ungrammatical profundity": C. S. King, "10 Commandments on Vietnam"; "amazingly intelligent": C. S. King, "10 Commandments on Vietnam."
76 "denied": Spillers, "Cross Currents and Discontinuities," 251; "vertical": Spillers, "Mama's Baby, Papa's Maybe," 218.
77 Wall, *Worrying the Line*, 10.
78 M. L. King, *Strength to Love*, 125. Pollard is also mentioned in "Letter from a Birmingham City Jail."
79 Newspaper accounts of the April 27, 1968, event put the number of demonstrators at between 60,000 and 100,000, depending on what part of the city the marchers, coming from not less than four major protest parades across New York City, were gathered in at any given time. In the Sheep Meadow, Central Park's parade ground, two parades from Fifth Avenue and Central Park West merged. Estimates by the *New York Times* had 60,000 in Sheep Meadow at the time of Coretta King's appearance. The *New York Amsterdam News* reported at least two more parades descending on Central Park from Harlem, one largely black and the other principally Puerto Rican, increasing the crowd size to approximately 100,000. See "Police Battle NY Marchers"; "87,000 March in War Protest Here; "Mrs. King at Anti-War Rally."
80 Spillers, "Mama's Baby, Papa's Maybe," 229. Spillers offers a succinct and forceful expression of why black feminist epistemology matters to black men's and boys' dreams of flourishing in the United States: "It is the heritage of the mother that the African American male must regain as an aspect of his own personhood—the power of 'yes' to the 'female' within" (228). Perhaps Coretta King's black feminist legacy is nothing less than a call to a full reckoning with the meaningfulness of such a historical revelation.
81 Cohen, *Duke Ellington's America*, 337.
82 Schwerin, *Got to Tell It*, 120. Emphasis added.
83 Goreau, *Just Mahalia, Baby*, 251.
84 Ellington, *Music Is My Mistress*, 181; Cohen, *Duke Ellington's America*, 230.
85 Lloyd, "Development of African American Gospel," 274n11.
86 Ellington, *Music Is My Mistress*, 256.
87 Jackson's a capella recording of "Come Sunday" appears as a bonus track only on the rereleases of the *Black, Brown and Beige* album.
88 Ellison, *Invisible Man*, 9; Ellison, *Living with Music*, 92.
89 Gumbs, *Spill*, 131.
90 Famously, Jackson said, "I'm used to singing in church where they don't stop me until the Lord comes." M. Jackson and Wylie, *Movin' On Up*, 108.
91 Jackson, *Movin' On Up*, 109.
92 Crawley, *Blackpentecostal Breath*, 10.
93 Daniels, "'Until the Power of the Lord Comes Down,'" 176.
94 Crawley, *Blackpentecostal Breath*, 159.
95 Crawley, *Blackpentecostal Breath*, 159.
96 Crawley, *Blackpentecostal Breath*, 136.
97 Ellison, *Living with Music*, 92.
98 Ellison, *Living with Music*, 92, 93, 94.
99 Heilbut, *Gospel Sound*, 94.

100 Admittedly, Ellison's reference to Jackson's "frame" is ambiguous. In *Spirit in the Dark*, for example, Josef Sorett casts it as "the specific context in which Mahalia Jackson's sound has been cultivated and sustained" (147). It is noncorporeal. And yet as Sorett himself argues, "Ellison had never been one to argue for just one reading of a single source, even if he was convinced his interpretation was best. Multiplicity and complexity were his signatures" (147). I agree with Sorett and it is owing precisely to this Ellisonian aesthetic that I take Jackson's "frame" to refer to her material body even if Sorett's interpretation is, technically speaking, "best." Ellison's praise for Jackson's 1956 *Bless This House*, particularly its "triumphal blending of popular dance movements with religious passion" that precedes his attention to "the frame within which she moves" by the fewest lines, encourages the corporeal valence I bring to the "multiplicity and complexity" of Jackson's moving—perhaps even dancing—"frame." Ellison, *Living with Music*, 94.
101 Heilbut, *Gospel Sound*, 92.
102 Schwerin, *Got to Tell It*, 4. Emphasis added.
103 Eidsheim, "Voice as Technology of Selfhood," 30, 1.
104 Schwerin, *Got to Tell It*, 4.
105 Heilbut, *Gospel Sound*, 94.
106 Ellison, *Living with Music*, 92.
107 The Adhan ("to listen") is the Islamic call to Friday prayer at the mosque. In the Hebrew tradition, the Barekhu ("Let us praise") serves a similarly convoking function among the devout. It is worth noting that while Jackson performed "Come Sunday" with Ellington on Thursday, festival organizers arranged for her to perform a full one-hour set Saturday at midnight, to sacralize Sunday morning with Jackson's singing. Just as the scheduling of her Saturday night/Sunday morning performance at Freebody Park aimed to call attention to Sunday's calendrical temporality in a nearly liturgical way, so did Thursday night's performance of "Come Sunday" invoke her free July 6, 1958, concert at Mt. Zion AME, and her priestly call or summoning to that space and performance.
108 Ellison, *Living with Music*, 93.
109 Ellison, *Living with Music*, 92, 93.
110 Emerson, "Mahalia Jackson Weaves a Spell with Gospel Singing at Festival."
111 Campt, *Listening to Images*, 9.
112 DeCarava, *The Sound I Saw*, n.p. An author's note at the end of the volume discloses that "this book was made with original photographs and text and finished in the early 1960s. It is published for the first time, [however,] by Phaidon Press in 2001."
113 Campt, *Listening to Images*, 8. Even as he laments how little attention has been paid to Mildred Falls's influence upon the swing style of early gospel piano play, Johari Jabir offers what is likely the most discerning reflection on Falls's part in Jackson's performances in the literature available on Falls. Paying particular attention to the work of Falls's left hand in providing "a walking baseline" and her right, carrying on "conversation with Mahalia's vocals, both in terms of Mahalia's melodies and her alternate vocalities," Jabir's reading of the partnership between Falls and Jackson on Jackson's "Didn't It Rain" is brief but penetrating. Jabir, "On Conjuring Mahalia," 656.

114 Jafa, "Black Visual Intonation," 267.
115 Jafa, "Black Visual Intonation," 267.
116 Jafa, "Black Visual Intonation," 268.
117 Jafa, "Black Visual Intonation," 267.
118 Ellison, *Living with Music*, 94.
119 On this, Moten is best. Discerned from performances by free jazz figures Cecil Taylor and Ed Blackwell, he deduced: "If the sensual dominant of a performance is visual (if you're there, live, at the club), then the aural emerges as that which is given in its fullest possibility by the visual.... Similarly, if the sensual dominant of the performance is aural (if you're at home, in your room, with the recording), then the visual emerges as that which is given its fullest possibility by the aural.... The visual and the aural are before one another." Moten, *In the Break*, 173.
120 Erin Manning takes up this important differentiation in her 2016 book *The Minor Gesture*. Any movement is understood to be volitional which is "intentional" and "tied to consciousness" (17). It is that which is thought to belong to the subject who directs the course of desire autonomously. Any movement is understood to be decisional which is "nonconscious" and decisional "in the sense that it is capable of altering the course of [an] event *in the event*" (19). It is movement that is open to improvisation. If dancers and athletes are exemplars of decisional movement, then decisional movement may be thought of, in the parlance of those two activities—dance and sport—as *flow* in its idealized manifestation. Manning, *Minor Gesture*.
121 S. M. Smith, *At the Edge of Sight*, 6.
122 S. M. Smith, *At the Edge of Sight*, 6.
123 S. M. Smith, *At the Edge of Sight*, 6.
124 S. M. Smith, *At the Edge of Sight*, 77.
125 S. M. Smith, *At the Edge of Sight*, 77.
126 S. M. Smith, *At the Edge of Sight*, 77.
127 S. M. Smith, *At the Edge of Sight*, 76–77.
128 S. M. Smith, *At the Edge of Sight*, 79–80.
129 Manning, *Minor Gesture*, 1–2.
130 Manning, *Minor Gesture*, 1.
131 Manning, *Minor Gesture*, 2.
132 Manning, *Minor Gesture*, 2.
133 Manning, *Minor Gesture*, 2.
134 "deferred": S. M. Smith, *At the Edge of Sight*, 81; "sites of dissonance": Manning, *Minor Gesture*, 2.
135 Crawley, *Blackpentecostal Breath*, 28.
136 Coretta Scott King, qtd. in Schwerin, *Got to Tell It*, 179.
137 McDaniel, "Funeralizing Mahalia Jackson," 254.
138 Coretta Scott King, qtd. in McDaniel, "Funeralizing Mahalia Jackson," 254.
139 This position is taken by Johari Jabir, whose reflections on Mahalia Jackson are personal and incisive. See, again, his "On Conjuring Mahalia," n120.
140 Recall "signifyin(g)" is a signal feature of Henry Louis Gates's theory of African American literature. In *The Signifying Monkey*, Gates posits the critical relationship

between black writers as "motivated" and "unmotivated," which is to say often parodic and thus implicitly argumentative (motivated) and, at other times, admiring and reverential (unmotivated). Perhaps not ironically, Gates analogizes the distinction between motivated and unmotivated signifyin(g) in black literary criticism from black musical practice. Unmotivated signifyin(g), in particular, might be most saliently reflected, he says, by "black jazz musicians who perform each other's standards . . . not to critique these but to engage in refiguration as an act of homage." Gates, *Signifying Monkey*, 21. Since Jackson and Franklin had a somewhat complicated personal relationship, one cannot discount Franklin's capacity for motivated signifyin(g) on Jackson's version of "Precious Lord." However, I choose to believe Franklin's singing on the event of Jackson's funeral was significantly more eulogistic (and unmotivated) than critical or argumentative (and therefore motivated).

141 Ritz, *Respect*, 54. Emphasis added.
142 Ritz, *Respect*, 58.
143 Öhman, "Sound Business," 222.
144 Franklin and Ritz, *Aretha*, 74. Some sources indicate that it was the local Detroit label JBV that first recorded Franklin in Oakland and later licensed these works to Chess Records (and their companion label, Checkers Records). JBV (later Battle Records) had previously cooperated with Chess Records in producing Rev. Franklin's sermons from New Bethel Baptist Church. It seems likely that Aretha Franklin's first recordings were issued according to a similar arrangement. For a good outline of the business relationships among Chess, JBV, and the Franklin family, see Öhman, "Sound Business," 188–243.
145 Ritz, *Respect*, 54–55.
146 Cox, *Shapeshifters*, 11.
147 Cox, *Shapeshifters*, 12.
148 *Womanish* is as close as I can come to conveying the liminal condition of black girls as already always "adults in the making," as Aimee Meredith Cox says. While *manchild* is available to describe black boys perceptually denied boyhood, no such analogous nominalization exists for black girls, as far as I can tell. Although usually identified with Alice Walker's *In Search of Our Mother's Gardens*, I prefer Walker's account of the term's derivation in a note appended to her 1979 short story "Coming Apart." There, she explains *womanish* as

> a word our mothers used to describe, and attempt to inhibit, strong, outrageous or outspoken behavior when we were children: "You're acting *womanish*!" A labeling that failed, for the most part, to keep us from acting "womanish" whenever we could, that is to say, like our mothers themselves, and like other women we admired.

Womanish, Walker's note suggests, names the child's will to adulthood as both a radical will to exceed childhood's containments and a traditionalist will to social convention by way of imitation and, to borrow an idea from Judith Butler, "citationality." Walker, "Coming Apart," 100.

149 Chatelain, *South Side Girls*, 4.
150 If "'black girls' narratives have not appeared in the bulk of scholarship on Migration," as Chatelain writes, then it is not only because research institutions are

generally uninterested in collecting materials from black girls who "by virtue of their race, gender and age" are believed not to have contributed much to migration history. Chatelain, *South Side Girls*, 5. More than that, few researchers have followed Farah Griffin, to take one example, in considering the musical modalities that, running parallel with black visual and literary forms of the period, also inform migration narratology, as she deftly showed in *"Who Set You Flowin?"*. In 1956, as in 1932, the journey motif of "Precious Lord" ("At the river, I stand / Guide my feet, hold my hand") could not have escaped the associative grip of migration's freedom-dreams in the modern black cultural imagination.

151 Cox, *Shapeshifters*, 193.
152 Erma Franklin, qtd. in Ritz, *Respect*, 24.
153 Erma Franklin, qtd. in Ritz, *Respect*, 25.
154 Erma Franklin, qtd. in Ritz, *Respect*, 26.
155 Spillers, "Mama's Baby, Papa's Maybe," 220.
156 Franklin, "Precious Lord (Part One)" and "Precious Lord (Part Two)."
157 Schwerin, *Got to Tell It*, 181.
158 Ritz, *Respect*, 54.
159 Not by a long shot. Two weeks earlier, Franklin teamed up with Reverend James Cleveland and the Southern California Community Choir to live-record *Amazing Grace*, the highest-selling of Franklin's thirty-eight studio and six live albums, and the best-selling live gospel recording of all time.
160 Hartman and Wilderson, "Position of the Unthought," 185; Spillers, "Mama's Baby, Papa's Maybe," 228.
161 Spillers, "Mama's Baby, Papa's Maybe," 229.

Chapter 6. King's Vibrato

1 Johnson and Adelman, *King*, 6.
2 S. Lewis, "Guest Editor's Note," 12.
3 Benjamin, "The Work of Art in the Age of Mechanical Reproduction," 236.
4 Both DeCarava and Jafa point toward an aural power in the ontology of photographs that Slovenian philosopher Slavoj Žižek has described as "seeing in the mode of hearing." See Decarava, *Sound I Saw*; Jafa, "Black Visual Intonation"; Žižek, "'I Hear You with My Eyes,'" 95.
5 Mitchell, *What Do Pictures Want?*
6 Žižek was specifically concerned with the human voice as the threshold to subjectivity and, following Lacan, set "voice" against silence as "figure [to] ground." Though not an equivalency exactly, I take "sound" to be the general condition of all "voices"—human, animal, and machine—coming online at once within a defined time and space such that "sound" too relates silence as "figure and ground." That is, "silence is not (as one would be prone to think) the ground against which the figure of a voice [i.e., a human sound object] emerges; quite the contrary, the reverberating sound itself provides the ground that renders visible the figure of silence"—in this case, the photograph or its image. Žižek, "'I Hear You with My Eyes,'" 93.

7 Moten, *Black and Blur*, viii.
8 S. M. Smith, *At the Edge of Sight*, 6.
9 S. M. Smith, *At the Edge of Sight*, 6.
10 Hartman and Wilderson, "Position of the Unthought."
11 Sontag, *On Photography*, 15.
12 Anderson, *Imagined Communities*, 12.
13 Žižek, "'I Hear You with My Eyes,'" 92.
14 Žižek, "'I Hear You with My Eyes,'" 93. Emphasis Žižek's.
15 Dolar, "Object Voice," 7.
16 Dolar, "Object Voice," 7.
17 Similarly, Tina Campt refers to the "quiet" dimensions of the photograph. "Quiet photography names a heuristic," she writes, "for attending to the lower range of intensities generated by images assumed to be mute." It "challenge[s] the equation of vision with knowledge by engaging photography through a sensory register that is critical to the Black Atlantic cultural formations: sound" (Campt, *Listening to Images*, 6). I am interested in the specific sounds (or sound objects) photographs repress and thus help us forget as a dimension of the photographic event. The history of that event is not silent; it noisily resounds.
18 B. J. Brueggemann, "On (Almost) Passing," 322. Emphases added.
19 B. J. Brueggemann, "On (Almost) Passing," 322.
20 Azoulay, *Civil Contract of Photography*, 16.
21 This latter category was evoked in a proposal, circa 1969, by the SCLC for "An Audio History of Martin Luther King, Jr." In support of its weekly, thirty-minute *Martin Luther King Speaks* radio program, the SCLC leadership, with the help of William S. Stein and the American Foundation of Nonviolence (AFON), called for "the collection, preservation, organization and dissemination of the auditory record of Martin Luther King, Jr.—in action—during the events which he helped to shape." The proposal aimed to solicit from "people involved in the Freedom Movement" their magnetic tape recordings of King. The proposal noted that there were "approximately twelve hundred tapes of Dr. King in circulation" with seven hundred already committed to the audio archive or in SCLC possession. The proposal is clear that its success would depend upon acquiring this representative volume of tapes from "several individuals [with] large tape collections of Dr. King" (Southern Christian Leadership Conference, "Proposal for an Audio History").
22 Baldwin, *Fire Next Time*, 306.
23 Žižek, "'I Hear You with My Eyes,'" 92.
24 "Never Again Where He Was," 13.
25 Žižek, "'I Hear You with My Eyes,'" 92.
26 M. L. King, "I've Been to the Mountaintop."
27 K. D. Miller, *Martin Luther King's Biblical Epic*, 62.
28 Hopkins, "United States Department of the Interior."
29 K. D. Miller, *Martin Luther King's Biblical Epic*, 63.
30 That Taylor was the architect responsible for Mason Temple's strikingly modernist plan is storied but difficult to verify beyond the building's cornerstone. There, the architect is indeed identified as "H. Taylor" while church records,

including a 1945 dedication booklet, give "Elder W. H. Taylor" architectural credit. Next to nothing is known of Taylor's life, professional training, or practice. What is known is that Elder Taylor, who was almost certainly African American, was a leading member of the Church of God in Christ (COGIC), as the appearance of his name embossed upon a permanent historical marker on church grounds implies. According to Hopkins, however, Taylor "was not in Memphis according to city directory sources and directories published by the Memphis branch of the Negro Chamber of Commerce in 1940" (Hopkins, "United States Department of the Interior," sec. 8, 4–5). Hopkins isn't entirely accurate. As *elder* is a pastoral designation in the COGIC lexicon, a search for Taylor under *Clergyman* is far more efficient than combing through the countless *Taylors* with first names beginning with *H* or *W* appearing as residents of Memphis. The "Business" section of the 1940 Memphis City Directory, on the other hand, includes listings for "Harry Taylor" *and* "Wm. H. Taylor" under the heading "Clergymen." Since "Wm. H. Taylor" is identified in the directory as Methodist, it is unlikely this Taylor is the architect Taylor appearing on the Mason Temple markers. "H. Taylor," on the other hand, is listed as a clergyman in the Church of God in Christ. It is likely that this Taylor, of "1367 E McLemore av" [sic], is the Taylor in question. In the *African-American Holiness Pentecostal Movement* compiled by Sherry S. DuPree, "Elder Harry Taylor" is identified as serving "Binghamton Church, Scott Street and Autumn Avenue, Memphis, Tennessee." Although Binghamton Church no longer survives to confirm it, it seems this Harry Taylor, a local COGIC pastor (elder) whose service was secured by Bishop R. F. Williams of Cleveland and Elder U. E. Miller of Cleveland—Mason Temple's building commissioner and superintendent of construction, respectively—was the architect. Nothing more is presently known of Taylor's life or design practices, remarkable as he had to have been as an African American professional (presumably) in the wartime South. Surprisingly, Taylor is not listed in Dreck Spurlock Wilson's tremendous *African-American Architects: A Biographical Dictionary, 1865–1945*. He clearly deserves historical attention. See DuPree, *African-American Holiness Pentecostal Movement*, 217.

31 K. Miller, "No Mason Temple, No 'Mountaintop' Speech."
32 K. D. Miller, *Martin Luther King's Biblical Epic*, 63.
33 K. Miller, "No Mason Temple, No 'Mountaintop' Speech."
34 K. Miller, "No Mason Temple, No 'Mountaintop' Speech."
35 *Electric modernisms* is an appropriation of Sandy Isenstadt's "electric modernism," which he grounds "in the formation of new sorts of spaces unique to an era of electric light." I use *electric modernisms* to refer to technological inventions and reinventions radically transforming social life and aesthetic expression in the modern age of electricity. Isenstadt, *Electric Light*, 12.
36 Schafer, *Soundscape*, 78.
37 Crawford, *Hum*, 68.
38 Williams and Miller, *Facts about the Temple*, 53.
39 Warner, "Preacher's Footing," 371.

40. Warner, "Preacher's Footing," 371. We might say that these are also the very dynamics obtaining to the antiphonal habits of black preaching which Albert Raboteau and Sterling Stuckey have located in slave religion. See Raboteau's foundational *Slave Religion*.
41. Sharpe, *In the Wake*, 104.
42. "Preview of ESSA Weather Bureau Forecast."
43. Sharpe, *In the Wake*, 104.
44. Details of the Atoka, Tennessee, tornado appeared in the Thursday, April 4, 1968, issue of Memphis's *Commercial Appeal* newspaper. Alongside "Tornado Strikes near Millington: At Least 30 Hurt," a second article, "King Challenges Court Restraint, Vows to March," betrays the early printing of this edition, as King will have been assassinated later that day.
45. M. L. King, "I've Been to the Mountaintop."
46. Powell, *Cutting a Figure*, 21.
47. Powell, *Cutting a Figure*. "Being" is indebted to Amiri Baraka. His *In Our Terribleness*, which Powell relies on here, has a cosmological conception of being/Being in mind as he writes of the transformation of black subjects from "themselves Thru to the Being." Baraka and Fundi, *In Our Terribleness*, n.p.
48. King had also addressed an audience at a freedom rally at Mason Temple in 1959.
49. M. L. King, "*All Labor Has Dignity*," 176.
50. I say "mostly" to acknowledge the recovery of "All Labor Has Dignity" for labor history by Michael Honey in 2011 (M. L. King, *All Labor Has Dignity* [2011]) and, more recently, by Cornel West (M. L. King, *Radical King* [2015]). Honey and West both collect the speech in volumes dedicated to the more progressive, even radical, speeches and writings in the King archive.
51. Moten, *In the Break*, 50.
52. Honey, "Editor's Note," in M. L. King, *All Labor Has Dignity*, xxxviii–xxxix.
53. The original manuscripts are available among the King papers at the Martin Luther King Jr. Center for Nonviolent Social Change in Atlanta. Some are archived in special collections at Stanford, Boston, Emory, and Atlanta University Center as well.
54. On the improvisational imperative in early gospel, Kenneth Morris, a contemporary of Thomas Dorsey, explained once: "I can play . . . the same song twenty times and never repeat myself, or twenty times I'll play it in a different way because I feel differently twenty times. That's soul. That's gospel. . . ." Morris, "'I'll Be a Servant for the Lord,'" 333.
55. Honey, "Editor's Note," xxxix.
56. Honey, "Editor's Note," xxxix.
57. Honey, "Editor's Note," xxxviii.
58. Moten, *In the Break*, 46.
59. Moten, *In the Break*, 47.
60. Moten, *In the Break*, 48.
61. Moten, *In the Break*, 48. It should be noted here that although it is not easy to distinguish the March 18 and April 3 images of King holding forth at Mason

Temple Church of God in Christ, differences in dress and audience are the best gauges of the earlier and later photographing. Two photographs of King at Mason Temple, including the one named in this chapter, credit Matthews. One Matthews image was reproduced for *Mother Jones* in 2018; the other for *NBC News* in 2013. Both date the event of the photograph as March 18, 1968, and, taken from an identical angle, show King attired in a suit that may or may not be shades lighter than the one worn weeks later on the occasion of "I've Been to the Mountaintop." If this difference in King's dress is not sufficient on the visual level alone to establish his earlier and later visits to Mason Temple, then the disparate subjects seated or standing in the photographic background make differentiating the occasions easier and undeniable. Even a casual study of figures seated to King's back reveals they do not capture the same event. Day, "50 Years after Their Historic Strike"; Caron, "MLK and Me."

62 Moten, *In the Break*, 48.
63 Davies, "Togate Statues and Petrified Orators," 72.
64 Davies, "Togate Statues and Petrified Orators," 51.
65 Davies, "Togate Statues and Petrified Orators," 53.
66 Brilliant, *Gesture and Rank in Roman Art*, qtd. in Davies, "Togate Statues and Petrified Orators," 53.
67 Here, I am following Kaja Silverman on Lacan's "mirror-stage" as "the threshold of the visible world" in Lacan's *Écrits*. See Silverman, *Threshold of the Visible World*, 2–3.
68 "The African American male has been touched, therefore, by the mother, *handed* by her in ways he cannot escape, and in ways that the white American male is allowed to temporize by a fatherly reprieve." Spillers, "Mama's Baby, Papa's Maybe," 228.
69 Agamben, "Notes on Gesture," 138.
70 Agamben, "Notes on Gesture," 139.
71 Campt, *Listening to Images*, 6.
72 Campt, *Listening to Images*, 7.
73 "mythical": Agamben, "Notes on Gestre," 153; "in and as vibration": Campt, *Listening to Images*, 7.
74 Manning, *The Minor Gesture*, 1.
75 Manning, *Minor Gesture*, 1–2.
76 Manning, *Minor Gesture*, 177.
77 Manning, *Minor Gesture*, 1.
78 Manning, *Minor Gesture*, 1.
79 Manning, *Minor Gesture*, 7, 2.
80 Manning, *Minor Gesture*, 71.
81 Manning, *Minor Gesture*, 15.
82 Manning, *Minor Gesture*, 7.
83 Manning, *Minor Gesture*, 1.
84 Seashore, "Introduction," 7.
85 Seashore, "Introduction," 9.
86 Seashore, "Introduction," 9.
87 Seashore, *Psychology of the Vibrato*, 53; Metfessel, "Vibrato in Artistic Voices," 73.

88   Shaler, "Negro Problem," 702.
89   Shaler, "Negro Problem," 702.
90   Shaler, "Science and the African Problem," 36, 38.
91   Shaler, "Science and the African Problem," 45, 44.
92   Shaler, "Science and the African Problem," 39, 44.
93   Shaler, "Science and the African Problem," 45.
94   Shaler, "Science and the African Problem," 40.
95   Shaler, "Science and the African Problem," 41.
96   Shaler, "Science and the African Problem," 43.
97   Seashore, *Psychology of the Vibrato*, 53.
98   Metfessel, "Vibrato in Artistic Voices," 14–15, 15.
99   Shaler, "Negro Problem," 700, 702, 701.
100 "problem for thought": Chandler, X, 11; "art of control": Seashore, "Introduction," 9.
101 Odum and Johnson, *Negro Workaday Songs*, 252.
102 Odum and Johnson, *Negro Workaday Songs*, 252. Even more exactly, Metfessel offered that "the apparatus consists of photographic instruments mounted within a suit case. In the interior there is a large wheel to which a crank is attached from the outside. Motion picture film is wound around the wheel, coming from a film magazine. In its passage from the magazine to the wheel, beams of light are concentrated upon it. These lights are reflected from tiny mirrors, which are attached to diaphragms." Next, "a sound wave photograph is made on the moving picture film by three light points. The diaphragms pick up the vibrations of sound, and the mirrors translate the vibrations into an up and down flashing of the light. The light flashes at the same rate at which the vocal cords are sounding." Metfessel, *Phonophotography in Folk Music*, 22.
103 Metfessel, *Phonophotography in Folk Music*, 20.
104 Metfessel, *Phonophotography in Folk Music*, 20.
105 Metfessel, *Phonophotography in Folk Music*, 20. Metfessel named researchers such as J. W. Work, Natalie Curtis-Burlin, and Dorothy Scarborough as those who concluded the black voice was beyond description.
106 Metfessel, *Phonophotography in Folk Music*, 26.
107 Moten, *Stolen Life*, 13.
108 Seashore, "Vibrato in Voice and Instrument," 150.
109 I have in mind "Did Rise" by Jessica Rae Bergamino.
110 Odum and Johnson, *Negro Workaday Songs*, 264.
111 Ellison, *Invisible Man*, 7.
112 Metfessel, *Phonophotography in Folk Music*, 37.
113 Metfessel, *Phonophotography in Folk Music*, 85.
114 Baker, *Modernism and the Harlem Renaissance*, 92.
115 Baker, *Modernism and the Harlem Renaissance*, 91, 92.
116 Baker, *Modernism and the Harlem Renaissance*, 104.
117 Metfessel, *Phonophotography in Folk Music*, 51.
118 Panagia, *Political Life of Sensation*, 92.
119 Panagia, *Political Life of Sensation*, 132–33.
120 Panagia, *Political Life of Sensation*, 125.

121 Figure 6.13 appears also in Seashore, "Vibrato in Voice and Instrument," 53.
122 Kersands's mouth was said to open so wide that he could place a cup and saucer in it. Hughes and Meltzer, *Black Magic*, 27.
123 On "orificiality," see Tompkins, *Racial Indigestion*, 194n20. Although Tompkins's neologism signifies the author's interest in "orality, in images of black ingestion or of the association of blackness with edibility," not public speech-making, "orificiality" may hail our attention nevertheless to its greater and lesser contortions in speech- and sound-making.
124 Johnson, "The Creation"; Baker, *Blues, Ideology, and Afro-American Literature*; Henderson, *Understanding the New Black Poetry*.
125 Panagia, *Political Life of Sensation*, 147.
126 M. L. King, "MLK Speech at Mason Temple, March 18th, 1968." The audio of "All Labor Has Dignity" is preferred here to Michael Honey's otherwise reliable transcription of King's speech as my transcription reflects the playful rhyming of "no-house" and "Mo-house" King was clearly seeking to effect in his delivery.
127 See Wilderson, "Gramsci's Black Marx," 225–40.
128 Wilderson, "Gramsci's Black Marx," 229; Du Bois, *Black Reconstruction in America*, 40.
129 Wilderson, "Gramsci's Black Marx," 230.
130 Wilderson, "Gramsci's Black Marx," 230.
131 Moten, *In the Break*, 42–43.
132 M. L. King, "All Labor Has Dignity," 172. Emphasis added.
133 M. L. King, "All Labor Has Dignity," 172.
134 M. L. King, "All Labor Has Dignity," 178.
135 Moten, *Stolen Life*, 45.
136 Moten, *Stolen Life*, 45.
137 Although the conclusion to "I Have a Dream" is commonly heard (and just as often read) as "Thank God Almighty, we are free at last!" the version of the speech copyrighted in 1963 by King and now housed in the National Archives ends "*Great* God a-mighty, we are free at last." Emphasis added.
138 Sexton, "Social Life of Social Death," 10.
139 Mitchell, *What Do Pictures Want?*, 33; Dunbar, "We Wear the Mask," 71.

Chapter 7. Dream Variations

1 This is King's phrase. He referred to Hughes with this honorific in his 1967 address at Riverside Church, "Beyond Vietnam: A Time to Break Silence."
2 W. J. Miller, *Origins of the Dream*, 2.
3 W. J. Miller, *Origins of the Dream*, 2.
4 "Resonant," "room," and "outdoors" are acoustic classifications posited by English musicologist Thurston Dart in *Interpretation of Music* (1960). Historically, musical acoustics, Dart argues, may be "roughly divided into" these three forms. Dart, *Interpretation of Music*, 57.
5 Ater, "Communities in Conflict," 35.
6 Elbert Lee, qtd. in "Rocky Mount Journal."

7   Ater, "Communities in Conflict," 33.
8   Erik Blome, qtd. in Upton Dell, *What Can and Can't Be Said*, 101.
9   Blome, qtd. in Dell, *What Can and Can't Be Said*, 103.
10 Here I am extrapolating from the observation of Karla FC Holloway in *Passed On*. There she reminds us that, past and present, the "embalming of black bodies often requires a repair job that masks the residue of violent death." Moreover, the black mortician's skill in facial reconstruction and restorative art techniques is "as old as the particularities involved in professional attention to the ways and means of black death in the United States," Holloway adds. "The generational circumstances may change, but the violence done to black bodies has had a consistent history." I argue that this "consistent" historical backdrop is key to understanding black opposition to the King statue in Rocky Mount, NC. See Holloway, *Passed On*, 27.
11 Rocky Mount "statue committee" member Kimberle Evans, qtd. in Dell, *What Can and Can't Be Said*, 101; Sharpe, *In the Wake*, 5.
12 Sharpe, *In the Wake*, 10.
13 Panagia, *Political Life of Sensation*, 92.
14 Blome, "Artist's Statement." The photograph Blome references is photographer Bob Fitch's iconic image of King standing stiffly in the foreground. Over his left shoulder is a framed portrait of a shawled Mahatma Gandhi. Enphasis added.
15 Evans, qtd. in Fears, "Depiction of King Divides N. C. City." In 2007, after many rounds of debate, talk of a new commission, and a change in the makeup of the city council, the Blome statue, languishing in a city warehouse since city officials had it removed from display in 2005, was erected a second time in Martin Luther King Jr. Park. Few opinions about the statue changed. Ultimately, Blome's vision of King, "quieter, calmer, pondering," prevailed.
16 Piehl, "White Use of Dr. Booker T. Washington," 84.
17 Piehl, "White Use of Dr. Booker T. Washington," 84.
18 Battle, qtd. in Piehl, "White Use of Dr. Booker T. Washington," 86.
19 Pope, *Chalk Dust*, 136.
20 Sterne, *Audible Past*, 303.
21 Sterne, *Audible Past*, 292.
22 Edison, "Phonograph and Its Future," 534.
23 Bohlman and McMurray, "Tape," 8. Emphasis added.
24 Bohlman and McMurray, "Tape," 7.
25 W. J. Miller, "King's First Dream."
26 Ernst, *Digital Memory and the Archive*, 181.
27 W. J. Miller, "King's First Dream."
28 B. Kane, "Relays," 74.
29 Sexton, "Social Life of Social Death," 5.
30 The death-bound subject is Abdul Jan Mohamed's formulation, inspired by Richard Wright, of the subject condition of black life in the United States; see Mohamed's *The Death-Bound Subject*. Quote from Moten, *Universal Machine*, 145.
31 Eidsheim, *Sensing Sound*, 151.
32 Eidsheim, *Sensing Sound*, 149.

33 Eidsheim, *Sensing Sound*, 149.
34 Eidsheim, *Sensing Sound*, 130, 149.
35 Eidsheim, *Sensing Sound*, 6, 151.
36 Eidsheim, *Sensing Sound*, 171.
37 Eidsheim, *Sensing Sound*, 171.
38 W. J. Miller, "King's First Dream," n87. Reverend D(urocher) L(on) Blakey was pastor of St. John AME Zion Church at the time of King's visit and served the church until 1965, when a new appointment took him to Kyle's Temple AME Zion Church in Durham, North Carolina. According to an announcement concerning Blakey's arrival there, Durham's black weekly, the *Carolina Times*, reported that Blakey had held pastoral appointments "in Birmingham, Ala., McGhee, Ark., Atlanta, Ga., Belmont and Lexington . . . North Carolina" ("New Pastor of Kyle Temple to Fill Pulpit Sunday Morning"). Blakey's memoir, *Sharing Divine Life*, was published in 1997.
39 Crawley, "That There Might Be Black Thought," 136.
40 Eidsheim, *Race of Sound*, 27–28. Her phrase is "listening to listening."
41 Titled "Birth of a New Age" in some earlier versions.
42 W. J. Miller, *Origins of the Dream*, 166–67.
43 W. J. Miller, "King's First Dream," n58.
44 W. J. Miller, "King's First Dream," n61.
45 W. J. Miller, "King's First Dream," n84.
46 I mean the distinctive pitch of black political longing discussed in chapter 3, "that the congregation finds in tune with its expectations and needs," as theorized by Evans Crawford in *The Hum* (68).
47 W. J. Miller, "King's First Dream." Recording times Miller's. Emphasis added.
48 I am revising Eidsheim ever so slightly. In *Sensing Sound* Eidsheim speaks of "moving and being moved" homologously with physical vibration and nonphysical inspiration (130).
49 W. J. Miller, "King's First Dream." Emphasis added.
50 Eidsheim, *Sensing Sound*, 148.
51 I am borrowing this line from Allison Pitinii Davis's "Function of Humor in the Neighborhood."
52 Davis, "Function of Humor in the Neighborhood."
53 Davis, "Function of Humor in the Neighborhood." Emphasis added. I recognize an alternative reading of this line, one that valorizes lament over laughter, rather than the inverse as I prefer to read it. In the latter case, to "choke on history" is to refuse its ingestion, while weeping, to use other terms in the poem, is "evasive," "a cop-out," "cheap"—a leisure, "a privilege."
54 In linguistics, hortative and imperative moods of verbal expression are homologous with encouragement and demand.
55 Recall that "echo" is a reflection of sound "distinguishable as a repetition *or partial repetition* of the original sound." Schafer, *Soundscape*, 218. Emphasis added.
56 John Wesley to Charles Wesley, qtd. in Leigh Eric Schmidt, "Sound Christians and Religious Hearing in Enlightenment," 234.

57 See Eidsheim, *Sensing Sound*, 68.
58 Keller, "Architecture for Community and Spectacle," 202.
59 Keller, "Architecture for Community and Spectacle," 197.
60 Keller, "Architecture for Community and Spectacle," 205.
61 Keller, "Architecture for Community and Spectacle," 207.
62 Cavanagh, "An Invitation . . . from the Mayor." Although the specific year of the brochure's publication appeared uncertain to archivists at Bentley Historical Library—they could only offer "196-"—I have determined, based on the membership of the Detroit City Council printed at the end of the brochure, that the brochure was likely printed between April and December 1963.
63 Carter, *Sound In Between*, 11.
64 Carter, *Sound In Between*, 13.
65 Carter, *Sound In Between*, 11.
66 Carter, *Sound In Between*, 12; also see Goffman, *Forms of Talk*.
67 Carter, *Sound In Between*, 12.
68 Carter, *Sound In Between*, 13.
69 Carter, *Sound In Between*, 12.
70 Eidsheim, *Sensing Sound*, 65.
71 Carter, *Sound In Between*, 168.
72 Carter, *Sound In Between*, 159.
73 Carter, *Sound In Between*, 168.
74 Carter, *Sound In Between*, 164.
75 Carter, *Sound In Between*, 169.
76 Carter, *Sound In Between*, 169.
77 For a succinct expression of the currency of "radical democracy" in contemporary political study and debate, see especially Adrian Little and Moya Lloyd's introduction to their edited volume *The Politics of Radical Democracy*, 1–11. See also Trend, "Democracy's Crisis of Meaning."
78 Carter, *Sound In Between*, 170.
79 Carter, *Sound In Between*, 170.
80 Carter, *Sound In Between*, 170.
81 Carter, *Sound In Between*, 16.
82 Carter, *Sound In Between*, 118.
83 Kelley, "Big, Glitzy Marches Are Not Movements." Emphasis added.
84 Rev. C. L. Franklin made seventy-five recordings in his career, the greater part on JBV and Chess Records. At the height of Franklin's popularity in the 1950s he commanded as much as four thousand dollars for an appearance. By comparison, Franklin's biographer, Nick Salvatore, reminds us that Elvis Presley commanded $7,500 in the same period. With a personal driver, an ample residence, and colorful sartorial tastes, Franklin's wealth and celebrity were ever on display. See Salvatore, *Singing in a Strange Land*.
85 King misidentifies the city of Sasser, Georgia, as "Sasser County, Georgia" and Rocky Mount, North Carolina, as "Rocky Mountain, North Carolina." W. Jason Miller argues for these errors as "intentional mistakes." See W. J. Miller, *Origins of the Dream*, 167–68.

86 On Detroit's program for urban renewal and the history of Black Bottom and Paradise Valley, see especially McGraw, "Bringing Detroit's Black Bottom Back to (Virtual) Life."
87 Among others, Grace Lee Boggs, James Boggs, Malcolm X, Albert Cleage, and the League of Revolutionary Black Workers were all active radicals in Detroit in 1963.
88 Boyle, "Ruins of Detroit," 109.
89 S. E. Smith, *Dancing in the Street*, 8.
90 S. E. Smith, *Dancing in the Street*, 8.
91 L. Jones, *Blues People*, 97.
92 S. E. Smith, *Dancing in the Street*, 13.
93 Jenkins, qtd. in S. E. Smith, *Dancing in the Street*, 12.
94 Gordy, qtd. in S. E. Smith, *Dancing in the Street*, 14.
95 Gordy, qtd. in S. E. Smith, *Dancing in the Street*, 40.
96 Gordy, qtd. in S. E. Smith, *Dancing in the Street*, 40.
97 Fumo and Handley, "Video."
98 Fumo and Handley, "Can We Create the Motown Sound?"
99 Fumo and Handley, "Video."
100 Fumo and Handley, "Video."
101 See Keller, "Architecture for Community and Spectacle," 261.
102 Carter, *Sound In Between*, 13.
103 Carter, *Sound In Between*, 13. Emphasis Carter's.
104 Carter, *Sound In Between*, 18.
105 Ward, *Just My Soul Responding*, 273.
106 Schafer, *Soundscape*, 9.
107 Schafer, *Soundscape*, 9.
108 C. B. Jones, Remarks at the New York Law School Review Symposium.
109 Here I acknowledge the widespread belief that King's "I Have a Dream" sequence was explicitly "called for" by gospel singer Mahalia Jackson. Now commonly taken for fact and no longer seen as apocryphal, Jackson's urging to "tell them about the dream, Martin" as she stood near him on the speakers' platform has not gone unchallenged, however. While Jones claims to have heard Jackson firsthand encourage King to abandon his prepared speech for the inspired set piece she was goading him toward, a recent *Time* contributor, Andrew R. Chow, pointed to "the Motown tape" for "its impeccable sound quality" and importance in "answer[ing] questions about the speech itself":

> One of the loudest voices that can be heard on the record is that of gospel singer Mahalia Jackson, who also performed that day. She contributes loudly and frequently, her utterances serving as exclamation points for King's most fiery sentences. But while Jackson's impact on King's energy is palpable, Motown's recording also deflates a popular theory set forth by Clarence Jones and others: that she prompted King to launch into the "Dream" portion of the speech by imploring him to "tell them about the dream."
>
> Jackson can be heard yelling "Yes!" the first time King says that he has a dream. But . . . she cannot be heard suggesting where the speech should go.

While Chow and distinguished King archivist Clayborne Carson are thus suspicious of Jackson's part in the history of "I Have a Dream," Chow's article comes short of disproving Jones insofar as he also reports that Gordy "gave the only master copy of the company's recording to King's widow" when he sold Motown to MCA in 1988. Chow's audio source, "the Motown tape" on which Jackson's voice is heard (but not heard goading King), is therefore not likely a master. Whether or not it is the same as that "copy which had been stored away in an [unspecified] archive" before being digitally restored is also unclear. This uncertain source, "the Motown tape," is therefore hardly reliable enough to disprove Jones. Nor does Chow seem to be willing to imagine the coaxing Jones alleges in other than the most explicit discourse by Jackson. For my part, I am willing to accept Jones's insistence on Jackson's push, even if she may not have used Jones's words. Chow, "A Dream Restored," 95.
110 Schoenbrod, "We Have a Dream," 13.
111 C. B. Jones and Connelly, *Behind the Dream*, 116.
112 "March on Washington."
113 "March on Washington."
114 Euchner, *Nobody Turn Me Around*, 8.
115 Rustin, qtd. in Euchner, *Nobody Turn Me Around*, 9.
116 "March on Washington for Jobs and Freedom; Part 2 of 17."
117 Schlesinger, *Thousand Days*, 969.
118 "Aural aggression" belongs to Ronda L. Seward. See her "Forced Listening."
119 Ahmann et al., "Statement by the Heads of the Ten Organizations."
120 Wilderson, "Do I Stank, or Was It Already Stanky in Here?"
121 Evers was not originally part of the program, nor was any woman slated to give an address. However, Anna Arnold Hedgeman of the National Council of Churches, the only woman on the march's organizing committee, argued for a woman speaker. Belatedly, Myrlie Evers, wife of the recently slain Mississippi civil rights leader Medgar Evers, was chosen as the only woman speaker among more than a dozen men slated to address the demonstrators. It was agreed she would deliver a short "Tribute to Negro Women Fighting for Freedom." When traffic in Washington was too congested for Evers to get to the stage in time to make the tribute, Arkansas journalist and civil rights figure Daisy Bates stood in. Anderson, too, would miss her scheduled part, though later march organizers deviated from the official program to insert Anderson singing "He's Got the Whole World" into the lineup.
122 Moten, *In the Break*, 102.
123 Shelley, "Analyzing Gospel," 211.
124 Shelley, "Analyzing Gospel," 209, 202.
125 McGann, *Precious Fountain*, 140.
126 M. L. King, "'I Have a Dream.'"
127 Jackson shouted the improvised "Hallelujah" just off mic as she turned to yield the podium.
128 It was not only Jackson's vocal affects (growls, glissandos, moans, vibrato) on "I've Been Buked and I've Been Scorned" that radicalized its performance at

the March on Washington; the lyrics she sang appear to be largely improvised. Nowhere in print do the spiritual's lyrics correspond to what Jackson sang. Even those represented by Charles Euchner, who covered Jackson singing at the march, rely on a cycle of lyrics from a print collection of traditional African American spirituals from which Jackson's live performance departed noticeably. Compare, for example, the lyrics Jackson sang at the Washington march to these archived at https://hymnary.org/text/ive_been_buked_an_ive_been_scorned:

> Dere is trouble
> all over dis worl', Yes!
> Dere is trouble
> all over dis worl', Children!
> Dere is trouble
> all over dis worl', Yes!
> Dere is trouble
> all over dis worl'.
> Ain' gwine lay my 'ligion down, No!
> Ain' gwine lay my 'ligion down, Children!
> Ain' gwine lay my 'ligion down, No!
> Ain' gwine lay my 'ligion down.

Or compare these archived at https://www.negrospirituals.com/songs/buked_and_scorned.htm:

> You may talk about me sure as you please
> Talk about me sure as you please, Children
> Talk about me sure as you please
> Your talk will
> never drive me down to my knees
> Jesus died to set me free
> Jesus died to set me free,
> Children
> Jesus died to set me free
> Nailed to that cross on Calvary.

Years later, in 1976, Jackson recorded a stirring a cappella version of "I Been Buked and I Been Scorned" on Columbia Records. Lyrically, it kept to Jackson's Washington performance, although it omitted the second and fifth stanzas of the live performance.

129 Jackson and Wylie, *Movin' On Up*, 198–99. Emphasis added.
130 Hansen, *Dream*, 42.
131 Hansen, *Dream*, 42.
132 Nancy, *Listening*, 2.
133 Hass, *Introduction to Computer Music*.
134 "March on Washington for Jobs and Freedom; Part 7 of 17."
135 Arendt, *Human Condition*, 198, 199.
136 Arendt, *Human Condition*, 198. Emphasis added.

137 Arendt, *Human Condition*, 12, 15.
138 Radovac, "Mic Check," 39.
139 Hansen, *Dream*, 122.
140 Hansen, *Dream*, 127.
141 Hansen, *Dream*, 123, 127.
142 See Wallace, "Print, Prosthesis, (Im)Personation."
143 Hansen, *Dream*, 128.
144 Weheliye, *Phonographies*, 28.
145 Hansen, *Dream*, 128.
146 Weheliye, *Phonographies*, 129.
147 Kahn, *Noise, Water, Meat*, 246.
148 Wagner, qtd. in Kahn, *Noise, Water, Meat*, 246.
149 Kahn, *Noise, Water, Meat*, 233.
150 Feld, "Acoustemology," 12.
151 Schafer, *Soundscape*, 217.
152 By Lincoln's "uncertain shadow" I mean to call attention on the one hand to the US president's heroic reputation as "a Great American" whose signature on the Emancipation Proclamation, King said, "came as a great beacon light of hope to millions of Negro slaves who had been seared in the flames of withering injustice." On the other hand, one cannot help but consider how the marble materials and Doric columns of the Lincoln cenotaph also cast carceral shadows which, when seen, underline the tragedy that was the fundamental thesis of King's speech that day: namely, "one hundred years later, the Negro still is not free." M. L. King, "'I Have a Dream. . . .'"
153 See Barrett, *Blackness and Value*, 94.
154 Nielsen, *Black Chant*, 30. Nielsen's title is, of course, borrowed from poet Ed Roberson's "The Calligraphy of Black Chant."

I am not unaware of Nielsen's differences with Barrett on the signing voice and the singing voice. I call on the distinction here to heuristic ends and do not dispute Nielsen's claim against Barrett that "orature is not opposed to writing: lecture is not opposed to listening." The relation of black orature to writing, however, is not necessarily dialectical. I argue that black writing is after oral expression—that is, black writing has been regularly in orality's pursuit, in search of its recording in scripted form. Black orality, though, has consistently demonstrated a fugitive will, escaping graphic signification to the degree that graphic representation can in no way *command* a mimetic reproduction of the sound it aimed to record. Almost as soon as written representation gets near the point of orality's capture, black orality gets away, takes flight. Of course, black writing goes on from there, self-consciously, to higher forms (to Robersonian "calligraphy," let's say) because orality demands it. This relationship is not oppositional, but dynamically appositional. It is black iron sharpening black iron and bending both. This matter, which deserves greater space than I have to give it here, would be well served by more deliberate attention to Édouard Glissant, especially I think, *Caribbean Discourse* (1989).
155 Branch, *Parting the Waters*, 881.

156 Arguably, the visual power of the Reflecting Pool was as important to King's speech-making as its sonic property. Whether or not King spied the scores of marchers—hundreds probably—who loudly avowed their accord with the sound of his vision from the edge of the Reflecting Pool is unclear. But not a few observers noticed the many shouting along with them, kicking their feet easily in the pool's water. It was a vivid contrast to the scene of water and black protest in Birmingham four months earlier. In 1970, Black Arts poet Lorenzo Thomas gave mythopoeic representation to the violence of the latter in the poem "The Bathers." Against the body-breaking force of the firefighter's water hose, Birmingham's blacks mustered a counterforce of fiery nonviolent resistance that radically altered the water's weaponized effect, to the extent that

> We turned to fire when the water hit
> Us. Something
> Berserk regained
> An outmoded regard for sanity
> . . . .
> It was in Birmingham. It happened.
>
> Week after week in the papers
> The proof appeared in their faces
>
> Week after week seeing the same moment grow clearer
> Raising the water.
> Filling the vessel.
> . . . .
> Down here in this place
> Crying for common privilege
> In a comfortable land
>
> Their anger is drawing the water.
> Their daughters is drawing the waters.
> . . . .
> Some threw the water
> On their heads
> They was Baptists
> . . . .
> And orisha walked amid the waters with hatchets
> Where Allah's useful white men
> Came there bearing the water
> And made our street Jordan
> And we stepped into our new land.

I mean to suggest that in the water of the Reflecting Pool, a similar fire was to be felt, the Reflecting Pool another "Jordan" to cross. To step into the Reflecting Pool as hundreds did that day was to step, as Thomas imagined, "into our new land"; it was to stand at the imagined shore of freedom's achievement. Visually, then, the people in the Reflecting Pool must have seemed like so many pilgrim-actors in exodus, intent on the Promised Land King dreamed in Rocky Mount and Detroit and would repeat in Washington. Thomas, *Bathers*, 59–62. See, too, Lipman, "Fifty Years Ago."

157 Branch, *Parting the Waters*, 881.
158 Glissant, *Caribbean Discourse*, 124.
159 "Martin Luther King, Jr. 'I Have a Dream.'"
160 Wald, "Soul Vibrations," 677.
161 Wald, "Soul Vibrations," 680.
162 Interview by Walter Nixon, The March on Washington Tapes. Digitized sound recordings of King delivering "I Have a Dream" may be found in the RCAAVC, tape cpb-aacip-528-nz80k27q07_01, and online at Internet Library, https://archive.org/details/MLKDream.

Epilogue

1 Lischer, *End of Words*, 5.
2 Lischer, *End of Words*, ix.
3 Muhammad, "On John Coltrane's 'Alabama.'"
4 Jesse Jackson, "Speech by Rev. Jesse Jackson [July 27]."
5 Heilbut, *Gospel Sound*, xxiii.
6 Muhammad, "On John Coltrane's 'Alabama.'"
7 Muhammad, "On John Coltrane's 'Alabama.'"
8 O'Neal, "George Floyd's Mother Was Not There."
9 McSpadden, "Michael Brown's Mom."
10 McSpadden, "Michael Brown's Mom."
11 Rankine, "'Condition of Black Life Is One of Mourning.'"
12 Rankine, "Condition of Black Life"; Moten, *In the Break*, 200.
13 Moten, *In the Break*, 200.
14 Moten, *In the Break*, 201.
15 W. Brueggemann, "Costly Loss of Lament," 62.
16 W. Brueggemann, "Costly Loss of Lament," 59.
17 Moten, *In the Break*, 201.
18 Moten, *In the Break*, 211.
19 Moten, *In the Break*, 198.

BIBLIOGRAPHY

Abernathy, Ralph. *And the Walls Came Tumbling Down*. New York: Harper and Row, 1989.

Agamben, Giorgio. "Notes on Gesture." In *Infancy and History: Essays on the Destruction of Experience*, translated by Liz Heron, 135–40. London: Verso, 1993.

Ahmann, Mathew, Eugene Carson Blake, James Farner, Martin Luther King Jr., John Lewis, Joachim Prinz, A. Philip Randolph, Walter Reuther, Roy Wilkins, and Whitney M. Young Jr. "Statement by the Heads of the Ten Organizations Calling for Discipline in Connection with the Washington March of August 28, 1963." Civil Rights Archive. Accessed May 15, 2020. https://www.crmvet.org/docs/mowprog.pdf.

"Along the Color Line." *Crisis* 11, no. 5 (March 1916): 215–24.

Anderson, Benedict. *Imagined Communities: Reflections on the Origins and Spread of Nationalism*. New York: Verso, 1991.

Angelou, Maya. "Still I Rise." In *And Still I Rise*, 41–42. New York: Random House, 1978.

Arendt, Hannah. *The Human Condition*. Chicago: University of Chicago Press, 1998.

Arnold, Taschereau. "Master Organ Is Dedicated at Ebenezer." *Atlanta Daily World*, November 2, 1940: 1.

Ater, Renée. "Communities in Conflict: Memorializing Martin Luther King, Jr. in Rocky Mount, North Carolina." *Indiana Magazine of History* 110, no. 1 (March 2014): 32–39.

"Atlanta, Georgia. Ebenezer Baptist Church. Hillgreen, Lane and Co. (Opus 1191, 1955) 2 manuals. 14 ranks." Organ Historical Society Pipe Organ Database. Accessed November 26, 2017. https://pipeorgandatabase.org/OrganDetails.php?OrganID=59770.

Attali, Jacques. *Noise: The Political Economy of Music*. Translated by Brian Massumi. Minneapolis: University of Minnesota Press, 1985.

Azaransky, Sarah. *The Worldwide Struggle: Religion and the International Roots of the Civil Rights Movement*. New York: Oxford University Press, 2017.

Azoulay, Ariella. *The Civil Contract of Photography*. New York: Zone, 2008.

The Babylonian Talmud. 18 vols. Translated by Isidore Epstein. London: Soncino Press, 1978 [1935–1948].

Bachelard, Gaston. *The Poetics of Space*. Translated by Maria Jolas. Boston: Beacon Press, 1969.

Baker, Houston. *Blues, Ideology, and Afro-American Literature: A Vernacular Theory*. Chicago: University of Chicago Press, 1984.

Baker, Houston A. *Critical Memory: Public Spheres, African American Writing, and Black Fathers and Sons in America*. Athens: University of Georgia Press, 2001.

Baker, Houston. *Modernism and the Harlem Renaissance*. Chicago: University of Chicago Press, 1987.

Baker, Houston. *Turning South Again: Re-Thinking Modernism/Re-Reading Booker T.* Durham, NC: Duke University Press, 2001.

Baldwin, James. *The Evidence of Things Not Seen*. New York: Holt, Rinehart and Winston, 1985.

Baldwin, James. *The Fire Next Time*. In *James Baldwin: Collected Essays*, edited by Toni Morrison, 291–349. New York: Library of America, 1998.

Baldwin, James. *Just above My Head*. New York: Laurel, 1979.

Baldwin, James. *No Name in the Street*. New York: Vintage, 2007.

Baldwin, James. "Notes of a Native Son." In *James Baldwin: Collected Essays*, edited by Toni Morrison, 63–84. New York: Library of America, 1998.

Baldwin, James. "On Language, Race, and the Black Writer." In *The Cross of Redemption: Uncollected Writings*, edited by Randall Kenan, 140–44. New York: Pantheon, 2010.

Bambara, Toni Cade. *These Bones Are Not My Child*. New York: Pantheon Books, 1999.

Baraka, Imamu Amiri (LeRoi Jones), and Fundi (Billy Abernathy). *In Our Terribleness (Some Elements and Meaning in Black Style)*. Indianapolis IN: Bobbs-Merrill, 1970.

Barr, Wayne A. "A History of the Pipe Organ in the Black Church." In *Readings in African American Church Music and Worship*, edited by James Abbingdon, 429–31. Chicago: GIA Publishing, 2001.

Barrett, Lindon. *Blackness and Value: Seeing Double*. New York: Cambridge University Press, 1999.

Barthes, Roland. "The Grain of the Voice." In *Image-Music-Text*, translated by Stephen Heath, 179–89 New York: Hill and Wang, 1977.

Basie, Count. *Good Morning Blues: The Autobiography of Count Basie*. Minneapolis: University of Minnesota Press, 1885.

Begbie, Jeremy S., and Steven R. Guthrie, *Resonant Witness: Conversations between Music and Theology*. Grand Rapids: William B. Eerdmans, 2011.

Benjamin, Walter. "Theses on the Philosophy of History." In *Illuminations*, edited by Hannah Arendt, translated by Harry Zohn, 253–64. New York: Schocken, 1969.

Benjamin, Walter. "The Work of Art in the Age of Mechanical Reproduction." In *Illuminations*, edited by Hannah Arendt, translated by Harry Zohn, 217–51. New York: Schocken, 1969.

Beranek, Leo L., and John W. Kopec. "Wallace C. Sabine, Acoustical Consultant." *Newsletter of the National Council of Acoustical Consultants* (Fall 2003): 3–12.

Bergamino, Jessica Rae. "Did Rise." Poem-a-Day. Academy of American Poets. January 9, 2020. https://poets.org/poem/did-rise.

Blakey, Dorocher Lon. *Sharing Divine Life: The Story of My Life and My Teaching in Zion Methodism*. [Chicago?]: Team Publishers, 1997.

Blome, Erik. "Artist's Statement." *Rocky Mount Telegram* (NC) (July 19, 2003): news sec.

Bohlman, Andrea F., and Peter McMurray. "Tape: Or, Rewinding the Phonographic Regime." *Twentieth-Century Music* 14, no. 1 (2017): 3–24.

Boyer, Horace Clarence. "'Take My Hand, Precious Lord, Lead Me On.'" In *We'll Understand It Better: Pioneering African American Gospel Composers*, edited by Bernice Johnson Reagon, 141–63. Washington, DC: Smithsonian Institution Press, 1992.

Boyer, Horace, and Lloyd Yearwood. *The Golden Age of Gospel*. Urbana: University of Illinois Press, 2000.

Boyle, Kevin. "The Ruins of Detroit: Exploring the Urban Crisis in the Motor City." *Michigan Historical Review* 27, no. 1 (Spring 2001): 109–27.

Bradley, Adam. *Ralph Ellison in Progress: The Making and Unmaking of One Writer's Great American Novel*. New Haven, CT: Yale University Press, 2010.

Branch, Taylor. *At Canaan's Edge: America in the King Years, 1965–1968*. New York: Simon and Schuster, 2006.

Branch, Taylor. *Parting the Waters: America in the King Years, 1954–63*. New York: Simon and Schuster, 1988.

Brilliant, Richard. *Gesture and Rank in Roman Art: The Use of Gestures to Denote Status in Roman Sculpture and Coinage*. New Haven, CT: Connecticut Academy of Arts and Sciences, 1963.

Brinkmann, Tobias. *Sundays at Sinai: A Jewish Congregation in Chicago*. Chicago: University of Chicago Press, 2012.

Broughton, Viv. *Black Gospel: An Illustrated History of the Gospel Sound*. Dorset, UK: Blandford Press, 1985.

Brown, Claude. "The Language of Soul," *Esquire* 69 (April 1968). Reprinted in *Mother Wit from the Laughing Barrel*, edited by Alan Dundes, 230–37. Englewood Cliffs, NJ: Prentice Hall, 1973.

Brueggemann, Brenda Jo. "On (Almost) Passing." In *The Disability Studies Reader*, 2nd ed., edited by Lennard J. Davis, 321–30. New York: Routledge, 2006.

Brueggemann, Walter. "The Costly Loss of Lament." *Journal for the Study of the Old Testament* 36 (1986): 57–71.

Bryant, Donald C., and Karl R. Wallace, *Fundamentals of Public Speaking*. New York: Prentice Hall, 1976.

Burns, Rebecca. *Burial for a King: Martin Luther King Jr.'s Funeral and the Week That Transformed Atlanta and Rocked the Nation*. New York: Scribner, 2011.

Burns, Rebecca. "Funeral: An Oral History of the Remarkable Behind-the-Scenes Effort to Stage Martin Luther King Jr.'s 1968 Funeral and Keep Peace in Atlanta While 110 Other Cities Burned." *Atlanta Magazine*, April 1, 2008. http://www.atlantamagazine.com/great-reads/mlk-funeral-1968/.

Burns, Rebecca Poyner. "Mourning and Message: Martin Luther King Jr.'s 1968 Atlanta Funeral as an Image Event." M.A. thesis, Georgia State University, 2008.

Cain, Lisa. *Art of the Spirit: The Culture of the Rural South, Self-Taught Artist Lisa Cain*. Bloomington: AuthorHouse, 2011.

Campbell, Charles L. *The Word before the Powers: An Ethic of Preaching*. Louisville, KY: Westminster John Knox Press, 2002.

Campt, Tina M. *Listening to Images*. Durham, NC: Duke University Press, 2017.
Caron, Christina. "MLK and Me: How Rookie Photographer Captured History." *NBC News*, April 4, 2013. http://photoblog.nbcnews.com/_news/2013/04/04/17603354-mlk-and-me-how-rookie-photographer-captured-history?lite.
Carson, Clayborne, ed. *The Papers of Martin Luther King, Jr.*, vol. 6. Berkeley: University of California Press, 1992.
Carson, Clayborne, Susan Carson, Susan Englander, Troy Jackson, and Gerald L. Smith, eds. *The Papers of Martin Luther King, Jr., Volume VI: Advocate of the Social Gospel, September 1948–March 1963*. Berkeley: University of California Press, 2007.
Carson, Clayborne, and Peter Holloran, eds. *A Knock at Midnight: Inspiration from the Great Sermons of Reverend Martin Luther King, Jr.* New York: Warner, 1998.
Carter, Paul. *The Sound in Between: Voice, Space, Performance*. Sydney: University of New South Wales, 1992.
Cavanagh, Jerome P. "An Invitation . . . from the Mayor." In *Cobo Hall: Detroit* (Detroit: Department Report and Information Committee, 1963). Bentley Historical Library, University of Michigan. http://hdl.handle.net/2027/mdp.39015071816834.
Chall, Malca. "Rabbi Edgar F. Magnin: Leader and Personality." Bancroft Library Regional Oral History Office. Berkeley: University of California, 1975.
Chandler, Nahum Dimitri. *X–The Problem of the Negro as a Problem for Thought*. New York: Fordham University Press, 2014.
Chatelain, Marcia. *South Side Girls: Growing Up in the Great Migration*. Durham, NC: Duke University Press, 2015.
"Chicago, Illinois. Sinai Temple. Casavant Frères Ltée. (Opus 454, 1911) 3 manuals. 67 ranks." The Organ Historical Society Pipe Organ Database. Accessed November 26, 2017. https://pipeorgandatabase.org/OrganDetails.php?OrganID=47100.
Chion, Michel. *Guide des objets sonores*. Translated by John Dack. Paris: Buchet/Chastel, 1983.
Chow, Andrew R. "A Dream Restored: The Sound of the Civil Rights Movement, Like It's Never Been Heard Before." *Time*, March 2–March 9, 2020, 92–95.
"Church History." First Baptist Church–Gainsboro, Roanoke, VA. Accessed December 21, 2018. https://fbcgrke.org/fbc/history-page1/history-page2/.
Cohen, Harvey G. *Duke Ellington's America*. Chicago: University of Chicago Press, 2010.
"'Come By Here, My Lord.'" *Newsweek*, November 30, 1964, 94.
Cooper, Brittney C. *Beyond Respectability: The Intellectual Thought of Race Women*. Urbana: University of Illinois Press, 2017.
Cooper, Brittney. *A Black Feminist Discovers Her Superpower*. New York: St. Martin's, 2018.
Corbin, Alain. *Village Bells: Sound and Meaning in the 19th-Century French Countryside*. Translated by Martin Thom. New York: Columbia University Press, 1998.
"'Coretta Scott King: Soprano' Program." The King Center. Accessed August 13, 2018. http://www.thekingcenter.org/archive/document/coretta-scott-king-soprano/.
Cox, Aimee Meredith. *Shapeshifters: Black Girls and the Choreography of Citizenship*. Durham, NC: Duke University Press, 2015.
Crawford, Evans, with Thomas H. Troeger. *The Hum: Call and Response in African American Preaching*. Nashville: Abingdon, 1995.

Crawley, Ashon T. *Blackpentecostal Breath: The Aesthetics of Possibility*. New York: Fordham University Press, 2017.
Crawley, Ashon. "That There Might Be Black Thought: Nothing Music and the Hammond B-3." *CR: New Centennial Review* 16, no. 2 (Fall 2016): 123–49.
Curry, Lynne. "Birthing Practices." *Encyclopedia of Chicago*. Accessed April 30, 2018. http://www.encyclopedia.chicagohistory.org/pages/139.html.
Curry, Lynne. *Modern Mothers in the Heartland: Gender, Health, and Progress in Illinois, 1900–1930*. Columbus: Ohio State University Press, 1999.
Cusick, Suzanne G. "Gender and the Cultural Work of a Classical Music Performance." *Repercussions* 3, no. 1 (Spring 1994): 77–110.
"Dameun Strange Interview on *Mother King*." *Studio Z Blog: A Project of Zeitgeist New Music*. December 12, 1016. http://www.studiozstpaul.com/blog/dameun-strange-interview-on-mother-king.
Daniels, David D. "'Until the Power of the Lord Comes Down': African American Pentecostal Spirituality and Tarrying." In *Contemporary Spiritualities: Social and Religious Contexts*, edited by Clive Ericker and Jane Ericker, 173–91. New York: Bloomsbury Publishing, 2001.
Darden, Robert. *Nothing but Love in God's Water: Black Sacred Music from the Civil War to the Civil Rights Movement*, vol. 1. University Park: Pennsylvania State University Press, 2014.
Dart, Thurston. *Interpretation of Music*. New York: Harper and Row, 1960.
Davies, Glenys. "Togate Statues and Petrified Orators." In *Form and Function in Roman Oratory*, edited by D. H. Berry and Andrew Erskine, 51–72. Cambridge: Cambridge University Press, 2010.
Davis, Allison Pitinii. "The Function of Humor in the Neighborhood." Poem-a-Day. Academy of American Poets. April 1, 2020. https://poets.org/poem/function-humor-neighborhood.
Day, Eli. "50 Years after Their Historic Strike, Memphis Sanitation Workers Are Still Fighting." *Mother Jones*, March 22, 2018. https://www.motherjones.com/politics/2018/03/memphis-sanitation-strike-martin-luther-king-assassination/.
DeCarava, Roy. *The Sound I Saw: Improvisation on a Jazz Theme*. New York: Phaidon Press, 2001.
Dell, Upton. *What Can and Can't Be Said: Race, Uplift and Monument Building in the Contemporary South*. New Haven, CT: Yale University Press, 2015.
Derrida, Jacques. *Specters of Marx: The State of the Debt, the Work of Mourning and the New International*. Translated by Peggy Kamuf. New York: Routledge, 1994.
Derrida, Jacques. *Speech and Phenomena and Other Essays on Husserl's Theory of Signs*. Translated by David Allison and Newton Garver. Evanston, IL: Northwestern University Press, 1973.
Derrida, Jacques. *The Work of Mourning*. Edited by Pascale-Anne Brault and Michael Naas. Chicago: University of Chicago Press, 2001.
Dolar, Mladen. "The Object Voice." In *Gaze and Voice as Love Objects*, edited by Renata Salecl and Slavoj Žižek, 7–31. Durham, NC: Duke University Press, 1996.
Drake, St. Clair, and Horace Cayton, *Black Metropolis: A Study of Negro Life in a Northern City*, vol. 2. Rev. ed. New York: Harcourt, Brace and World, 1962.

"Dr. King's Funeral Service." YouTube. Uploaded by msremmu. April 3, 2008. https://youtu.be/lQbLW9mDdbI.

Du Bois, W. E. B. *Black Reconstruction in America, 1860-1880*. New York: Simon and Schuster, 1999 [1935].

Du Bois, W. E. B. *The Souls of Black Folk*. New York: New American Library, 1982.

Dunbar, Paul Laurence. "Sympathy." In *The Collected Poetry of Paul Laurence Dunbar*, edited by Joanne M. Braxton, 102. Charlottesville: University Press of Virginia, 1993.

Dunbar, Paul Laurence. "We Wear the Mask." In *The Collected Poetry of Paul Laurence Dunbar*, edited by Joanne M. Braxton, 71. Charlottesville: University Press of Virginia, 1993.

DuPree, Sherry S. *African-American Holiness Pentecostal Movement: An Annotated Bibliography*. New York: Garland, 1996.

"Ebenezer Baptist Church Has New Pipe Organ." *Atlanta Daily World*, October 28, 1940, 3.

"Ebenezer Choir Scores at Gala 'GWTW' Ball." *Atlanta Daily World*, December 15, 1939, 1.

Edison, Thomas. "The Phonograph and Its Future." *North American Review* 126, no. 262 (1878): 527-36.

Edwards, Erica. *Charisma and the Fictions of Black Leadership*. Minneapolis: University of Minnesota Press, 2012.

Eidsheim, Nina Sun. *The Race of Sound: Listening, Timbre, and Vocality in African American Music*. Durham, NC: Duke University Press, 2019.

Eidsheim, Nina Sun. *Sensing Sound: Singing and Listening as Vibrational Practice*. Durham, NC: Duke University Press, 2015.

Eidsheim, Nina Sun. "Voice as Technology of Selfhood: Toward an Analysis of Racialized Timbre and Vocal Performances." PhD diss., University of California, San Diego, 2008.

"87,000 March in War Protest Here: 160 Demonstrators Are Seized, Many in Washington Sq. Class." *New York Times*, April 28, 1968, 1.

Ellington, Edward Kennedy. *Music Is My Mistress*. New York: Doubleday, 1973.

Ellison, Ralph. "A Song of Innocence." *Iowa Review* 1 (Spring 1970): 30-40.

Ellison, Ralph. "As the Spirit Moves Mahalia." In *Shadow and Act*, 213-20. New York: Random House, 1964.

Ellison, Ralph. *Invisible Man*. New York: Vintage Books, 1995 [1952].

Ellison, Ralph. "Living with Music." In Ellison, *Living with Music*, edited by Robert G. O'Meally, 3-14.

Ellison, Ralph. *Living with Music: Ralph Ellison's Jazz Writings*. Edited by Robert G. O'Meally. New York: Modern Library, 2001.

Ellison, Ralph. "Ralph Ellison's Territorial Vantage." In *Living with Music: Ralph Ellison's Jazz Writings*, edited by Robert G. O'Meally, 15-33.

Ellison, Ralph. *Three Days before the Shooting. . . .* Edited by John F. Callahan and Adam Bradley. New York: Modern Library, 2010.

Emerson, Clara F. "Mahalia Jackson Weaves a Spell with Gospel Singing at Festival." *Newport Daily News*, July 7, 1958, n.p.

Ernst, Wolfgang. *Digital Memory and the Archive*. Minneapolis: University of Minnesota Press, 2013.

Euchner, Charles C. *Nobody Turn Me Around: A People's History of the 1963 March on Washington.* Boston: Beacon Press, 2010.

Fanon, Frantz. "This Is the Voice of Algeria." In *A Dying Colonialism*, 69–98. New York: Monthly Review, 1964 [1959].

Fears, Darryl. "Depiction of King Divides N. C. City." *Washington Post*, January 19, 2004, A3.

Feaster, Patrick. "Pictures of Sound: One Thousand Years of Educed Audio, 980–1980." YouTube video, 2011. https://www.youtube.com/watch?v=Kx_WANIVOcM.

Feld, Steven. "Acoustemology." In *Keywords in Sound*, edited by David Novak and Matt Sakakeeny, 12–21. Durham, NC: Duke University Press, 2015.

Franklin, Aretha. "Precious Lord (Part One)" and "Precious Lord (Part Two)." 7-inch vinyl recordings. Chicago: Checkers Records, 1960. https://www.youtube.com/watch?v=korCFV2etT8.

Franklin, Aretha, and David Ritz, *Aretha: From These Roots*. New York: Villard, 1999.

Friedenberg, Robert V. *"Hear O Israel": The History of American Jewish Preaching, 1654–1970.* Tuscaloosa: University of Alabama Press, 1989.

Fuentes, Venessa. "Forever Free." Song performed by the character AD in Strange and Fuentes, "Mother King."

Fuentes, Venessa. "I AM." Song performed by the character Alberta in Strange and Fuentes, "Mother King."

Fuentes, Venessa. "Jesus Leads Me All the Way." Song performed by the character Jennie in Strange and Fuentes, "Mother King."

Fuentes, Venessa. "Preacher King." Song performed by the character MLK Sr. in Strange and Fuentes, "Mother King."

Fumo, Dante, and Joel Handley. "Can We Create the Motown Sound?" YouTube. October 3, 2019. https://youtu.be/TysRGMSjtpQ.

Fumo, Dante, and Joel Handley. "Video: What Makes Motown Sound Like Motown." *Reverb*. October 3, 2019. https://reverb.com/news/video-what-makes-motown-sound-like-motown.

"Funeral Service for Dr. Martin Luther King, Jr., April 9, 1968, Ebenezer Baptist Church." Southern Christian Leadership Conference records. Stuart A. Rose Manuscript, Archives, and Rare Book Library (MARBL), Emory University.

Gamble, Vanessa Northington. *Making a Place for Ourselves: The Black Hospital Movement, 1920–1945.* New York: Oxford University Press, 1995.

Garrow, David J. *Bearing the Cross: Martin Luther King, Jr., and the Southern Christian Leadership Conference.* New York: Perennial, 1986.

Gates, Henry Louis, Jr. *The Signifying Monkey: A Theory of African American Literary Criticism.* New York: Oxford University Press, 1988.

George, Nelson. *The Death of Rhythm and Blues.* New York: Penguin, 2003.

Glissant, Édouard. *Caribbean Discourse: Selected Essays.* Translated by J. Michael Dash. Charlottesville: University Press of Virginia, 1989.

Goffman, Erving. *Forms of Talk.* Philadelphia: University of Pennsylvania Press, 1981.

Gookin, Frederick William. *The Chicago Literary Club: A History of Its First Fifty Years.* Chicago: Chicago Literary Club, 1926.

Gordon, Avery F. *Ghostly Matters: Haunting and the Sociological Imagination*, 2nd ed. Minneapolis: University of Minnesota Press, 2008.
Goreau, Laurraine. *Just Mahalia, Baby: The Mahalia Jackson Story*. Gretna, LA: Pelican, 1984.
Griffin, Farah Jasmine. *"Who Set You Flowin'?": The African-American Migration Narrative*. New York: Oxford University Press, 1995.
Gumbs, Alexis Pauline. *Spill: Scenes of Black Feminist Fugitivity*. Durham, NC: Duke University Press, 2016.
Hansen, Drew. *The Dream: Martin Luther King, Jr., and the Speech that Inspired a Nation*. New York: Ecco, 2003.
Harney, Stephano, and Fred Moten. *The Undercommons: Fugitive Planning and Black Study*. New York: Minor Compositions, 2013.
Harris, Michael W. *The Rise of Gospel Blues: The Music of Thomas Andrew Dorsey in the Urban Church*. New York: Oxford University Press, 1994.
Hartman, Saidiya. *Wayward Lives, Beautiful Experiments: Intimate Histories of Social Upheaval*. New York: Norton, 2019.
Hartman, Saidiya V., and Frank B. Wilderson III. "The Position of the Unthought." *Qui Parle* 13, no. 2 (Spring/Summer 2003): 183–201.
Hass, Jeffery. *Introduction to Computer Music: An Electronic Textbook*. Bloomington: Center for Electronic and Computer Music, Indiana University. 2020. https://cmtext.indiana.edu/index.php.
Heilbut, Anthony. *The Gospel Sound: Good News and Bad Times*. New York: Simon and Schuster, 1971.
Henderson, Stephen. *Understanding the New Black Poetry*. New York: William Morrow, 1973.
Hirsch, Emil G. "The Concordance of Judaism and Americanism: An Address Preached at the Memorial Celebration in Sinai Temple, Sunday, Nov 26, 1905." No. 18. In *Twenty Discourses*, 2–20. New York: Bloch, 1906.
Holloway, Karla FC. *BookMarks: Reading in Black and White: A Memoir*. New Brunswick, NJ: Rutgers University Press, 2006.
Holloway, Karla FC. *Codes of Conduct: Race, Ethics, and the Color of Our Character*. New Brunswick, NJ: Rutgers University Press, 1995.
Holloway, Karla FC. *Passed On: African American Mourning Stories*. Durham, NC: Duke University Press, 2002.
Holy Trinity Archives Committee, comp. "History of the Organs at Holy Trinity Episcopal Church, Gainesville, Florida." Holy Trinity Episcopal Church. 2012. Accessed November 10, 2021. https://static1.squarespace.com/static/5f68d8890eea3d7fc84735da/t/60105223343bcd08ffbfec30/1611682358930/final-2nd-ed-printed-hist-of-organs-corrected-booklet-wrb-12-200_3.pdf.
Honey, Michael K. "Editor's Note." In M. L. King, *"All Labor Has Dignity,"* xxxviii–xxxix.
Honey, Michael K. *Going down Jericho Road: The Memphis Strike, Martin Luther King's Last Campaign*. New York: Norton, 2007.
Hopkins, John Linn. "United States Department of the Interior, National Park Service National Register of Historic Places Registration Form, Mason Temple Church of God in Christ." NPS Form 109-00 (September 15, 1991).

Hughes, Langston. "Drum." In *The Collected Poems of Langston Hughes*, edited by Arnold Rampersad and David Roessel, 137. New York: Knopf, 2004.

Hughes, Langston. "Mother to Son." In *The Collected Poems of Langston Hughes*, edited by Arnold Rampersad and David Roessel, 30. New York: Vintage Books, 1994.

Hughes, Langston, and Milton Meltzer. *Black Magic: A Pictorial History of the African-American in the Performing Arts*. New York: Da Capo, 1990 [1967].

Hurston, Zora Neale. *The Sanctified Church*. Berkeley, CA: Marlowe, 1981.

Ihde, Don. *Listening and Voice: A Phenomenology of Sound*. Athens: Ohio University Press, 1976.

"The Institutional Church." *Chicago Defender* (November 16, 1912): 5.

Isenstadt, Sandy. *Electric Light: An Architectural History*. Cambridge, MA: MIT Press, 2018.

Jabir, Johari. "On Conjuring Mahalia: Mahalia Jackson, New Orleans, and the Sanctified Swing." *American Quarterly* 61, no. 3 (September 2009): 649–69.

Jackson, Jerma. *Singing in My Soul: Black Gospel Music in a Secular Age*. Chapel Hill: University of North Carolina Press, 2004.

Jackson, Jesse. "Speech by Rev. Jesse Jackson [July 27]." On Aretha Franklin, *One Lord, One Faith, One Baptism*. 12-inch vinyl double album. New York: Arista Records, 1987.

Jackson, Mahalia, and Evan Mcleod Wylie. *Movin' On Up*. Chicago: Hawthorne, 1966.

Jafa, Arthur. "Black Visual Intonation." In *The Jazz Cadence in American Culture*, edited by Robert O'Meally, 264–68. New York: Columbia University Press, 1998.

Jeffers, Honorée Fanoone. "Selah." Poem-a-Day. Academy of American Poets. July 17, 2020. https://poets.org/poem/selah.

Johnson, Charles, and Bob Adelman. *King: A Photobiography of Martin Luther King, Jr.* New York: Viking Studio, 2000.

Johnson, James Weldon. "The Creation." Poets.org. Accessed April 26, 2022. https://poets.org/poem/creation.

Johnson, James Weldon. "O Black and Unknown Bards." In *The Book of American Negro Poetry*, edited by James Weldon Johnson, 114–16. Auckland: Floating Press, 2008 [1922].

Jones, Bessie. "It's a Rough and Rocky Road Before You Get to Heaven." Sound recording. Association for Cultural Equity. Bessie Jones VII 10/61. Accessed October 1, 2017. http://research.culturalequity.org/get-audio-detailed-recording.do?recordingId=23476.

Jones, Clarence B. Remarks at the New York Law School Review Symposium: Remembering the Dream, Renewing the Dream: Celebrating the 50th Anniversary of Dr. Martin Luther King Jr's "I Have a Dream" Speech at the March on Washington (September 13, 2013). Qtd. In David Schoenbrod, "We Have a Dream," *New York Law School Review* 59 (2014–2015): 13.

Jones, Clarence B., and Stuart Connelly. *Behind the Dream: The Making of the Speech That Transformed a Nation*. New York: St. Martin's Press, 2011.

Jones, LeRoi. *Blues People: Negro Music in White America*. New York: William Morrow, 1963.

Jones, Tayari. *Leaving Atlanta*. New York: Warner, 2002.

Jones, Tommy H. "Ebenezer Baptist Church: Historic Structure Report." National Park Service, Cultural Resources, Southeast Regional Office (2001).

Jordan, June. "The Mountain and the Man Who Was Not a God." In *Some of Us Did Not Die: New and Selected Essays*, 143–56. New York: Basic/Civitas Books, 2002.

Kahn, Douglass. *Noise, Water, Meat: A History of Sound in the Arts*. Cambridge, MA: MIT Press, 1999.

Kane, Brian. "Relays: Audiotape, Material Affordances, and Cultural Practice." *Twentieth-Century Music* 14, no. 1 (2017): 65–75.

Kane, Brian. *Sound Unseen: Acousmatic Sound in Theory and Practice*. New York: Oxford University Press, 2014.

Kane, Thomas H. "Last Acts: Automortography and the Cultural Performance of Death in the United States, 1968–2001." PhD diss., University of Virginia, 2003.

Keeling, Kara, and Josh Kun. "Introduction: Listening to American Studies." *American Quarterly* 63, no. 3 (September 2011): 445–59.

Keller, William B. "Architecture for Community and Spectacle: The Roofed Arena in North America, 1853–1968." PhD diss., University of Pennsylvania, 2007.

Kelley, Robin D. G. "Big, Glitzy Marches Are Not Movements." *Boston Review*, August 28, 2013. http://bostonreview.net/us/robin-kelley-big-glitzy-marches-are-not-movements.

Kilde, Jeanne Halgren. *When Church Became Theatre: The Transformation of Evangelical Architecture and Worship in Nineteenth-Century America*. New York: Oxford University Press, 2002.

King, Coretta Scott. *My Life with Martin Luther King, Jr.* New York: Holt, Rinehart and Winston, 1969.

King, Coretta Scott. "10 Commandments on Vietnam." American Rhetoric: Online Speech Bank. Accessed November 10, 2021. https://www.americanrhetoric.com/speeches/corettascottkingvietnamcommandments.htm.

King, Coretta Scott, and Barbara Reynolds. *My Life, My Love, My Legacy*. New York: Henry Holt, 2017.

King, Martin Luther Jr. *"All Labor Has Dignity."* Edited by Michael K. Honey. Boston: Beacon, 2011.

King, Martin Luther Jr. "The Drum Major Instinct." In *A Knock at Midnight: Inspiration from the Great Sermons of Reverend Martin Luther King, Jr.*, edited by Clayborne Carson and Peter Holloran, 165–86. New York: Warner, 1998.

King, Martin Luther Jr. "'I Have a Dream . . .': Speech by the Rev. Martin Luther King at the 'March on Washington.'" Accessed May 19, 2020. https://www.archives.gov/files/press/exhibits/dream-speech.pdf.

King, Martin Luther Jr. "I've Been to the Mountaintop." Delivered April 3, 1968, Mason Temple (Church of God in Christ Headquarters), Memphis, Tennessee. Accessed May 19, 2020. American Rhetoric: Online Speech Bank. https://www.americanrhetoric.com/speeches/mlkivebeentothemountaintop.htm.

King, Martin Luther Jr. "A Knock at Midnight." In *Strength to Love*, 58–68. Philadelphia: Fortress Press, 1981 [1963].

King, Martin Luther King Jr. *A Knock at Midnight: A Sermon Delivered at the Mt. Zion Baptist Church in Cincinnati, Ohio*. Part 1. Creed Records, 1968.

King, Martin Luther Jr. "Letter from a Birmingham City Jail." In *A Testament of Hope: The Essential Writings of Martin Luther King, Jr.*, edited by James M. Washington, 289–302. New York: HarperCollins, 1986.

King, Martin Luther Jr. "Martin Luther King, Jr. 'I Have a Dream' Delivered 28 August 1963, at the Lincoln Memorial, Washington D.C." American Rhetoric: Online Speech Bank. Accessed April 26, 2022. https://www.americanrhetoric.com/speeches/mlkihaveadream.htm.

King, Martin Luther Jr. "MLK Speech at Mason Temple, March 18th, 1968." Accessed May 20, 2020. https://vimeo.com/281521134.

King, Martin Luther Jr. *The Radical King* (*King Legacy*). Edited by Cornel West. Boston: Beacon Press, 2015.

King, Martin Luther Jr. *Strength to Love*. Philadelphia: Fortress, 1963.

King, Martin Luther Jr. "The Un-Christian Christian." *Ebony*, August 1965, 77–80.

King, Martin Luther Jr. *Where Do We Go from Here: Chaos or Community?* Boston: Beacon Press, 2010 [1967].

King, Martin Luther Jr. "'Why Jesus Called a Man a Fool' Sermon (Mt. Pisgah Missionary Baptist Church, 8/26/67, Chicago, IL." Accessed November 4, 2017. https://youtu.be/6CENN9f12yQ.

KMT, Joy. "We Stay in Love with Our Freedom: An Interview with Alexis Pauline Gumbs." *LARB: Los Angeles Review of Books*, February 4, 2018. https://lareviewofbooks.org/article/we-stay-in-love-with-our-freedom-a-conversation-with-alexis-pauline-gumbs/#!.

Landon, John W. *Behold the Mighty Wurlitzer: The History of the Theatre Pipe Organ*. Westport, CT: Greenwood Press, 1983.

Leiffermann, Henry. "'Profession: Concert Singer, Freedom Movement Lecturer.'" *New York Times*, November 26, 1972.

Lewis, David Levering. "W. E. B. Du Bois: A Biography of Race." *C-SPAN*. Accessed November 4, 2017. https://www.c-span.org/video/?53447-1/web-du-bois-biography-race.

Lewis, Sara. "Guest Editor's Note." *Aperture* 223, Special Issue: Vision and Justice (Summer 2016): 12.

Lipman, Don. "Fifty Years Ago: A Day to Remember, the Weather on the Day of the MLK Dream Speech." *Washington Post*, August 28, 2013. https://www.washingtonpost.com/news/capital-weather-gang/wp/2013/08/28/fifty-years-ago-a-day-to-remember-the-weather-on-the-day-of-the-mlk-dream-speech/.

Lischer, Richard. *The End of Words: The Language of Reconciliation in a Culture of Violence*. Grand Rapids, MI: Wm. B. Eerdmans, 2005.

Lischer, Richard. *The Preacher King: Martin Luther King, Jr. and the Word That Moved America*. New York: Oxford University Press, 1995.

Little, Adrian, and Moya Lloyd, eds. *The Politics of Radical Democracy*. Edinburgh: Edinburgh University Press, 2009.

Lloyd, Johnny. "Development of African American Gospel Piano Style, 1926–1960: A Socio-Musical Analysis of Arizona Dranes and Thomas A. Dorsey." PhD diss., University of Pittsburgh, 2009.

Lordi, Emily. *Black Resonance: Iconic Women Singers and African American Literature*. New Brunswick, NJ: Rutgers University Press, 2013.

Luccock, Halford E. *In the Minister's Workshop*. New York: Abingdon, 1944.

Malcolm X. "The Ballot or the Bullet." 1964. In *Say It Loud: Great Speeches on Civil Rights and African American Identity*, edited by Catherine Ellis and Stephen Smith, 1–18. New York: New Press, 2010.

Manning, Erin. *The Minor Gesture*. Durham, NC: Duke University Press, 2016.
"March on Washington for Jobs and Freedom; Part 2 of 17 [August 28, 1963]." WGBH Media Library and Archives. May 12, 2020. http://openvault.wgbh.org/catalog/A_313 5488CBB9E467B9F0684BC930E6498.
"March on Washington for Jobs and Freedom; Part 7 of 17 [August 28, 1963]." WGBH Media Library and Archives. May 26, 2020. http://openvault.wgbh.org/catalog/A_ 3135488CBB9E467B9F0684BC930E6498.
"March on Washington." WRVR-FM, Riverside Church, New York. August 28, 1963. The Riverside Church Archives, Audio Visual Collection. WRVR-FM Series. The March on Washington Tapes.
Markovitch, Jeremy. "Dawn of the Dream." *Our State: Celebrating North Carolina Magazine*, January 2, 2019. https://www.ourstate.com/dawn-of-the-dream/.
Marovich, Robert. *A City Called Heaven: Chicago and the Birth of Gospel Music*. Urbana: University of Illinois Press, 2015.
"Martin Luther King, Jr. Funeral Services." C-SPAN Video Library: A Digital Archive of C-SPAN Video, Created by Cable, Offered as a Public Service. [s.n.]: National Cable Satellite Corporation.
Matthews, Henry B. "Provident Hospital—Then and Now." *Journal of the National Medical Association* 53, no. 3 (May 1961): 209–24.
McAfee, Cleland Boyd. "The Worshipful Element in Music." *Homiletic Review* 52 (1906): 358–60.
McClary, Susan. *Feminine Endings: Music, Gender, and Sexuality*. Minnesota: University of Minnesota Press, 2002 [1991].
McDaniel, Charles-Gene. "Funeralizing Mahalia Jackson." *Christian Century* 89, no. 9 (March 1, 1972): 253–54.
McDowell, Deborah E. *Leaving Pipe Shop: Memories of Kin*. New York: Scribner, 1996.
McGann, Mary E. *A Precious Fountain: Music in the Worship of an African American Catholic*. Collegeville, MN: Liturgical Press, 2004.
McGraw, Bill. "Bringing Detroit's Black Bottom Back to (Virtual) Life (Special to the Free Press)." *Detroit Free Press*, February 28, 2017. https://www.freep.com/story/news /local/michigan/detroit/2017/02/27/detroit-black-bottom-neighborhood/98354122/.
McSpadden, Lezley. "Michael Brown's Mom, on Alton Sterling and Philando Castile." *New York Times*, July 7, 2016. https://www.nytimes.com/2016/07/08/opinion /michael-browns-mom-on-alton-sterling-and-philando-castile.html.
The Mello-Tones. "Rough and Rocky Road." *Forever Mello-Tones*. CD. Magnitud Records, 2013.
Metfessel, Milton. *Phonophotography in Folk Music: American Negro Songs in New Notation*. Chapel Hill: University of North Carolina Press, 1928.
Metfessel, Milton. "The Vibrato in Artistic Voices." In *University of Iowa Studies: Studies in the Psychology of Music. Vol. 1: The Vibrato*, edited by Carl E. Seashore, 14–117. Iowa City: University of Iowa Press, 1932.
Meyer, Michael A. *Response to Modernity: A History of the Reform Movement in Judaism*. Detroit: Wayne State University Press, 1995.
Miller, Keith D. *Martin Luther King's Biblical Epic: His Final, Great Speech*. Jackson: University Press of Mississippi, 2012.

Miller, Keith. "No Mason Temple, No 'Mountaintop' Speech." *Commercial Appeal*, April 2, 2018. https://www.commercialappeal.com/story/opinion/contributors/2018/04/02/opinion-no-mason-temple-no-mountaintop-speech/474823002/.

Miller, Keith D. *Voice of Deliverance: The Language of Martin Luther King, Jr. and Its Sources*. New York: Free Press, 1992.

Miller, W. Jason. "King's First Dream: November 27, 1962." King's First Dream. Accessed March, 23, 2020. http://kingsfirstdream.com/history/.

Miller, W. Jason. *Origins of the Dream: Hughes's Poetry and King's Rhetoric*. Gainesville: University Press of Florida, 2015.

Mitchell, W. J. T. *What Do Pictures Want? The Lives and Loves of Images*. Chicago: University of Chicago Press, 2005.

Mohamed, Abdul Jan. *The Death-Bound Subject*. Durham, NC: Duke University Press, 2005.

Morris, Kenneth. "'I'll Be a Servant for the Lord': A 1987 Interview Conducted and Edited by Bernice Johnson Reagon." In *We'll Understand It Better: Pioneering African American Gospel Composers*, edited by Bernice Johnson Reagon, 329–41. Washington, DC: Smithsonian Institution Press, 1992.

Morrison, Toni. *Sula*. New York: Knopf, 1974.

Moten, Fred. *Black and Blur*. Durham, NC: Duke University Press, 2017.

Moten, Fred. "Black Kant (Pronounced Chant): A Theorizing Lecture at Kelly Writers House, February 27, 2007." Philadelphia: PennSound, 2007. https://media.sas.upenn.edu/pennsound/authors/Moten/KWH_022-70-7/moten-fred_KWH_theorizing%20lecture_022-70-7.mp3.

Moten, Fred. "The Case of Blackness." *Criticism* 50, no. 2 (Spring 2008): 177–218.

Moten, Fred. *In the Break: The Aesthetics of the Black Radical Tradition*. Minneapolis: University of Minnesota Press, 2003.

Moten, Fred. "Knowledge of Freedom." *CR: The Centennial Review* 4, no. 2 (2004): 269–310.

Moten, Fred. *Stolen Life*. Durham, NC: Duke University Press, 2019.

Moten, Fred. *The Universal Machine*. Durham, NC: Duke University Press, 2018.

"*Mother King* by Dameun Strange." New Music Events in Minnesota. July 21, 2017. http://newmusicmn.org/event/mother-king-dameun-strange/2017-07-21/.

"Mrs. King at Anti-War Rally." *New York Amsterdam News*, April 27, 1968, 2.

Muhammad, Ismail. "On John Coltrane's 'Alabama.'" *Paris Review*, June 17, 2020. https://www.theparisreview.org/blog/2020/06/17/on-john-coltranes-alabama/.

Murphet, Julian, Helen Groth, and Penelope Hone, eds. *Sounding Modernism: Rhythm and Sonic Mediation in Modern Literature and Film*. Edinburgh: Edinburgh University Press, 2017.

Nancy, Jean-Luc. *Listening*. Translated by Charlotte Mandell. New York: Fordham University Press, 2007 [2002].

"Never Again Where He Was." *Time*, January 3, 1964, 13–27.

"New Pastor of Kyle Temple to Fill Pulpit Sunday Morning." *Carolina Times*, November 13, 1965, 1.

Nielsen, Aldon Lynn. *Black Chant: Languages of African-American Postmodernism*. New York: Cambridge University Press, 1997.

Nierenberg, George T., dir. *Say Amen, Somebody*. 100 mins. New York: GTN Pictures, 1982.
Nixon, Walter. The March on Washington Tapes. August 28, 1963. The Riverside Church Archives, Audio Visual Collection, WRVR-FM Series.
Ochse, Orpha. *The History of the Organ in the United States*. Bloomington: Indiana University Press, 1975.
Odum, Howard, and Guy Johnson, *Negro Workaday Songs*. Chapel Hill: University of North Carolina Press, 1926.
Öhman, Nina Christina. "Sound Business: Great Women of Gospel Music and the Transmission of Tradition." PhD diss., University of Pennsylvania, 2017.
"The OHS Pipe Organ Database." The Organ Historical Society. 2016. https://www.pipeorgandatabase.org/OrganDetails.php?OrganID=16177.
"On Anniversary of MLK's Death, the Sax, the Story behind His Last Words." *USA Today*, April 4, 2017. https://www.usatoday.com/story/news/nation-now/2017/04/04/martin-luther-king-jr-death-anniversary-saxophone/100014402/?hootPostID=497b2a7755721311d673908e4d141c08e.
O'Neal, Lonnae. "George Floyd's Mother Was Not There, But He Used Her As a Sacred Invocation." *The Undefeated*, May 28, 2020. https://theundefeated.com/features/george-floyds-death-mother-was-not-there-but-he-used-her-as-a-sacred-invocation.
Panagia, Davide. *The Political Life of Sensation*. Durham, NC: Duke University Press, 2009.
Piehl, Charles K. "The White Use of Dr. Booker T. Washington: Rocky Mount, North Carolina, 1910." *Journal of Negro History* 70, nos. 3–4 (Summer–Autumn 1985): 82–88.
"Police Battle NY Marchers; Scores Beaten." *New York Times*, April 28, 1968, 7.
Pope, Oliver R. *Chalk Dust*. New York: Pageant Press, 1967.
Powell, Richard. *Cutting a Figure: Fashioning Black Portraiture*. Chicago: University of Chicago Press, 2008.
"Preview of ESSA Weather Bureau Forecast." *Commercial Appeal* (Memphis), April 3, 1968, 28.
Price, Peter. *Resonance: Philosophy for Sonic Art*. New York: Atropos, 2011.
Raboteau, Albert. *Slave Religion: The "Invisible Institution" in the Antebellum South*. New York: Oxford University Press, 2004.
Radovac, Lillian. "Mic Check: Occupy Wall Street and the Space of Audition." *Communication and Critical/Cultural Studies* 11, no. 1 (March 2014): 34–41.
Rampersad, Arnold. *Ralph Ellison: A Biography*. New York: Knopf, 2007.
Rankine, Claudia. *Citizen: An American Lyric*. Minneapolis: Graywolf Press, 2015.
Rankine, Claudia. "'The Condition of Black Life Is One of Mourning.'" *New York Times Magazine*, June 22, 2015. https://www.nytimes.com/2015/06/22/magazine/the-condition-of-black-life-is-one-of-mourning.html.
Ridgeway, Benjamin C. *Atlanta's Ebenezer Baptist Church*. Charleston, SC: Arcadia, 2009.
Ritz, David. *Respect: The Life of Aretha Franklin*. New York: Little, Brown, 2014.
"Rocky Mount Journal: King Statue, a Unity-Symbol, Severely Tests the Dream." *New York Times*, December 13, 2003, A 11.

Rosenbaum, Nancy. "The Strange Music of Mother King" (audio interview). KFAI'S MinneCulture: Minnesota Arts, Culture, and History. Accessed August 23, 2018. http://ampers.org/mn-art-culture-history/the-strange-music-of-mother-king/.

Salvatore, Nick. *Singing in a Strange Land: C. L. Franklin, the Black Church and the Transformation of America.* New York: Little, Brown, 2005.

Schaeffer, Pierre. *Traité des Objets Musicaux: Essai Interdisciplines.* Paris: Éditions du seuil, 1966.

Schafer, R. Murray. *The Soundscape: Our Sonic Environment and the Tuning of the World.* Rochester, VT: Destiny, 1994 [1977].

Schlesinger, Arthur. *A Thousand Days: John F. Kennedy in the White House.* Boston: Houghton Mifflin, 1965.

Schmidt, Leigh Eric. *Hearing Things: Religion, Illusion, and the American Enlightenment.* Cambridge, MA: Harvard University Press, 2000.

Schmidt, Leigh Eric. "Sound Christians and Religious Hearing in Enlightenment." In *Hearing History: A Reader*, edited by Mark M. Smith, 221–46. Athens: University of Georgia Press, 2004.

Schoenbrod, David. "We Have a Dream." In *New York Law School Review* 59 (2014–2015): 11–15.

Schwartz, S. D. "Emil Gustave Hirsch." *American Jewish Year Book* 27 (September 1925–September 1926): 230–37.

Schwerin, Jules. *Got to Tell It: Mahalia Jackson, Queen of Gospel.* New York: Oxford University Press, 1992.

Seashore, Carl E. "Introduction." In *University of Iowa Studies: Studies in the Psychology of Music. Vol. 1: The Vibrato,*, edited by Carl E. Seashore, 7–13. Iowa City: University of Iowa Press, 1932.

Seashore, Carl E., ed. *University of Iowa Studies: Studies in the Psychology of Music. Vol. 3: The Psychology of the Vibrato in Voice and Instrument.* Iowa City: University of Iowa Press, 1936.

Seltzer, Mark. *Bodies and Machines.* New York: Routledge, 1992.

Seward, Ronda L. "Forced Listening: The Contested Use of Loudspeakers for Commercial and Political Messages in the Public Soundscape." *American Quarterly* 63, no. 3, Sound Clash: Listening to American Studies (September 2011): 761–80.

Sexton, Jared. "The Social Life of Social Death: On Afro-Pessimism and Black Optimism." *InTensions* 5 (Fall–Winter 2011): 1–47.

Shakespeare, William. *Hamlet.* Camberwell, VIC: Penguin Australia, 2010.

Shaler, Nathanial S. "Science and the African Problem." *Atlantic Monthly* 66 (1890): 36–45.

Shaler, N. S. "The Negro Problem." *Atlantic Monthly* 54 (1884): 696–709.

Sharpe, Christina. *In the Wake: On Blackness and Being.* Durham, NC: Duke University Press, 2018.

Shelley, Braxton D. "Analyzing Gospel." *Journal of American Musicology* 72, no. 1 (2019): 181–243.

Silverman, Kaja. *The Threshold of the Visible World.* New York: Routledge, 1996.

Smith, Mark M. "Introduction: Onward to Audible Pasts." In *Hearing History: A Reader*, edited by Mark M. Smith, ix–xxii. Athens: University of Georgia Press, 2004.

Smith, Shawn Michelle. *At the Edge of Sight: Photography and the Unseen.* Durham, NC: Duke University Press, 2013.

Smith, Suzanne E. *Dancing in the Street: Motown and the Cultural Politics of Detroit.* Cambridge, MA: Harvard University Press, 1999.

Smith, Ted A. *The New Measures: A Theological History of Democratic Practice.* New York: Cambridge University Press, 2007.

Sontag, Susan. *On Photography.* New York: Farrar, Straus and Giroux, 1977.

Sorett, Josef. *Spirit in the Dark: A Religious History of Racial Aesthetics.* New York: Oxford University Press, 2016.

Southern Christian Leadership Conference (SCLC). "A Proposal for an Audio History of Martin Luther King, Jr." Manuscript, Archives, and Rare Book Library (MARBL), Southern Christian Leadership Conference Records, box 593, folder 4, Emory University.

Spillers, Hortense. "Cross Currents and Discontinuities." In *Conjuring: Black Women, Fiction and Literary Tradition,* edited by Hortense Spillers and Marjorie Pryse, 248–61. Bloomington: Indiana University Press, 1985.

Spillers, Hortense J. "Interstices: A Small Drama of Words." In *Black, White, and in Color: Essays on American Literature and Culture,* 152–73. Chicago: University of Chicago Press, 2003.

Spillers, Hortense J. "Mama's Baby, Papa's Maybe: An American Grammar Book." In *Black, White, and in Color: Essays on American Literature and Culture,* 203–29. Chicago: University of Chicago Press, 2003.

Spillers, Hortense J. "Moving on Down the Line: Variations on the African American Sermon." In *Black, White, and in Color: Essays on American Literature and Culture,* 251–76. Chicago: University of Chicago Press, 2003.

Spillers, Hortense J. "'The Permanent Obliquity of an In(pha)llibly Straight': In the Time of the Daughters and the Fathers." In *Black, White, and in Color: Essays on American Literature and Culture,* 230–50. Chicago: University of Chicago Press, 2003.

Stars of Harmony. "(There's a) Rough and Rocky Road." *The History of Rhythm and Blues, 1942–1952.* 4-CD compilation. London: Rhythm and Blues Records, 2009.

State of Illinois, Department of Public Health, Division of Vital Statistics. Coroner's Certificate of Death, No. 25300, "NETTIE DORSEY" (September, 30, 1932).

Sterne, Jonathan. *The Audible Past: Cultural Origins of Sound Reproduction.* Durham, NC: Duke University Press, 2006.

Stone, Peter, and Ellen Harold. "Bessie Jones." Cultural Equity. Accessed October 1, 2017. http://www.culturalequity.org/alanlomax/ce_alanlomax_profile_jonesb.php.

Strange, Dameun, and Venessa Fuentes. "Mother King." Opera presented at Public Functionary, Minneapolis, July 20–22 and July 27–29, 2017.

Street, Seán. *The Memory of Sound: Preserving the Sonic Past.* New York: Routledge, 2015.

Stuckey, Sterling. *Slave Culture: Nationalist Theory and the Foundations of Black America.* New York: Oxford University Press, 1987.

Sundquist, Eric J. *King's Dream.* New Haven, CT: Yale University Press, 2009.

Thomas, Lorenzo. *The Bathers.* New York: Reed, 1981.

Thompson, Emily. *The Soundscape of Modernity: Architectural Acoustics and the Culture of Listening in America, 1900–1933.* Cambridge, MA: MIT Press, 2002.

Tiffen, Joseph. "Phonophotograph Apparatus." In *University of Iowa Studies: Studies in the Psychology of Music. Vol. 1: The Vibrato*, edited by Carl E. Seashore, 118-33. Iowa City: University of Iowa Press, 1932.

Tompkins, Kyla Wazana. *Racial Indigestion: Eating Bodies in the 19th Century*. New York: NYU Press, 2012.

"Tornado Strikes near Millington; At Least 30 Hurt." *Commercial Appeal* (Memphis), April 4, 1968, 1.

Townes, Emilie. "They came because of the wailing." In *Deeper Shades of Purple: Womanism in Religion and Society*, edited by Stacey M. Floyd-Thomas, 251. New York: NYU Press, 2006.

Trend, David. "Democracy's Crisis of Meaning." In *Radical Democracy: Identity, Citizenship, and the State*, 7-18. New York: Routledge, 1996.

Turner, William C. "The Musicality of Black Preaching: Performing the Word." In *Performance in Preaching: Bringing the Sermon to Life*, edited by Jana Childers and Clayton J. Schmit, 191-209. Grand Rapids, MI: Baker Academic, 2008.

Van Rijn, Guido. *Roosevelt's Blues: African-American Blues and Gospel Songs on FDR*. Jackson: University Press of Mississippi, 1997.

Virginia Foundation for the Humanities. "First Baptist Church, Roanoke." African American Historic Sites Database. Accessed December 21, 2018. http://www.aahistoricsitesva.org/items/show/142.

Wald, Gayle. "Soul Vibrations: Black Music and Black Freedom in Sound and Space." *American Quarterly* 63, no. 3 (September 2011): 673-96.

Walker, Alice. "Coming Apart." In *Take Back the Night: Women on Pornography*, edited by Laura Lederer, 95-104. New York: Morrow, 1980.

Wall, Cheryl. *Worrying the Line: Black Women Writers, Lineage and Literary Tradition*. Chapel Hill: University of North Carolina Press, 2005.

Wallace, Maurice O. "Print, Prosthesis, (Im)Personation: Morrison's *Jazz* and the Limits of Literary History." *American Literary History* 20, no. 4 (2008): 794-806.

Ward, Brian. *Just My Soul Responding: Rhythm and Blues, Black Consciousness, and Race Relations*. London: UCL Press, 1998.

Warner, Michael. "The Preacher's Footing." In *This Is Enlightenment*, edited by Clifford Siskin and William Warner, 368-83. Chicago: University of Chicago Press, 2010.

Washington, Booker T. *Up from Slavery*. New York: Oxford University Press, 1995 [1901].

Washington, James Melvin, ed. *Conversations with God: Two Centuries of Prayers by African Americans*. New York: Harper Perennial, 1994.

Webb, Stephen. *The Divine Voice: Christian Proclamation and the Theology of Sound*. Eugene, OR: Wipf and Stock, 2004.

Weheliye, Alexander G. *Phonographies: Grooves in Sonic Afro-Modernity*. Durham, NC: Duke University Press, 2005.

Whitman, Walt. "Song of the Banner at Day-break." In *Leaves of Grass*, 235-39. New York: New American Library, 1980 [1865].

Wilderson, Frank B., III. "Do I Stank, or Was It Already Stanky in Here? or, Notes from an Impossible Negro." Closing comments, Black Thought in the Age of Terror Symposium, University of California, Irvine, May 2006.

Wilderson, Frank B., III. "Gramsci's Black Marx: Whither the Slave in Civil Society." *Social Identities* 9, no. 2 (2003): 225–40.

Wilkerson, Isabel. *The Warmth of Other Suns: The Epic Story of America's Great Migration*. New York: Random House, 2010.

Williams, R. F., and U. E. Miller. *Facts about the Temple: Mason Temple-Memphis, Tennessee*. Cleveland, OH: self-published, 1945.

Wilson, Drek Spurlock. *African American Architects: A Biographical Dictionary, 1865-1945*. New York: Routledge, 2004.

Younge, Gary. *The Speech: The Story behind Martin Luther King Jr.'s Dream*. Chicago: Haymarket Books, 2013.

Žižek, Slavoj. "'I Hear You with My Eyes'; or, the Invisible Master." In *Gaze and Voice and Love Objects*, edited by Renata Salecl and Slavoj Žižek, 90–126. Durham, NC: Duke University Press, 1996.

INDEX

Note: References to King alone are to Martin Luther King Jr. Page numbers in italics indicate figures.

Abernathy, Ralph: autobiography, 24; and Jesse Jackson, 300n95; King's memorial service, 22–24, 33, 41, 283nn5–6; in Memphis with King, 195–96; national civil rights organization, 2; SCLC leadership expectations, 283nn5–6; West Hunter Baptist Church pastorship, 297n45
acousmatic listening, 33–34, 38, 286n45, 286n48
acousmatic vs. acoustical sound, 33–34, 286n45, 286n48
acoustic architecture: Booker T. Washington High School gym (Rocky Mount, NC), 241–42; Cobo Hall, 242–43, 245–46, 251; Ebenezer Church (Atlanta), 33, 41, 47, 50–51; in-between sounds, 243–46, 251, 266; Mason Temple, 197–99; Mt. Pisgah Missionary Baptist Church, 72–73, 75, 79–81, 83–84, 88, 295n66; National Mall (Washington, DC), 260–61, 265–68, 270, 322–23n156; phenomenological voice, 32–33; Sinai Congregation, 78–81; *vox dei* effects, 32–33; wall voices, 78–79
acoustic ecologies in black Protestantism, 72. *See also* Ebenezer sound
acoustic memory, 71–93
Adler, Dankmar, 125
Afro-Protestant soundscapes, 69
Agamben, Giorgio, 207–8
airs, 67–68, 73
"All Labor Has Dignity" (King), 202–4, 208, 217, 219, 311n50; aurality, 224, 226–27; hauntology, 224; King's vibrato, 217, 219, 224; politics, 223–26; as precursor to "I've Been to the Mountaintop," 228; reception, 226; transcriptions, 226, 314n126

Alschuler, Alfred S., 72, 79–81, 83, 293n25
an-archic sounds, 83, 93, 246
Anderson, Benedict, 191
Anderson, Marian, 148, 270–71, 319n121
"And Still I Rise" (Angelou), 156, 303n68
Angelou, Maya, 156, 303n68
architecture: auditorium designs, 46–47; black religious modernism, 44; Cobo Hall, Detroit, 242–43; ecclesial, 44–48; ensoniment, 45–46; Gothic Revivalism, 45, 47, 50, 288n6; Mason Temple COGIC, 197–98; phenomenological voice, 32–33. *See also* acoustic architecture
Arendt, Hannah, 262–63
Arnold, Taschereau, 64, 290nn59–60
Ater, Renée, 231
Atlanta, GA: early African American churches, 292n3
Atlanta child murders, 30–31
Attali, Jacques, 6, 185
audiences: echoic, 244–45; "I Have a Dream," 253–55, 267, 269–70; laughter, 238–41
audition, 14, 90–91. *See also* black audition
aurality: black mourning, 275–80; epistemology, 6; gesturalism and, 205–7; history's, 6–7; "I Have a Dream" (King), 227; modernity's, 48–49. *See also* music; photographic aurality; sound
Avery Chapel AME, 52, 288n31
Azaransky, Sarah, 28
Azoulay, Ariella, 193

Bagley, Edythe Scott, 283n6
Baker, Ella, 2

Baker, Houston: African American literature, 223; black modernism, 13–14, 99; cultural performance, 44; deformation of mastery, 220–22; Ralph Ellison, 53–55; *Modernism and the Harlem Renaissance*, 13–14; mulatto modernism, 67
Baldwin, James, 24, 31, 120–21, 194
Baraka, Amiri (LeRoi Jones): African traditions and gender, 139; being/Being, 311n47; "Black Dada Nihilismus," 257; black sound, 7; blues, 113–14; *Blues People*, 97, 113–14, 139, 291n71
Barr, Wayne A., 289n29
Barett, Lindon, 267, 321n154
Barthes, Roland, 5–6, 88
Basie, Count, 63, 288n31
Bates, Daisy, 319n121
Battle, Thomas H., 233
Benjamin, Walter, 8, 169, 186
"Beyond Vietnam: A Time to Break Silence" (King), 157
Birmingham bombings, 4–5
black audition, 1, 5–6, 236; acoustemology of freedom, 237; audience laughter, 240–41; the body and, 237–38; Ebenezer Sound, 47; and ethical listening, 237; "Facing the Challenge of a New Age" recording, 237–38, "I Have a Dream" (King), 253; listening-for vs. listening-against, 236–37; visuality and, 168
black boyhood, 307n148
black chant, 267, 321n154
black children: mortality, 123; precarity, 30–31; public performances, 141. *See also* Atlanta child murders
black feminist resonance, 140, 301n9
black girlhood, 179, 307n148, 307n150
black grief. *See* black mourning
black modernism, 14; architecture, 44; the Ebenezer sound, 47, 51, 63; improvisation, 54; internationalism, 28; pipe organs and, 49, 51–52, 63; print vs. proclamation, 112; religious, 44, 47, 49–51, 63–70, 73, 75; socio-economic class, 69; strategies, 99; "Why Jesus Called a Man a Fool" (King), 81–82
black mortality, 116, 121, 123
black mourning, 120, 136, 273–80; aural expressions, 275–80; laments, 116, 124, 278–79; mothers for sons, 277–79; Muhammad's writings on Coltrane, 273–75; *One Lord, One Faith, One Baptism* (record album; A. Franklin), 275–76; police murders, 273–78; politics, 279–80; video's impact, 278; as visual protest, 278–79. *See also* gospel blues; gospel music; King's memorial service;

mother-loss; "Take My Hand, Precious Lord" (Dorsey)
black poetry, 75–76
black preaching: bio-material effects, 230; echoic communication, 244–45; C. L. Franklin, 177–78, 247–48, 307n144, 317n84; in "Mother King" (Strange), 146; social change, 113; women, 139. *See also* King's preaching
black sound studies, 7
black voices: empirical racialized studies, 210, 212–14, 217, 219–22, 313n105; enslaved subject expressions, 224–25; photographic aurality, 223–24, 228
black womanism, 125, 298n82
black women: childbirthing experiences, 121–23; expressiveness and gospel blues, 123–24; feminine ideals, 151; gospel music, 116, 123–26, 298n82; intellectuals, 157–59, 303n72; loss, 125, 128, 135; modernity, 56–57; mortality, 116, 121, 123; mothers, 143, 182, 277–79, 301n20; musical labor, 147–48; preachers, 139; resistance, 135; "Take My Hand, Precious Lord" responses, 125–26; witnesses to death, 278. *See also* black women vocalists; mother-loss
black women vocalists, 147, 150–51, 155. *See also* Franklin, Aretha; Jackson, Mahalia; King, Coretta Scott
Blakey, D. L. (Durocher Lon), 237–41, 247, 315n38
Bland, Sandra, 279
Blome, Erik, 231–33, 315n14
blues music, 97, 113–14, 249. *See also* gospel blues
Blues People (Baraka), 97, 113–14, 139, 291n71
Bohlman, Andrea, 235
Boyer, Horace Clarence, 100, 102–3, 296n13
Bradley, Adam, 60
Branch, Ben, 128–31, 133–34, 300n96
Branch, Taylor, 110, 267–68
Brault, Pascale-Anne, 37, 283n5
Brinkmann, Tobias, 84–85, 293n48
Broughton, Viv, 300n94
Brown, Claude, 9–10, 12
Brown, John, 49, 288n16
Brown, Michael, 277
Brueggemann, Brenda J., 193
Brueggemann, Walter, 279
Bryant, Donald C., 218–19
Burns, Rebecca, 24, 283n6
Byron, L. B., 67

Cain, Lisa, 124
calling narratives, 93
Campbell, Charles L., 110–13
Campt, Tina, 167–68, 207, 309n17
Carmichael, Stokely, 27, 111–12
Carnegie, Andrew, 51

Carson, Clayborne, 72, 292n18
Carter, Paul, 243-46, 251, 266
Cayton, Horace, 69
Chandler, Nahum, 213
Chatelain, Marcia, 179-80, 307n150
Chauvin, Derek, 274
Chicago: black children mortality, 123; black healthcare access, 121-23, 298n72; black women mortality, 123; gospel blues, 73-74, 97-100; the Great Migration, 97, 122, 298n72; King's activism in, 292n9. *See also* Mt. Pisgah Missionary Baptist Church; Sinai Congregation
childhood public performances, 140-42
Chinampus (Taylor), 38-39
Chion, Michel, 33-34, 286n45
Chow, Andrew R., 318n109
Cleage, Albert, 243
Cleveland, James, 308n159
Cole, Echol, 224
Coltrane, John, 273-76, 278
"Come Sunday" (Ellington and Jackson), 160-64
Connelly, Stuart, 229
Cook County Hospital, 122
Cooper, Brittney, 158, 296n34, 303n72
Cox, Aimee Meredith, 179-80, 307n148
Crawford, Evans, 88, 225
Crawley, Ashon, 68, 119, 124, 163-64, 238; gospel shouting, 124; King's speech-making, 238; nothing music, 119, 126; religious tarrying, 163
Cusick, Suzanne G., 150-52, 154

Daniels, David, 163
Darden, Robert, 98
Dart, Thurston, 314n4
Davies, Glenys, 206
Davis, Allison Pitinii, 240, 316n51, 316n53
death-bound subjects, 236, 315n30
DeCarava, Roy, 167, 171, 188, 202, 305n112, 308n4
Deleuze, Gilles, 170
democratic relationality, 245-46
Derrida, Jacques: hauntology, 1, 39-40; mourning, 37-39, 283n15; phantomatic production, 21; *Specters of Marx*, 39-40; survivance, 36-37, 88; voice, 32
Detroit: auto industry, 249; Cobo Hall, 242-43, 244, 251; Motown sound, 248-52; political activism, 248, 317n87; tourist promotion, 243, 316n62; Walk to Freedom rally, 243, 256. *See also* "Facing the Challenge of a New Age" (King; Detroit)
DeWolf, L. Harold, 22
"diacritical noise," 12
disability studies, 208

Dolar, Mladen, 192
Dorsey, E. H., 24
Dorsey, Nettie, 117-18, 120-22, 125-27, 134
Dorsey, Thomas: biographical overview, 73-74; black women's expressiveness, 123-24; elegiac expressiveness, 114; gospel blues, 73-74, 99-104, *105*, *106*, 113-20; gospel's teleology, 125; "If You See My Savior Tell Him That You Saw Me," 114-16; *Say Amen, Somebody* (documentary), 118-19, *120*; "Take My Hand, Precious Lord," 114, 116-21, 123-28, 298n62, 299n87, 300n94; teaching gospel, 101; wife and child's death, 117-18
Douglass, Frederick, 185
Drake, St. Clair, 69
dream speeches, 229-30. *See also* "I Have a Dream"
"Drum" (Hughes), 41
"Drum Major Instinct, The" (King): acoulogical properties, 35-36, 42; death, 29-30, 36-37; deliveries, 27-28; dying words, 35-36; influences, 27-28, 36; jazz impulse, 38-39; recording played at memorial service, 24-35, 37-38, 41-43, 234, 283n6, 285n41
Du Bois, W. E. B.: black sound, 7; general strike as open revolt of slaves, 224; gospel shouting, 124; and Emil Gustav Hirsch, 293n45; pipe organs, 51; *The Souls of Black Folk*, 13, 51; voice, 12, 282n33
Dunbar, Paul Laurence, 58
DuPree, Sherry S., 309n30
dying words, meaning, 35-36

Ebenezer Baptist Church (Atlanta): Afro-Protestantism, 69; architecture, 33, 41, 45, 47, 50-51; class, 69, 291n73; cultural performance, 44; "The Drum Major Instinct" (King) delivery, 27-28, 36; gospel of, 28; history, 44-45; King's copastorate, 71. *See also* Ebenezer sound; King's memorial service
Ebenezer Church (Chicago), 99-100, 123, 125-26
"Ebenezer gospel" (Lischer), 27-28, 71-72, 136
Ebenezer sound (Atlanta), 43-70, 72; acoustic architecture, 33, 41, 47, 50-51; black religious modernism, 47, 51, 63; black women's laments, 116; choir, 64-66; church dedication event, 63-67; class, 69; elements comprising, 47-48; influence on King's preaching, 51, 69-71; neon sign, 51, 288n24; vs. other churches, 72; pipe organs, 47-51, 63-67, 69, 288n16, 288n22, 290n57
echoic sounds, 241-42, 245, 250-52, 316n55
Edison, Thomas, 235
Edwards, Erica, 147, 150, 302n34
Edwards, J. H., 284n17

Eidsheim, Nina Sun, 164, 237–38, 240, 245, 316n48
electric modernisms, 198, 310n35
Ellington, Duke, 160–61, 165, 305n107. *See also* "Come Sunday"
Ellison, Ralph: black cultural memory, 54; black sound, 7; *Invisible Man*, 52–59, 161, 185, 220; on Mahalia Jackson, 161, 164–68, 304n100; "Living with Music," 56; pipe organs, 52, 54–55, 57–62, 288n31; reputation and criticisms, 52–54; *Three Days before the Shooting . . .* , 54, 59–62
epistemology, aural vs. visual, 6
ethics of preaching, 110–13
Euchner, Charles, 319n128
eulogies, phonographic, 22–25
Evans, Clay, 131
Evers, Medgar, 248, 319n121
Evers, Myrlie, 319n121

"Facing the Challenge of a New Age" (King; Detroit): acoustic architecture (Cobo Hall), 242–43, 245–46, 251; democratic relationality, 245–46; echoic communication, 251–52; C. L. Franklin acknowledgment, 247; geographic errors, 248, 317n85; "I have a dream" set piece, 248, 252; in-between sounds, 245–47, 251; keynote sounds, 252–53; "Let freedom ring" refrain, 248; recording, 247–48, 250–52
"Facing the Challenge of a New Age" (King; Rocky Mount, NC), 233; acoustic architecture (Booker T. Washington High School), 241–42; audience laughter, 238–41; black audition, 237–38; historicity, 236; "How long? Not long" sequence, 238–39, 241; as "I Have a Dream" precursor, 236, 238; "Let freedom ring" refrain, 239, 241, 248; photographs, 233–34; recordings, 234–38; transcriptions, 238–39
Falla, Manuel de, 111–12
Falls, Mildred, 160, 167, 305n113
Fanon, Frantz, 7
Farris, Christina King, 23, 283n6
Feld, Steven, 266
feminine endings, 134–35, 140, 142, 300n104
Fernandez, Benedict J., 186, *187*
First Baptist Church–Gainsboro, 51–52
First Baptist Church–Roanoke, 51, *53*, 289n27
Floyd, George, 274–78
Ford, Henry, 249
Franklin, Aretha: *Amazing Grace*, 308n159; "Ave Maria," 276–78; black feminist resonance, 140; childhood recordings, 177–78, 307n144; mother-loss, 178, 180–81; *One Lord, One Faith, One Baptism* (album), 275–76; "Take My Hand, Precious Lord" (Dorsey), 176–82, 306n140
Franklin, Barbara Siggers, 177, 180–81
Franklin, C. L.: Detroit Walk to Freedom, 243, 247; personal life, 180, 182; popularity as preacher, 177–78, 247–48, 307n144, 317n84
Franklin, Erma, 180
freedom concerts, 147–57, 302n55
Friedenberg, Robert V., 86–87, 294n49, 294n57
Frye, Theodore R., 99–100, 123
Fuentes, Venessa, 144, 147
Fumo, Dante, 250

Gaines, Charles, 111–12
Gates, Henry Louis, 306n140
gender: historiography, 144, 147; musical performance, 149–52, 155
George, Nelson, 301n9
gesturalism, 170–71, 205–9
Gettysburg Address (Lincoln), 141–42
"Give Us the Ballot" (King), 190
Glissant, Édouard, 268
Goffman, Erving, 200, 244–45
Gordon, Avery F., 1, 21, 127–28
Gordy, Berry, 132, 247–52
gospel blues: black loss, 114; black women's expressiveness, 123–24; Chicago, 73–74, 97–100; Theodore R. Frye, 99–100, 123; King's preaching, 113, 136–37; Roberta Martin, 99, 101; mother-loss, 135; origins, 73–74; popularity, 100–2; song sheets, 100–4; teachers, 101. *See also* Dorsey, Thomas
gospel modernism, 99–113, 117–37
gospel music, 138–82; James Baldwin on, 120–21; feminist histories, 126–27, 137, 182; Great Migration, 97–99; and hapticality, 125; improvisation, 99, 101–4, 311n54; "I've Been Buked and I've Been Scorned," 257–59, 264–65, 319n128; laments, 116, 124; meter-mood tensions, 66; moans, 276; notation, 102–4; origins, 97–98; politics, 98, 123; "Rough and Rocky Road," 64–67, 291n60; shouting, 123–26, 298n82; "Take My Hand, Precious Lord" (Dorsey), *105*, 106, 114, 116–21, 123–27, 133–34, 136–37; vamps, 257–58. *See also* Franklin, Aretha; gospel blues; Jackson, Mahalia; King, Alberta Williams
Gothic Revivalist architecture, 45, 47, 50, 288n6
Great Migration, the, 73, 97–99, 122, 299n72
Griffin, Farah, 307n150
Groth, Helen, 14
Guattari, Félix, 170
Gumbs, Alexis Pauline, 135–36, 162–63, 220
Gurley, Mary, 28, 285n22
Guthrie, Steven R., 51

Hamilton, J. Wallace, 27, 36, 284n18
Handley, Joel, 250
Hansen, Drew, 229, 260, 263
hapticality, 125–26
Harney, Stephano, 125, 132
Harren, J. B., 233
Harris, Michael W., 66, 73–74, 115–16, 298n62
Hartman, Saidiya V., 189
hauntology, 1, 39–42, 127–28, 224
hearing: historicist, 236; and seeing, 188–89, 308n4, 308n6; and speaking, 90, 92. *See also* listening
Hedgeman, Anna Arnold, 319n121
Heilbut, Anthony: gospel music, 98, 276; gospel sheet music publications, 100–1; interview with Thomas Dorsey, 114–15; on Mahalia Jackson, 164–65
Henderson, Stephen, 223
Henry, Thomas, 90–93
Hirsch, Emil Gustav, 79–81, 84–88, 90, 293n45, 293n48
historiography, 7, 144, 147
history, aural vs. visual, 6–7
Holloran, Peter, 72
Holloway, Karla FC, 30–31, 140–42, 315n10
Hone, Penelope, 14
Honey, Michael, 204–5, 311n50, 314n126
Hopkins, John Linn, 309n30
"House I Live In, The" (Robinson and Meeropol), 154–55
Hughes, Langston, 41, 157–59, 229–30, 314n11
Hurston, Zora Neale, 7

"I Call It Pretty Music But the Old People Call It the Blues" (Wonder), 131–33
"If You See My Savior Tell Him That You Saw Me" (Dorsey), 114–16
"I Have a Dream" (King; Washington, DC): vs. Marian Anderson's concert, 270–71; audience, 253–55, 267, 269–70; aurality, 227; conclusion, 314n137; delivery, 263–67, 269–71; delivery location, 190, 265–68, 270, 321n156, 321n152; footing, 264; freedom, 258–59; Langston Hughes connections, 229–30; "I have a dream" sequence, 268–69; improvisation, 264, 267–68; Mahalia Jackson, 256–61, 264–65, 318n109, 319nn127–28; precursor addresses, 228, 230, 236, 238; sound system for, 254–55; transcriptions, 263–64
Ihde, Don, 87–88
improvisation: black modernism, 54; gospel music, 99, 101–4, 311n54; "I Have a Dream" (King), 264, 267–68; King's preaching, 98–99, 111; "A Knock at Midnight" (King), 111–13; movement, 306n120

in-between sounds, 243–47, 251, 266
Invisible Man (Ellison), 52–59, 161, 185, 220
Ira Aldridge Theater, 52, 288n31
Isenstadt, Sandy, 310n35
"I've Been Buked and I've Been Scorned" (song), 257–59, 264–65, 319n128
"I've Been to the Mountaintop" (King; Memphis), 194; Ralph Abernathy's introduction, 195–96; as civil address, 286n51; delivery, 194–95; gesturalism, 205–8; King's physicality, 200–2; Mason Temple's acoustic architecture, 197–99; photographs, 202, 205–8, 228, 311n61; precursor addresses, 228; sonic environment, 199–200

Jabir, Johari, 129, 305n113, 306n139
Jackson, Graham Washington, 63–64, 290n55, 290n57
Jackson, Jerma A., 126
Jackson, Jesse, 275–76, 278, 300n95
Jackson, Mahalia: black feminist resonance, 140; church singing, 304n90; "Come Sunday," 160–64; death and funeral, 172, 176–77, 182, 306n140; Ralph Ellison on, 161, 164–68, 304n100; and Mildred Falls, 160, 167, 305n113; "The House I Live In," 154; March on Washington performance, 256–61, 264–65, 319nn127–28; music critics on her body, 164–65, 304n100; Newport jazz festival performances, 164–69, 172, 305n107, 305n113; photographs of, 166–71, 172, 173, 174, 175; "Take My Hand, Precious Lord" recording, 170–71, 306n139
Jafa, Arthur, 167–68, 188, 308n4
Jeffers, Honorée, 71
Jenkins, Bobo, 249
Jewish Reform movement, 83–88, 294n49, 294n57
Johnson, Charles, 185–86, 188
Johnson, Guy, 219
Jones, Bessie, 66
Jones, Clarence B., 229, 253–54, 264, 318n109
Jones, LeRoi. *See* Baraka, Amiri
Jordan, June, xv
Judaism, 78, 83–87
Just above My Head (Baldwin), 120–21

Kahn, Douglas, 13–14, 266
Kane, Brian, 34, 236, 286n45, 286n48
Karenga, Ron, 27
Keighton, Robert E., 107–9
Keller, William B., 242
Kelley, Robin D. G., 247
Kersands, Billy, 222, 313n122
keynotes, 7–8

keynote sounds, 8, 68, 139, 252-53, 301n6
Kilde, Jeanne Halgren, 45-47
King, A. D., 30, 285n27
King, Alberta Williams, 49; influence on King's preaching, 140, 143-44, 147; King's recollections of, 143, 301n20; "Mother King" (opera; Strange), 144-46; murder, 139, 301n8; musical performances with King (childhood), 140-41, 145, 302n28; organ playing at Ebenezer, 64-65, 138-40, 143, 147, 302n28
King, Bernice, 30-32, 38
King, Coretta Scott: activism, 152, 154; black feminist legacy, 304n80; Central Park address, 156-59, 304n79; as intellectual, 157-58; Mahalia Jackson's funeral, 172, 176; King's chauvinism, 148-49, 154, 203; King's memorial service, 22-23, 26, 30-31, 33, 283n6, 285n27; musical education, 150; performance of poise, 155-56; singing (freedom concerts), 147-57, 302n55; woman power, 156-57
King, Martin Luther, Jr.: aesthetic funerals of, 186; assassination, 128, 138; and Branch's playing of "Take My Hand, Precious Lord" (Dorsey), 128-30, 134, 300n96; chauvinism, 148-49, 154, 203; hauntology, 40-42; on Mahalia Jackson, 172, 176; and Marxism, 287n70; name, 301n7; politics, 225-28; Rocky Mount, NC, monument, 230-33, 315n10, 315nn14-15; statues, 207, 228, 232; voice, 9-11, 70, 88, 136-37, 139. See also King's memorial service; King's preaching; photographs of King
King, Martin Luther Sr., 49, 69-70, 301n7, 302n28
King's memorial service, 21-42, 282n1; architecture of the church, 32-33; "The Drum Major Instinct" playback, 24-35, 37-38, 41-43, 234, 283n6, 285n41; eulogy, lack of, 22-24; hauntology, 39-42; King's children, 30-32; procession, 42; readings of King's works, 23; soundscape, 35
King's preaching, 1-2; aesthetics, 109; assertiveness, 113; black motherliness, 138-39; education, 218-19; footing, 200-2, 204; gospel blues, 113-14; importance to his identity, 111, 139, 297n36; improvisation, 98-99, 111; influences, 51, 69-71, 139-44, 147; manuscripts, 104, 204, 296n32, 311n53; vs. oratory, 9; recordings, 193, 309n21; reproduction in print, 11; sound, 5, 7; super-scripting, 78, 81, 83, 98-99; training, 107-9; transcription challenges, 204-5; vibrato, 9, 12-13, 75, 83, 143, 199, 208, 217-19, 224. See also "All Labor Has Dignity"; "Beyond Vietnam: A Time to Break Silence"; "Drum Major Instinct, The"; "Facing the Challenge of a New Age" (Rocky Mount, NC); "I Have a Dream"; "I've Been to the Mountaintop"; "Knock at Midnight, A"; "Man Who Was a Fool, The"; *Preacher King, The* (Lischer)

"Knock at Midnight, A" (King): deliveries, 98-99, 104, 107, 109-10, 296n32, 297n45; dialectical method, 108; form, 108; gospel's influence, 98-99, 104, 107, 113; improvisation, 111-13; politics, 109-10; print version, 107-9, 111, 297n33; tone, 110-11

labor, 195. See also "All Labor Has Dignity" (King)
Lacan, Jacques, 192, 206
"Language of Soul, The" (Brown), 9-10, 12
Last Request: Ben Branch and the Operation Breadbasket Orchestra and Choir, The (album), 131
Lee, Albert, 231
L'Enfant, Pierre Charles, 261
Levinson, Stanley, 253, 264
Lewis, David Levering, 282n33
Lewis, John, 260
Lewis, Sara, 186
Librettos (Gaines), 111-12
Lischer, Richard: black women preachers, 139; "dead ends of language," 142; King's birth name, 301n7; Benjamin Mays, 292n76; preaching in the age of mass violence, 274-75; prophecy, 36. See also *Preacher King, The*
listening: acousmatic, 33-34, 38, 286n45, 286n48; direct, 33-34; ethical, 237-38; for vs. against, 236-37; historicist, 236; politics of, 90, 92; prayer as, 91; reduced, 38. See also hearing
"Living with Music" (Ellison), 56
Lomax, Alan, 66
Lordi, Emily, 52, 140, 147, 223
Lowery, Joseph, 2
Luccock, Halford, 107-9
Luther, Michael, 139

Maddox, Lester, 42
Magnin, Edgar F., 293n45
Malcolm X, 189
Manning, Erin, 170-71, 208-9, 306n120
"Man Who Was a Fool, The" (King), 77, 83
March on Washington: acoustic architecture, 260-61; Mahalia Jackson's performance, 256-61, 264-65, 319nn127-28; location, 255; male speakers, 254, 256; militancy, 256; peacefulness, 254-56; Joachim Prinz, 261-63, 267; A. Philip Randolph, 256, 263; Reflecting Pool, 265-68, 270, 322-23n156; Bayard Rustin, 254-56, 260, 285n22; sound system, 254-55, 260, 265; women speakers, 256, 319n121. See also "I Have a Dream" (King)

Marovich, Robert, 127–28
Martin, Roberta, 99, 101
Martin, Sallie, 101
Martin Luther King Speaks (radio program), 2
Marx, Karl, 39–41
Mason, Charles H., 198
Mason Temple Church, Memphis, 197–99, *201*, 202, 309n30, 311n48
Mathews, Vernon, 202, 205–7, 220, 228, 311n61
Mays, Benjamin, 28, 284n22, 292n76
McAfee, Cleland Boyd, 129–30
McClary, Susan, 134–35, 177, 300n104
McDonald, Dora, 283n6
McDowell, Deborah E., 141–42
McMurray, Peter, 235
McSpadden, Lezley, 277–78
Meeropol, Abel, 154
Mello-Tones, The, 63, 291n60
Memphis, King in: freedom rallies, 311n48; march, 195; Mason Temple photographs, 202, 205–8, 228, 311n61; reasons for going, 195, 202, 224. *See also* "All Labor Has Dignity" (King); "I've Been to the Mountaintop" (King)
Memphis labor strikes, 195, 224
Metfessel, Milton: phonophotography, 213–14, *215*, 313n102; racialized studies of black voices, 210, 212–14, 217, 219–22
Miller, Keith D., 108–9, 197–98
Miller, W. Jason, 229–30, 237–39, 317n85
"minor gestures" (Manning), 170–71, 208–9
Mitchell, W. J. T., 188, 228
modernism: black culture's impact, 13; electric, 198, 310n35; gospel, 97–137; sound, 13–14; technological, 219–20, 250. *See also* black modernism; Ebenezer sound
Mohamed, Abdul Jan, 315n30
Morris, Kenneth, 102–3, 311n54
Morrison, Toni, 117
Moten, Fred, 11, 75–76, 125, 185, 204–5, 225, 237, 279–80, 286n50, 296n34, 306n119; on Charles Gaines's *Librettos*, 111–12; knowledge of freedom, 226–27; stolen life, 286n41
"Mother King" (Strange), 144–47
mother-loss, 128, 135; Aretha Franklin, 178, 180–81; Alberta King, 139; "Mother King"(opera; Strange), 145; *Spill* (Gumbs), 135–36; "Take My Hand, Precious Lord" (Dorsey), 124–25, 138. *See also* black mourning; black women; King, Alberta Williams
"Mother to Son" (Hughes), 157–59, *158–59*
Motown, 248–52
mountain tropes, 241. *See also* "I've Been to the Mountaintop" (King)

mouths, as organs of political articulation, 222, 232
Mt. Pisgah Missionary Baptist Church: acoustic architecture, 72–75, 79–81, 83–84, 88, 295n66; photographs, 89; sanctuary, 88. 295n66; sonic memory, 78–79, 81, 84, 90. *See also* "Why Jesus Called a Man a Fool" (King)
Muhammad, Ismail, 273–76
Murphet, Julian, 14
music: black, 256; black preaching, 146; black women's labor, 147–48; blues, 97, 113–14, 249; canned, 26; commercialization of black, 301n9; feminine endings, 134–35, 140, 300n104; gender and performance, 149–52, 155; Motown, 248–52; pretty, 128–137; white criticism of black, 133, 150–51; white empirical studies of black musicality, 211–12. *See also* gospel blues; gospel music
Muybridge, Eadweard, 169–71

Naas, Michael, 37, 283n5
Nancy, Jean-Luc, 260
National Baptist Convention, 101
Nielsen, Aldon, 267, 321n154
Niles, D. T., 297n45
Nirenberg, George T., 118–19, *120*
noise, political economy of (Atali), 6–7, 12
Norman, Jessye, 151–52, 154
nothing music (Crawley), 119

Ochs, Michael, 166, 168
Odum, Howard, 219
Öhman, Nina, 177
Operation Breadbasket Band, 128, 130–31
oratory, classical, 206–7
organology, 43–70. *See also* pipe organs
orificiality, 223, 313n123

Panagia, Davide, 222–23, 232
Parker, John A., 44
Paul, Clarence, 132
Payne, Larry, 195
performativity: black cultural, 44; black religious modernism, 69, 75; black visual intonation, 167–68; music and gender, 149–52, 155
phenomenological voice, 32–33
phonography, 25–36, 234–35
phonophotography, 213–17, 219–20, 226, 313n102
photographic aurality, 188–89, 308n6; the aural unconscious, 189–93; black voices, 223–24, 228; criticism, 186, 188; gesture, 205–7; Mahalia Jackson, 166–68; King, 186, 188, 190, 192–94, 205, 207–8, 228; memories of, 188; Emmett Till's murder, 279

photographs: Frederick Douglass, 185; Mahalia Jackson, 166–71, *172, 173, 174, 175*; memory, 189; motion, 168–71; mouths pictured in, 221–23; Eadweard Muybridge's, 169–70; as partial records, 169; vs. statues, 207, 228. *See also* photographic aurality; photographs of King; photography

photographs of King: aesthetic funerary, 186; aurality, 186, 188, 190, 192–94, 205, 207–8, 228; Chicago Coliseum New Politics Convention, 222–23; "Facing the Challenge of a New Age," 233–34; gesturalism, 205–6; Lincoln Memorial, 190–91; Mason Temple Church, 202, 205–8, 228, 311n61; as misremembering, 192; optical unconscious, 191; as symbolic violence, 190–92; ubiquity, 185–86, 188; use in birthday commemorations, 189; "Vendor in New York City, New York" (Fernandez), 186, *187*

photography: aural unconscious, 189–93; hearing, 192–93; optical unconscious, 169, 186, 188–89, 191, 205; phono-, 213–17, 219–20, 226, 313n102; quiet, 309n17; vs. shooting, 191; sound waves, 214; violence of, 190

Pickett, Ludie, 93

pipe organs: an-archic potentialities, 62, 64; black airs, 68–69; black cultural modernity, 62; black religious life, 49, 51–52, 63, 289n29, 289n31; John Brown-made, 49, 288n16; the Ebenezer sound, 47–51, 63–67, 69, 288n16, 288n22, 290n57; Ralph Ellison's fiction, 52, 54–55, 57–62, 288n31; Graham Washington Jackson's playing, 63–64, 290n55, 290n57; Sinai Congregation (Chicago), 87; Wurlitzer Company, 49–50, 288n22

politics of race and place, 229–71

Powell, Richard, 201, 228, 311n47

prayer as listening, 91

Preacher King, The (Lischer), 1, 15; "The Drum Major Instinct" (King), 28; Ebenezer Baptist Church, 69–70, 291n73; Ebenezer gospel, 71; on King's vibrato, 12–13; militancy, 38–39; musical education, 140–41; reproduction of King's preaching, 11, 282n27; sermons vs. civil religious addresses, 286n51; strategies of style, 5; *Strength to Love* (King), 108–9; voice, 9–11, 70

preaching, 110–13. *See also* black preaching; sermons

preaching, reform, 71–93

"Precious Lord" (Dorsey). *See* "Take My Hand, Precious Lord"

pretty music, 128–137

Prinz, Joachim, 261–63, 267

Pritchard, Norman H., 76, 78, 114

"Proposal for an Audio History of Martin Luther King, Jr." (SCLC), 2–3
Provident Hospital, 122, 298n72

Raboteau, Albert, 311n40
Rampersad, Arnold, 56
Randolph, A. Philip, 4, 256, 263
Rankine, Claudia, 30, 278
Ray, James Earl, 26, 130, 138
recording, early audio, 25–26, 32, 234–35. *See also* phonography
Reed-Veal, Geneva, 279
Reuther, Walter, 255
Ritz, David, 177–78, 181
Roberson, Ed, 83
Robeson, Paul, 148
Robinson, Earl, 154
Rocky Mount, NC, 230–33, 315n10, 315nn14–15. *See also* "Facing the Challenge of a New Age" (King; Rocky Mount, NC)
Roosevelt, Franklin Delano, 63, 290n55
Rosenwald, Julius, 293n45
"Rough and Rocky Road" (song), 64–67, 291n60
Rustin, Bayard, 2, 28, 254–56, 260, 285n22

Saarinen, Eero, 242–43
Saarinen, Eliel, 242–43
Sabine, Wallace C., 79–81, 293n25
Say Amen, Somebody (Nirenberg), 118–19, *120*
Schaeffer, Pierre, 33–34, 286n45, 286n48
Schafer, R. Murray, 8, 68, 198, 252–53, 301n6
Schmidt, Leigh Eric, 90–93
Schutzer, Paul, 190–91, *193*
Schwerin, Jules, 164–65
Scripto Pen strike, 285n22
Seashore, Carl E., 209–10, 212–17, 219, 222
Seltzer, Mark, 55
sermons: vs. civil religious addresses, 286n51; King's printed, 108; self-eulogizing, 25, 234; structure, 107–9. *See also* preaching
Sexton, Jared, 227, 236
Shaler, Nathanial S., 210–12
Sharpe, Christina, 114, 199–200, 232, 277
Shelley, Braxton, 257–58
Shuttlesworth, Fred, 2, 297n45
Silverman, Kaja, 312n67
Sims, Frank Kentworth, 100
Sinai Congregation: anti-racism, 85–86, 293n48; Germanness, 84–85; modernism, 85; and the NAACP, 85; progressivism, 84–86. *See also* Hirsch, Emil Gustav; Mt. Pisgah Missionary Baptist Church
Smith, Francis Manuel, 239, 241
Smith, James Howard Lorenzo, 99–100
Smith, Mark, 6–7

350 INDEX

Smith, Samuel Francis, 270
Smith, Shawn Michelle, 168–71, 189
Smith, Suzanne E., 249–50
Smith, Ted A., 294n57
Smith, Willie Mae Ford, 125
Sontag, Susan, 190
Sorett, Josef, 304n100
sound: acousmatic vs. acoustical, 33–34, 286n45, 286n48; an-archic, 83, 93, 246; black, 6–7, 12; echoic, 241–42, 245, 250–52, 316n55; epistemology, 6; haptic capacity, 207; historical temporalities, 49; in-between, 243–47, 251, 266; keynote, 8, 68, 139, 252–53, 301n6; King's preaching, 5, 7; laughter, 238–41; motile ontology, 256; noise and political economy, 6–7, 12; signal, 8; vibration, 238, 316n48; water's effects, 265–66. *See also* acoustic architecture; audition; aurality; Ebenezer sound (Atlanta); music; photographic aurality; pipe organs; voice
Sousa, John Philip, 26
Southern Christian Leadership Conference (SCLC): audio archive proposal, 2–3, 309n21; Chicago Freedom Movement, 98; King's presidency, 76; Memphis garbage collectors' strike, 226; Operation Breadbasket, 128, 300n95
Spillers, Hortense, 1, 56–58, 143, 151, 155, 304n80, 312n68; singers, 149–50
spoken soul, 9–10, 12
Stars of Harmony, 64, 291n60
statues, 200–2, 206–7, 228, 230–33, 315n10, 315nn14–15; vs. photographs, 207, 228
Stein, William S., 2–3
Sterling, Alton, 277–78
Sterne, Jonathan, 25–26, 234–35
Strange, Dameun, 144–47
Strayhorn, Billy, 160
Street, Seán, 78–79
Strength to Love (King): "Antidotes for Fear" (King), 159; goals, 109; "A Knock at Midnight" (King), 107–9, 111, 297n33; sermon structures, 108–9; "Why Jesus Called a Man a Fool," 77, 83
Stuckey, Sterling, 311n40
Sundquist, Eric, 4, 229
super-scripting, 78, 81, 83, 98–99

"Take My Hand, Precious Lord" (Dorsey): as black feminist elegy, 131; Ben Branch's Memphis performance, 128–31, 134, 300n96; Ben Branch's recorded version, 131, 133; Thomas Dorsey, 114, 116–21, 123–28, 298n62, 299n87, 300n94; Aretha Franklin, 176–82, 306n140; Mahalia Jackson's recording, 170–71, 306n139; King's affection for, 128–30, 134, 137–38, 300n96
Taylor, Cecil, 38–39
Taylor, H., 198, 309n30
"10 Commandments on Vietnam" (C. S. King), 156–57, 159
Thomas, Lorenzo, 322–23n156
Thompson, Emily, 48–49
Three Days before the Shooting . . . (Ellison), 54, 59–62
Thurman, Howard, 28, 285n22
Till, Emmett, 248, 278–79
Till-Mobley, Mamie, 278–79
Tompkins, Kyla Wazana, 223, 313n123
Townes, Emilie, 298n82
transcriptions of King's speeches: "All Labor Has Dignity," 226, 314n126; challenges, 204–5; "Facing the Challenge of a New Age," 238–39; "I Have a Dream," 263–64
Tuskegee Institute, 293n48

(un)dying performativity, 134, 138
Up from Slavery (Washington), 13

vibration, 238, 316n48
vibrato: empirical racialized studies, 212–16, 217, 219–20; empirical studies, 209–10, 213; film studies, 219–20; as musical gesture, 209; phono-photography studies, 213–17, 219–20, 226, 313n102
Vietnam, 109–10, 156–57, 274
visual oratory, 188–99, 200–8, 223–24, 228
voice: acoustic architecture, 32–33, 78–79; Jacques Derrida, 32; W. E. B. Du Bois's, 12, 282n33; grain of, 5–6; King's, 9–11, 70, 88, 136–37, 139. *See also* black voices; vibrato

Wald, Gayle, 270
Walker, Alice, 307n148
Walker, Robert, 224
Wall, Cheryl, 158–59
Wallace, Karl R., 218–19
Ward, Brian, 252
Warner, Michael, 199–201
Washington, Booker T., 13–14, 233, 293n45
Washington, DC. *See* "I Have a Dream" (King); March on Washington
Washington, James, 92, 295n72
Webb, Stephen, 146
Weheliye, Alexander, 15, 265
Wells, Joseph, 76–77
Wesley, John, 241
West, Cornel, 228, 311n50
Where Do We Go from Here: Chaos or Community (King), 109

White, Graham, 7
White, Shane, 7
"Why Jesus Called a Man a Fool" (King; Mt. Pisgah Church): acoustic architecture, 72–73, 78–81, 83–84, 93; black modernism, 81–82; delivery, 83; eschatology, 92–93; hearing and speaking, 90–92; incantatory mode, 75–76, 78, 83, 295n66; Jewish reform preaching, 83–84, 88; kitchen table epiphany, 88, 91–92; prayer in, 91–92; precursors, 77–78, 292n18; printings, 83, 92, 295n72; sound of King's voice, 88

Why We Can't Wait (King), 109
Wilderson, Frank B., III, 189, 224, 256
Williams, Adam Daniel (AD), 44–45, 146, 302n28
Williams, Daniel Hale, 122
Wise, Isaac Mayer, 87
Wonder, Stevie, 131–33

Young, Andrew, 24
Younge, Gary, 229

Žižek, Slavoj, 188–89, 192, 194–95, 308n4, 308n6

www.ingramcontent.com/pod-product-compliance
Lightning Source LLC
Chambersburg PA
CBHW051047230426
43666CB00012B/2601